A DREAM DEFERRED

READINGS IN AMERICAN HISTORY
EDITED BY LOUIS WILLIAMS AND ANGELA HOLDER

VOLUME II

SIMON & SCHUSTER CUSTOM PUBLISHING

Cover photo courtesy of The New York Convention & Visitors Bureau.

Printed in the United States of America

10 9 8 7 6 5 4 3 2 1

Please visit our website at www.sscp.com

ISBN 0–536–02019–1

BA 98660

SIMON & SCHUSTER CUSTOM PUBLISHING
160 Gould Street/Needham Heights, MA 02494
Simon & Schuster Education Group

Copyright Acknowledgments

Contents

Harlem

Langston Hughes

What happens to a dream deferred?

Does it dry up
like a raisin in the sun?
Or fester like a sore—
And then run?
Does it stink like rotten meat?
Or crust and sugar over—
like a syrupy sweet?

Maybe it just sags
like a heavy load.

Or does it explode?

I, Too

Langston Hughes

I, too, sing America.

I am the darker brother.
They send me to eat in the kitchen
When company comes,
But I laugh,
And eat well,
And grow strong.

Tomorrow,
I'll be at the table
When company comes.
Nobody'll dare
Say to me,
"Eat in the kitchen,"
Then.

Besides,
They'll see how beautiful I am
And be ashamed—

I, too, am America.

Mother to Son

Langston Hughes

Well, son, I'll tell you:
Life for me ain't been no crystal stair.
It's had tacks in it,
And splinters,
And boards torn up,
And places with no carpet on the floor—
Bare.
But all the time
I'se been a-climbin' on,
And reachin' landin's,
And turnin' corners,
And sometimes goin' in the dark
Where there ain't been no light.
So boy, don't you turn back.
Don't you set down on the steps
'Cause you finds it's kinder hard.
Don't you fall now—
For I'se still goin', honey,
I'se still climbin',
And life for me ain't been no crystal stair.

Reading 1

Abraham Lincoln and the Second American Revolution

James M. McPherson

The foremost Lincoln scholar of a generation ago, James G. Randall, considered the sixteenth president to be a conservative on the great issues facing the country, Union and slavery. If conservatism, wrote Randall, meant "caution, prudent adherence to tested values, avoidance of rashness, and reliance upon unhurried peaceable evolution, [then] Lincoln was a conservative." His preferred solution of the slavery problem, Randall pointed out, was a program of gradual, compensated emancipation with the consent of the owners, stretching over a generation or more, with provision for the colonization abroad of emancipated slaves to minimize the potential for racial conflict and social disorder. In his own words, Lincoln said that he wanted to "stand on middle ground," avoid "dangerous extremes," and achieve his goals through "the spirit of compromise . . . [and] of mutual concession." In essence, concluded Randall, Lincoln believed in evolution rather than revolution, in "planting, cultivating, and harvesting, not in uprooting and destroying." Many historians have agreed with this interpretation. To cite just two of them: T. Harry Williams maintained that "'Lincoln was on the slavery question, as he was on most matters, a conservative"; and Norman Graebner wrote an essay entitled "Abraham Lincoln: Conservative Statesman," based on the premise that Lincoln was a conservative because "he accepted the need of dealing with things as they were, not as he would have wished them to be."

Yet as president of the United States, Lincoln presided over a profound, wrenching experience which, in Mark Twain's words, "uprooted institutions that were centuries old, changed the politics of a people, transformed the social life of half the country, and wrought so profoundly upon the entire national character that the influence cannot be measured short of two or three generations." Benjamin Disraeli, viewing this experience from across the Atlantic in 1863, characterized "the struggle in America" as "a great revolution. . . . [We] will see, when the waters have subsided, a different America." The *Springfield* (Mass.) *Republican*, an influential wartime newspaper, predicted that Lincoln's Emancipation Proclamation would accomplish "the greatest social and political revolution of the age." The historian Otto Olsen has labeled Lincoln a revolutionary because he led the nation in its achievement of this result.

As for Lincoln himself, he said repeatedly that the right of revolution, the "right of any people" to "throw off, to revolutionize, their existing form of government, and to establish such other in its stead as they may choose" was "a sacred right—a right, which we may hope and believe, is to liberate the world." The Declaration of Independence, he insisted often, was the great "charter of freedom" and in the example of the American Revolution "the world has found . . . the germ . . . to grow and expand into the universal liberty of mankind." Lincoln championed the leaders of the European revolutions of 1848; in turn, a man who knew something about those revolutions—Karl Marx—praised Lincoln in 1865 as "the single-minded son of the working class" who had led his "country through the matchless struggle for the rescue of an enchained race and the reconstruction of a social world."

What are we to make of these contrasting portraits of Lincoln the conservative and Lincoln the revolutionary? Are they just another example of how Lincoln's words can be manipulated to support any position, even diametrically opposed ones? No. It is a matter of interpretation and emphasis within the context of a fluid and rapidly changing crisis situation. The Civil War started out as one kind of conflict and ended as something quite different. These apparently contradictory positions about Lincoln the conservative versus Lincoln the revolutionary can be reconciled by focusing on this process. The attempt to reconcile them can tell us a great deal about the nature of the American Civil War.

That war has been viewed as a revolution—as the second American Revolution—in three different senses. Lincoln played a crucial role in defining the outcome of the revolution in each of three respects.

The first way in which some contemporaries regarded the events of 1861 as a revolution was the frequent invocation of the right of revolution by southern leaders to justify their secession—their declaration of independence—from the United States. The Mississippi convention that voted to secede in 1861 listed the state's grievances against the North, and proclaimed: "For far less cause than this, our fathers separated from the Crown of England." The governor of Tennessee agreed that unless the North made concessions to the South, "the only alternative left to us [will be] to follow the example of our fathers of 1776." And an Alabama newspaper asked rhetorically: Were not "the men of 1776, who withdrew their allegiance from George III and set up for themselves . . . Secessionists?"

Southerners created the Confederacy to protect their "rights" against a perceived northern threat to those rights. If we remain in the Union said a Virginia slaveholder, "we will be deprived of that right for which our fathers fought in the battles of the revolution." From "the high and solemn motive of defending and protecting the rights . . . which our fathers bequeathed to us," declared Jefferson Davis, let us "renew such sacrifices as our fathers made to the holy cause of constitutional liberty." In the middle of the war, a Confederate army officer declared that he had "never believed the Constitution recognized the right of secession. I took up arms, sir, upon a broader ground—the right of revolution. We were wronged. Our properties and liberties were about to be taken from us. It was a sacred duty to rebel." A Confederate songster contained a stirring tune that linked the two revolutions, titled "Seventy-Six and Sixty-One." Another song contained the following words:

> *Rebels* before,
> Our fathers of yore,
> *Rebel's* the righteous name
> *Washington* bore.
> Why, then, be ours the same.

Northerners were unimpressed by these claims of revolutionary legitimacy. The principal right and liberty that southerners feared would be threatened if they remained in a Union governed by "Black Republicans" was their right to own slaves and their liberty to take them where they pleased in territories of the United States. "Will you consent to be robbed of your property," secession leaders asked their fellow Mississippians, or will you "strike bravely for liberty, property, honor and life?" A Georgia secessionist declared dramatically that if the South stayed in a Union "ruled by Lincoln and his crew . . . in TEN years or less our children will be the *slaves* of negroes. For emancipation must follow and negro equality is the same result." William Cullen Bryant, antislavery editor of the *New York Evening Post,* cited such statements to ridicule southern claims to be following in the footsteps of their revolutionary forebears. That "is a libel upon the whole character and conduct of men of '76," said Bryant. The founders fought "to establish the rights of man . . . and principles of universal liberty." The South was rebelling "not in the interest of general humanity, but of a domestic despotism. . . . Their motto is not liberty, but slavery." Thomas Jefferson's Declaration of Independence, added the *New York Tribune,* invoked "Natural Rights against Established Institutions," while "Mr. Jeff. Davis's caricature thereof is made in the interest of an unjust, outgrown, decaying Institution against the apprehended encroachments of Natural Human Rights." It was, in short, not a revolution but rather a counterrevolution "reversing the wheels of progress . . . to hurl everything backward into deepest darkness . . . despotism and oppression."

Many secessionists conceded that their movement was essentially a counterrevolution against the anticipated revolutionary threat to slavery. Indeed, they proudly affirmed it. "We are not revolutionists," insisted James B. D. DeBow, the South's leading journalist; "we are resisting revolution." It was "an abuse of language" to call secession a revolution, said Jefferson Davis. "Ours is not a revolution." We left the Union "to save ourselves from a revolution" that threatened to make "property in slaves so insecure as to be comparatively worthless. . . . Our struggle is for inherited rights." The Black Republicans were the real revolutionaries, southerners insisted, "a motley throng of Sans culottes . . . Infidels and freelovers, interspersed by Bloomer women, fugitive slaves, and amalgamationists . . . active and bristling with terrible designs and as ready for bloody and forcible realities as ever characterized the ideas of the French revolution." Secession was therefore a "political revolution," explained a Georgian in 1860, to forestall the "social revolution" sure to come if the South remained in the Union. In 1861 the Confederate secretary of state advised foreign governments that southern states had formed a new nation "to preserve their old institutions" from "a revolution [that] threatened to destroy their social system."

Northerners could scarcely have denied to the South the right of revolution for just cause, since Yankees were as much heirs of the legacy of 1776 as southerners were. But that phrase, "for just cause," is crucial. "It may seem strange," said Lincoln of Confederate leaders, "that any men should dare to ask a just God's assistance in wringing their bread from the sweat of other men's faces." Secession was not a just revolution, but an unjust counterrevolution. As Lincoln phrased it in the summer of 1861, "the right of revolution, is never a legal right . . . At most, it is but a moral right, when exercised for a morally justifiable cause. When exercised without such a cause revolution is no right, but simply a wicked exercise of physical power."

In Lincoln's view, secession was just such a wicked exercise. The event that precipitated it was his own election, which had been achieved by a constitutional majority according to constitutional procedures. The Republicans had done nothing against the law, had violated nobody's constitutional rights. Indeed, seven states had seceded and formed the Confederacy a month before Lincoln even took office. As northerners saw it, the South, having controlled the national government for most of the previous two generations through its domination of the Democratic party, now decided to leave the Union just because it had lost an election.

For Lincoln it was the *Union,* not the Confederacy, that was the true heir of the Revolution of 1776. That revolution had established a republic, a democratic government of the people by the people. This republic was a fragile experiment in a world of kings, emperors, tyrants, and theories of aristocracy. If secession were allowed to succeed, it would destroy that experiment. It would set a fatal precedent by which the minority could secede whenever it did not like what the majority stood for, until the United States fragmented into a dozen pitiful, squabbling countries, the laughing stock of the world. The successful establishment of a slaveholding Confederacy would also enshrine the idea of inequality, a contradiction of the ideal of equal natural rights on which the United States was founded. "This issue embraces more than the fate of these United States," said Lincoln on another occasion. "It presents to the whole family of man, the question, whether a constitutional republic, or a democracy . . . can, or cannot, maintain its territorial integrity." Nor is the struggle "altogether for today; it is for a vast future . . . On the side of the Union it is a struggle for maintaining in the world that form and substance of government whose leading object is to elevate the condition of men . . . to afford all an unfettered start, and a fair chance in the race of life."

To *preserve* the Union and *maintain* the republic: these verbs denote a conservative purpose. If the Confederacy's war of independence was indeed a revolution, Lincoln was most certainly a conservative. But if secession was an act of counterrevolution to forestall a revolutionary threat to slavery posed by the government Lincoln headed, these verbs take on a different meaning and Lincoln's intent to conserve the Union becomes something other than conservatism. But precisely what it would become was not yet clear in 1861.

The second respect in which the Civil War is viewed as a revolution was in its abolition of slavery. This was indeed a revolutionary achievement—not only an expropriation of the principal form of property in half the country, but a destruction of the institution that was basic to the southern social order, the political structure, the culture, the way of life in this region. But in 1861 this revolutionary achievement was not part of Lincoln's war aims.

From the beginning of the war, though, abolitionists and some Republicans urged the Lincoln administration to turn the military conflict into a revolutionary crusade to abolish slavery and create a new order in the South. As one abolitionist put it in 1861, although the Confederates "justify themselves under the right of revolution," their cause "is not a revolution but a rebellion against the noblest of revolutions." The North must meet this southern counterrevolution by converting the war for the Union into a revolution for freedom. "WE ARE THE REVOLUTIONISTS," he proclaimed. The principal defect of the first American Revolution, in the eyes of abolitionists, had been that while it freed white Americans from British rule it failed to free black Americans from slavery. Now was the time to remedy that defect by proclaiming emancipation and inviting the slaves "to share in the *glorious second American Revolution.*" And Thaddeus Stevens, the grim-visaged old gladiator who led the radical Republicans in the House of Representatives, pulled no punches in this regard. "We must treat this [war] as a radical revolution," he declared, and "free every slave—slay every traitor—burn every rebel mansion, if these things be necessary to preserve" the nation.

Such words grated harshly on Lincoln's ears during the first year of the war. In his message to Congress in December 1861 the president deplored the possibility that the war might "degenerate into a violent and remorseless revolutionary struggle." It was not that Lincoln *wanted* to preserve slavery. On the contrary, he said many times: "I am naturally anti-slavery. If slavery is not wrong, nothing is wrong." But as president he could not act officially on his private "judgment [concerning] the moral question of slavery." He was bound by the Constitution, which protected the institution of slavery in the states. In the first year of the war the North fought to preserve this Constitution and restore the Union as it had existed before 1861. Lincoln's theory of the war held that since secession was illegal, the Confederate states were still legally in the Union although temporarily under the control of insurrectionists. The government's purpose was to suppress this insurrection and restore loyal Unionists to control of the southern states. The conflict was therefore a limited war with the limited goal of restoring the status quo ante bellum, not an unlimited war to destroy an enemy nation and reshape its society. And since, in theory, the southern states were still in the Union, they continued to enjoy all their constitutional rights, including slavery.

There were also several political reasons for Lincoln to take this conservative position in 1861. For one thing, the four border slave states of Missouri, Kentucky, Maryland, and Delaware had remained in the Union; Lincoln desperately wanted to keep them there. He would like to have God on his side, Lincoln supposedly said, but he *must* have Kentucky. In all of these four states except Delaware a strong pro-Confederate faction existed. Any rash action by the northern government against slavery, therefore, might push three more states into the Confederacy. Moreover, in the North itself nearly half of the voters were Democrats, who supported a war for the Union but might oppose a war against slavery. For these reasons, Lincoln held at bay the Republicans and abolitionists who were calling for an antislavery war and revoked actions by two of his generals who had proclaimed emancipation by martial law in areas under their command.

Antislavery Republicans challenged the theory underlying Lincoln's concept of a limited war. They pointed out that by 1862 the conflict had become in theory as well as in fact a full-fledged war between nations, not just a police action to suppress an uprising. By imposing a blockade on Confederate ports and treating captured Confederate soldiers as prisoners of war rather than as criminals or pirates, the Lincoln administration had in effect recognized that this was a war rather than a mere domestic insurrection. Under international law, belligerent powers had the right to seize or destroy enemy resources used to wage war—munitions, ships, military equipment, even food for the armies and crops sold to obtain cash to buy armaments. As the war escalated in scale and fury and as Union armies invaded the South in 1861, they did destroy or capture such resources. Willy-nilly the war was becoming a remorseless revolutionary conflict, a total war rather than a limited one.

A major Confederate resource for waging war was the slave population, which constituted a majority of the southern labor force. Slaves raised food for the army, worked in war industries, built fortifications, dug trenches, drove army supply wagons, and so on. As enemy property, these slaves were subject to confiscation under the laws of war. The Union Congress passed limited confiscation laws in August 1861 and July 1862 that authorized the seizure of this human property. But pressure mounted during 1862 to go further than this—to proclaim emancipation as a *means* of winning the war by converting the slaves from a vital war resource for the South to allies of the North, and beyond that to make the abolition of slavery a *goal* of the war, in order to destroy the institution that had caused the war in the first place and would continue to plague the nation in the future if it was allowed to survive. By the summer of 1861, most Republicans wanted to turn this limited war to restore the old Union into a revolutionary war to create a new nation purged of slavery.

For a time Lincoln tried to outflank this pressure by persuading the border slave states remaining in the Union to undertake voluntary, gradual emancipation, with the owners to be compensated by the federal government. With rather dubious reasoning, Lincoln predicted that such action would shorten the war by depriving the Confederacy of its hope for the allegiance of these states and thereby induce the South to give up the fight. And though the compensation of slaveholders would be expensive, it would cost much less than continuing the war. If the border states adopted some plan of gradual emancipation such as northern states had done after the Revolution of 1776, said Lincoln, the process would not radically disrupt the social order.

Three times in the spring and summer of 1862 Lincoln appealed to congressmen from the border states to endorse a plan for gradual emancipation. If they did not, he warned in March, "it is impossible to foresee all the incidents which may attend and all the ruin which may follow." In May he declared that the changes produced by his gradual plan "would come gently as the dews of heaven, not rending or wrecking anything. Will you not embrace it? . . . You can not, if you would, be blind to the signs of the times." But most of the border-state representatives remained blind to the signs. They questioned the constitutionality of Lincoln's proposal, objected to its cost, bristled at its veiled threat of federal coercion, and deplored the potential race problem they feared would come with a large free black population. In July, Lincoln once more called border-state congressmen to the White House. He admonished them bluntly that "the unprecedentedly stern facts of the case" called for immediate action. The limited war was becoming a total war; pressure to turn it into a war of abolition was growing. The slaves were emancipating themselves by running away from home and coming into Union lines. If the border states did not make "a decision at once to emancipate *gradually* . . . the institution in your states will be extinguished by mere friction and abrasion—by the mere incidents of the war." In other words, if they did not accept an evolutionary plan for the abolition of slavery, it would be wiped out by the revolution that was coming. But again they refused, rejecting Lincoln's proposal by a vote of twenty to nine. Angry and disillusioned, the president decided to embrace the revolution. That very evening he made up his mind to issue an emancipation proclamation. After a delay to wait for a Union victory, he sent forth the preliminary proclamation on September 22—after the battle of Antietam—and the final proclamation on New Year's Day 1863.

The old cliché, that the proclamation did not free a single slave because it applied only to the Confederate states where Lincoln had no power, completely misses the point. The proclamation announced a revolutionary new war aim—the overthrow of slavery by force of arms if and when Union armies conquered the South. Of course, emancipation could not be irrevocably accomplished without a constitutional amendment, so Lincoln threw his weight behind the Thirteenth Amendment, which the House passed in January 1865. In the meantime two of the border states, Maryland and Missouri, which had refused to consider gradual, compensated emancipation in 1862 came under control of emancipationists who pushed through state constitutional amendments that abolished slavery without compensation and went into effect immediately—a fate experienced by the other border states, Kentucky and Delaware, along with the rest of the South when the Thirteenth Amendment was ratified in December 1865.

But from the time the Emancipation Proclamation went into effect at the beginning of 1863, the North fought for the revolutionary goal of a new Union without slavery. Despite grumbling and dissent by some soldiers who said they had enlisted to fight for the Union rather than for the "nigger," most soldiers understood and accepted the new policy. A colonel from Indiana put it this way: whatever their opinion of slavery and blacks, his men "desire to destroy everything that gives the rebels strength!" Therefore "this army will sustain the emancipation proclamation and enforce it with the bayonet." Soon after the proclamation came out, General-in-Chief Henry W. Halleck wrote to General Ulysses S. Grant near Vicksburg, that "the character of the war has very much changed within the last year. There is now no possible hope of reconciliation with the rebels. . . . We must conquer the rebels or be conquered by them. . . . Every slave withdrawn from the enemy is the equivalent of a white man put *hors de combat.*" One of Grant's field commanders explained that "the policy is to be terrible on the enemy. I am using negroes all the time for my work as teamsters, and have 1,000 employed."

Lincoln endorsed this policy of being "terrible on the enemy." And the policy soon went beyond using freed slaves as teamsters and laborers. By early 1863 the Lincoln administration committed itself to enlisting black men in the army. Arms in the hands of slaves constituted the South's ultimate nightmare. The enlistment of black soldiers to fight and kill their former masters was by far the most revolutionary dimension of the emancipation policy. And, after overcoming his initial hesitation, Lincoln became an enthusiastic advocate of this policy. In March 1863 he wrote to Andrew Johnson, military governor of occupied Tennessee: "The bare sight of fifty thousand armed, and drilled black soldiers on the banks of the Mississippi, would end the rebellion at once. And who doubts that we can present that sight, if we but take hold in earnest?" By August 1863, when the Union army had organized 50,000 black soldiers and was on the way to enlistment of 180,000 before the war was over, Lincoln declared in a public letter that "the emancipation policy, and the use of colored troops, constitute the heaviest blow yet dealt to the rebellion."

When, conservatives complained of the revolutionary nature of these heavy blows, Lincoln responded that the nation could no longer pursue "a temporizing and forbearing" policy toward rebels. "Decisive and extensive measures must be adopted." Conservatives who did not like it should blame the slaveholders and fire-eaters who started the war. They "must understand," said Lincoln in an angry tone, "that they cannot experiment for ten years trying to destroy the government, and if they fail still come back into the Union unhurt." In a metaphor that he used several times, Lincoln said that "broken eggs cannot be mended." The egg of slavery was already broken by 1862;

if the South continued fighting it must expect more eggs to be broken, so the sooner it gave up "the smaller [would] be the amount of that which will be beyond mending." Lincoln's fondness for this metaphor is interesting, for modern revolutionaries sometimes use a similar one to justify the use of violence to bring about social change: you cannot make an omelet, they say, without breaking eggs—that is, you cannot make a new society without destroying the old one.

Another way of illustrating how Lincoln came to believe in this revolutionary concept is to quote from his inaugural address, delivered at a time when the war had gone on for almost four terrible years. On the one hand were the famous words of the second inaugural calling the binding up of the nation's wounds, with malice toward none and charity for all. With these words Lincoln invoked the New Testament lesson of forgiveness; he urged peace once the war was over. But although he believed in a soft peace, it could be won only by a hard war. This was an Old Testament concept, and for Lincoln's Old Testament vision of a hard war, examine *this* passage from the second inaugural: "American Slavery is one of those offences which in the providence of God . . . He now wills to remove [through] this terrible war, as the woe due to those by whom the offence came. . . . Fondly do we hope—fervently we pray—that this mighty scourge of war may speedily pass away. Yet if God wills that it continue, until all the wealth piled by the bondman's two hundred and fifty years of unrequited toil shall be sunk, and until every drop of blood by drawn with the lash, shall be paid by another drawn with the sword, as was said three thousand years ago, so still it must be said 'the judgments of the Lord, are true and righteous altogether.' "

This was the language not only of the Old Testament, but also of revolution. In the second respect in which the Civil War has been viewed as a revolution—its achievement of the abolition of slavery—Lincoln fits the pattern of a revolutionary leader. He was a reluctant one at first, to be sure, but in the end he was more radical than Washington or Jefferson or any of the leaders of the first revolution. They led a successful struggle for independence from Britain but did not accomplish a fundamental change in the society, they led. Lincoln did preside over such a change. Indeed, as he put it himself, also in the second inaugural, neither side had anticipated such "fundamental and astounding" changes when the war began.

These words introduce the third respect in which the Civil War can be viewed as a revolution: it destroyed not only slavery but also the social structure of the old South that had been founded on slavery, and it radically altered the power balance between the North and the South. It changed the direction of American development. This was what Mark Twain meant when he wrote that the war had "uprooted institutions that were centuries old . . . transformed the social life of half the country, and wrought so profoundly upon the entire national character." It was what Charles A. Beard meant when he wrote (as quoted in the preceding essay) that the Civil War was a "social cataclysm . . . making vast changes in the arrangement of classes, in the distribution of wealth, in the course of industrial development."

The war ended seventy years of southern domination of the national government and transferred it to Yankee Republicans who controlled the polity and economy of the United States for most of the next seventy years. It increased northern wealth and capital by 50 percent during the 1860s while destroying 60 percent of southern wealth. The output of southern industry in proportion to that of the North was cut in half by the war; the value of southern agricultural land in relation to that of the North was cut by three-fourths.

These changes occurred because when the Civil War became a total war, the invading army intentionally destroyed the economic capacity of the South to wage war. Union armies ripped up thousands of miles of southern railroads and blew up hundreds of bridges; Confederate cavalry raids and guerrilla operations behind Union lines in the South added to the destruction. More than half of the South's farm machinery was wrecked by the war, two-fifths of its livestock was killed, and one-quarter of its white males of military age—also the prime age for economic production—were killed, a higher proportion than suffered by any European power in World War I, that holocaust which ravaged a continent and spread revolution through many of its countries.

Union generals William Tecumseh Sherman and Philip Sheridan saw more clearly than anyone else the nature of modern total war, a war between peoples rather than simply between armies, a war in which the fighting left nothing untouched or unchanged. "We are not only fighting hostile armies, but a hostile people," wrote Sherman in the middle of the war. "We cannot change the hearts of those people of the South," he said in 1864 as his army began its march from Atlanta to the sea, "but we can make war so terrible . . . that generations would pass away before they again appeal to it." While Sherman's army was marching through Georgia and South Carolina destroying everything in its path, Sheridan's army cut a similar swath through the Shenandoah Valley making sure that it, like Georgia and South Carolina, would produce no more food or munitions for Confederate forces.

Although Abraham Lincoln was a compassionate man who deplored this destruction and suffering, he nevertheless assented to it as the only way to win the war. After all, he had warned southerners two years earlier that the longer they fought, the more eggs would be broken. Now, in 1864, he officially conveyed to Sheridan the "thanks of the nation, and my own personal admiration and gratitude, for [your] operations in the Shenandoah Valley"; he sent Sherman and his army "grateful acknowledgments" for their march through Georgia.

The second American Revolution, as Charles Beard viewed it, involved not only this destruction of the southern plantation gentry but also the consolidation of the northern entrepreneurial capitalist class in national power, supported by its rural and urban middle-class allies. Legislation passed by the Union Congress during the war promoted this development. The Republican party had inherited from its Hamiltonian and Whig forebears a commitment to the use of government to foster economic development through tariffs 'to protect industry, a centralized and regulated banking system, investment subsidies and land grants to high-risk but socially beneficial transportation enterprises, and government support for education. By 1860 the Republican party had also pledged itself to homestead legislation to provide farmers with an infusion of capital in the form of free land. Before 1860, the southern-dominated Democratic party that controlled the federal government had repeatedly defeated or frustrated these measures. During the war, Republicans passed them all: a higher tariff in 1861; a homestead act, a land-grant college act, and a Pacific railroad act providing loans and land grants for a transcontinental railroad in 1862; and a national banking act in 1863, which, along with the legal tender act of the previous year authorizing the issuance of a federal currency, the famous greenbacks, gave the national government effective control over the nation's currency for the first time. In addition, to finance the war the government marketed huge bond issues to the public and passed an Internal Revenue Act which imposed a large array of federal taxes for the first time, including a progressive income tax.

This astonishing blitz of laws, most of them passed within the span of less than one year, did more to reshape the relation of the government to the economy than any comparable effort except perhaps the first hundred days of the New Deal. This Civil War legislation, in the words of one historian, created a "blueprint for modern America." It helped promote what another scholar termed "the last capitalist revolution" whereby the Civil War destroyed the "older social structure of plantation slavery" and installed "competitive democratic capitalism" in unchallenged domination of the American economy and polity. That this capitalism itself became a form of entrenched conservatism exploiting labor and resisting change a generation or two later does not nullify the revolutionary meaning of its triumph over the slave South and plantation agriculture in the 1860s. And as a former Whig who had favored these measures to promote banking, transportation, and industry as a means of bringing a higher standard of living to all Americans, and who believed that the abolition of slave labor would enhance the dignity and value of free labor, Abraham Lincoln was one of the principal architects of this capitalist revolution.

What conclusions can we draw, then, that make sense of those contrasting pictures of Lincoln the conservative and Lincoln the revolutionary quoted at the beginning of this essay? Although it may seem like an oxymoron, Lincoln can best be described as a conservative revolutionary. That is, he wanted to conserve the Union as the revolutionary heritage of the founding fathers. Preserving this heritage was the *purpose* of the war; all else became a means to achieve this end. As Lincoln phrased it in his famous public letter to Horace Greeley in August 1862, "My paramount object in this struggle *is* to save the Union, and is *not* either to save or to destroy slavery. . . . What I do about slavery and the colored race, I do because I believe it helps to save the Union." By the time he wrote these words, Lincoln had made up his mind that to save the Union he must destroy slavery. The means always remained subordinated to the end, but the means did become as essential to the northern war effort as the end itself. In that sense perhaps we could describe Lincoln as a pragmatic revolutionary, for as a pragmatist he adapted the means to the end. Thus we can agree with the historian Norman Graebner who was quoted earlier as stating that Lincoln "accepted the need of dealing with things as they were, not as he would have wished them to be." But instead of concluding, as Graebner did, that this made Lincoln a conservative, we must conclude that it made him a revolutionary. Not an ideological revolutionary, to be sure—Lincoln was no Robespierre or Lenin with a blueprint for a new order—but he was a pragmatic revolutionary who found it necessary to destroy slavery and create a new birth of freedom in order to preserve the Union.

"The dogmas of the quiet past," Lincoln told Congress in December 1862, "are inadequate to the stormy present. As our case is new, we must think anew, and act anew." It was *the war itself,* not the ideological blueprints of Lincoln or any other leader, that generated the radical momentum that made it a second American revolution. Like most wars that become total wars, the Civil War snowballed into huge and unanticipated dimensions and took on a life and purpose of its own far beyond the causes that had started it. As Lincoln said in his second inaugural address, neither side, "expected for the war the magnitude or the duration which it has already attained." Or as he put it on another occasion, "I claim not to have controlled events, but confess plainly that events have controlled me." But in conceding that the war rather than he had shaped the thrust and direction of the revolution, Lincoln was perhaps too modest. For it was his own superb leadership, strategy, and sense of timing as president, commander in chief, and head of the Republican party that determined the pace of the revolution and ensured its success. With a less able man as president, the North might have lost the war or ended it under the leadership of Democrats who would have given its outcome a very different shape. Thus in accepting "the need of dealing with things as they were," Lincoln was not a conservative statesman but a revolutionary statesman.

Reading 2

The Robber Barons

Harvey Wasserman

The Civil War made a few businessmen very rich.

The North and the South both gave army deferments to the rich. The Confederacy exempted owners of more than fifty slaves; the Union let those who had it buy their way out for $300.

Among those who paid their $300 were J. Pierpont Morgan, John D. Rockefeller, Andrew Carnegie, James Mellon, Philip Armour, and Jay Gould. Mellon just listened to his father, who told him in a letter that "a man may be a patriot without risking his own life or sacrificing his health. There are plenty of lives less valuable."

Accordingly, young Mellon bought his way out and joined a few thousand men like J. P. Morgan and Jay Cooke in the business of war profiteering.

To Cooke the war meant about $3 million a year in commissions alone. A wealthy banker and speculator, he wormed his way into the government as official promoter of Union bonds. After four years of war the national debt had skyrocketed from $75 million to almost $3 billion. Cooke became a multimillionaire and the most powerful banker in the country. The national debt, he announced, was "a national blessing."

J. P. Morgan, son of a millionaire banker, took his cut dealing gold and guns. Through a middleman, the 24-year-old Morgan bought obsolete carbines from the War Department at $3.50 apiece. His partner then resold them to Union General Fremont at $22.00 each.

Meanwhile Philip Armour supplied the Union Army with beef. Jay Gould speculated gold and securities while Cornelius Vanderbilt dealt rotten hulks to the Navy and began putting together a railroad empire. Jim Fisk ran **contraband** southern cotton through the Union blockade, and John D. Rockefeller piled up profits as a Cleveland merchant and invested them in oil refineries.

America's first crop of "war millionaires" was taking shape. Mellon wrote his father that there were men starting in business who "continue growing richer and don't care when the war closes."

The War Profiteers Play Monopoly

For the millions who actually fought or who watched the two war machines wreck their farms, towns, and lives, the Civil War meant unimaginable horror, four years of unmitigated slaughter and devastation. Five hundred thousand people died, and the romantic spirit of the thirties and forties was consumed into a mangled, bloody mess.

---

contraband: Goods prohibited by law or treaty from being imported or exported. Smuggled goods.

The economic root of the war was a collision of the rising factory owners of the North against the slave-owning ruling caste of the South. Both wanted control of the federal government and both wanted the land west of the Mississippi, then being taken from the Indians.

Between them were the growing agrarian masses, who wanted free land for homesteading. After four decades of political strife, in the midst of a collapsed railroad boom and a national depression, the small farmers joined the industrialists to elect Abraham Lincoln on the slogan "Vote Yourself a Farm!" War over slavery, union, and control of the Mississippi River and the West followed almost immediately.

With the slaveowners out of Washington, the farmers and factory owners speeded construction of the national industrial machine and prepared to open the West. A homestead act was passed as well as an immigration act, high tariffs, and a reform of the national banking system.

Industrial entrepreneurs poured into the capitol for huge "grants" of money and land. The Pacific Railway Act of 1862 gave the promoters of the Union Pacific and Central Pacific Railways five square miles of land for every mile of track they would lay across the west.

Two years later, after an amazing round of bribery, the members of Congress decided to up the grant to ten square miles in addition to the allotment of as much as $48,000 for every mile of track.

By 1872 a bought Congress had given various industrial con artists more than $700 million and 200 million acres of public land, an area roughly the size of Maine, New Hampshire, Vermont, Massachusetts, Rhode Island, Connecticut, New York, and Pennsylvania. Grants by the individual states swelled the money and land totals even higher, and by the time land grant colleges and independent speculators got through, virtually all the homestead land was in the hands of eastern finance.

Actual construction of the railroads was also quite profitable. The directors of the Union Pacific, which began cross-country construction in Omaha, hired the Credit Mobilier Corporation to do the road work. The directors of the Union Pacific also happened to control the Credit Mobilier, which charged the UP about $23 million more than construction had actually cost, money which came out of the federal subsidy and the public sale of worthless stock. The Central Pacific ring of California did even better, picking up $121 million for $58 million in actual construction.

Thus, with the railroad grants as their key capital base, a few men began to carve giant private empires out of public money and land. Many of them, like Rockefeller, Vanderbilt, Carnegie, and Jim Hill, had begun life in dire poverty. Most were of Scottish or old Yankee descent.

Vanderbilt was one of the few who got his start before the Civil War. He was born to Dutch parents in 1794. As a youth he ran a ferry boat from Staten Island to Manhattan, slowly building capital to buy more boats. By the 1850s he was a full-fledged pioneer in the free-enterprise system, whose methods he perfected. "Whenever his keen eye detected a line that was making a large profit," wrote a biographer, "he swooped down and drove it to the wall by offering better service and lower rates."

Then, with the competition driven out of business, "he would raise his rates without pity, to the lasting misery of his clients."

Vanderbilt slowly collected a fleet of ships, and in the crazed years of the Gold Rush he made a fortune running the prospectors from New York across Nicaragua by boat and stage and then on to California. He was at his best in the jungles, where he drove his men to the breaking point, setting the example by fourteen to sixteen hours a day of sleepless vigilance and labor.

> The engineers were appalled but on he went. Sometimes he got over the rapids by putting on all steam; sometimes, when this did not avail, he extended a heavy cable to great trees up stream and warped the boat over. . . . The engineers reported that he "tied down the safety-valve and 'jumped' the obstructions, to the great terror of the whole party."

The tall, gaunt Commodore swelled his fortune by carrying the mail, studiously keeping postage rates high through his power in Congress.

During the Civil War he began piecing together a railway system with capital from his fleet, capital he added to by buying boats like the *Niagara* for the Union Navy. Gustavus Myers wrote *in Great American Fortunes* that

> Vanderbilt was one of the few men in the secret of the Banks' expedition; he knew that the ships had to make an ocean trip. Yet he bought for $10,000 the *Niagara*, an old boat that had been built nearly a score of years before for trade on Lake Ontario. "In perfectly calm weather," reported Senator Grimes, of Iowa, "with a calm sea, the planks were ripped out of her and exhibited to the gaze of the indignant soldiers on board, showing that her timbers were rotten. The committee have in their committee room a large sample on one of the beams of this vessel to show that it has not the slightest capacity to hold a nail."

As early as 1853 the dour, semiliterate Commodore was worth about $11 million, little of which he spent on his wife and nine children, who led a notably sparse existence. His son William, whom he considered stupid, was shipped off to a farm on Staten Island.

One day, however, William cheated his father in a small business deal; Cornelius then considered his son "fit" and brought him into the business, eventually leaving him around $100 million. "Law!" the Commodore once screamed, "What do I care about the Law! Hain't I got the power?"

Vanderbilt's early foe in the railroad game was "Uncle" Dan Drew, a financial manipulator of whom an admirer noted "no hardships or privations could deter him from the pursuit of money."

Like most of his contemporaries, Drew was deeply religious, an avid churchgoer, and a sponsor of cathedrals and seminaries. "He holds the honest people of the world to be a pack of fools," said Henry Clews, a Wall Street contemporary. "When he has been unusually lucky in his trade of fleecing other men, he settles accounts with his conscience by subscribing toward a new chapel or attending a prayer meeting."

Drew got his start as a cattle drover, buying the animals from the midwestern farmers and driving them over the Alleghenies to market. It was as a drover that Drew pioneered the practice of "stock-watering."

During the long drive to market Drew kept the cows from getting water and often, in fact, fed them salt. Then, just before selling them, he let the thirst-crazed animals bloat themselves, multiplying their weight and price but adding nothing of value.

Drew perfected financial "stock-watering" on the Erie Railroad, the first truck line from New York City to the Great Lakes. The road was built at a cost of around $15 million, and its completion in 1851 brought celebrations and "tremendous barbecues" all over the country. The Erie was hailed as a monument at once of "engineering skill and commercial enterprise."

Unfortunately, the rails were made of weak iron which had to be replaced, and the engines and cars were rickety and cheap. Furthermore, $26 million in stock—watered stock—was issued on around half that in real assets. The difference went to men on the inside, like Drew.

In the late sixties Vanderbilt squared off against Drew, Jim Fisk, and Jay Gould for control of the Erie. Vanderbilt wanted to add it to his New York Central; the "Erie Ring" wanted it for their stock-watering games and their thriving business into New York City, which they multiplied by dealing through Tammany Hall and by blackmailing farmers and merchants along the road who had no other way to get their goods to market.

When Vanderbilt tried to buy up the Erie stock the Ring began printing fresh shares like confetti. Certificates flew all over Wall Street, followed by court injunctions which each side got from their own judges.

Suddenly, Vanderbilt took the upper hand—

> At ten o'clock the astonished police saw a throng of panic-stricken railway directors—looking more like a frightened gang of thieves, disturbed in the division of their plun-

der, than like the wealthy representatives of a great corporation—rush headlong from the doors of the Erie office and dash off in the direction of the Jersey ferry. In their hands were packages and files of papers, and their pockets were crammed with assets and securities. One individual bore away with him in a hackney-coach bales containing six millions of dollars in greenbacks. Other members of the board followed under cover of the night; some of them, not daring to expose themselves to publicity of a ferry, attempted to cross in open boats concealed by darkness and a March fog.

The Erie directors holed up in the Taylor Hotel in Jersey City, which they surrounded with armed guards. When a rumor spread that Vanderbilt was offering $50,000 reward for the return of Drew to New York, "a standing army was organized from the employees of the road, and a small navy equipped. The alarm spread through Jersey City; the militia was held in readiness; in the evening the stores were closed and the citizens began to arm; while a garrison of about one hundred and twenty-five men entrenched themselves around the directors, in their hotel."

But it was a false alarm, and a little later a rumor circulated that Gould had left for Ohio. Soon thereafter he surfaced in Albany with a valise containing $500,000 for "legal expenses." There, said Charles Francis Adams, he undertook the task of cultivating a thorough understanding between himself and the members of the legislature—

Fabulous stories were told of the amounts which the contending parties were willing to expend; never before had the market quotations of votes and influence stood as high.

Faced with an apparently endless expense, the Commodore called a truce. He let Drew back into New York and agreed to a temporary settlement. "Vanderbilt allus told me that I acted very foolish in goin' to Jersy City," said Uncle Dan. "I tole him I didn't know but what I was circumstanced in an ockered light."

After the Vanderbilt fight, Drew played a smaller and smaller role on Wall Street and eventually died a pauper.

The following year—1869—Fisk and Gould fought Pierpont Morgan for the Albany & Susquehanna, a key link to some rich Pennsylvania coal fields. In a snowstorm of legal paper, Fisk, now known as "the Prince of Erie," sauntered into a stockholder's meeting with a gang of thugs, expecting to take over.

A group of Morgan men (recruited from the Bowery) met him and threw him down a flight of stairs, where he was "arrested" and taken to the local police station. The "policeman" that "arrested" him turned out to be a Morgan man in costume, and Fisk walked out of jail a little later.

Soon Morgan took control of the Albany terminal of the road, while the Erie Ring held the station at Binghamton. With injunctions flying right and left both sides sent out a trainload of thugs. The two locomotives rammed each other at a tunnel fifteen miles east of Binghamton, where "there was a crash and a smash, and the Albany locomotive rolled off the track, leaving the other without cowcatcher, headlight, or smokestack."

A pitched battle ensued, which the better-armed Morgan men won. The Erie Army retreated into the tunnel and regrouped. Morgan's men charged but were afraid to attack in the dark. Night fell, the militia marched in and the battle reverted to the courts, where Morgan eventually won.

That same year Gould cornered the national gold exchange and sent the price skyrocketing. When it peaked he poured his gold onto the open market, taking a gigantic profit and incidentally crashing the entire economy. "Let everyone carry out his own corpse!" yelled the irrepressible Fisk.

The Crash of '73

Four years later eastern speculators noticed their money was drying up again, as it had in 1819, 1837, and 1857. This time the Franco-Prussian War had thrown European money sources into disarray, while the postwar orgy of speculation in the United States put thousands of operators out on a limb, holding paper empires with nothing real under them.

Jay Cooke was sunk deep over his head in the Northern Pacific Railroad. Morgan, whose father had just arranged a $50 million loan to save the French government, wanted to add the NP to his expanding empire. He began publishing stories in his newspaper aimed at undermining the market value of Cooke's stock.

Under the strain Cooke's cash reserves disappeared. He was forced to duel Morgan on the floor of Congress for a $300 million "loan." Morgan won.

On September 17, 1873, President Ulysses S. Grant visited Cooke's palace in Philadelphia and spent the night. In the morning, while Grant slept, oblivious to what was going on, Cooke rode downtown and closed the doors of his bank. The national money supply disappeared. Millions of farmers and workers were thrown into a desperate struggle for existence. Mortgage money dried up, unemployment skyrocketed, families wandered from city to city in search of work.

For Morgan, Vanderbilt, and a few others with big money, crash meant good times. Labor was cheap. Giant factories stood idle, waiting to be picked off for next to nothing. With Cooke out of the way Morgan became the most powerful banker in the country. Vanderbilt and Gould added property after property to their empires while Rockefeller put the final touches on his oil kingdom. Bit by bit they took it all—

> Just as a number of German barons planted their castles along the banks of the Rhine, in order to tax the commerce between East and West, which was obliged to make use of this highway, so it is with these economic narrows. Wherever they are found, monopolies plant themselves in the shape of "rings," "corners," "pools," "syndicates," or "trusts."

Rockefeller's position was pretty well set by the 1873 depression. Rising as a merchant during the Civil War, he invested his capital in Cleveland oil refineries, taking care as he grew to commandeer all the railroad support he could get. By the early seventies he was the most powerful oil man in Cleveland.

Like Drew, Rockefeller was deeply religious. He read the Bible every night before retiring to bed, where he would discuss the day's business with himself. "These intimate conversations with myself had a great influence upon my life," he wrote in his autobiography.

The Baron of Oil had "the soul of a bookkeeper," kept all his accounts in his head, and was exceedingly **taciturn**, almost never displaying any emotion of any kind. On making a large profit, however, Rockefeller was known to clap his hands with delight, or throw his hat in the air and yell "I'm bound to be rich! *Bound to be rich!*"

With ruthless precision Rockefeller trimmed waste from his refineries while forcing rebates from the roads that carried his oil, carefully insuring that they charged his competitors more—

> Wilkerson and Company received car of oil Monday 13th—70 barrels which we suspect slipped through at the usual fifth class rate—in fact we might say we know it did—paying only $41.50 freight from here. Charges $57.40. Please turn another screw.

In the depression of the seventies Rockefeller consolidated virtually the entire oil industry in his own hands. Dominating the railroad, underselling and, in at least one instance, blowing up would-be competitors, Standard Oil simply strong-armed the rest of the industry out of existence. "I tried to make friends with these men," explained John D. "I admitted their ability and the value of their enterprise. I worked to convince them that it would be better for both to cooperate."

By 1880 Rockefeller refined 80 percent of the nation's oil. Its gigantic capital fund allowed the Standard machine to pile railroads, ore mines, shipping companies, pipelines, state governments, and

---

taciturn: Habitually untalkative.

U.S. senators one on top of the other into a mushrooming empire that was probably the most powerful single organization in the world.

By the 1880s Standard and the other baronies growing with it—Carnegie Steel, the Morgan and Mellon Banks, James Duke's American Tobacco Company, Swift and Armour Meat Packing, the railroads of Gould, Jim Hill, Tom Scott, and the Central Pacific ring—filled every corner of American life.

The Big Three

The wreckage of the 1893 collapse left three barons in control of the heart of the economy—Morgan, Rockefeller, and Carnegie, the baron of steel.

Morgan was born in Hartford in 1847. Cold and colorless, he studied mathematics in Germany and then settled into his father's banking business. In his old age his face was disfigured by a rare disease that made his nose swollen and red. He had the mind of a computer, the passion of a Swiss watch.

Morgan, in his position as the leading banker on Wall Street, had taken to "reorganizing" as many railroads as he could get his hands on, which by the nineties was about half the track in the country.

After the Erie War of 1869 he worked himself and his father's capital into the role of "peace-maker" among warring corporations. When a major struggle loomed he would invite the directors to his yacht *Corsair (Corsair II,* 204 feet long, was sold to the navy for use in conquering Cuba) and preside over a settlement. Any new stocks or bonds that resulted were handled by the House of Morgan and often interlocking directorates were created. A typical settlement occurred when General Electric and Westinghouse threatened to engage in "ruinous competition." Morgan settled the fight, took a directorship in both corporations, and the two companies pooled their patents.

The only man as big as Morgan was Rockefeller. Allied with E. H. Harriman of the Illinois Central, Rockefeller in the 1890s sat atop complete control of the oil industry, a widespread network of controlled or affiliated railroads, huge coal and iron mining interests, and a gigantic yearly income that allowed him to buy properties, ruin competitors, and manipulate national prices and markets at will.

Between Morgan and Rockefeller, Andrew Carnegie held the key. Outgoing, well-read and articulate, the lively Scotsman was known to the world as a philanthropist, to his associates as a pirate, and to the workers in his factories as a killer. An outspoken advocate of peace and human community, Carnegie built an empire on the tools of war and paid other men to use them. He was a pioneer preacher of the gospel of wealth, a leader of men "who in the words of Jack London invoked the name of the Prince of Peace in their diatribes against war, and who put rifles in the hands of Pinkertons with which to shoot down strikers in their own factories."

Carnegie built his empire of steel from the untiring efforts of a few devoted engineers who helped him cash in on the Bessemer process. Later he brought Henry Frick, the coke king, into his operation as plant manager, thus tying most of his raw materials under one roof. By the nineties he held undisputed control over the nation's key growth industry.

In 1899 friction developed between Carnegie and the Pennsylvania Railroad, where he had begun as an office boy. He threatened to "go to war" and build his own railroad to the Great Lakes, a move that upset both Rockefeller and Morgan.

Rockefeller offered to buy him out but the deal fell through. In 1900 Morgan told Carnegie to name his price and then paid over $492 million.

Quickly Morgan added his own steel holdings to the Carnegie properties and on April Fool's Day, 1901, the House of Morgan offered the first billion dollar trust—the United States Steel Corporation—for public consumption. *Cosmopolitan* magazine declared it a turning point in American economic history—

The old competitive system, with its ruinous methods, its countless duplications, its wastefulness of human effort, and its relentless business warfare, is hereby abolished.

King Dollar

As the wealth of the barons mushroomed, so did their power. From the days of Jackson the spoils system carried through the Civil War to the "Great Barbeque" of Grant, when the flood of corporate money into the government became a tidal wave. With amazing speed an efficient, loosely centralized political machine grew out of corporate money. "It was simple," wrote William Allen White—

> A state boss collected money from the railroads, the packing houses, the insurance companies, and the banks in his state.
>
> This money he sent to his henchmen in the counties, who distributed the largesse to their followers, who controlled the county conventions. The object and aim of all county conventions was to control the nomination of those Republicans who would run for the legislature and the state senate. When they were elected, as all good Republicans were, they would follow the boss.
>
> On most matters they were free; but where legislation touched the banks, the railroads, the insurance companies, or the packing houses, they were bound in honor to vote with the boss, and on his candidate for United States senator and for the tie-up he made with a candidate for state printer.
>
> The two united made a winning majority. So, over the United States, our senators went to Washington obligated to the large corporate interests of their states. . . .
>
> The railroad lobbyists and bosses in Washington amalgamated their forces. Thus the plutocracy built its mighty fortress.

In mass elections "votes" equaled "dollars." No candidate could win without a political party and thus real issues were eliminated because "the same monopolies that run the Republican run the Democratic party." A political party, explained Secretary of State William Seward, was "a joint-stock company in which those who contribute the most direct the action and management of the concern."

The parties were essentially rival corporations competing for the spoils of power. The bigger barons usually contributed to both, often supporting candidates against each other to cover their bets.

Washington was a bad joke. Congress was "transformed into a mart where the price of votes was haggled over, and laws, made to order, were bought and sold." In 1877, after troops crushed a bloody national rail strike, President Rutherford B. Hayes looked in amazement at what had become of American government—

> Shall the railroads govern the country, or shall the people govern the railroads? . . . This is a government of the people, by the people, and for the people no longer. It is a government of corporations, by corporations, and for corporations. How is this?
>
> At the turn of the century the U.S. Senate—ninety men—included no less than 25 of the country's 4000 millionaires.

The Legal Backstop

Nonetheless, as early as the seventies popular hostility to the money power was too great to be denied by electoral manipulation. At all levels of government the American people demanded that the corporations be brought under some degree of popular control.

This pushed the issue to the last line of legal defense—the Supreme Court.

After the Civil War, Congress passed the Fourteenth Amendment, guaranteeing the right of exslaves by forbidding any state to "deprive any person of life, liberty, or property without due process of law. . . ."

In 1886 the Supreme Court voided some 230 state laws meant to regulate corporations on the ground that they deprived the corporations of their property "without due process of law."

This insane ruling meant that a corporation—an organization of property—got the same legal rights as a human being. At the same time the corporations were never held liable on a human basis for criminal offenses—maltreatment of human beings and murder, for example, as literally thousands of workers were killed in factories where safety devices were "unprofitable."

In 1874, in *Schulenburg v. Harriman,* the Court stopped an attempt to take back a public land grant from a railroad which had not completed its contract. In 1895 the Court ruled an income tax law unconstitutional.

In 1887 Congress passed the Interstate Commerce Act to regulate the railroads and other businesses dealing across state lines. Almost immediately the law became the tool of the corporations themselves. Richard Olney, a lawyer for the Boston & Maine and Attorney General under Cleveland, advised a railroad president that

> The Commission, as its functions have now been limited by the courts, is, or can be made, of great use to the railroads. It satisfies the public clamor for a government supervision of railroads, at the same time that that supervision is almost entirely nominal.
>
> Further, the older such a commission gets to be, the more inclined it will be found to take the business and railroad view of things. It thus becomes a sort of barrier between the railroad corporations and the people. . . .

The Sherman Anti-Trust Act, passed in 1890, served the same function. Republican Senator Orville Platt of Connecticut explained why Congress bothered to pass it at all—

> The conduct of the Senate . . . has not been in the line of honest preparation of a bill to prohibit and punish trusts. It has been in the line of getting some bill with that title that we might go to the country with.
>
> The questions of whether the bill would be operative, of how it would operate, . . . have been whistled down the wind in this Senate as idle talk, and the whole effort has been to get some bill headed: "A Bill to Punish Trusts" with which to go to the country.

If there was ever any doubt, the Supreme Court wiped out the Sherman Act's effectiveness against the trusts five years after its passage. In 1895 it ruled that the E. C. Knight Company, which refined 98 percent of the nation's sugar, restrained trade only "indirectly."

But from 1890 to 1897 the Sherman Act was used twelve times to break labor strikes. "What looks like a stone wall to a layman," said the humorist Mr. Dooley, "is a triumphal arch to a corporation lawyer."

The Barrel of the Gun

But if the system seemed to run on money and legalities, there was no mistaking that ultimately it rested on brute force. From the thirties on, federal, state, and local armies, militia, and police were in ceaseless use breaking up demonstrations, strikes, labor unions. In the name of property, law, and order, jails were constantly filled and official violence brought down on those who advocated worker control of factories, the right to organize, a black-white alliance in the South, and a redistribution of wealth and power.

In a pinch the barons also had their private armies of Pinkerton "detectives," professional guards, strikebreakers, vigilantes, and citizen's leagues to handle the untidy work of doing away with rebels.

In a nation with a solid unemployment rate and an average income below the subsistence level, a man like Jay Gould wasn't kidding when he boasted "I can hire one-half the working class to kill the other half!"

Atop this flexible tyranny sat the Four Hundred, a group of four to six hundred families centered in New York and including the biggest of the barons and their entourage—a self-proclaimed "nobility of wealth." Frederick Townshend Martin spoke their creed in *The Passing of the Idle Rich*—

> The class I represent, care nothing for politics . . . it matters not one iota what political party is in power or what president holds the reigns of office.
>
> We are not politicians or public thinkers; we are the rich; we own America; we got it, God knows how, but we intend to keep it if we can by throwing all the tremendous weight of our support, our influence, our money, our political connections, our purchased senators, our hungry congressmen, our public-speaking demagogues, into the scale against any legislature, any political platform, any presidential campaign that threatens the integrity of our estate.

The Machine

The American industrial machine was clearly becoming the biggest in the world. Each landmark of growth, each statistic of wealth, was hailed by the barons with excitement and pride.

Upon completion of the transcontinental railroad in 1869, Jay Gould could hardly control his delight. "WE have made the country rich," he yelled. "WE have developed the country, coal mines and cattle raising, as well as cotton . . . WE have created this earning power by developing the system!"

With great national fanfare the Union and Central Pacific lines were joined at Promontory Point, Utah. A gold and a silver spike were to be driven into the final tie by one of the many dignitaries carried to Utah for the ceremony. But none of them could handle a sledgehammer. A construction worker had to be called out of the crowd to knock in the spikes.

By 1888 the American industrial system was killing 100 workers every day—around 35,000 were killed each year, with over 500,000 reported injured.

More than 700,000 American workers were killed in industrial "accidents" from 1888 to 1908. Nearly a million industrial injuries were reported in 1913. The railroads alone killed ten workers a day, the coal mines about the same. If you only get maimed you were lucky—

> A brakeman with both hands and all his fingers was either remarkably skillful, incredibly lucky or new on the job.

A substantial part of the work force was made up of children, especially in the mines and in the textile mills of New England towns like Lawrence, Massachusetts, where half the workers were girls between the ages of fourteen and eighteen—

> A considerable number of the boys and girls die within the first two or three years after beginning work . . . Thirty-six of every 100 of all the men and women who work in the mill die before or by the time they are twenty-five years of age.

The life-span of the average mill worker in Lawrence was twenty-two years shorter than that of an owner.

To help guarantee a large work force for their factories, the barons advertised American all over Europe as the land of the rich, where anyone "good enough" could become wealthy in no time. The plains of Montana were hailed as fertile, jungle-like farmland and became known as "Jay Cooke's Banana Belt." Steamship companies and rail lines starving for passengers uplifted entire peasant villages and set them down in the West.

For the immigrants the voyage to America was a journey of hope, an escape from the poverty of Europe's dying peasant culture. America meant a new chance at life. But for Andrew Carnegie, himself an immigrant, people coming to America meant a "cheap and mobile labor force," as he pointed out in 1905—

> Taking the cost, the value of a man, a woman or a child, in this Republic as low as you put the slave, and that was average of about $1000, you are getting 400,000 a year and that means $4,000,000 cash value.

Utterly powerless and confused, piled into the ghettoes of New York, Chicago, Philadelphia, Baltimore, and Boston, or shuttled to the crippled western farm community, the new arrivals were at the disposal of employers without whom they literally could not get food, clothing, housing. The bitter prewar diatribe of a South Carolina senator began to make a perverted sort of sense—

> The difference between us is that our slaves are hired for life. . . . Yours are hired by the day, not cared for, and scantily compensated which may be proved in the most deplorable manner, at any hour in any street of your large towns. . . .

American industry was paid for in the broken backs and dead eyes of men, women, and children who were valued only as fuel. "Men are cheap and machinery is dear," explained Woodrow Wilson. "You can discard your man and replace him; there are others ready to come into his place; but you can't without great cost, discard your machine and put a new one in its place."

Who Do You Trust?

At the turn of the century it was generally accepted that the free enterprise system had finally passed away. It was hoped by many that the "community of interest" arrangements between the banks and the big trusts would help rationalize the economy. Wasteful competition would be eliminated, and professional, "progressive" management would take charge.

But the trusts brought no basic changes. From its very beginning the long-awaited United States Steel Corporation was half water. Morgan floated $1.4 billion in stock over $5,682 million in real assets and took a $62 million "commission" for handling the issue. By 1903 U.S. Steel stock had dropped from 40 to 8. The price of a ton of the company's steel jumped from $24 to $28 soon after the trust was formed.

As for efficiency, the giant corporations were at best unwieldy, impersonal bureaucracies. And they turned out to be powerful, destructive barriers to technological progress.

For while many of them could and did conduct expensive scientific research, they also used their power to buy up new inventions and bury them in the patent office, keeping them out of the hands of the public.

Small innovations were indeed used to cut short-range production costs. But major changes that might require expensive retooling or complicated reorganization were suppressed time and again. "A huge organization," wrote *Engineering News*, "is too clumsy to take up the development of an original idea. With the market closely controlled and profits certain by following standard methods, those who control our trusts do not want the bother of developing anything new."

Woodrow Wilson, before he became President, agreed—

> I am not saying that all invention has been stopped by the growth of the trusts, but I think it is perfectly clear that invention in many fields has been discouraged . . . and that mankind has been deprived of many comforts and conveniences, as well as the opportunity of buying at lower prices.

Reading 3

Plessy v. Ferguson:
The Birth of Jim Crow

C. Vann Woodward

In the spring of 1885, Charles Dudley Warner, Mark Twain's friend, neighbor, and onetime collaborator from Hartford, Connecticut, visited the International Exposition at New Orleans. He was astonished to find that "white and colored people mingled freely, talking and looking at what was of common interest," that blacks "took their full share of the parade and the honors," and that the two races associated "in unconscious equality of privileges." During his visit he saw "a colored clergyman in his surplice seated in the chancel of the most important white Episcopal church in New Orleans, assisting in the service."

It was a common occurrence in the 1880s for foreign travellers and northern visitors to comment, sometimes with distaste and always with surprise, on the freedom of association between white and black people in the South. Yankees in particular were unprepared for what they found and sometimes estimated that conditions below the Potomac were better than those above. There was discrimination, to be sure, and blacks were often excluded from first-class public accommodations—as they were in the North. But that was done on the responsibility of private owners or managers and not by requirement of law. According to the Supreme Court's decision in the Civil Rights Cases of 1883 the federal law gave no protection from such private acts.

Where discrimination existed it was often erratic and inconsistent. On trains the usual practice was to exclude blacks from first-class or "ladies'" cars but to permit them to mix with whites in second-class or "smoking" cars. In the old seaboard states of the South, however, blacks were as free to ride first class as whites. In no state was segregation on trains complete, and in none was it enforced by law. The age of Jim Crow was still to come.

The first genuine Jim Crow law requiring railroads to carry blacks in separate cars or behind partitions was adopted by Florida in 1887. Mississippi followed this example in 1888; Texas in 1889; Louisiana in 1890; Alabama, Arkansas, Georgia, and Tennessee in 1891; and Kentucky in 1892. The Carolinas and Virginia did not fall into line until the last three years of the century.

Blacks watched with despair while the legal foundations for the Jim Crow system were laid and the walls of segregation mounted around them. Their disenchantment with the hopes based on the Civil War amendments and the Reconstruction laws was nearly complete by 1890. The American commitment to equality, solemnly attested by three amendments to the Constitution and by elaborate civil rights acts, was virtually repudiated. The "compromise of 1877" between the Hayes

Republicans and the southern conservatives had resulted in the withdrawal of federal troops from the South and the formal end of Reconstruction. What had started then as a retreat had within a decade turned into a rout. Northern radicals and liberals had abandoned the cause; the courts had rendered the Constitution helpless; the Republican party had forsaken the cause it had sponsored. A tide of racism was mounting in the country unopposed.

The black community of New Orleans, with its strong infusion of French and other nationalities, was in a strategic position to furnish leadership for the resistance against segregation. Many of these people had culture, education, and some wealth, as well as a heritage of several generations of freedom. Unlike the great majority of blacks, they were city people with an established professional class and a high degree of literacy. By ancestry as well as by residence they were associated with Latin cultures at variance with Anglo-American ideas of race relations. Their forebears had lived under the Code Noir decreed for Louisiana by Louis XIV, and their city faced out upon Latin America.

When the Jim Crow car bill was introduced in the Louisiana legislature, New Orleans blacks organized to fight it. Blacks were still voting in large numbers, and there were sixteen black senators and representatives in the Louisiana General Assembly. On May 24, 1890, that body received "A Protest of the American Citizens' Equal Rights Association of Louisiana Against Class Legislation." An organization of black people, the association protested that the pending bill was "unconstitutional, unamerican, unjust, dangerous and against sound public policy." It would, declared the protest, "be a free license to the evilly-disposed that they might with impunity insult, humiliate, and otherwise maltreat inoffensive persons, and especially women and children who should happen to have a dark skin."

On July 10, 1890, the Assembly passed the bill, the governor signed it, and it became law. Entitled "An Act to promote the comfort of passengers," the new law required railroads "to provide equal but separate accommodations for the white and black races." Two members of the Equal Rights Association, L. A. Martinet, editor of the *New Orleans Crusader,* and R. L. Desdunes, placed heavy blame on the sixteen colored members of the Assembly for the passage of the bill. According to Martinet, "they were completely the masters of the situation." They had but to withhold their support for a bill desired by the powerful Louisiana Lottery Company until the Jim Crow bill was killed. "But in an evil moment," he added, "our Representatives turned their ears to listen to the golden siren," and "did so for a 'consideration.'"

Putting aside recriminations, the *Crusader* declared: "The Bill is now a law. The next thing is what we are going to do?" The editor spoke testily of boycotting the railroads, but concluded that "the next thing is . . . to begin to gather funds to test the constitutionality of this law. We'll make a case, a test case, and bring it before the Federal Courts." On September 1, 1891, a group of eighteen men of color formed a "Citizens' Committee to Test the Constitutionality of the Separate Car Law."

Money came in slowly at first, but by October 11, Martinet could write that the committee had already collected $1,500 and that more could be expected "after we have the case well started." Even before the money was collected, Martinet had opened a correspondence about the case with Albion Winegar Tourgée of Mayville, New York, and in October to the Citizens' Committee formally elected Tourgée "leading counsel in the case, from beginning to end, with power to choose associates."

This action called back into the stream of history a name prominent in the annals of Reconstruction. Albion Tourgée was in 1890 probably the most famous surviving carpetbagger. His fame was due not so much to his achievements as a carpetbagger in North Carolina, significant though they were, as to the six novels about his Reconstruction experiences that he had published since 1879. Born in Ohio, of French Huguenot descent, he had served as an officer in the Union Army, and moved to Greensboro, North Carolina, in 1865 to practice law. He soon became a leader of the Radical Republican party, took a prominent part in writing the Radical Constitution of North Carolina, and served as a judge of the superior court for six years with considerable distinction. He brought to the fight against segregation in Louisiana a combination of zeal and ability that the Citizens' Committee of New Orleans would have found it hard to duplicate. They had reason to write him, "we know we have a friend in you & we know your ability is beyond question." He was informed that the committee's decision was made "spontaneously, warmly, & gratefully."

Tourgée's first suggestion was that the person chosen for defendant in the test case be "nearly white," but that proposal raised some doubts. "It would be quite difficult," explained Martinet, "to have a lady *too* nearly white refused admission to a 'white' car." He pointed out that "people of tolerably fair complexion, even if unmistakably colored, enjoy here a large degree of immunity from the accursed prejudice. . . . To make this case would require some tact." He would volunteer himself, "but I am one of those whom a fair complexion favors. I go everywhere, in all public places, though well-known all over the city, & never is anything said to me. On the cars it would be the same thing. In fact, color prejudice, in this respect does not affect me. But, as I have said, we can try it, with another."

Railroad officials proved surprisingly co-operative. The first one approached, however, confessed that his road "did not enforce the law." It provided the Jim Crow car and posted the required sign, but told its conductors to molest no one who ignored instructions. Officers of two other roads "said the law was a bad and mean one; they would like to get rid of it," and asked for time to consult counsel. "They want to help us," said Martinet, "but dread public opinion." The extra expense of separate cars was one reason for railroad opposition to the Jim Crow law.

It was finally agreed that a white passenger should object to the presence of a black in a "white" coach, that the conductor should direct the black passenger to go to the Jim Crow car, and that he should refuse to go. "The conductor will be instructed not to use force or molest," reported Martinet, "& *our* white passenger will swear out the affidavit. This will give us our *habeas corpus* case, I hope." On the appointed day, February 24, 1892, Daniel F. Desdunes, a young black man, bought a ticket for Mobile, boarded the Louisville & Nashville Railroad, and took a seat in the white coach.

All went according to plan. Desdunes was committed for trial to the Criminal District Court in New Orleans and released on bail. On March 21, James C. Walker, a local attorney associated with Tourgée in the case, filed a plea protesting that his client was not guilty and attacking the constitutionality of the Jim Crow law. He wrote Tourgée that he intended to go to trial as early as he could.

Between the lawyers there was not entire agreement on procedure. Walker favored the plea that the law was void because it attempted to regulate interstate commerce, over which the Supreme Court held that Congress had exclusive jurisdiction. Tourgée was doubtful. "What we want," he wrote Walker, "is not a verdict of not guilty, nor a defect in this law but a decision whether such a law can be legally enacted and enforced in any state and we should get everything off the track and out of the way for such a decision." Walker confessed that "it's hard for me to give up my pet hobby that the law is void as a regulation of interstate commerce," and Tourgée admitted that he "may have spoken too lightly of the interstate commerce matter.

The discussion was ended abruptly and the whole approach altered before Desdunes' case came to trial by a decision of the Louisiana Supreme Court handed down on May 25. In this case, which was of entirely independent origin, the court reversed the ruling of a lower court and upheld the Pullman Company's plea that the Jim Crow law was unconstitutional in so far as it applied to interstate passengers.

Desdunes was an interstate passenger holding a ticket to Alabama, but the decision was a rather empty victory. The law still applied to intrastate passengers, and since all states adjacent to Louisiana had by this time adopted similar or identical Jim Crow laws, the exemption of interstate passengers was of no great importance to the blacks of Louisiana, and it left the principle against which they contended unchallenged. On June 1, Martinet wired Tourgée on behalf of the committee, saying that

"Walker wants new case wholly within state limits," and asking Tourgée's opinion. Tourgée wired his agreement.

One week later, on June 7, Homer Adolph Plessy bought a ticket in New Orleans, boarded the East Louisiana Railroad bound for Covington, a destination "wholly within the state limits," and took a seat in the white coach. Since Plessy later described himself as "seven-eighths Caucasian and one-eighth African blood," and swore that "the admixture of colored blood is not discernible," it may be assumed that the railroad had been told of the plan and had agreed to co-operate. When Plessy refused to comply with the conductor's request that he move to the Jim Crow car, he was arrested by Detective Christopher C. Cain "and quietly accompanied the officer." The *New Orleans Times-Democrat* remarked that "It is generally believed that Plessy intends testing the law before the courts."

In due course Homer Plessy's case became *Plessy v. Ferguson*. The latter name belonged to John H. Ferguson, Judge of Section A of the Criminal District Court for the Parish of New Orleans, who overruled the plea of Tourgée and Walker, the defendant's counsel, that the Jim Crow law was null and void because it was in conflict with the Constitution of the United States. Plessy then applied to the State Supreme Court for a writ of prohibition and certiorari and was given a hearing in November, 1892. The court recognized that neither the interstate commerce clause nor the question of equality of accommodations was involved and held that "the sole question" was whether a law requiring "separate but equal accommodations" violated the Fourteenth Amendment. Citing numerous decisions of lower federal courts to the effect that accommodations did not have to be identical to be equal, the court as expected upheld the law.

"We have been at pains to expound this statute," added the court, "because the dissatisfaction felt with it by a portion of the people seems to us so unreasonable that we can account for it only on the ground of some misconception."

Chief Justice Francis Redding Tillou Nicholls, heading the court that handed down this decision in 1892, had signed the Jim Crow act as governor when it was passed in 1890. Previously he had served as the "Redeemer" governor who took over Louisiana from the carpetbaggers in 1877 and inaugurated a brief regime of conservative paternalism. In those days Nicholls had denounced race bigotry, appointed blacks to office, and attracted many of them to his party.

L. A. Martinet wrote Tourgée that Nicholls in those years had been "fair & just to colored men" and had, in fact, "secured a degree of protection to the colored people not enjoyed under Republican Governors." But in November, 1892, the wave of Populist rebellion among the white farmers was reaching its crest in the South, and Judge Nicholls' change of course typified the concessions to racism that conservatives of his class made in their efforts to forestall or divert the rebellion. Nonetheless, at a further hearing Nicholls granted Plessy's petition for a writ of error that permitted him to seek redress before the Supreme Court of the United States.

The brief that Albion Tourgée submitted to the Supreme Court in behalf of Plessy breathed a spirit of equalitarianism that was more in tune with his carpetbagger days than with the prevailing spirit of the mid-nineties.

At the very outset, he advanced an argument in behalf of his client that unconsciously illustrated the paradox that had from the start haunted the American attempt to reconcile strong color prejudice with deep equalitarian commitments.

Plessy, he contended, had been deprived of property without due process of law. The "property" in question was the "reputation of being white." It was "the most valuable sort of property, being the master-key that unlocks the golden door of opportunity." Intense race prejudice excluded any man suspected of having black blood "from the friendship and companionship of the white man," and therefore from the avenues to wealth, prestige, and opportunity. "Probably most white persons if given the choice," he held, "would prefer death to life in the United States as *colored persons.*"

Since Tourgée had proposed that a person who was "nearly white" be selected for the test case, it may be presumed that he did so with this argument in mind. But this was not a defense of the black man against discrimination by whites, but a defense of the "nearly" white man against the penalties of color. The argument, whatever its merits, apparently did not impress the Court.

Tourgée went on to develop more relevant points. He emphasized especially the incompatibility of the segregation law with the spirit and intent of the Thirteenth and particularly the Fourteenth amendments. Segregation perpetuated distinctions "of a servile character, coincident with the institution of slavery." He held that "slavery was a caste, a legal condition of subjection to the dominant class, a bondage quite separable from the incident of ownership." He scorned the pretense of impartiality and equal protection advanced in the defense of the "separate but equal" doctrine.

"The object of such a law," he declared, "is simply to debase and distinguish against the inferior race. Its purpose has been properly interpreted by the general designation of 'Jim Crow Car' law. Its object is to separate the blacks from the whites in public conveyances for the gratification and recognition of the sentiment of white superiority and white supremacy of right and power." He asked the members of the Court to imagine the tables turned and themselves ordered into a Jim Crow car. "What humiliation, what rage would then fill the judicial mind!" he exclaimed.

The clue to the true intent of the Louisiana statute was that it did not apply "to nurses attending the children of the other race." On this clause Tourgée shrewdly observed:

> The exemption of nurses shows that the real evil lies not in the color of the skin but in the relation the colored person sustains to the white. If he is a dependent it may be endured: if he is not, his presence is insufferable. Instead of being intended to promote the general comfort and moral well-being, this act is plainly and evidently intended to promote the happiness of one class by asserting its supremacy and the inferiority of another class. Justice is pictured blind and her daughter, the Law, ought at least to be color-blind.

Tourgée then asked the Court to look to the future. Should the separate-car law be upheld, he inquired, "what is to prevent the application of the same principle to other relations?" Was there any limit to such laws? "Why not require all colored people to walk on one side of the street and whites on the other? . . . One side of the street may be just as good as the other. . . . The question is not as to the *equality* of the privileges enjoyed, but *the right of the State to label one citizen as white and another as colored* in the common enjoyment of a public highway."

The Supreme Court did not get around to handing down a decision on *Plessy v. Ferguson* until 1896. In the years that intervened between the passage of the Louisiana segregation law in July, 1890, and the time of the eventual decision on its constitutionality in 1896, the retreat from the commitment to equality had quickened its pace in the South and met with additional acquiescence, encouragement, and approval in the North. Two states had already disfranchised the black citizen, and several others, including Louisiana, were planning to take the same course. In 1892 Congress defeated the Lodge Bill, designed to extend federal protection to elections, and in 1894 it wiped from the federal statute books a mass of Reconstruction laws for the protection of equal rights. And then, on September 18, 1895, Booker T. Washington delivered a famous speech embodying the so-called "Atlanta Compromise," which was widely interpreted as an acceptance of subordinate status for the black citizen by the foremost leader of the race.

On May 18, 1896, Justice Henry Billings Brown, a resident of Michigan but a native of Massachusetts, delivered the opinion of the Court in the case of *Plessy v. Ferguson*. His views upholding the defendant's case that the "separate but equal" doctrine was constitutional—were in accord with those of all his brothers, with the possible exception of Justice David Josiah Brewer, who did not participate, and the certain exception of Justice John Marshall Harlan, who vigorously dissented in phrases that often echoed Tourgée's arguments. In approving, to all intents and purposes, the principle of segregation, Justice Brown followed not only the trend of the times, but a host of state judicial precedents, which he cited at length. That there were no federal judicial precedents to the contrary only added to the technical strength of his position. Just as telling, perhaps, was Brown's mention of the action of Congress in establishing segregated schools for the District of Columbia, an action endorsed by Radical Republicans who had supported the Fourteenth Amendment, and sustained in regular congressional appropriations ever since.

Similar laws, wrote Brown, were adopted by "the legislatures of many states, and have been generally, if not uniformly, sustained by the courts." The validity of such segregation laws, he maintained, depended on their "reasonableness." And in determining reasonableness, the legislature "is at liberty to act with reference to the established usages, customs, and traditions of the people, and with a view to the promotion of their comfort, and the preservation of the public peace and good order."

In addition to judicial precedent and accepted practice, Justice Brown ventured into the more uncertain fields of sociology and psychology for support of his opinion. He wrote:

> We consider the underlying fallacy of the plaintiff's argument to consist in the assumption that the enforced separation of the two races stamps the colored race with a badge of inferiority. If this be so, it is not by reason of anything found in the act, but solely because the colored race chooses to put that construction upon it. . . . The argument also assumes that social prejudices may be overcome by legislation, and that equal rights cannot be secured by the negro except by an enforced commingling of the two races. We cannot accept this proposition . . . Legislation is powerless to eradicate racial instincts, or to abolish distinctions based upon physical differences, and the attempt to do so can only result in accentuating the difficulties of the present situation. If the civil and political rights of both races be equal, one cannot be inferior to the other civilly or politically. If one race be inferior to the other socially, the constitution of the United States cannot put them upon the same plane.

One of the most fascinating paradoxes in American jurisprudence is that the opinion of a native son of Massachusetts, Brown, should have bridged the gap between the radical equalitarian commitment of 1868 and the reactionary repudiation of that commitment in 1896; and that Harlan, a southerner, should have bridged the greater gap between the repudiation of 1896 and the radical rededication to the equalitarian idealism of 1868 in 1954. For the dissenting opinion of Justice Harlan, embodying many of the arguments of Plessy's ex-carpetbagger counsel, foreshadowed the Court's eventual repudiation of the *Plessy v. Ferguson* decision, and the doctrine of "separate but equal" more than half a century later—a repudiation in which, fittingly enough, Harlan's grandson and namesake on the Warren Court wholly concurred.

The elder John Marshall Harlan is correctly described by Robert Cushman as "a Southern gentleman and a slave-holder, and at heart a conservative." A Kentuckian of the Whig persuasion, Harlan had opposed secession and fought in the Union Army, but at the same time he opposed both the emancipation of the slaves and the passage of civil rights laws to protect the rights of the freedmen. Shocked by Ku Klux excesses, he experienced a sudden conversion, renounced his former views, became a Republican in 1868, and was appointed to the Supreme Court by President Hayes in 1877.

After his conversion Harlan became one of the most outspoken champions of black rights of his time, and during his thirty-four years on the bench he lifted his voice repeatedly against denial of those rights by the dominant opinion of the Court. His famous dissent in the Civil Rights Cases of 1883 had denounced the "subtle and ingenious verbal criticism" by which "the substance and spirit of the recent amendments of the Constitution have been sacrificed." And in 1896 he was ready to strike another blow for his adopted cause.

Harlan held the Louisiana segregation law in clear conflict with both the Thirteenth and the Fourteenth amendments. The former "not only struck down the institution of slavery," but also "any burdens or disabilities that constitute badges of slavery or servitude," and segregation was just such a burden or badge. Moreover, the Fourteenth Amendment "added greatly to the dignity and glory of American citizenship, and to the security of personal liberty," and segregation denied to blacks the equal protection of both dignity and liberty. "The arbitrary separation of citizens, on the basis of race, while they are on a public highway," he said, "is a badge of servitude wholly inconsistent with the civil freedom and the equality before the law established by the constitution. It cannot be justified upon any legal grounds."

Harlan was as scornful as Tourgée had been of the claim that the separate-car law did not discriminate against the black citizen. "Every one knows," he declared, that its purpose was "to exclude colored people from coaches occupied by or assigned to white persons." This was simply a poorly disguised means of asserting the supremacy of one class of citizens over another. The justice continued:

> But in view of the constitution, in the eye of the law, there is in this country no superior, dominant, ruling class of citizens. There is no caste here. Our constitution is color-blind, and neither knows nor tolerates classes among citizens. In respect of civil rights, all citizens are equal before the law. The humblest is the peer of the most powerful. The law regards man as man, and takes no account of his surroundings, or of his color when his civil rights as guaranteed by the supreme law of the land are involved. . . . We boast of the freedom enjoyed by our people above all other peoples. But it is difficult to reconcile that boast with a state of law which, practically, puts the brand of servitude and degradation upon a large class of our fellow citizens,—our equals before the law. The thin disguise of "equal" accommodations for passengers in railroad coaches will not mislead any one, nor atone for the wrong this day done.

"The present decision, it may well be apprehended," predicted Harlan, "will not only stimulate aggressions, more or less brutal and irritating, upon the admitted rights of colored citizens, but will encourage the belief that it is possible, by means of state enactments, to defeat the beneficent purposes which the people of the United States had in view when they adopted the recent amendments of the constitution. . . ." For if the state may so regulate the railroads, "why may it not so regulate the use of the streets of its cities and towns as to compel white citizens to keep on one side of a street, and black citizens to keep on the other," or, for that matter, apply the same regulations to streetcars and other vehicles, or to courtroom, the jury box, the legislative hall, or to any other place of public assembly?

"In my opinion," the Kentuckian concluded, "the judgment this day rendered will, in time, prove to be quite as pernicious as the decision made by this tribunal in the Dred Scott Case."

But Harlan was without allies on the Court, and the country as a whole received the news of its momentous decision upholding the "separate but equal" doctrine in relative silence and apparent indifference. Thirteen years earlier the Civil Rights Cases had precipitated pages of news reports, hundreds of editorials, indignant rallies, congressional bills, a Senate report, and much general debate. In striking contrast, the *Plessy* decision was accorded only short, inconspicuous news reports and virtually no editorial comment outside the black press. A great change had taken place, and the Court evidently now gave voice to the dominant mood of the country. Justice Harlan had spoken for the forgotten convictions of a bygone era.

The racial aggressions he foresaw came in a flood after the decision of 1896. Even Harlan indicated by his opinion of 1899 in *Cummings v. Board of Education* that he saw nothing unconstitutional in segregated public schools. Virginia was the last state in the South to adopt the separate-car law, and she resisted it only until 1900. Up to that year this was the only law of the type adopted by a majority of the southern states. But on January 12, 1900, the editor of the *Richmond Times* was in full accord with the new spirit when he asserted: "It is necessary that this principle be applied in every relation of Southern life. God Almighty drew the color line and it cannot be obliterated. The negro must stay on his side of the line and the white man must stay on his side, and the sooner both races recognize this fact and accept it, the better it will be for both."

With a thoroughness approaching the incredible, the color line *was* drawn and the Jim Crow principle was applied even in those areas that Tourgée and Harlan had suggested a few years before as absurd extremes. In sustaining all these new laws, courts universally and confidently cited *Plessy v. Ferguson* as their authority. They continued to do so for more than half a century.

On April 4, 1950, Justice Robert H. Jackson wrote old friends in Jamestown, New York, of his surprise in running across the name of Albion W. Tourgée, once a resident of the nearby village of Mayville, in connection with segregation decisions then pending before the Supreme Court. "The *Plessy* case arose in Louisiana," he wrote, "and how Tourgée got into it I have not learned. In any event, I have gone to his old brief, filed here, and there is no argument made today that he would not make to the Court. He says, 'Justice is pictured blind and her daughter, the Law, ought at least to be color-blind.' Whether this was original with him, it has been gotten off a number of times since as original wit. Tourgée's brief was filed April 6, 1896 and now, just fifty-four years after, the question is again being argued whether his position will be adopted and what was a defeat for him in '96 be a postmortem victory."

Plessy v. Ferguson remained the law of the land for fifty-eight years lacking one day from May 18, 1896, to May 17, 1954, when the Supreme Court at last renounced it in the school segregation cases of *Brown et al. v. Board of Education of Topeka, et al.* In that decision could indeed be found, at long last, a vindication, "a post-mortem victory"—not only for the ex-carpetbagger Tourgée but for the ex-slaveholder Harlan as well.

Reading 4

Russian Jews in the United States

J. William T. Youngs

America has long been a place of refuge for the outcasts of other lands. Puritans fleeing religious persecution and Irish families escaping famine immigrated to the New World to begin their lives anew. Waves of immigrants from Northern Europe peopled the United States in the early years, but the greatest influx came during the years 1880 to 1915 when millions of people from Eastern and Southern Europe came to America and created ethnic communities. The Russian Jews and other immigrants faced many hardships in the United States, but none more difficult than maintaining their cultural identity in an America that both stimulated and undermined their traditional ways.

When did America begin? The American national holiday celebrates the events of 1776 in Philadelphia, Pennsylvania. But the United States is not exclusively the product of the Revolution. America had many births—after 1776 as well as before; her origins lay in the streets of Dublin, the villages of Russia, the fields of China, and the fjords of Norway, as well as in the farms and towns of the thirteen colonies. In 1900, 15 percent of the people living in the United States had been born elsewhere. Between 1840 and 1914 more than 30 million people came from foreign countries to settle in the United States. The Great Migration of Puritans to Massachusetts Bay from 1630 to 1640 brought about forty thousand people; late in the nineteenth and early in the twentieth centuries, as many immigrants frequently passed through Ellis Island in a week. In the years 1905, 1906, and 1907 more people came to America than the whole population of the United States at the time of the Revolution. Ireland, Great Britain, Scandinavia, Russia, Italy, and Germany each gave birth to more than a million future Americans between 1840 and 1915.

These immigrants were changed by the United States, but America was changed by them at the same time. The story does not lend itself to neat chronological boundaries or to the listing of key episodes; it is much more subtle and amorphous than the history of an individual or event. But the story of one group will help clarify this gradual, fundamental change. The Russian Jewish experience is remarkable in itself, but is the more important because it is not unique; a dozen or more immigrant sagas have similar scope. The Chinese in San Francisco, the Irish in Boston, the Scandinavians in Wisconsin and Minnesota, and scores of other groups combined immigrant backgrounds with an American future.

The Russian Jews who began arriving in the United States in large numbers after 1880 were not the earliest members of the Jewish faith to arrive. The first Jews came to America in 1654 and settled in New Amsterdam. At the time of the American Revolution, some two thousand Jews were in the United States, with congregations in Newport, New York, Philadelphia, Richmond, and

Savannah. In the next thirty years the population climbed slowly, but after 1820 Jewish immigration began to increase rapidly. By 1850 the Jewish population was 50,000; in 1860 it reached 150,000. Most of the new immigrants were refugees from political and social turmoil in Germany. They mainly engaged in trade and settled throughout the United States.

Just before 1900, immigration to the United States changed dramatically. Hitherto most immigrants, non-Jewish as well as Jewish, had been from Central and Northern Europe: France, Germany, Scandinavia, Great Britain, and Ireland. But now "new immigrants" began to arrive from Southern and Eastern Europe: Austria-Hungary, Poland, Russia, Romania, Italy, and Greece. Most Jewish immigrants after 1880 were from Eastern Europe.

At first the German Jews were ambivalent about the arrival of their religious fellows from Eastern Europe. On the one hand, they sympathized with Jews escaping from oppression. On the other, they were embarrassed by the curious customs of the new immigrants: the men with long, curly beards; the women with wigs; the strange accents; the poverty; the reputation of some for radicalism. The old Jews commonly feared that the strange new immigrants would damage their own image of respectability. But despite these reservations, the German Jews became active in immigrant aid societies and lobbied to keep immigration policies liberal. Between 1881 and 1914 more than 2 million Jews immigrated to America. More than three-fourths of these came from Russia; most of the remainder from other regions of Eastern Europe, especially Austria-Hungary and Romania. Most new immigrants settled in, or at least passed through, New York's Lower East Side. Between 1880 and 1910 the Jewish population in New York City increased from 80,000 to 1,250,000.

The Jews who came to the United States had no nation of their own but lived scattered across Europe and through other quarters of the globe. Wherever they lived they depended on their host nation to allow them to worship in peace. In Germany, Italy, Austria-Hungary, Russia, and elsewhere, they provided services as artisans and businessmen and accordingly were tolerated. But their position was always precarious. They usually had no political power and often were oppressed by hostile citizens and rulers.

The Russian Jews were mainly the descendants of men and women who had settled in Poland in the thirteenth and fourteenth centuries. There they had become moneylenders, tax collectors, innkeepers, artisans, and grain merchants. For several centuries they lived in relative peace, but in the eighteenth century Poland was partitioned—divided among Russia, Prussia, and Austria—and many Polish Jews came under Russian domination.

Under the tsars the position of the Jews rapidly deteriorated. They were not allowed to live outside of a region known as the Pale of Settlement, which consisted of Poland, Lithuania, Byelorussia, and the Ukraine. Within the Pale itself, their political and economic activities were restricted. They were usually not allowed to own land, and they were barred from higher education by restrictive quotas and tests. Early in the nineteenth century, Jews were drafted into the Russian army for twenty-five-year periods of service and were expected to become Christians. Those who managed to preserve their faith through this long ordeal became heroes among their people.

For civilians as well as for soldiers, the challenge of maintaining Judaism in a hostile environment strengthened faith. Religion provided the Jewish people with a sense of community, integrity, and purpose. Being a Jew involved not only special forms of worship but also distinctive patterns of dress, behavior, and speech—most spoke Yiddish, a composite of Hebrew and other languages. They observed special holidays, prayers, and laws. Religious learning was the essential part of education: young men frequently spent many years studying Jewish law, and the scholar was highly esteemed.

Thus, the Russian Jews were effectively a nation within a nation, drawn together by a common faith and driven together by Russian prejudice. But despite their disadvantages they established strong, healthy communities within the Pale. Most lived in towns that dotted the predominantly agricultural landscape. Barred from landownership, they provided goods for the agrarian population by working as artisans, small manufacturers, and merchants. In the Russian population as a whole, a much larger proportion of Jews than Gentiles was involved in manufacturing, commerce, and the professions. These economic activities provided a livelihood but not great riches. Some 5 to 10 percent of Russian Jews were moderately wealthy; 20 percent were impoverished; the majority lived in modest comfort with simple food, clothing, shelter, and furnishings.

Still, by several measures of achievement the Russian Jews may be said to have prospered. They maintained close family ties, had high standards of hygiene, and experienced no problem with alcoholism. These indications of personal and communal health are reflected in Russian vital statistics: the Jewish death rate was much lower than that of other Russians. The caliber of Jewish life is reflected also in a relatively high literacy rate: twice as many Russian Jews as non-Jews could read at the end of the nineteenth century.

The life of the Russian Jew with its mixture of hardship and triumph is told in the story of a girl who migrated from the Pale to the United States. After a few years of life in the New World she decided to write an account of her youth, not, as she indicated in her preface, because it was unique, but because it was "typical of many." Her American name was Mary Antin, and the title of her book was *The Promised Land*.

Mary was born in Polotzk, a village some three hundred miles west of Moscow. Her father was a prosperous merchant who provided well for his family: his daughter remembered embroidered linen, silver candlesticks, kitchen shelves "lined with copper and brass," and "featherbeds heaped halfway to the ceiling." It was a world in which matchmakers arranged marriages, and people wore a ribbon around the neck to ward off disease. Above all, it was a world tinctured by the Jewish faith. Religion touched almost every corner of Mary's life. Whenever her mother discovered a peculiar mark on a chicken she was preparing to cook, she would send it to the rabbi, who would "look in his big books" and decide whether the chicken could be eaten. The Antins observed the Sabbath with a rigor that even the early American Puritans could not have matched. On the Sabbath, Mary was not allowed to work or even to touch any instrument of labor or commerce, such as an ax or a coin. It was "forbidden to light a fire, or to touch anything that contained a fire, or had contained fire, were it only a cold candlestick or a burned match."

As a little girl Mary learned that "The world was divided between Jews and Gentiles." A girl named Vanka threw mud at her; her mother brushed off the dirt and explained that there was nothing to do because Vanka was a Gentile, and "The Gentiles do as they like with us Jews." Mary learned quickly, and later when Vanka spat at her she wiped her face and, she writes, "thought nothing at all. I accepted ill-usage from the Gentiles as one accepts the weather."

As she grew older, she saw other signs of prejudice. Jewish merchants had to pay special fees for the right to travel on business. A local capmaker went to a city to practice his trade, passed the proper tests, and paid his fees, but the authorities claimed he had not done so. He returned impoverished to Polotzk. The young men of Polotzk were drafted into an army that made no provision for their faith. Many sought to avoid the service by inflicting injuries on themselves. Mary Antin recalled that the deformities often proved incurable, so that "there were many men in Polotzk blind of one eye, or hard of hearing, or lame, as a result of these secret practices."

If such hardships were the daily bread of Jews in the Pale of Settlement, they lived always with the fear of much worse oppression. At any moment the Gentiles in a community might take it into their heads to massacre the Jews. These outbreaks of mass violence, known as pogroms, were frequently encouraged by priests, police, and even by the tsar. They were rare under the benevolent rule of Alexander II (1855–81), but they occurred much more often after his assassination in 1881. In the following year the government instigated a massacre of Jews at Nizhny Novgorod. During the next few years Jews were slain or driven from their homes in scores of local pogroms throughout Russia.

Fear haunted the Jews in Polotzk, especially on Christian holidays; then they locked their doors and stayed inside, "knowing that the least disturbance might start a riot, and a riot lead to a pogrom." Mary Antin recalled seeing people who had been caught in pogroms. "Jews who escaped the pogroms," she writes, "came to Polotzk with wounds on them, and horrible, horrible stories, of little babies torn limb from limb before their mothers' eyes. Only to hear these things made one sob and sob and choke with pain. People who saw such things never smiled any more, no matter how long they lived; and sometimes their hair turned white in a day, and some people became insane on the spot."

To be a Jew in the Pale of Settlement was to be constantly humiliated and threatened by hostile neighbors and a hostile regime. Yet it was an economic crisis rather than fear of oppression that finally drove the Antins to migrate to America. During the nineteenth century large new industries had forced many East Europeans out of work. Simultaneously, the rapidly growing population strained the resources of food and shelter. The Jews were especially injured by these changes. Between 1800 and 1900 the number of Russian Jews increased from 1 million to 4 million. Many Jewish artisans lost their jobs when factories began to produce goods more cheaply than they could. At the same time, government regulations prevented most Jews from becoming industrialists.

Mary Antin's father was ruined by these changes. At first Antin was a successful merchant, but then he became ill and was no longer able to support his family. To survive, the Antins had to sell many of their belongings, and Mary's mother had to go to work as a peddler. When the father finally recovered, economic conditions were so bad that he could not reestablish himself in business. Like millions of other Europeans, he began to think of America.

Russian Jews could not go to Moscow, Kiev, or Saint Petersburg to improve their condition. But they could go to New York, Boston, or Chicago to find more economic opportunities and fewer prejudicial restrictions. Prior to 1880 very few East Europeans had come to America, but in the next thirty-five years one Russian Jew in three would make the trip. Steamship companies encouraged them by offering rapid passage at a low fare. The first settlers helped others by sending back information and money and by establishing households and neighborhoods in America where the immigrant could settle among friends.

After 1880 the migration developed an astonishing momentum. Between 1881 and 1914, when World War I interrupted the flow of immigrants, more than 1.5 million Russian Jews came to the United States. Migration became an obsession in the Pale of Settlement. Mary Antin recounts:

> America was in everybody's mouth. Businessmen talked of it over their accounts; the market women made up their quarrels that they might discuss it from stall to stall; people who had relatives in the famous land went around reading their letters for the enlightenment of less fortunate folk . . . children played at emigrating.

Mary's father listened carefully to such talk. If others could go, then so too might he. Finally he gathered his courage and set out alone for America. He could not afford to bring his family, but in America he borrowed the necessary money and wrote for the family to join him. Mary was ecstatic. "So at last," she writes, "I was going to America! Really, really going at last! The boundaries burst. The arch of heaven soared. A million suns shone out for every star. The winds rushed in from outer space, roaring in my ears, 'America! America!'" Mary compared going to America with going to Jerusalem or crossing the Red Sea. It was not merely a journey—it was the fulfillment of life's promise.

With such thoughts, Mary Antin and hundreds of thousands of other East Europeans set out for America. The trip was filled with hardships. First one must pack together the few belongings that could be easily carried on a long journey by cart, rail, and ship. With these possessions—pots and pans, a samovar, and perhaps goose-down bedding—the emigrant departed from the native village into a world whose language and customs were unfamiliar. At every step were unscrupulous trainmen, innkeepers, and government officials who might prey on the ignorant. At the borders many had to cross illegally, because the tsar often denied passports to Jews. Many a refugee crossed into Germany or Austria in the black of night and on foot, following a guide through isolated fields or forests.

Once outside Russia, the immigrants boarded trains, usually riding in fourth-class accommodations that were little better than boxcars, and journeyed on to port cities such as Hamburg or Bremen. Even then the ordeal was frequently prolonged, as they lived in prisonlike quarantine enclosures while waiting for their vessels. Finally, on the voyage to America the passengers were exposed to acute discomfort. They commonly traveled in crowded steerage quarters deep in the bowels of the ship, which were poorly ventilated and shook with the engines' vibrations. Many travelers recalled the poor food, filthy toilets, and the constant stench of vomit. One man echoed the feelings of many when he described the journey as "a kind of hell that cleanses a man of his sins before coming to the land of Columbus."

The Antins experienced many hardships on their travels. After journeying across Russia they learned that they could not enter Germany unless they purchased second-class rail tickets (instead of the fourth-class tickets they held). They could not afford the extra cost and had to remain in a border town until a friend helped them across. They then passed through Germany, packed like cattle into a fourth-class car. Once all the passengers were unceremoniously removed from the train and forced to take showers, apparently as a precaution against disease, though no explanation was given. At their destination they were herded into a building where they had to wait for many days before boarding a ship.

Finally they went to sea for a sixteen-day voyage. Crowded together with other passengers as seasick as themselves, they encountered storms that tossed passengers from their beds. "We frightened immigrants," writes Mary Antin, "turned our faces to the wall and awaited our watery graves." Despite such difficulties, the voyage was not entirely painful. When the weather cleared there were "happy hours on deck, with fugitive sunshine, birds atop the crested waves, band music and dancing and fun." And then there was the fine moment when the ship finally neared the American shore.

At Ellis Island, where most of the immigrants entered America, they came face to face with the first of the blunt realities that would shape their new lives. This immigrant depot, a huge brick edifice lying just off Manhattan in New York Harbor, was opened in 1892, a year after the United States government had taken over supervision of immigration from the states. As immigrants disembarked, they were given numbers and herded into a great central hall where they were formed into lines and led past several doctors who scrutinized them for disease. The laws of that time imposed no quotas on immigrants but did stipulate that entrants be in good health and be able to provide for themselves. Those who appeared to be sick with tuberculosis, venereal disease, ringworm, or other serious ailments were marked with chalk and held for further examination. The immigrants who passed the medical tests were then asked a barrage of questions about their character, politics, skills, money, and family status. Frequently their assimilation began here at the hands of clerks who simplified East European names into shorter Anglo-Saxon forms. Most were allowed to leave Ellis Island after a day. Others had to remain for one or two weeks for further examination. The least fortunate—between 1 and 2 percent of the immigrants between 1880 and 1914—had to return to Europe.

The ordeal at Ellis Island was softened for Jewish immigrants by the Hebrew Immigrant Aid Society, founded in 1892. Its representatives, identified by the letters HIAS on their blue caps, helped the immigrants answer questions and served as advocates for those the government sought to exclude. They also provided information on housing and jobs.

After completing their examinations on Ellis Island, the immigrants boarded one of the ferries that ran twenty-four hours a day between the island and Manhattan. A short voyage past the Statue of Liberty took the travelers to Battery Park. Behind them now were the loathsome railroad and steamship accommodations and intimidating customs and immigration officials. Disembarking amid the cries of seagulls and the throb of the ferry engine, the immigrants were finally set free in America.

But who were they now? Where would they go? How would they make a living? Because immigrants landed in New York with an average of only $8 in their pockets, the end of the long journey from Europe was only the beginning of a much longer struggle to make a living in America.

The Russian Jews who came to America were mostly young, and many came with their families. The majority were skilled laborers; 40 percent were clothing workers. After an abortive Russian revolution in 1905, a higher proportion of wealthy and educated Jews began to immigrate. Some artisans were able to use their European skills in America, but many found that the industrial forces that rendered their crafts obsolete in Europe were also at work in America.

Whatever their backgrounds, the immigrants had first to search for shelter and work. Some went to other cities—Boston, Cleveland, Detroit, even Los Angeles—but most stayed in New York. Of the Jews who landed at Ellis Island, three-fourths remained in the city. New York was vital in shaping the East European Jewish experience in America.

New York had grown rapidly during the nineteenth century. In 1800 its population was 60,000; by 1850 it had climbed to 515,000; and in 1900, after it absorbed Brooklyn and other outlying areas, the population was more than 3 million. The city owed its growth in part to the forces that were redistributing the American population from farm to city across the country. With new railroads, telegraphs, and steamships, urban centers acquired greater importance. Cities became centers of manufacturing, distribution and finance in an economy where interdependence was rapidly replacing self-sufficiency.

Even without the immigrants New York would have grown in the nineteenth century, but newly arriving Americans greatly accelerated the expansion. Once Russian Jews had arrived in Manhattan they had reasons to stay. New York had jobs in manufacturing enterprises, department stores, and printshops. Opportunities for individual enterprise were there, too; one could easily become a street peddler or proprietor of a small store. Another attraction was one's fellow immigrants, a whole neighborhood with tens of thousands of men and women who had grown up in Russia, bringing with them Yiddish newspapers, plays, stores, doctors. They created a comfortable, familiar community in the midst of a strange land.

Most East Europeans lived on the Lower East Side of New York, an area that had become a Jewish ghetto the past eighty years. Early in the nineteenth century a small colony of Jewish immigrants settled there. In the 1830s and 1840s, Dutch, German, and Polish Jews followed them. With the later arrival of East European Jews, the Lower East Side became a nation within a nation—or, more accurately, a cluster of nations within a nation. A map of the settlement patterns of Russian, Galician, Austro-Hungarian, Romanian, and Levantine Jews reveals boundaries among the groups as distinct as national frontiers. By 1900 the Lower East Side was one of the most crowded places in the world, with more than a half million Jews in concentrations of as many as seven hundred per acre. This was the most crowded section of the city, containing only about one-eightieth of the land, but one-sixth of the population. One observer wrote: "The architecture seemed to sweat humanity at every window and door."

Such crowding was made possible in part by new building techniques and in part by forbearance by the inhabitants. New York City lots were twenty-five feet wide and roughly a hundred feet deep. The first tenements consisted of private houses that were converted into apartments. But with increased crowding, a more efficient system was required. In 1879 a contest was held with the prize going to the best apartment design. The winning plan was the now infamous "dumbbell" tenement, so named because it was shaped like a weightlifter's bar and weights.

The typical dumbbell tenement had from six to seven stories, each floor with four apartments containing a kitchen, a sitting room, and one or two bedrooms. Only the rooms facing the street or the ten-foot-deep backyard had fresh air. Other rooms faced a foul air shaft or had no windows. One toilet served all the inhabitants on each floor. Under the best of conditions these rooms would seem confining, even for a small family. But many were occupied by families with five or six children. Also there were boarders, individuals or whole families, who shared an apartment with the renters, sleeping in the kitchen or sharing the other rooms and helping to pay the rent of $10 to $20 a month. Through the summer men and women slept in the yards or on roofs or fire escapes to avoid the stifling closeness of the tenement apartments. In one week during August 1896 the temperature averaged 90 degrees and 420 New Yorkers died of the heat.

With all its limitations, the tenement apartment still offered shelter, both physical and psychological, from the abrasive world in which the immigrant must find work. The search for steady employment was frequently the most trying and disorienting feature of immigrant life. Many artisan immigrants had to find work in new areas. Some went to work in sweatshops, small manufacturing establishments producing clothing, cigars, and other products. Others became small merchants—with a pushcart and a bushel of apples one could easily become a peddler on the busy ghetto streets. With a little more money, one could rent a small street-front store with a tenement apartment in the rear.

Reading 5

The Atlanta Exposition Address

Booker T. Washington

The Atlanta Exposition, at which I had been asked to make an address as a representative of the Negro race, was opened with a short address from Governor Bullock. After other interesting exercises, including an invocation from Bishop Nelson, of Georgia, a dedicatory ode by Albert Howell, Jr., and addresses by the President of the Exposition and Mrs. Joseph Thompson, the President of the Woman's Board, Governor Bullock introduced me with the words, "We have with us to-day a representative of Negro enterprise and Negro civilization."

When I arose to speak, there was considerable cheering, especially from the coloured people. As I remember it now, the thing that was uppermost in my mind was the desire to say something that would cement the friendship of the races and bring about hearty cooperation between them. So far as my outward surroundings were concerned, the only thing that I recall distinctly now is that when I got up, I saw thousands of eyes looking intently into my face. The following is the address which I delivered:—

MR. PRESIDENT AND GENTLEMEN OF THE BOARD OF DIRECTORS AND CITIZENS.

One-third of the population of the South is of the Negro race. No enterprise seeking the material, civil, or moral welfare of this section can disregard this element of our population and reach the highest success. I but convey to you, Mr. President and Directors, the sentiment of the masses of my race when I say that in no way have the value and manhood of the American Negro been more fittingly and generously recognized than by the managers of this magnificent Exposition at every stage of its progress. It is a recognition that will do more to cement the friendship of the two races than any occurrence since the dawn of our freedom.

Not only this, but the opportunity here afforded will awaken among us a new era of industrial progress. Ignorant and inexperienced, it is not strange that in the first years of our new life we began at the top instead of at the bottom; that a seat in Congress or the state legislature was more sought than real estate or industrial skill; that the political convention or stump speaking had more attractions than starting a dairy farm or truck garden.

A ship lost at sea for many days suddenly sighted a friendly vessel. From the mast of the unfortunate vessel was seen a signal, "Water, water; we die of thirst!" The answer from the friendly vessel at once came back, "Cast down your bucket where you are." A second time the signal, "Water,

water; send us water!" ran up from the distressed vessel, and was answered, "Cast down your bucket where you are." And a third and fourth signal for water was answered "Cast down your bucket where you are." The captain of the distressed vessel, at last heeding the injunction, cast down his bucket, and it came up full of fresh, sparkling water from the mouth of the Amazon River. To those of my race who depend on bettering their condition in a foreign land or who underestimate the importance of cultivating friendly relations with the Southern white man, who is their next-door neighbour, I would say: "Cast down your bucket where you are"—cast it down in making friends in every manly way of the people of all races by whom we are surrounded.

Cast it down in agriculture, mechanics, in commerce, in domestic service, and in the professions. And in this connection it is well to bear in mind that whatever other sins the South may be called to bear, when if comes to business, pure and simple, it is in the South that the Negro is given a man's chance in the commercial world, and in nothing is this Exposition more eloquent than in emphasizing this chance. Our greatest danger is that in the great leap from slavery to freedom we may overlook the fact that the masses of us are to live by the productions of our hands, and fail to keep in mind that we shall prosper in proportion as we learn to dignify and glorify common labour and put brains and skill into the common occupations of life; shall prosper in proportion as we learn to draw the line between the superficial and the substantial, the ornamental gewgaws of life and the useful. No race can prosper till it learns that there is as much dignity in tilling a field as in writing a poem. It is at the bottom of life we must begin, and not at the top. Nor should we permit our grievances to overshadow our opportunities.

To those of the white race who look to the incoming of those of foreign birth and strange tongue and habits for the prosperity of the South, were I permitted I would repeat what I say to my own race, "Cast down your bucket where you are." Cast it down among the eight millions of Negroes whose habits you know, whose fidelity and love you have tested in days when to have proved treacherous meant the ruin of your firesides. Cast down your bucket among these people who have, without strikes and labour wars, tilled your fields, cleared your forests, builded your railroads and cities, and brought forth treasures from the bowels of the earth, and helped make possible this magnificent representation of the progress of the South. Casting down your bucket among my people, helping and encouraging them as you are doing on these grounds, and to education of head, hand, and heart, you will find that they will buy your surplus land, make blossom the waste places in your fields, and run your factories. While doing this, you can be sure in the future, as in the past, that you and your families will be surrounded by the most patient, faithful, law-abiding, and unresentful people that the world has seen. As we have proved our loyalty to you in the past, in nursing your children, watching by the sick-bed of your mothers and fathers, and often following them with tear-dimmed eyes to their graves, so in the future, in our humble way, we shall stand by you with a devotion that no foreigner can approach, ready to lay down our lives, if need be, in deference of yours, interlacing our industrial, commercial, civil, and religious life with yours in a way that shall make the interests of both races one. In all things that are purely social we can be as separate as the fingers, yet one as the hand in all things essential to mutual progress.

There is no defence or security for any of us except in the highest intelligence and development of all. If anywhere there are efforts tending to curtail the fullest growth of the Negro, let these efforts be turned into stimulating, encouraging, and making him the most useful and intelligent citizen. Effort or means so invested will pay a thousand per cent interest. These efforts will be twice blessed—"blessing him that gives and him that takes."[1]

There is no escape through law of man or God from the inevitable:—
     The laws of changeless justice bind
          Oppressor with oppressed;
     And close as sin and suffering joined
          We march to fate abreast.[2]

Nearly sixteen millions of hands will aid you in pulling the load upward, or they will pull against you the load downward. We shall constitute one-third and more of the ignorance and crime of the South, or one-third its intelligence and progress; we shall contribute one-third to the business and industrial prosperity of the South, or we shall prove a veritable body of death, stagnating, depressing, retarding every effort to advance the body politic.

Gentlemen of the Exposition, as we present to you our humble effort at an exhibition of our progress, you must not expect overmuch. Starting thirty years ago with ownership here and there in a few quilts and pumpkins and chickens (gathered from miscellaneous sources), remember the path that has led from these to the inventions and production of agricultural implements, buggies, steam-engines, newspapers, books, statuary, carving, paintings, the management of drug-stores and banks, has not been trodden without contact with thorns and thistles. While we take pride in what we exhibit as a result of our independent efforts, we do not for a moment forget that our part in this exhibition would fall far short of your expectations but for the constant help that has come to our educational life, not only from the Southern states, but especially from Northern philanthropists, who have made their gifts a constant stream of blessing and encouragement.

The wisest among my race understand that the agitation of questions of social equality is the extremest folly, and that progress in the enjoyment of all the privileges that will come to us must be the result of severe and constant struggle rather than of artificial forcing. No race that has anything to contribute to the markets of the world is long in any degree ostracized. It is important and right that all privileges of the law be ours, but it is vastly more important that we be prepared for the exercises of these privileges. The opportunity to earn a dollar in a factory just now is worth infinitely more than the opportunity to spend a dollar in a opera-house.

In conclusion, may I repeat that nothing in thirty years has given us more hope and encouragement, and drawn us so near to you of the white race, as this opportunity offered by the Exposition; and here bending, as it were, over the altar that represents the results of the struggles of your race and mine, both starting practically empty-handed three decades ago, I pledge that in your effort to work out the great and intricate problem which God has laid at the doors of the South, you shall have at all times the patient, sympathetic help of my race; only let this be constantly in mind, that, while from representations in these buildings of the product of field, of forest, of mine, of factory, letters, and art, much good will come, yet far above and beyond material benefits will be that higher good, that, let us pray God, will come, in a blotting out of sectional differences and racial animosities and suspicions, in a determination to administer absolute justice, in a willing obedience among all classes to the mandates of law. Thus, this, coupled with our material prosperity, will bring into our beloved South a new heaven and a new earth.

The first thing that I remember, after I had finished speaking, was that Governor Bullock rushed across the platform and took me by the hand, and that others did the same. I received so many and such hearty congratulations that I found it difficult to get out of the building. I did not appreciate to any degree, however, the impression which my address seemed to have made, until the next morning, when I went into the business part of the city. As soon as I was recognized, I was surprised to find myself pointed out and surrounded by a crowd of men who wished to shake hands with me. This was kept up on every street on to which I went, to an extent which embarrassed me so much that I went back to my boarding-place. The next morning I returned to Tuskegee. At the station in Atlanta, and at almost all of the stations at which the train stopped between that city and Tuskegee, I found a crowd of people anxious to shake hands with me.

The papers in all parts of the United States published the address in full, and for months afterward there were complimentary editorial references to it. Mr. Clark Howell, the editor of the Atlanta *Constitution,* telegraphed to a New York paper, among other words, the following, "I do not exaggerate when I say that Professor Booker T. Washington's address yesterday was one of the most notable speeches, both as to character and as to the warmth of its reception, ever delivered to a Southern audience. The address was a revelation. The whole speech is a platform upon which blacks and whites can stand with full justice to each other."

The Boston *Transcript* said editorially: "The speech of Booker T. Washington at the Atlanta Exposition, this week, seems to have dwarfed all the other proceedings and the Exposition itself. The sensation that it has caused in the press has never been equalled."

I very soon began receiving all kinds of propositions from lecture bureaus, and editors of magazines and papers, to take the lecture platform, and to write articles. One lecture bureau offered me fifty thousand dollars, or two hundred dollars a night and expenses, if I would place my services at its disposal for a given period. To all these communications I replied that my life-work was at Tuskegee; and that whenever I spoke it must be in the interests of the Tuskegee school and my race, and that I would enter into no arrangements that seemed to place a mere commercial value upon my services.

Some days after its delivery I sent a copy of my address to the President of the United States, the Hon. Grover Cleveland. I received from him the following autograph reply:—

Gray Gables, Buzzard's Bay, Mass.,
October 6, 1895.
BOOKER T. WASHINGTON, ESQ.:

My DEAR SIR: I thank you for sending me a copy of your address delivered at the Atlanta Exposition.

I thank you with much enthusiasm for making the address. I have read it with intense interest, and I think the Exposition would be fully justified if it did not do more than furnish the opportunity for its delivery. Your words cannot fail to delight and encourage all who wish well for your race; and if our coloured fellow-citizens do not from your utterances gather new hope and form new determinations to gain every valuable advantage offered them by their citizenship, it will be strange indeed.

Yours very truly,

GROVER CLEVELAND.

---

1. William Shakespeare, *The Merchant of Venice* 4.1.187.

2. See "The Song of the Negro Boatmen" in *At Port Royal* (1862) by the American antislavery poet John Greenleaf Whittier.

Reading 6

Of Mr. Booker T. Washington and Others

W. E. B. Du Bois

> From bird till death enslaved; in word, in deed, unmanned!
> Hereditary bondsmen! Know ye not
> Who would be free themselves must strike the blow?[1]
>
> *Byron*

Easily the most striking thing in the history of the American Negro since 1876 is the ascendancy of Mr. Booker T. Washington. It began at the time when war memories and ideals were rapidly passing; a day of astonishing commercial development was dawning; a sense of doubt and hesitation overtook the freedmen's sons,—then it was that his leading began. Mr. Washington came, with a simple definite programme, at the psychological moment when the nation was a little ashamed of having bestowed so much sentiment on Negroes, and was concentrating its energies on Dollars.[2] His programme of industrial education, conciliation of the South, and submission and silence as to civil and political rights, was not wholly original; the Free Negroes from 1830 up to wartime had striven to build industrial schools,[3] and the American Missionary Association had from the first taught various trades; and Price[4] and others had sought a way of honorable alliance with the best of the Southerners. But Mr. Washington first indissolubly linked these things; he put enthusiasm, unlimited energy, and perfect faith into this programme, and changed it from a by-path into a veritable Way of Life. And the tale of the methods by which he did this is a fascinating study of human life.

It startled the nation to hear a Negro advocating such a programme after many decades of bitter complaint; it startled and won the applause of the South, it interested and won the admiration of the North; and after a confused murmur of protest, it silenced if it did not convert the Negroes themselves.

To gain the sympathy and cooperation of the various elements comprising the white South was Mr. Washington's first task; and this, at the time Tuskegee[5] was founded, seemed, for a black man, well-nigh impossible. And yet ten years later it was done in the word spoken at Atlanta: "In all things purely social we can be as separate as the five fingers, and yet one as the hand in all things essential to mutual progress." This "Atlanta Compromise"[6] is by all odds the most notable thing in Mr. Washington's career. The South interpreted it in different ways: the radicals received it as a complete surrender of the demand for civil and political equality; the conservatives, as a generously conceived working basis for mutual understanding. So both approved it, and to-day its author is certainly the most distinguished Southerner since Jefferson Davis,[7] and the one with the largest personal following.

Next to this achievement comes Mr. Washington's work in gaining place and consideration in the North. Others less shrewd and tactful had formerly essayed to sit on these two stools and had fallen between them; but as Mr. Washington knew the heart of the South from birth and training, so by singular insight he intuitively grasped the spirit of the age which was dominating the North. And so thoroughly did he learn the speech and thought of triumphant commercialism, and the ideals of material prosperity, that the picture of a lone black boy poring over a French grammar amid the weeds and dirt of a neglected home soon seemed to him the acme of absurdities. One wonders what Socrates and St. Francis of Assisi[8] would say to this.

And yet this very singleness of vision and thorough oneness with his age is a mark of the successful man. It is as though Nature must needs make men narrow in order to give them force. So Mr. Washington's cult has gained unquestioning followers, his work has wonderfully prospered, his friends are legion, and his enemies are confounded. To-day he stands as the one recognized spokesman of his ten million fellows, and one of the most notable figures in a nation of seventy millions. One hesitates, therefore, to criticise a life which, beginning with so little, has done so much. And yet the time is come when one may speak in all sincerity and utter courtesy of the mistakes and shortcomings of Mr. Washington's career, as well as of his triumphs, without being thought captious or envious, and without forgetting that it is easier to do ill than well in the world.

The criticism that has hitherto met Mr. Washington has not always been of this broad character. In the South especially has he had to walk warily to avoid the harshest judgments,—and naturally so, for he is dealing with the one subject of deepest sensitiveness to that section. Twice—once when at the Chicago celebration of the Spanish-American War he alluded to the color-prejudice that is "eating away the vitals of the South," and once when he dined with President Roosevelt[9]—has the resulting Southern criticism been violent enough to threaten seriously his popularity. In the North the feeling has several times forced itself into words, that Mr. Washington's counsels of submission overlooked certain elements of true manhood, and that his educational programme was unnecessarily narrow. Usually, however, such criticism has not found open expression, although, too, the spiritual sons of the Abolitionists have not been prepared to acknowledge that the schools founded before Tuskegee, by men of broad ideals and self-sacrificing spirit, were wholly failures or worthy of ridicule. While, then, criticism has not failed to follow Mr. Washington, yet the prevailing public opinion of the land has been but too willing to deliver the solution of a wearisome problem into his hands, and say, "If that is all you and your race ask, take it."

Among his own people, however, Mr. Washington has encountered the strongest and most lasting opposition, amounting at times to bitterness, and even to-day continuing strong and insistent even though largely silenced in outward expression by the public opinion of the nation. Some of the opposition is, of course, mere envy; the disappointment of displaced demagogues and the spite of narrow minds. But aside from this, there is among educated and thoughtful colored men in all parts of the land a feeling of deep regret, sorrow, and apprehension at the wide currency and ascendancy which some of Mr. Washington's theories have gained. These same men admire his sincerity of purpose, and are willing to forgive much to honest endeavor which is doing something worth the doing. They cooperate with Mr. Washington as far as they conscientiously can; and, indeed, it is no ordinary tribute to this man's tact and power that, steering as he must between so many diverse interests and opinions, he so largely retains the respect of all.

But the hushing of the criticism of honest opponents is a dangerous thing.[10] It leads some of the best of the critics to unfortunate silence and paralysis of effort, and others to burst into speech so passionately and intemperately as to lose listeners. Honest and earnest criticism from those whose interests are most nearly touched,—criticism of writers by readers, of government by those governed, of leaders by those led,—this is the soul of democracy and the safeguard of modern society. If the best of the American Negroes receive by outer pressure a leader whom they had not recognized before, manifestly there is here a certain palpable gain. Yet there is also irreparable loss,—a loss of that peculiarly valuable education which a group receives when by search and criticism it finds and commissions its own leaders. The way in which this was done is at once the most elementary and the nicest problem of social growth. History is but the record of such group-leadership; and yet how infinitely changeful is its type and character! And of all types and kinds, what can be more instructive than the leadership of a group within a group?—that curious double movement where real progress may be negative and actual advance be relative retrogression. All this is the social student's inspiration and despair.

Now in the past the American Negro has had instructive experience in the choosing of group leaders, founding thus a peculiar dynasty which in the light of present conditions is worth while studying. When sticks and stones and beasts form the sole environment of a people, their attitude is largely one of determined opposition to and conquest of natural forces. But when to earth and brute is added an environment of men and ideas, then the attitude of the imprisoned group may take three main forms,—a feeling of revolt and revenge; an attempt to adjust all thought and action to the will of the greater group; or, finally, a determined effort at self-realization and self-development despite environing opinion. The influence of all of these attitudes at various times can be traced of the American Negro, and in the evolution of his successive leaders.

Before 1750, while the fire of African freedom still burned in the veins of the slaves, there was in all leadership or attempted leadership but the one motive of revolt and revenge,—typified in the terrible Maroons, the Danish blacks, and Cato of Stono, and veiling all the Americas in fear of insurrection.[11] The liberalizing tendencies of the latter half of the eighteenth century brought, along with kindlier relations between black and white, thoughts of ultimate adjustment and assimilation. Such aspiration was especially voiced in the earnest songs of Phyllis, in the martyrdom of Attucks, the fighting of Salem and Poor, the intellectual accomplishments of Banneker and Derham, and the political demands of the Cuffes.[12]

Stern financial and social stress after the war cooled much of the previous humanitarian ardor. The disappointment and impatience of the Negroes at the persistence of slavery and serfdom voiced itself in two movements. The slaves in the South, aroused undoubtedly by vague rumors of the Haytian revolt, made three fierce attempts at insurrection,—in 1800 under Gabriel in Virginia, in 1822 under Vesey in Carolina, and in 1831 again in Virginia under the terrible Nat Turner.[13] In the Free States, on the other hand, a new and curious attempt at self-development was made. In Philadelphia and New York color-prescription led to a withdrawal of Negro communicants from white churches and the formation of a peculiar socio-religious institution among the Negroes known as the African Church,[14]—an organization still living and controlling in its various branches over a million of men.

Walker's wild appeal[15] against the trend of the times showed how the world was changing after the coming of the cotton-gin. By 1830 slavery seemed hopelessly fastened on the South, and the slaves thoroughly cowed into submission. The free Negroes of the North, inspired by the mulatto immigrants from the West Indies, began to change the basis of their demands; they recognized the slavery of slaves, but insisted that they themselves were freemen, and sought assimilation and amalgamation with the nation on the same terms with other men. Thus, Forten and Purvis of Philadelphia, Shad of Wilmington, Du Bois of New Haven, Barbadoes of Boston, and others strove singly and together as men, they said, not as slaves; as "people of color," not as "Negroes."[16] The trend of the times, however, refused them recognition save in individual and exceptional cases, considered them as one with all the despised blacks, and they soon found themselves striving to keep even the rights they formerly had of voting and working and moving as freemen. Schemes of migration and colonization arose among them; but these they refused to entertain, and they eventually turned to the Abolition movement as a final refuge.

Here, led by Remond, Nell, Wells-Brown, and Douglass,[17] a new period of self-assertion and self-development dawned. To be sure, ultimate freedom and assimilation was the ideal before the leaders, but the assertion of the manhood rights of the Negro by himself was the main reliance, John Brown's raid was the extreme of its logic.[18] After the war and emancipation, the great form of Frederick Douglass, the greatest of American Negro leaders, still led the host. Self-assertion, especially in political lines, was the main programme, and behind Douglass came Elliot, Bruce, and Langston, and the Reconstruction politicians, and, less conspicuous but of greater social significance, Alexander Crummell and Bishop Daniel Payne.[19]

Then came the Revolution of 1876,[20] the suppression of the Negro votes, the changing and shifting of ideals, and the seeking of new lights in the great night. Douglass, in his old age, still bravely stood for the ideals of his early manhood,—ultimate assimilation *through* self-assertion, and on no other terms. For a time Price arose as a new leader, destined, it seemed, not to give up, but to restate the old ideals in a form less repugnant to the white South. But he passed away in his prime. Then came the new leader. Nearly all the former ones had become leaders by the silent suffrage of their fellows,[21] had sought to lead their own people alone, and were usually, save Douglass, little known outside their race. But Booker T. Washington arose as essentially the leader not of one race but of two,—a compromiser between the South, the North, and the Negro. Naturally the Negroes resented, at first bitterly, signs of compromise which surrendered their civil and political rights, even though this was to be exchanged for larger chances of economic development. The rich and dominating North, however, was not only weary of the race problem, but was investing largely in Southern enterprises, and welcomed any method of peaceful cooperation. Thus, by national opinion, the Negroes began to recognize Mr. Washington's leadership; and the voice of criticism was hushed.

Mr. Washington represents in Negro thought the old attitude of adjustment and submission; but adjustment at such a peculiar time as to make his programme unique. This is an age of unusual economic development, and Mr. Washington's programme naturally takes an economic cast, becoming a gospel of Work and Money[22] to such an extent as apparently almost completely to overshadow the higher aims of life. Moreover, this is an age when the more advanced races are coming in closer contact with the less developed races, and the race-feeling is therefore intensified; and Mr. Washington's programme practically accepts the alleged inferiority of the Negro races. Again, in our own land, the reaction from the sentiment of war time has given impetus to race-prejudice against Negroes, and Mr. Washington withdraws many of the high demands of Negroes as men and American citizens. In other periods of intensified prejudice all the Negro's tendency to self-assertion has been called forth; at this period a policy of submission is advocated. In the history of nearly all other races and peoples the doctrine preached at such crises has been that manly self-respect is worth more than lands and houses, and that a people who voluntarily surrender such respect, or cease striving for it, are not worth civilizing.

In answer to this, it has been claimed that the Negro can survive only through submission. Mr. Washington distinctly asks that black people give up, at least for the present, three things,—

First, political power,

Second, insistence on civil rights,

Third, higher education of Negro youth,—and concentrate all their energies on industrial education, the accumulation of wealth, and the conciliation of the South. This policy has been courageously and insistently advocated for over fifteen years, and has been triumphant for perhaps ten years. As a result of this tender of the palm-branch, what has been the return? In these years there have occurred:

1. The disfranchisement of the Negro.
2. The legal creation of a distinct status of civil inferiority for the Negro.
3. The steady withdrawal of aid from institutions for the higher training of the Negro.

These movements are not, to be sure, direct results of Mr. Washington's teachings; but his propaganda has, without a shadow of doubt, helped their speedier accomplishment. The question then comes: Is it possible, and probable, that nine millions of men can make effective progress in economic lines if they are deprived of political rights, made a servile caste, and allowed only the most meagre chance for developing their exceptional men? If history and reason give any distinct answer to these questions, it is an emphatic *No.* And Mr. Washington thus faces the triple paradox of his career:

1. He is striving nobly to make Negro artisans business men and property-owners; but it is utterly impossible, under modern competitive methods, for workingmen and property-owners to defend their rights and exist without the right of suffrage.

2. He insists on thrift and self-respect, but at the same time counsels a silent submission to civic inferiority such as is bound to sap the manhood of any race in the long run.

3. He advocates common-school and industrial training, and depreciates institutions of higher learning; but neither the Negro common-schools, nor Tuskegee itself, could remain open a day were it not for teachers trained in Negro colleges, or trained by their graduates.

This triple paradox in Mr. Washington's position is the object of criticism by two classes of colored Americans. One class is spiritually descended from Toussaint the Savior, through Gabriel, Vesey, and Turner, and they represent the attitude of revolt and revenge; they hate the white South blindly and distrust the white race generally, and so far as they agree on definite action, think that the Negro's only hope lies in emigration beyond the borders of the United States. And yet, by the irony of fate, nothing has more effectually made this programme seem hopeless than the recent course of the United States toward weaker and darker peoples in the West Indies, Hawaii, and the Philippines,—for where in the world may we go and be safe from lying and brute force?[23]

The other class of Negroes who cannot agree with Mr. Washington has hitherto said little aloud. They deprecate the sight of scattered counsels of internal disagreement; and especially they dislike making their just criticism of a useful and earnest man an excuse for a general discharge of venom from small-minded opponents. Nevertheless, the questions involved are so fundamental and serious that it is difficult to see how men like the Grimkes, Kelly Miller, J. W. E. Bowen,[24] and other representatives of this group, can much longer be silent. Such men feel in conscience bound to ask of this nation three things:

1. The right to vote.
2. Civic equality.
3. The education of youth according to ability.

They acknowledge Mr. Washington's invaluable service in counselling patience and courtesy in such demands; they do not ask that ignorant black men vote when ignorant whites are debarred, or that any reasonable restrictions in the suffrage should not be applied; they know that the low social level of the mass of the race is responsible for much discrimination against it, but they also know, and the nation knows, that relentless color-prejudice is more often a cause than a result of the Negro's degradation; they seek the abatement of this relic of barbarism, and not its systematic encouragement and pampering by all agencies of social power from the Associated Press to the Church of Christ. They advocate, with Mr. Washington, a broad system of Negro common-schools supplemented by thorough industrial training; but they are surprised that a man of Mr. Washington's insight cannot see that no such educational system ever has rested or can rest on any other basis than that of the well-equipped college and university, and they insist that there is a demand for a few such institutions throughout the South to train the best of the Negro youth as teachers, professional men, and leaders.

This group of men honor Mr. Washington for his attitude of conciliation toward the white South; they accept the "Atlanta Compromise" in its broadest interpretation; they recognize, with him, many signs of promise, many men of high purpose and fair judgment, in this section; they know that no easy task has been laid upon a region already tottering under heavy burdens. But, nevertheless, they insist that the way to truth and right lies in straightforward honesty, not in indiscriminate flattery; in praising those of the South who do well and criticising uncompromisingly those who do ill; in taking advantage of the opportunities at hand and urging their fellows to do the same, but at the same time in remembering that only a firm adherence to their higher ideals and aspirations will ever keep those ideals within the realm of possibility. They do not expect that the free right to vote, to enjoy civic rights, and to be educated, will come in a moment; they do not expect to see the bias and prejudices of years disappear at the blast of a trumpet; but they are absolutely certain that the way for a people to gain their reasonable rights is not by voluntarily throwing them away and insisting that they do not want them; that the way for a people to gain respect is not by continually belittling and ridiculing themselves; that, on the contrary, Negroes must insist continually, in season and out of season, that voting is necessary to modern manhood, that color discrimination is barbarism, and that black boys need education as well as white boys.[25]

In failing thus to state plainly and unequivocally the legitimate demands of their people, even at the cost of opposing an honored leader, the thinking classes of American Negroes would shirk a heavy responsibility,[26]—a responsibility to themselves, a responsibility to the struggling masses, a responsibility to the darker races of men whose future depends so largely on this American experiment, but especially a responsibility to this nation,—this common Fatherland. It is wrong to encourage a man or a people in evil-doing; it is wrong to aid and abet a national crime simply because it is unpopular not to do so. The growing spirit of kindliness and reconciliation between the North and South after the frightful differences of a generation ago ought to be a source of deep congratulation to all, and especially to those whose mistreatment caused the war; but if that reconciliation is to be marked by the industrial slavery and civic death of those same black men, with permanent legislation into a position of inferiority, then those black men, if they are really men, are called upon by every consideration of patriotism and loyalty to oppose such a course by all civilized methods, even though such opposition involves disagreement with Mr. Booker T. Washington. We have no right to sit silently by while the inevitable seeds are sown for a harvest of disaster to our children, black and white.[27]

First, it is the duty of black men to judge the South discriminatingly. The present generation of Southerners are not responsible for the past, and they should not be blindly hated or blamed for it. Furthermore, to no class is the indiscriminate endorsement of the recent course of the South toward Negroes more nauseating than to the best thought of the South. The South is not "solid"; it is a land in the ferment of social change, wherein forces of all kinds are fighting for supremacy; and to praise the ill the South is to-day perpetrating is just as wrong as to condemn the good. Discriminating and broad-minded criticism is what the South needs,—needs it for the sake of her own white sons and daughters, and for the insurance of robust healthy mental and moral development.[28]

To-day even the attitude of the Southern whites toward the blacks is not as so many assume, in all cases the same; the ignorant Southerner hates the Negro, the workingmen fear his competition, the money makers wish to use him as a laborer, some of the educated see a menace in his upward development, while others—usually the sons of the masters—wish to help him to rise. National opinion has enabled this last class to maintain the Negro common-schools, and to protect the Negro partially in property, life, and limb. Through the pressure of the moneymakers, the Negro is in danger of being reduced to semi-slavery, especially in the country districts; the workingmen, and those of the educated who fear the Negro, have united to disfranchise him, and some have urged his deportation; while the passions of the ignorant are easily aroused to lynch and abuse any black man. To praise this intricate whirl of thought and prejudice is nonsense; to inveigh indiscriminately against "the South" is unjust; but to use the same breath in praising Governor Aycock, exposing Senator

Morgan, arguing with Mr. Thomas Nelson Page, and denouncing Senator Ben Tillman, is not only sane, but the imperative duty of thinking black men.[29]

It would be unjust to Mr. Washington not to acknowledge that in several instances he has opposed movements in the South which were unjust to the Negro; he sent memorials to the Louisiana and Alabama constitutional conventions, he has spoken against lynching, and in other ways has openly or silently set his influence against sinister schemes and unfortunate happenings. Notwithstanding this, it is equally true to assert that on the whole the distinct impression left by Mr. Washington's propaganda is, first, that the South is justified in its present attitude toward the Negro because of the Negro's degradation; secondly, that the prime cause of the Negro's failure to rise more quickly is his wrong education in the past and, thirdly, that his future rise depends primarily on his own efforts. Each of these propositions is a dangerous half-truth. The supplementary truths must never be lost sight of: first, slavery and race prejudice are potent if not sufficient causes of the Negro's position; second, industrial and common-school training were necessarily slow in planting because they had to await the black teachers trained by higher institutions,—it being extremely doubtful if any essentially different development was possible, and certainly a Tuskegee was unthinkable before 1880; and, third, while it is a great truth to say that the Negro must strive and strive mightily to help himself, it is equally true that unless his striving be not simply seconded, but rather aroused and encouraged, by the initiative of the richer and wiser environing group, he cannot hope for great success.

In his failure to realize and impress this last point, Mr. Washington is especially to be criticised. His doctrine has tended to make the whites, North and South, shift the burden of the Negro problem to the Negro's shoulders and stand aside as critical and rather pessimistic spectators; when in fact the burden belongs to the nation, and the hands of none of us are clean if we bend not our energies to righting these great wrongs.

The South ought to be led, by candid and honest criticism, to assert her better self and do her full duty to the race she has cruelly wronged and is still wronging. The North—her co-partner in guilt—cannot salve her conscience by plastering it with gold. We cannot settle this problem by diplomacy and suaveness, by "policy" alone. If worse come to worst, can the moral fibre of this country survive the slow throttling and murder of nine millions of men?

The black men of America have a duty to perform, a duty stern and delicate,—a forward movement to oppose a part of the work of their greatest leader. So far as Mr. Washington preaches Thrift, Patience, and Industrial Training for the masses, we must hold up his hands and strive with him, rejoicing in his honors and glorying in the strength of this Joshua[30] called of God and of man to lead the headless host. But so far as Mr. Washington apologizes for injustice, North or South, does not rightly value the privilege and duty of voting, belittles the emasculating effects of caste distinctions, and opposes the higher training and ambition of our brighter minds,—so far as he, the South, or the Nation, does this,—we must unceasingly and firmly oppose them. By every civilized and peaceful method we must strive for the rights which the world accords to men, clinging unwaveringly to those great words which the sons of the Fathers would fain forget: "We hold these truths to be self-evident: That all men are created equal; that they are endowed by their Creator with certain unalienable rights; that among these are life, liberty, and the pursuit of happiness."[31]

Notes

1. The verse is Lord Byron, "Childe Harold's Pilgrimage," Canto 2, stanza 74, line 710; stanza 76, fines 720–21. The music is a Negro spiritual, "A Great Camp Meeting in the Promised Land."

2. The historical "moment" Du Bois captures here is the Gilded Age of the 1880s and 1890s.

3. Industrial schools, as well as a variety of other self-improvement efforts, had been widely discussed at antebellum black conventions, especially one held in Rochester, New York, in July 1853. See, for example, Frederick Douglass, "The Industrial College," *Frederick Douglass's Paper,* January 2, 1854, in *Life*

and Writings of Frederick Douglass, ed. Philip S. Foner (New York: International Publishers, 1950), 2:272–75. Indeed, much of the debate over the purpose and character of black education, which became central to the Du Bois–Washington dispute in the early twentieth century, had been publicly addressed, often with similar controversy, among black leaders of the pre–Civil War generation.

4. Joseph C. Price (1854–1893) was born in Elizabeth, North Carolina, the son of a slave father and a free mother. Price graduated from Lincoln University in Pennsylvania in 1881 and became an A.M.E. Zion minister and a pioneering black educator in North Carolina. He founded Zion Wesley College in 1882 and Livingstone College in Salisbury, North Carolina, in 1885. A captivating orator, successful fundraiser among wealthy whites, and a proponent of liberal arts education, Price was seen as offering an alternative to the educational leadership of Booker T. Washington until his early death at age forty. In *The Crisis,* March 22, 1922, Du Bois declared that had Price lived, Livingstone College would have been the "black Harvard."

5. Washington founded Tuskegee Institute as a normal school (what today is called a secondary school) in 1881 in Tuskegee, Alabama. He served as principal until his death in 1915. The institute grew into a college of industrial education and training for southern black schoolteachers and became the most prominent and successful black educational institution.

6. The "Atlanta Compromise" was the most famous speech of Washington's life, delivered at the Cotton States Exposition in Atlanta on September 18, 1895. Washington argued that blacks should stay in the South, "cast down their buckets" where they were, pursue economic self-development and industrial education, and renounce political and civil rights in the Jim Crow South. The speech is reprinted as chapter 14 in Washington's autobiography, *Up From Slavery* (1901).

7. Jefferson Davis (1808–1889) was president of the Confederate States of America during the Civil War. He was a veteran of the Mexican War (1846–48) and had been secretary of war (1853–57) and a U.S. senator from Mississippi (1847–51, 1857–61).

8. Socrates (469?–399 B.C.) was a Greek philosopher, founder of the Socratic method of philosophical inquiry. St Francis of Assisi (1182–1226) founded the order of Franciscan monks in Assisi, Italy. He completely embraced poverty, attempting in every way possible to model Christ's life. His writings endure as expressions of love and human kindness.

9. Washington met and dined with President Theodore Roosevelt at the White House on October 16, 1901. See Louis Harlan, *Booker T. Washington: The Wizard of Tuskegee, 1901–1915* (New York: Oxford University Press, 1984), 2:304–24.

10. By "hushing of the criticism" Du Bois refers to the growing concern by 1903 that Washington's power extended to paying "hush money" to certain black newspaper editors to make them conform to Washington's point of view on many issues. Hence the accusation by some black intellectuals and activists that Washington operated as a type of "boss politician" through the "Tuskegee Machine."

11. Maroons were guerrilla bands of escaped slaves in the West Indies and in Central and South America in the eighteenth century. They formed colonies, often in mountainous regions as in Jamaica, and in some cases became formidable military forces. Cato of Stono was one of the leaders of the first major slave rebellion in the colonial American South. The rebellion occurred along the Stono River in South Carolina in 1739.

12. Phyllis Wheatley (c. 1753–1784), a poet, was born in West Africa, brought to America at age eight and sold to John Wheatley of Boston. Her first book of verse, *Poems on Various Subjects, Religious and Moral,* was published in London in 1773. She is widely regarded as the first African American writer-poet of distinction. Crispus Attucks (1723–1770) was an escaped slave, a dockworker, a black patriot, and one of the victims killed in the Boston Massacre on March 5, 1770. Peter Salem (c. 1750–1816) was a Massachusetts slave who gained his freedom by fighting in the American forces in the Revolution, especially at the Battle of Bunker Hill, June 17, 1775. Salem Poor (1747–?) was a free black who also fought in the American forces in the Revolution. Benjamin Banneker (1731–1806) was a free black born in Maryland; he became a prominent mathematician, scientist, and architect and published an

almanac for farmers (1792–1802). James C. Derham (c. 1762–?) was born a slave in Philadelphia, learned the art of medicine from his owner-physician, bought his own freedom in 1783, and established a successful medical practice in New Orleans. Paul Cuffe (1759–1817) was born in Boston of an African father and an American Indian mother. He became a ship captain and merchant seaman out of Nantucket and an early proponent of black emigration to Africa.

13. Gabriel Prosser (d. 1800) was a slave who led an unsuccessful insurrection conspiracy in Richmond, Virginia, in 1800. The revolt was betrayed by fellow slaves as well as ruined by thunderstorms. Prosser and other leaders were executed. Denmark Vesey (d. 1822) was an ex-slave from Haiti who led an aborted rebellion in Charleston, South Carolina, in 1822. Betrayed, he and other leaders were executed or deported. Nat Turner (1800–1831) was the leader of the bloodiest slave insurrection in North America, which occurred in Southampton County, Virginia, in August 1831. A religious visionary, his *Confessions* became an important part of the lore and literature of the antebellum crisis over slavery. Turner's rebellion, which killed nearly sixty whites in forty-eight hours, contradicted the myth of the contented slave in southern society.

14. The African Methodist Episcopal Church. See page 213, note 12.

15. David Walker (1785–1830) was a black abolitionist born free in North Carolina who achieved an education by unknown means. He moved to Boston by the mid-1820s and wrote *An Appeal to the Coloured Citizens of the World* (1829), one of the earliest and most militant antislavery documents. The *Appeal* drew upon the natural rights tradition, the Bible, and concepts of black nationalist self-reliance to warn America of its doom if slavery was not abolished. Walker was found dead outside his clothing shop in 1830.

16. James Forten (1766–1842) was a Revolutionary War veteran and a wealthy black sailmaker and abolitionist in Philadelphia. He is known as the earliest black philanthropist, as the author of some of the earliest antislavery petitions and public letters, and as a cofounder of the American Anti-Slavery Society (1833). Robert Purvis (1810–1898) was a black Philadelphia businessman, the son-in-law of James Forten. He was active in founding the American Anti-Slavery Society and became one of the leading abolitionists and proponents of black civil rights in the antebellum period. Shad is either Abraham D. Shadd (1801–1882), a free black leader in Wilmington, Delaware, and a staunch opponent of colonization, or Shadd's even more prominent daughter Mary Ann Shadd (1823–1893), who traveled north, became a teacher and an abolitionist, moved to Canada, edited the *Provincial Freeman,* and led an emigration campaign in the 1850s to induce fugitive slaves to move to Canada. James G. Barbadoes (1796–1841) was a free black, a Boston clothier and barber, and a cofounder of the American Anti-Slavery Society. He led an unsuccessful emigration campaign to Jamaica in 1840–1841. Alexander Du Bois was Du Bois's paternal grandfather, born in the Bahamas, a free person of color, he lived much of his life as a small merchant and ship steward in New Haven, Connecticut. Young Will Du Bois first met his grandfather in August 1883 in New Bedford, Massachusetts. Alexander Du Bois had been for a time the treasurer of St. Luke's Episcopal Church in New Haven, when Alexander Crummell was its pastor (c. 1840). For the ways in which Du Bois used his grandfather as a means to construct a half-mythical family past, see Lewis, *W. E. B. Du Bois,* 40–47.

17. Charles Lenox Remond (1810–1873) was a Boston black abolitionist and a prominent traveling lecturer. He belonged to the Garrisonian wing of the American Anti-Slavery Society, a radical faction devoted to abolition and black civil rights. William Cooper Nell (1816–1874), a Boston black abolitionist and staunch Garrisonian, led the campaign to integrate the Boston schools in the 1840s and wrote a pioneering history, *Colored Patriots of the American Revolution* (1855). William Wells Brown (1814–1884) was a fugitive slave who became a lecturer and the author of a novel, *Clotel, or the President's Daughter* (1853), and a work of history, *The Black Man: His Antecedents, His Genius, and His Achievements* (1863). Frederick Douglass (1818–1895) was a slave, abolitionist, orator, editor, and author of three prominent slave narratives. The most famous of his books was the first, the *Narrative of the Life of Frederick Douglass, An American Slave* (1845). Douglass edited his own newspaper for sixteen years (1847–1863) and became the most important black leader and thinker of the nineteenth century. In his voluminous

lectures and writings Douglass was a leading proponent of the integrationist vision of African American destiny. He insisted on American citizenship and civil and political rights for blacks throughout his life.

18. John Brown's raid, in October 1859, was a pivotal event in the coming of the Civil War. Brown was a white abolitionist who led a small guerrilla band in the capture of the federal arsenal at Harpers Ferry, Virginia. He was captured and later executed in a celebrated hanging in November 1859, but the raid had great symbolic and real significance in the crisis of disunion in 1860–1861.

19. Robert Brown Elliot (1841–1884) was a black politician and newspaper editor educated in Boston and London. He was elected to numerous offices in South Carolina during Reconstruction, including the U.S. Congress. John Mercer Langston (1829–1897) was a slave, born in Virginia, freed by his owner, and educated at Oberlin College in Ohio. He was elected Virginia's first black congressman during Reconstruction and became dean of the Howard University Law School. Blanche K. Bruce (1841–1898) was a slave who escaped in 1861 and was educated in the North. He moved to Mississippi during Reconstruction, became a planter, and was elected the first black U.S. senator as a member of the Republican Party. Alexander Crummell (1819–1898) was a black Episcopal clergyman and theologian. Denied admission to major American colleges, he was educated at Cambridge University in England. He became a missionary to Africa and lived in Liberia (1853–1871). When Crummell returned to America he became rector of St. Luke's Church in Washington, D.C., and helped found the American Negro Academy. Daniel Alexander Payne (1811–1893) was a black educator, founder of Wilberforce College in 1863, a prominent religious writer, and bishop of the AME Church. By "Reconstruction politicians," Du Bois refers generally to the nearly four hundred blacks who served in all levels of state government in the South, as well as in the U.S. Congress, during Reconstruction.

20. The Revolution of 1876: See page 197, note 15.

21. The term "silent suffrage" refers to the fact that most black leaders in the nineteenth century lacked elective sanction from their people because the vast majority of blacks could not vote.

22. A "gospel of Work and Money" may refer to Andrew Carnegie's *Gospel of Wealth,* a book published in 1900 that celebrated business enterprise, laissez-faire individualism, moneymaking, and philanthropy.

23. As a result of the Spanish-American War in 1898, the United States gained overseas possessions in Hawaii and the Philippines.

24. Archibald H. Grimké (1849–1930) and his brother, Francis J. Grimké (1850–1937), were born slaves in South Carolina. They were the nephews of Sarah Grimké, one of the early female abolitionists. Archibald became a lawyer, a prominent writer, and the leader of the NAACP's Washington, D.C., branch. Francis became a prominent minister and was active in the affairs of Howard University in Washington, D.C. Kelly Miller (1863–1939) was born the son of a Confederate soldier and a slave mother. He became a mathematics and sociology professor at Howard University and a noted essayist on black history and sociology. John Wesley Edward Bowen (1855–1933) was a Methodist minister and educator. He received a Ph.D. in religion from Boston University in 1887 and taught at Gammon Theological Seminary in Atlanta, Georgia.

25. This paragraph forms, perhaps, the heart of Du Bois's emerging attack on Washington's leadership; it addresses Washington's educational philosophy and the question of civil and political rights. It also anticipates some of Du Bois's other writings in the struggle against Washington, especially "The Parting of the Ways," *World Today* 6 (April 1904): 521–23, and "The Niagara Movement: Address to the Country," published as a pamphlet in 1906.

26. "Thinking classes" refers to Du Bois's concept of the "Talented Tenth," the idea that an educated black elite (10 percent) ought to lead and provide an uplifting example for the masses of the race. Also see page 100. Possibly he first formally named this concept in "Of the Training of Black Men," *Atlantic Monthly* 90 (September 1902): 296, which he revised as chapter 6 of *Souls.*

27. Here Du Bois states succinctly his sense that the nature of sectional reconciliation was at stake in the debates over Washington's leadership.

28. Du Bois demonstrates that he does not believe in collective guilt, yet he believes that the nation as a whole should assume responsibility for the deeds of the past. His generosity toward the white South is especially interesting given the sour state of race relations in 1903.

29. Charles Aycock (1859–1912) was governor of North Carolina (1901–1905) and an educational reformer. John Tyler Morgan (1824–1907) was a white supremacist U.S. senator from Alabama (1876–1907). Thomas Nelson Page (1853–1922) was a white southern novelist essayist, and popular short story writer who did much to create the romanticized "plantation school" of American literature. Benjamin R. Tillman (1847–1919) was a populist orator, a virulent white supremacist governor of South Carolina (1890–1894), and a U.S. senator (1894–1918).

30. Joshua was Moses' minister. After Moses' death God spoke directly to Joshua and called on him to lead the children of Israel over the River Jordan. See Joshua 1–3.

31. The preamble of the Declaration of Independence, 1776.

Reading 7

The Bitter Cry of the Children

John Spargo

VI

According to the census of 1900, there were 25,000 boys under sixteen years of age employed in and around the mines and quarries of the United States. In the state of Pennsylvania alone,—the state which enslaves more children than any other,—there are thousand of little "breaker boys" employed, many of them not more than nine or ten years old. The law forbids the employment of children under fourteen, and the records of the mines generally show that the law is "obeyed." Yet in May, 1905, an investigation by the National Child Labor Committee showed that in one small borough of 7000 population, among the boys employed in breakers 35 were nine years old, 40 were ten, 45 were eleven, and 45 were twelve—over 150 boys illegally employed in one section of boy labor in one small town! During the anthracite coal strike of 1902, I attended the Labor Day demonstration at Pittston and witnessed the parade of another at Wilkesbarre. In each case there were hundreds of boys marching, all of them wearing their "working buttons," testifying to the fact that they were *bona fide* workers. Scores of them were less than ten years of age, others were eleven or twelve.

Work in the coal breakers is exceedingly hard and dangerous. Crouched over the chutes, the boys sit hour after hour, picking out the pieces of slate and other refuse from the coal as it rushes past to the washers. From the cramped position they have to assume most of them become more or less deformed and bent-backed like old men. When a boy has been working for some time and begins to get round-shouldered, his fellows say that "He's got his boy to carry round wherever he goes." The coal is hard, and accidents to the hands such as cut, broken, or crushed fingers, are common among the boys. Sometimes there is a worse accident: a terrified shriek is heard, and a boy is mangled and torn in the machinery, or disappears in the chute to be picked out later smothered and dead. Clouds of dust fill the breakers and are inhaled by the boys, laying the foundations for asthma and miners' consumption. I once stood in a breaker for half an hour and tried to do the work a twelve-year-old boy was doing day after day, for ten hours at a stretch, for sixty cents a day. The gloom of the breaker appalled me. Outside the sun shone brightly, the air was pellucid, and the birds sang in chorus with the trees and the rivers. Within the breaker there was blackness, clouds of deadly dust enfolded everything, the harsh, grinding roar of the machinery and the ceaseless rushing of coal through the chutes filled the ears. I tried to pick out the pieces of slate from the hurrying stream of coal, often missing them; my hands were bruised and cut in a few minutes; I was covered from head to foot with coal dust, and for many hours afterwards I was expectorating some of the small particles of anthracite I had swallowed.

I could not do that work and live, but there were boys of ten and twelve years of age doing it for fifty and sixty cents a day. Some of them had never been inside of a school; few of them could read a child's primer. True, some of them attended the night schools, but after working ten hours in the breaker the educational results from attending school were practically *nil*. "We goes fer a good time, an' we keeps de guys wots dere hoppin' all de time," said little Owen Jones, whose work I had been trying to do. How strange that barbaric patois sounded to me as I remembered the rich, musical language I had so often heard other little Owen Joneses, speak in faraway Wales. As I stood in that breaker I thought of the reply of the small boy to Robert Owen. Visiting an English coal-mine one day, Owen asked a twelve-year-old lad if he knew God. The boy stated vacantly at his questioner: "God?" he said, "God ? No, I don't. He must work in some other mine." It was hard to realize amid the danger and din and blackness of that Pennsylvania breaker that such a thing as belief in a great All-good God existed.

From the breakers the boys graduate to the mine depths, where they become door tenders, switch-boys, or mule-drivers. Here, far below the surface, work is still more dangerous. At fourteen or fifteen the boys assume the same risks as the men, and are surrounded by the same perils. Nor is it in Pennsylvania only that these conditions exist. In the bituminous, mines of West Virginia, boys of nine or ten are frequently employed. I met one little fellow ten years old in Mt. Carbon, W. Va., last year, who employed as a "trap boy." Think of what it means to be a trap boy at ten years of age. It means to sit alone in a dark mine passage hour after hour, with no human soul near; to see no living creature except the mules as they pass with their loads, or a rat or two seeking to share one's meal; to stand in water or mud that covers the ankles chilled to the marrow by the cold draughts that rush in when you open the trap-door for the mules to pass through; to work for fourteen hours—waiting—opening and shutting a door—then waiting again—for sixty cents; to reach the surface when all is wrapped in the mantle of night, and to fall to the earth exhausted and have to be carried away to the nearest "shack" to be revived before it is possible to walk to the farther shack called "home."

Boys twelve years of age may be *legally* employed in the mines of West Virginia, by day or by night, and for as many hours as the employers care to make them toil or their bodies will stand the strain. Where the disregard of child life is such that this may be done openly and with legal sanction, it is easy to believe what miners have again and again told me—that there are hundreds of little boys of nine and ten of age employed in the coal-mines of this state.

VII

It is not my purpose to deal specifically with all the various forms of child labor. That would require a much larger volume than this to be devoted exclusively to the subject. Children are employed at a tender age in hundreds of occupations. In addition to those already enumerated, there were in 1900, according to the census, nearly 12,000 workers under sixteen years of age employed in the manufacture of tobacco and cigars, and it is certain that the number actually employed in that most unhealthful occupation was much greater. In New Jersey and Pennsylvania, I have seen hundreds of children, boys and girls, between the ages of ten and twelve years, at work in the factories belonging to the "Cigar Trust." Some of these factories are known as "kindergartens" on account of the large number of small children employed in them. It is by no means a rare occurrence for children in these factories to faint or to fall asleep over their work, and I have heard a foreman in one of them say that it was "enough for one man to do just to keep the kids awake." In the domestic manufacture of cheap cigars, many very young children are employed. Often the "factories" are poorly lighted, ill-ventilated tenements in which work, whether for children or adults, ought to be absolutely prohibited. Children work often as many as fourteen or even sixteen hours in these little "home factories," and in cities like Pittsburgh, Pa., it is not unusual for them, after attending school all day, to work from 4 P.M. to 12.30 A.M., making "tobies" or "stogies," for which they receive from eight to ten cents per hundred.

In the wood-working industries, more than 10,000 children were reported to be employed in the census year, almost half of them in saw-mills, where accidents are of almost daily occurrence, and where clouds of fine sawdust fill the lungs of the workers. Of the remaining 50 per cent, it is probable that more than half were working at or near dangerous machines, such as steam planers and lathes. Over 7000 children, mostly girls, were employed in laundries; 2000 in bakeries; 138,000 as servants and waiters in restaurants and hotels; 42,000 boys as messengers; and 20,000 boys and girls in stores. In all these instances there is every reason to suppose that the actual number employed was much larger than the official figures show.

In the canning and preservation of fish, fruit, and vegetables mere babies are employed during the busy season. In more than one canning factory in New York State, I have seen children of six and seven years of age working at two o'clock in the morning. In Oneida, Mr. William English Walling, formerly a factory inspector of Illinois, found one child four years old, who earned nineteen cents in an afternoon stringing beans, and other children from seven to ten years of age. There are over 500 canning factories in New York State, but the census of 1900 gives the number of children employed under sixteen years of age as 219. This is merely another illustration of the deceptiveness of the statistics which are gathered at so much expense. The agent of the New York Child Labor Committee was told by the foreman of one factory that there were 300 children under fourteen years of age in that one factory! In Syracuse it was a matter of complaint, in the season of 1904, on the part of the children, that "The factories will not take you *unless you are eight years old.*"

In Maryland there are absolutely no restrictions placed upon the employment of children in canneries. They may be employed at any age, by day or night, for as many hours as the employers choose, or the children can stand and keep awake. In Oxford, Md., I saw a tiny girl, seven years old, who had worked for twelve hours in an oyster-canning factory, and I was told that such cases were common. There were 290 canning establishments in the state of Maryland in 1900, all of them employing young children absolutely without legal restriction. And I fear that it must be added with little or no moral restriction either. Where regard for child life does not express itself in humane laws for its preservation, it may generally be presumed to be non-existent.

In Maine the age limit for employment is twelve years. Children of that age may be employed by day or night, provided that girls under eighteen and boys under sixteen are not permitted to work more than ten hours in the twenty-four or sixty hours in a week. In 1900 there were 117 establishments engaged in the preservation and canning of fish. Small herrings are canned and placed upon the market as "sardines." This industry is principally confined to the Atlantic coast towns,—Lubec and Eastport; in Washington County, being the main centres. I cannot speak of this industry from personal investigation, but information received from competent and trustworthy sources gives me the impression that child slavery nowhere assumes a worse form than in the "sardine" canneries of Maine. Says one of my correspondents in a private letter: "In the rush season, fathers, mothers, older children, and babies work from early morn till night—from dawn till dark, in fact. You will scarcely believe me, perhaps, when I say 'and babies,' but it is literally true. I've seen them in the present season, no more than four or five years old, working hard and beaten when they lagged. As you may suppose, being out here, far away from the centre of the state, we are not much troubled by factory inspection. I have read about the conditions in the Southern mills, but nothing I have read equals for sheer brutality what I see right here in Washington County."

In the sweatshops and, more particularly, the poorly paid home industries, the kindergartens are robbed to provide baby slaves. I am perfectly well aware that many persons will smile incredulously at the thought of infants from three to five years old working. "What can such little babies do?" they ask. Well, take the case of little Anetta Fachini, for example. The work she was doing when

I saw her, wrapping paper around pieces of wire, was very similar to the play of better-favored children. As play, to be put aside whenever her childish fancy wandered to something else, it would have been a very good thing for little Anetta to do. She was compelled, however, to do it from early morning till late at night and even denied the right to sleep. For her, therefore, what might be play for some other child became the most awful bondage and cruelty. What can four-year-old babies do? Go into the nursery and watch the rich man's four-year-old child, seated upon the rug, sorting many-colored beads and fascinated by the occupation for half an hour or so. That is play—good and wholesome for the child. In the public kindergarten, other four-year-old children are doing the same thing with zest and laughing delight. But go into the dim tenement yonder; another four-year-old child is sorting beads, but not in play. Her eyes do not sparkle with childish glee; she does not shout with delight at finding a prize among the beads. With tragic seriousness she picks out the beads and lays them before her mother, who is a slipper-beader—that is, she sews the beaded designs upon ladies' fancy slippers. She works from morn till night, and all the while the child is seated by her side, straining her little eyes in the dim light, sorting the beads or stringing them on pieces of thread.

Reading 8

The Diplomacy of Discrimination: Chinese Exclusion, 1876–1882

David L. Anderson

"The Chinese must go!" cried angry Pacific Coast workingmen in the 1870's who rioted against the influx of Chinese immigrants to the United States.[1] Although fueled by essentially domestic grievances which had little to do with China itself, their anti-Chinese movement, whose avowed goal was total exclusion of the Chinese from the United States, held serious implications for American-Chinese international relations and Western businessmen and missionaries in China. The eventual resolution between conflicting domestic demands and diplomatic treaty agreements in the 1880's— a solution involving complicated diplomatic and political maneuvers—a revealing study of how domestic issues and partisan politics have influenced America's foreign policy.

In 1868 the American diplomat Anson Burlingame, traveling as China's envoy to the nations of the Western world, had negotiated a treaty in Washington, D.C., with then Secretary of State William H. Seward. The resulting Burlingame Treaty had guaranteed free immigration and legal protection to Chinese people in America,[2] it was claimed, of American's friendship for China. The burgeoning domestic movement to exclude Chinese immigrants from the United States, however, clearly violated both the letter and the spirit of the Burlingame Treaty's policy of respect for the Chinese government and Chinese people in America.

This increasingly violent agitation for exclusion posed a grave threat to America's diplomatic position in China. Any unilateral American restriction of Chinese treaty rights in the United States, which was essentially what exclusionists demanded, could lead to retaliation by China. All of the legal rights and privileges held by Americans and Europeans in China rested on a system of so-called "unequal treaties," which British and French naval power had forced upon China after the Opium War of 1839–42. These treaties gave to Westerners in China commercial, judicial, and territorial privileges which flagrantly insulted and undermined the sovereignty of the Chinese government. Under the terms of the treaties, China was forbidden to set its own tariffs, to arrest and prosecute foreigners for violations of laws, and to deny to one Western nation any treaty or privilege granted to another nation.[3] Geographically and culturally isolated from Europe, the Chinese had agreed to these one-sided treaties not only because of military pressure, but also out of ignorance of Western international law and practices.

As the years passed the Chinese saw how Western diplomats had used the tenets of international law to justify demands for ever-increasing rights and privileges in China. The treaties, for example, had legalized penetration of China by Western merchants and missionaries. By the 1870's sizable foreign enclaves existed in China's major coastal cities, and Western missionaries were busily evangelizing far into the interior of China. After more than three decades of official treaty relations with Western nations, the Chinese had learned enough about Western diplomatic practice not only to be more cautious but also to attempt to turn it to their own use. If the United States prevented Chinese immigration into California, the Chinese government might move to exclude American and European merchants and missionaries from China.

The Chinese citizens who had traveled to the United States with Burlingame in 1868 had been somewhat of a curiosity in the East, but by 1870 the Chinese in America, particularly in the western states, were viewed as the "yellow peril." Their numbers had increased from 35,000 in 1860 to over 105,000 in 1880, with 99 percent of these immigrants concentrated in the Pacific Coast region.[4] Originally, capitalist entrepreneurs had welcomed the Chinese as a cheap labor source, but by the mid-1870's the completion of the transcontinental railroad, the growth of the white labor force in the West, and nation-wide economic depression had encouraged white workingmen to turn against Chinese workers. White Californians deeply resented competing with what they considered to be Chinese "slave" labor. Although the Chinese immigrants were not slaves, most did come to the United States as contract laborers who worked for extremely low wages. "Chinamen" were also unacceptable because they were not Caucasian. Many Californians viewed the filth, crime, opium-smoking, and crowded conditions of local Chinatowns as racial stereotypes rather than manifestations of poverty. Economic and racial hysteria, then, helped make Chinese exclusion an urgent political issue in California.[5]

Both the Democratic and Republican parties included a plank on "Mongolian immigration" in their national platforms in 1876, because they were courting California's votes in the upcoming presidential election which they expected to be a close race. The Democrats forthrightly recommended exclusion, and the Republicans proposed that Congress investigate the effects of Chinese immigration. The Republican candidate, Rutherford B. Hayes, avoided the issue throughout the campaign, however, because his party was split on the question. Many northern and eastern Republicans, such as Hannibal Hamlin, Lincoln's first vice-president, opposed exclusion as racially prejudiced and contrary to America's liberal traditions. Republicans from the western states such as California Senator Aaron Sargent, on the other hand, led the fight for restrictive immigration laws.[6]

While Hayes equivocated, Sargent tried to prompt congressional action limiting the influx of Chinese. The Senate and House refused to move quickly but did set up a joint committee to investigate the question. Because of the illness and eventual death of the chairman, Oliver P. Morton of Indiana, Sargent headed the investigation. After extensive testimony, more than half of which was favorable to the Chinese and immigration, Sargent submitted a report for the committee which unequivocally recommended exclusion. Morton's notes, published posthumously and based upon same testimony, concluded that the investigation failed to prove that California had suffered either morally or economically from the presence of the Chinese. In fact, Morton argued, the state had benefited from its Chinese population.[7]

Living in far-off China, George Frederick Seward, United States minister plenipotentiary in Peking and nephew of the former secretary of state, did not consider the domestic anti-Chinese movement a problem. The number of Chinese emigrating to United States would never be very large, he predicted, because the Orientals did not want to live in America. They were deterred in part by the hostile reception they received in California, but the primary reason, according to Seward, was that they "shrink from contact with our restless, energetic civilization." Only the lure of money had prompted them to relocate in America, in the minister's view, and "when the call for labor ceases to be an urgent one, the Chinaman will stop his migration in that direction."[8]

The increasing number of anti-Chinese incidents in the United States in early 1876, however, prompted the Tsungli Yamen, or Chinese foreign office, to address Minister Seward on the subject. Copying the language and arguments used innumerable times by Western diplomats, the Chinese officials reminded Seward of his nation's treaty obligations. They cited the fifth and sixth articles of the Burlingame Treaty, which guaranteed free immigration and protection to Chinese in America, and requested that Seward communicate their views to Washington, D.C. The American minister's reply read like those written by the Tsungli Yamen when faced with protests of treaty violations in China. Seward pointed out the difficulties of the situation in California, assured the Chinese that his government anxiously sought a solution to the problem, and promised to convey the foreign office's concerns to Washington.[9]

It was not until 1878 that Seward finally became concerned about the effect of the exclusion effort on American-Chinese diplomatic relations. Serious anti-Chinese rioting had occurred in San Francisco in the summer of 1877, and petitions from the California legislature had buttressed the joint congressional committee's findings in favor of exclusion. Under this pressure both houses of Congress passed resolutions urging President Hayes to seek changes in the existing treaties. At this same time China sent its first permanent envoys to the United States, and Seward feared that the Chinese ministers would:

> send back to this Government some very unpleasant reports in regard to the treatment
> of Chinese in California, and they may in turn deal in a very cavalier way with all our
> efforts to secure redress for wrongs suffered by our countrymen here.[10]

Further, Seward expressed concern that a national anti-Chinese law might threaten the entire Western treaty system in China. Although some congressmen believed that the United States could abrogate through legislation those portions of the American treaties which guaranteed free immigration and protection to the Chinese, the minister contended that such unilateral action by the United States would set a dangerous precedent. The Chinese did not like the existing treaties, he reminded the new secretary of state, William M. Evarts, and they would welcome justification for declaring null and void all the provisions which they found to be objectionable.[11]

Seward believed, however, that Washington could convince the Tsungli Yamen to revise the American treaty provisions on immigration. The minister reasoned that despite the incidents in California, the Chinese in America enjoyed substantially more rights than did Americans in China. Although there was an element of sophistry in his failure to acknowledge the unequal treaties, technically he was correct in his assessment. Using this "lack of reciprocity" as a bargaining point, Seward continued, the United States could demand that China either extend more privileges to Americans or approve the desired changes in the treaty. The minister predicted:

> It is very certain that China would not consent to the extension of the privileges enjoyed
> by foreigners in this country, and it is possible that, rather than do this, she would agree
> to such a revision of our treaties as I have indicated.[12]

Seward's fears of unilateral congressional action were realized in January, 1879, when the House passed a bill permitting only fifteen Chinese people to enter the United States on any one ship docking on the West Coast. The Senate concurred and added an amendment authorizing the president to abrogate Articles V and VI of the Burlingame Treaty.[13] The western congressmen had finally managed to force action on exclusion.

Many other Americans, however, began to push for a presidential veto. Most eastern newspaper editors and politicians contended that the fifteen-passenger bill violated the sanctity of treaties and reversed America's traditional open-door immigration policy. The *New York Times*, for example, argued that "the enactment of this bill into a law would violate all the principles upon which our government is founded."[14] Religious and commercial groups complained that the bill invited "the danger of retaliatory action" against American missionaries and businessmen in China.[15]

Not surprisingly, President Hayes vetoed the bill. His concern, however, was not with the substance of the legislation but with the method of limitation. Hayes indicated privately that he considered the Chinese "labor invasion" to be "pernicious," classifying the Chinese as one of the "weaker races," along with Negroes and Indians who would be oppressed in the United States and would make their oppressors "hoodlums or vagabonds." Hayes therefore favored the limitation of Chinese immigration—but by some means consistent with the treaties and with recognized international practices.[16] In reaching this decision Hayes may have conferred with Minister Seward, who was in Washington in February, 1879, because several of the minister's views appeared in the president's public and private statements on the exclusion issue. While preparing to veto the bill Hayes recorded in his diary:

> We have accepted the advantages which the treaty gives us. Our traders, missionaries and travelers are domiciled in China. Important interests have grown up under the treaty, and rest upon faith in its observance. One of the parties to a treaty cannot rightfully by legislation violate it.[17]

In his veto message to Congress, the president noted that if the United States abrogated part of the treaty, the Chinese would be free to renounce the Treaty of Tientsin of 1858 upon which rested all American rights in China.[18]

After successfully blocking unilateral action, Hayes began his own diplomatic steps to limit Chinese immigration. "It should be made certain *by proper methods,*" he wrote in his diary, "that such an invasion [of Chinese workers] can not permanently over-ride our people. It cannot safely be admitted into the bosom of our American society."[19] Accordingly, Hayes' Secretary of State Evarts instructed Seward to enter into preparatory discussions with the Chinese government on the subject of immigration and to allay their concern about the growing exclusion movement. Evarts also requested facts on the contract labor system and as the number of criminals and other undesirables who emigrated from China. His instructions did not authorize Seward to make any specific treaty proposals, because Hayes and Evarts themselves hoped to draft some revisions acceptable to Americans both at home and in China.[20]

Seward welcomed the opportunity to discuss the immigration question with the Chinese, but he bent his instructions to conform to his own views. Considering massive immigration unlikely, he therefore deemed exclusion an unnecessary complication of the American position in China. Although Seward had frequently ignored the Tsungli Yamen when he found their objections to Western activity troublesome, in this case he exceeded his instructions by assuring the Chinese officials that he sympathized with their grievances. From the perspective of the legation in Peking, antagonizing the Chinese with restrictive legislation would stupidly exacerbate the chronic Oriental hostility and suspicion toward the West. Meeting with the Tsungli Yamen, Seward boldly expressed the hope that the imperial government would voluntarily limit the emigration of paupers, criminals, and prostitutes to the United States, and thereby he violated his instructions to make no specific proposals to the Chinese. He also refused to raise the question of contract labor, despite Evarts' request for information on this point. In Seward's estimation the Chinese were sensitive to criticism on contract emigration (the so-called "coolie trade"), and broaching the subject would only further irritate an already difficult situation. Instead he chose to be almost apologetic about the anti-Chinese incidents in California and to assure the Tsungli Yamen of America's devotion to "liberal" government and humanity."[21] Following his meeting with the Chinese Officials, Seward informed Washington in July that

> the sooner we rise to the idea of dealing with this Government as being actuated by very much the same motives of dignity, patriotism and public policy which actuates other governments, the sooner we shall be able to place our relations upon an enduring basis of good will and common interests.[22]

Seward may have echoed the Burlingame Treaty's doctrine of respect for the Chinese, but he spoke from expediency, not principle. As United States consul general in Shanghai for thirteen years before advancing to the post of minister in 1876, Seward had consistently promoted Western commercial interests. By both inclination and instinct, he thought in terms of what would best serve the needs of Westerners in China, not justice for the Chinese. "Our people in this part of the world, merchants and missionaries," he reiterated in August, "would be much reassured if they could know even that the disruption of our relations with China may be averted."[23]

Seward's official efforts to resolve the immigration issue came to an abrupt halt in 1880. With national elections approaching in the United States, the Hayes administration identified Seward as a political liability. The minister's refusal to pursue vigorously the immigration issue with the Tsungli Yamen began costing the Republicans potential votes in Pacific Coast states. Moreover, a concerted, although unsuccessful, the preceding year in the House of Representatives to impeach Seward for peculation and other offenses in China also made him a political detriment to his party.[24] Accordingly, Evarts asked Seward for his resignation. When the minister stubbornly refused, Hayes formally recalled Seward from his post. Before leaving China, however, Seward made a parting attempt to thwart the exclusion movement. In a farewell gathering he tried to prejudice a high-ranking Chinese official against revision of the Burlingame Treaty by telling him that only the "Irish rabble" in the United States favored exclusion. Further, the exiting minister predicted that future American proposals on Chinese immigration would insult the dignity of the imperial government.[25]

Upon his return home Seward wrote a book refuting the pro-exclusion arguments, contending that there was no basis for America's fears of a massive influx of Chinese, that the Chinese had been of great service on the West Coast, and that lawful remedies already existed for such problems as crime in Chinatowns. Seward's book, however, made him seem more liberal and enlightened than he actually was. Although he wrote, for example, that "all men under the sun are worthy in the measure of their intelligence and moral excellence, and not according to their grade in life or the hue of their skin,"[26] a few years earlier he had also written that "the darker races fall successively before the Caucasian" and that "in the long run the Chinese cannot prove the exception."[27] Seward's main consideration, then, was the promotion of foreign interests in China.[28]

Seward left China maintaining that Washington did not understand or appreciate his efforts and that it was ignoring Peking's reaction to American discrimination against Chinese immigrants. Convinced that his diplomatic effort had been terminated for no good reason, Seward pronounced the following potshot valedictory on the role of being an American minister:

> The field of labor is so distant and so obscure that effort cannot be expected to win for the given officer adequate compensation. . . . It may . . . bring him into collision with his own Government . . . and the given Government may unwittingly sacrifice its best interests, overruling and condemning its Minister to its own damage.[29]

Secretary of State Evarts named James Burrill Angell as the new American minister plenipotentiary to China. He also designated Angell a treaty commissioner and assigned to him the task of amending the free immigration provisions of the Burlingame Treaty. Selecting Seward's replacement very carefully, Evarts believed that Angell, a midwesterner, would be more acceptable to the Chinese than a representative of either the West Coast exclusionists or the East Coast mercantilists. Angell was also an educator and the president of the University of Michigan, a background the secretary thought would appeal to the Chinese. Although Angell had no practical diplomatic experience, he knew a great deal about international law, or what President Hayes referred to as "proper methods." In addition, his personal qualities were ideally suited to his delicate assignment. The man who would ask the Chinese government to allow its subjects to be discriminated against by American immigration laws was a sensitive, intelligent, and urbane gentleman. Angell occasionally employed stereotypes in his speech, but his private as well as public writings were singularly lacking in racial aspersions, especially compared to those of Seward.[30]

The cautious Angell did not immediately accept the post. He first sought assurance that the appointment as treaty commissioner would be only temporary because he wanted to return quickly to the university. He also expressed serious doubts about reversing America's traditional policy of welcoming immigrants. Angell feared, however, that Congress would eventually pass restrictive legislation despite the Burlingame Treaty and that such unilateral action might cause Chinese retaliation against American treaty rights in China. Some kind of treaty revision permitting congressional regulation was therefore necessary. He informed Evarts that he would accept the position, but only if his instructions did not require him to seek absolute prohibition of Chinese immigration.[31]

To assist Angell, the State Department appointed two other commissioners plenipotentiary to participate in the treaty negotiations. John F. Swift, who was a San Francisco assemblyman, advocated total exclusion of Chinese immigrants from the U.S.; William H. Trescot of South Carolina, on the other hand, viewed exclusion with professional caution reflecting his considerable diplomatic experience in the service of both the United States and Confederate States of America. All three commissioners were Republicans. Chester Holcombe, the secretary of the legation in Peking and interpreter to the treaty negotiations, later termed the composition of the commission a master political move for the party. The Democrats in Congress grumbled about how this move stole their thunder on the exclusion issue which they had long supported, but they did not dare oppose it.[32]

In May, 1880, Secretary Evarts met several times with Angell and Trescot in Washington to discuss the mission. The secretary gave them no specific instructions—a fact which suggests that the commission was established to relieve exclusionist political pressure on the administration rather than to implement any considered policy. The three men agreed that the Chinese immigrants' lack of interest in assimilation created a social problem, but that the United States wanted to be "just and generous" to the Chinese government. Although the meetings dealt with a broad range of potential treaty questions, the three men reached no conclusions. In fact Angell and Trescot learned from Evarts only that the Burlingame Treaty must be revised, that the State Department had no specific changes in mind, that it was the commission's job to make some revisions, and that in doing so they must seek to please people on both sides of the Pacific.[33]

Evarts' written instructions to Angell and his colleagues consisted only of a series of points to be considered during the negotiations with the Chinese. Nor did he provide them with any draft provisions. The secretary told the commissioners only to take into account sentiment on the Pacific coast, United States commercial relations with China, American traditions of liberal admission of foreigners, and the opposition of certain religious groups to exclusion. Evarts sent the commissioners copies of the Democratic and Republican party platform planks on Chinese immigration.[34]

Enroute to Peking, Angell stopped for several days in San Francisco where he talked with Frederick F. Low, a former United States minister to China and former governor of California, and with several other local spokesmen. He also visited Chinatown and met the leaders of San Francisco's Chinese community. Angell determined that although most men in California favored some limitation of immigration because of the problem of non-assimilation, Californians thought that the Chinese should be well treated. The new minister also found neither deplorable conditions in Chinatown nor widespread white unemployment in California, and he concluded that most of the exclusion agitation had been politically motivated and created by the press. In his opinion a few demagogues had exploited the white agricultural "tramps" who poured into San Francisco after the harvest to become "bummers and sand lot politicians."[35]

The American commission arrived in Peking in August, 1880, and held its own caucus before making its initial proposals to the Chinese. Swift, the Californian, wanted a treaty which absolutely prohibited Chinese immigration into the United States. Angell and Trescot disagreed, arguing that the treaty should only give Congress the discretion to regulate immigration as it deemed necessary. Although Swift continued to advocate his position vigorously in this session and later meetings, the majority ruled. Trescot accordingly drafted a memorandum to the Chinese asking that [the United States] shall be allowed to judge for itself to what extent the immigration of Chinese labor is useful and advantageous, and that whenever . . . it feels that its social or industrial interests require a limitation or prohibition of such immigration, it shall have the authority . . . to regulate it as is most consonant with those interests.[36]

At the first negotiating session with the Chinese on October 1, the two Chinese treaty commissioners proposed to leave the Burlingame Treaty unchanged and to make Seward's proposals concerning the limiting of certain classes of people, such as paupers and prostitutes, the basis for discussion. Trescot countered that Seward's suggestion had been made without the authorization of government and that the present commission had come specifically to revise the Burlingame Treaty. The Chinese cooperatively agreed to consider the issues and indicated that they thought a settlement feasible. Trescot thought that the Chinese were stalling. Angell and Swift, however, left the meeting thinking that the emperor's representatives would negotiate on a basis of limitation of immigration, but not prohibition. Although the Americans were prepared to waive prohibition, they decided to wait a while longer before revealing their hand.[37]

Several days later the Chinese called a meeting and presented the Americans with a full project or draft for a treaty. This draft applied immigration restrictions only to California, exempted "artisans" from the excluded class of "laborers," and proposed what amounted to an imperial veto over any regulations which Congress might adopt. The Americans expressed their objections, to the articles, but the conference adjourned on a cordial note. After this meeting the Americans decided to play their trump and resubmit their own project asking only for limitation, not prohibition.[38]

The decisive treaty session occurred on November 5, 1880, slightly more than a month after the first official meeting. With both projects before them, the Chinese and American commissioners turned to the first article which dealt with regulating immigration. The two drafts were at such variance that Swift and Trescot were ready to abandon the entire effort, but Angell believed that the Chinese were prepared to negotiate in earnest and counseled patience. "Let us leave this article," he suggested, "and take up the last. Let the fish chew the bait awhile." Turning to other provisions, the two sides quickly came to agreement on several minor points. Returning to the first article and "having now gotten into the mood of agreeing," the commissioners succeeded in "dovetailing" together the two drafts, and the work was done.[39]

The commissioners agreed to the final wording of the treaty on November 8 and signed the document on November 17. Genuine bargaining had taken place between the American commissioners and their Chinese counterparts, and the rapidity of the settlement must have set a record for Sino-Western diplomatic dealings under conditions other than duress. A simultaneous border controversy with Russia may have prompted China to come to quick agreement, but more likely the Chinese simply were not concerned enough about emigration to quibble.[40]

Article I of the Treaty of 1880 allowed the United States to "regulate, limit, or suspend" but "not absolutely prohibit" the immigration of Chinese laborers. The other three articles provided specifically for the entrance of Chinese students, merchants, and tourists into the United States; for protection of Chinese people already residing in America; and for communication to the Chinese government of any laws passed in accordance with the treaty.[41]

Angell, Swift, and Trescot believed that the Chinese only agreed to these terms because of their belief in America's friendship for their country. In their summary report to Washington, the three commissioners concluded that once the Chinese granted that the United States should have discretionary power over immigration to the Western country, they assumed that America would "exercise that discretion with justice, and spirit of friendship." "We were fortunate enough," continued the commissioners, "to satisfy the Chinese commissioners not only of the justice of our views, but of the entire good faith in which they were advanced."[42] The Chinese apparently trusted that future American restrictions and behavior would be reasonable, and Angell considered the immigration treaty a good solution of the "Chinese question," as it was called in the United States.

Angell's expectation that the United States would find hardly "any need of availing itself of the power conceded it," however, proved sadly inaccurate.[43] The ink was barely dry on the treaty's signatures when Congress began debate on seven different exclusion bills, and the goals of politics and diplomacy continued to be exactly opposite on the immigration question. Congress tended to view the Angell Treaty not as a international accommodation on a sensitive issue but rather as a carte blanche for luring constituents' votes at the expense of Chinese immigrants. Congressional debate centered not on whether to suspend immigration but rather over how long the suspension should be. The negotiated treaty, purposefully vague, allowed the United States to close immigration for a "reasonable" period, but even the American treaty commissioners did not agree on the timetable. Angell contended that five years was a reasonable period, but Swift maintained that forty years was not excessive.[44]

The first exclusion bill approved by Congress in 1882 under the aegis of the new treaty provided for a twenty-year suspension of immigration of Chinese laborers. It also created an elaborate system of regulations which would have effectively impeded the immigration of merchants, students, and other Chinese whom the treaty had specifically exempted from such restrictions. During the debate on this bill, which had been authored by Senator John F. Miller of California, Senator Joseph Hawley of Connecticut perceptively summarized the ironic history of Sino-Western relations: "We are asked to deny to the Chinaman the right [of immigration and residence which] he was bombarded into accepting" for foreigners in his own country.[45]

President Chester A. Arthur vetoed this twenty-year suspension bill for much the same reason that President Hayes had vetoed the earlier fifteen-passenger-limit bill. The new president agreed with the purpose of the bill but thought that the twenty-year period and onerous regulations were unreasonable and hence indefensible under both the new Angell Treaty and accepted international practices. Unsuccessful at overriding the veto, Congress quickly passed a second bill establishing a ten-year exclusion period and modifying but not removing the provisions affecting the supposedly exempted classes of Chinese. Arthur thought that this substitute bill also went beyond the suspension period and regulations permitted by the Angell Treaty, but he yielded to political pressure for some type of exclusion and signed the law.[46]

In the face of the United States' quick moves to restrict all Chinese immigration to America, the government of China was incapable of responding with anything more than formal remonstrances. Plagued by difficulties much more serious than the treatment of its emigrants in America, China faced increasing pressures from other countries for economic and territorial concessions as well as insurmountable internal problems ranging from pervasive poverty to political upheaval. China's government, economy, and entire way of life were collapsing under the weight of these burdens, and the Chinese were thus unable to retaliate by restricting the rights of foreigners in China as Seward and Angell had once thought they might.

Washington's move to discriminate against Chinese immigrants in the 1870's and 1880's illustrated more than the way in which domestic political considerations could complicate the nation's diplomatic goals. Its decision to exclude immigrants revealed one of the most unsavory and unequal aspects of Western policy toward China in the nineteenth century: namely, the invocation of treaties and international law to give legitimacy to arbitrary actions against the weak Chinese government. Earlier in the century the Western nations had invaded China's centuries-old isolation, using international conventions and practices to justify their own penetration of Chinese society. The American Treaty of 1880, however, led to an ironic reapplication of diplomatic principles. Again using the sanctimonious shroud of a treaty, the United States in 1882 blocked the entry of the Chinese into American society.

Notes

1. Neil L. Shumsky, "San Francisco's Workingmen Respond to the Modern City," *California Historical Quarterly,* 55 (Spring, 1976): 46–51, and the accompanying pictorial history, "The Workingmen's Party in California, 1877–1882," 58–73. See also Roger Olmsted, "The Chinese Must Go!" *California Historical Quarterly,* 50 (Sept., 1971): 285–94.

2. Charles I. Bevans, ed., *Treaties and Other International Agreements of the United States of America 1776–1949* (Washington, 1968–74), 6: 680–84.

3. *Treaties, Conventions, etc., Between China and Foreign States* (Shanghai, 1908), I:29–46, 159–64, 212–29, 238–42, 509–23, 602–23, 673–78.

4. The statistics on Chinese immigration are approximate. See Mary R. Coolidge, *Chinese Immigration* (New York, 1909), pp. 425, 501; Elmer C. Sandmeyer, *The Anti-Chinese Movement in California* (Urbana, Ill., 1939), P. 17

5. Sandmeyer, *Anti-Chinese Movement,* 25–39; Alexander Saxton, *The Indispensable Enemy: Labor and the Anti-Chinese Movement in California* (Berkeley, Los Angeles, and London, 1971). pp. 258–65; Robert McClellan, *The Heathen Chinee* (Columbus, Ohio, 1971), pp. 1–6; Tyler Dennett, *Americans in Eastern Asia* (New York, 1922), pp. 535–40; Stuart Creighton Miller, *The Unwelcome Immigrant: The American Image of the Chinese, 1785–1882* (Berkeley, Los Angeles, and London, 1969). pp. 3–15, argues that anti-Chinese sentiments were not limited to California and the West Coast.

6. Gary Pennanen, "Public Opinion and the Chinese Question, 1876–1879," *Ohio History,* 77 (Winter, Spring, Summer, 1968): 141.

7. Coolidge, *Chinese Immigration,* 96–104, 132–33; John W. Foster, *American Diplomacy in the Orient* (Boston, 1903), pp. 283–93. For Sargent's report, see Senate, *Report No. 689,* 44 Cong., 2 Sess. For Morton's notes see Senate, *Miscellaneous Document No. 20,* 45 Cong., 2 Sess.

8. George F. Seward to Secretary of State Hamilton Fish, March 22, 1876, Despatches from United States Ministers to China, National Archives (hereafter cited as China Despatches).

9. Seward to Fish, June 29, 1876, ibid.

10. Seward to Fish, March 13, 1878, ibid; Coolidge, *Chinese Immigration* 83–84, 114–16, 133–34; Pennanen, "Public Opinion," 141–43.

11. Seward to Evarts, March 22, 1878, China Despatches; House, *Report No. 240,* 45 Cong., 2 Sess.

12. Ibid.

13. *Congressional Record,* 45 Cong., 3 Sess., 791–801, 1264–76, 1299–1316, 1383–1400, 1796–97; House, *Report No. 62,* 45 Cong., 3 Sess.

14. *The New York Times,* February 24, 1879.

15. Pennanen, "Public Opinion," 143–45.

16. T. Harry Williams, ed., *Hayes: The Diary of a President, 1875–1881* (New York, 1964), pp. 187–88.

17. Ibid., 189.

18. James D. Richardson, comp., *A Compilation of the Messages and Papers of the Presidents* (New York, 1913), 6:4466–72.

19. Williams, *Hayes Diary,* 192. Emphasis added.

20. Evarts to Seward, April 23, 1879, Diplomatic Instructions of the Department of State, China, National Archives (hereinafter cited as China Instructions).

21. Seward to Evarts, July 21, 1879, China Despatches.

22. Ibid.

23. Seward to Evarts, Aug. 1, 1879, ibid.

24. Denny to Angell, Aug. 10, 1880, James B. Angell Papers, Michigan Historical Collections of the

University of Michigan; "James B. Angell Diaries Concerning his Service in China from 1880 to 1881" (hereafter cited as Angell Diary), 1:8, James B. Angell Papers, Michigan Historical Collections of the University of Michigan; House, *Report No. 134, 45* Cong., 3 Sess.

25. Evarts to Seward, telegram, Dec. 27, 1879, China Instructions; Evarts to Seward, June 5, 1880, ibid; Seward to Evarts, Jan. 26, 18 1880, China Despatches; Commission to Evarts, Oct. 11 18 1880, ibid.

26. George F. Seward, *Chinese Immigration* (New York, 1881), p. 158.

27. Seward to Davis, July 18, 1874, Despatches from United States Consuls in Shanghai, National Archives.

28. Ibid.; Seward, *Chinese Immigration,* v–vi, 11–13.

29. Seward to Evarts, May 6, 1880, China Despatches.

30. Angell Diary, 1:3, 59.

31. James Burrill Angell, *Reminiscences* (New York, 1912), p. 131; Shirley W. Smith, *James Burrill Angell: An American Influence* (Ann Arbor, Mich., 1954), pp. 119–22; Coolidge, *Chinese Immigration,* 152.

32. Smith, Angell, 122–23; Coolidge, Chinese *Immigration*, 153.

33. Angell Diary, 1:7–11; Smith, *Angell*, 124–25; Brainerd Dyer, *The Public Career of William M. Evarts* (Berkeley, 1933), p. 222.

34. Evarts to Commission, June 7, 1880, China Instructions; Evarts to Commission, July 23, 1880, ibid.

35. Angell Diary, 1:17–18.

36. Memorandum enclosed in Commission to Evarts, Oct. 11, 1880, China Despatches; Angell Diary, 1:59–60.

37. Commission to Evarts, Oct. 23, 1880, China Despatches; Angell Diary, 1:66–67.

38. Commission to Evarts, Nov. 3, 1880, China Despatches; Angell Diary, 1:70–72.

39. Angell Diary, 1:72–75; Angell, *Reminiscences*, 143–45; Commission to Evarts, Nov. 6, 1880, China Despatches.

40. Angell to his son (Alexis Angell), Aug. 14, 1880, and Nov. 21, 1880, James B. Angell Papers.

41. Bevans, *Treaties*, 6:68–87.

42. Commission to Evarts, Nov. 17, 1880, China Despatches.

43. Angell Diary, 1:80.

44. Coolidge, *Chinese Immigration,* 164–69.

45. *Congressional Record,* 47 Cong., 1739

46. Thomas C. Reeves, Gentleman Boss: *The Life of Chester Alan Arthur* (New York, 1975), pp. 278–79; Coolidge, *Chinese Immigration,* 169–78; Senate, *Executive Document No. 148,* 47 Cong., 1. Sess.

Reading 9

"Whackety Whack, Don't Talk Back": The Glorification of Violence Against Females and the Subjugation of Women in Nineteenth-Century Southern Folk Music

C. Kirk Hutson

All violence is worthy of scholarly attention. Violence against women gives historians a unique insight into mentally reinforced gender inequality and control in the nineteenth century. Because few historical sources deal with the beating or killing of southern women, particularly those in the nineteenth century, and because battered women have not historically spoken out for fear of violent consequences and social condemnation, music offers a way of discerning this hidden problem in the South. Violence is not a uniquely southern phenomenon however, as several prominent social scientists and historians have shown, the South has traditionally condoned the use of violence more than any other section of the United States. Historically, for example, the region has consistently led the nation in the number of homicides per 100,000 inhabitants. Similarly, even though violence against women occurred throughout society, on certain occasions southern culture sanctioned its use more than other areas of the country. In 1824, for example, the Supreme Court of Mississippi was the first state court to recognize a husband's right to beat his wife. Moreover, between 1882 and 1927, seventy-six African-American women and sixteen white women were lynched in the United States, all but two in the South. In fact, one scholar pointed out that in the nineteenth-century South, violence was viewed as "an essential fact life somehow built into relationships." In such an environment, women could easily be physically and psychologically abused.[1]

The southerner's penchant for violence was also reflected the region's music. Both the North and the South, for example, published hundreds of tunes during the Civil War, but there were some major differences in how the messages were communicated. Southern ditties, for example, were less humorous, and more "ferocious and savage" than, those of the North. In fact, homicide was one of the region's most popular song themes. Love melodies that described fatal bloodshed, for example, outnumbered nonviolent love songs "about ten to one." In fact, no matter how sensational these folksongs might appear to contemporary observers, the stories were not inconceivable to the listeners. When songs dealt with vicious female murders, such events could occur. Most of the local tunes were, indeed, factual.[2]

Folksongs show the extent of violence against women in the rural South. Lyrics are of value to historians because they are artifacts of a community and culture, permitting "an unobtrusive view into the issues, values, [and] ideas" of the time period in which the lyrics were written and sung. When dealing with gender issues, for instance, lyrics illustrate how both males and females thought and acted, or were expected to act. The study of southern folksong lyrics is also important because the words demonstrate how southern men understood particular issues.[3]

Even though it is clear that southern folk music reflects cultural attributes, a hotly debated topic in scholarly research is whether media affects culture. Modern studies have shown that men use violence against women because it works. When a male abuses a female, it "puts a quick stop to an emotional argument or a situation that is getting out of control." Men who are abusive to women often "learn that women are the 'appropriate' recipients" of violence. According to social learning theorists, male violence is not an "innate personality characteristic" but a learned behavior; therefore, music can be seen as a vital element in the learning process. Since violent anti-female ballads were extremely popular in the region among all classes of individuals, southern males continually heard that male authority could be maintained with violence.[4]

After many investigations, "researchers have reached a consensus on the effects of mass media on violence." Under "certain circumstances, subjects exposed to portrayals of violence typically display more aggressive behavior." Moreover, many psychological studies indicate that if the events seem real, if the aggressors are rewarded and not punished, if the violent acts are not condemned, if the acts seem socially acceptable, exciting, and justified, and if the person committing the crime is portrayed as aggressive and is seen as "intending to injure his victim," the media story is "most likely to be imitated in the laboratory." Similarly, if the aggressor is depicted as similar to the laboratory subjects and if the violent acts contain "cues" which "match cues in the real life environment," the subjects will act more aggressively.[5]

Although some scholars maintain that laboratory experiments can never duplicate real life, others, such as social psychologist George Comstock, maintain that such experiments are the "most rigorous" methods to use. When combined with nonlaboratory evidence, these experiments demonstrate the existence of positive correlations between viewing violence and behavior. Moreover, recent nonlaboratory "settings not vulnerable to criticisms in terms of laboratory artificiality" have increased in the last decade, and they clearly demonstrate that when violence against women is portrayed as "having positive consequences," a male's "acceptance of interpersonal violence against women" increases.[6]

Nineteenth-century folk music contains the criteria psychologists contend must be present to provoke aggressive behavior. These songs appear to portray real events. In fact, many of the tunes related actual occurrences, as reported in the newspapers. In addition, to make imported songs seem more real, they were often reset in familiar locations. Moreover, when performed, singers incorporated them into their own life stories, making them seem even more authentic. According to folklorist G. Malcolm Laws, balladeers often took these songs and personalized them until the "first person becomes more and more intrusive." In fact, a good singer could make audience members cry, believing the event had happened in his own family.[7] The fact that a singer might not know who composed a particular tune was irrelevant, because the "song belonged as much to him as to the first man who sang it." When discussing tunes from 1865 to 1895, for instance, one scholar stated that songs were such a "part of the day-to-day living itself" that it would have been "absurd" to ask the singer or the community who wrote the songs if the events portrayed were real. One old-time singer verified this statement when asked where he had learned a particular tune, "Why, I've known them all my life. I didn't learn them—I grew up with them." These songs were old tunes his "grandmother" had sung to him.[8]

When acts of violence were depicted they were often shown to be exciting, and the aggressive people were sometimes rewarded and seldom punished. The violent deeds were not condemned, and the brutal acts seemed socially acceptable and justifiable. Many types of folk tunes fit some of these criteria and adultery killings fit all. First, respectable and supposedly knowledgeable persons, such as medical doctors, endorsed such behavior in the songs. In "The Dumb Wife," for example, a doctor told a man that in order to "make a scolding wife hold her tongue," he should beat her with a hickory stick. Similarly, well-respected local individuals frequently sang these tunes at community events. Second, men were neither taken to court nor condemned by the community. In fact, they were applauded for their acts. Even when they were punished by the victims themselves, this bit of information was shrewdly omitted. In addition, the violence was rewarded. The man doing the beating or killing got what he wanted. His fists, for example, made his "nagging" wife shut up. Men who were able to keep females under their control were portrayed as macho.[9]

Psychological studies have generally shown that when the media portrays violence against women, male audience members will view women more negatively and increase their "aggression against them." The more such songs were sung, the less violent and less degrading the acts probably seemed to most southern males. Research shows that if males are bombarded with images of violence against females, over time this continual degradation of women will have violent repercussions for women. Although no historian can prove that a particular nineteenth-century southern male who listened to a singer glorify his abuse of his nagging wife immediately went home and beat his own wife, the prolonged psychological effects of such music cannot be discounted. Modern studies have shown that even if there is no immediate effect, long-range negative consequences can occur.[10] The continual barrage of such songs helps explain why males become desensitized to violence against women. When exposed to messages that depict aggression, "antagonistic orientations" towards women develops. Recent studies have shown at such negative "beliefs are a significant predictor of aggression against women." This form of aggression increases in environments where women are portrayed as less powerful and "justifiable targets of aggression."[11]

Even though these studies all deal with forms of mass media popular in the twentieth century, it is reasonable to suppose that violence in nineteenth-century folk music had similar effects. Folk music was especially important in the lives of rural southerners. It was a primary form of entertainment, and it broke down some of the barriers associated with rural isolation. It was not countered by opera and classical music. Although the so-called musically sophisticated ignored the rural fiddler, banjo picker, or dulcimer player, rural society did not. In fact, the folk musician was as "important as the parson," and received as much respect as the minister. In addition, music enabled many people to earn respect and some extra income. Moreover, music uplifted the spirits in a segment of the population that faced extreme poverty.[12]

Instead of only hearing songs on the radio, like later twentieth-century listeners, nineteenth-century men, women, and children were exposed to these tunes live and in a communal setting. Rural southerners, for example, habitually sang homicide tunes while attending "quiltin', house raisin', bean stringin' and corn huskin' parties." In fact, many of these songs remained in the oral tradition for generations. Musical lyrics transmit social norms and are a significant socializing element. The music of the nineteenth-century South informed men, women, and children about culturally acceptable behavior. Children especially look to music for "cultural cues to determine what attitudes, behaviors, and characteristics are a part of belonging to a particular sex."[13]

The most violent act is murder, and imported ballads that described the killing of women were often more popular in the South than other sections of the United States. These tunes came from various locations, including England, Scotland, and Norway, as well as other regions of the United States. They were popular with both African-American and white rural southerners from the Florida Everglades to the Ozark mountains. Although imported ballads indicate that southern males were not the only men to beat women, their popularity reinforces the view that many southern men overwhelmingly approved of the practice.[14]

According to interviews, female murder tunes were not only popular in the South but a major part of the oral tradition. In fact, such imported murder ballads were found in every southern state. Examination of the most important southern folklore collections attests to their prevalence. In the Frank C. Brown Collection of North Carolina approximately 47 percent of the imported murder ballads involved the murder of women. In John Harrington Cox's monumental study of folksongs in the South, approximately 44 percent of the murder tunes involved the death of women. Similarly, in Arthur Kyle Davis, Jr.'s *Traditional Ballads of Virginia,* approximately 42 percent of the murder ballads portrayed women killed. In the tunes Vance Randolph collected in northern Arkansas and southern Missouri, the figure is approximately 42 percent. Finally, in Oliver Dame Campbell and Cecil J. Sharp's *English Folk Songs from the Southern Appalachians,* a similar statistic of 43 percent is found. Although more men were portrayed as murder victims in folk music, there were significant gender differences.[15]

Although not every imported song that depicted the murder of a woman was popular throughout the South, several violent ballads and their numerous variations were prevalent in one or more southern states. There are several reasons for their popularity. First, for rural southerners, murder and violence were integral parts of the culture. Second, southern folksingers, like all folksingers, often strengthened their audience's belief in the reality of those stories by changing some facet of the old tune. Typically they assigned the song a regional name and a local setting. For instance a West Virginia version of the "Boston Burglar," instead of being from the northeast, the thief was said to have been "born in West Virginia, a place we all know well."[16]

Since only songs that mirrored some essential element of southern culture survived the region's oral tradition, it is important to analyze which events remained unchanged in imported murder tunes. What was the crucial element in these songs that enabled them to endure in the South, sometimes for generations after they ceased to be sung in Europe, while other tunes simply faded from the region's collective memory? First, although several southern versions of a particular female murder ballad might differ in tone or location, one thing remained the same—a woman was killed. By examining the murder ballads in folklorist Michael E. Bush's thesis, "Murder Ballads in Appalachia," it is apparent that material not essential to the murder did not survive. Similarly, in folklorist Arthur Kyle Davis Jr.'s examination of the only North American version of "Jellon Grame'," he supplied various European and Virginia versions of the text. The central theme, the killing of the woman, stayed, but the Scottish dialect and uncommon words were changed or omitted.[17]

Although imported ballads that depicted violence against women were popular in southern music, the South did not depend on outside regions to supply these tunes. In fact, violence against women was one of the most prevalent themes in nineteenth-century music that originated in the rural South. Over half of the murder ballads originating in North Carolina involved the murder of women.[18] In fact, femicide was one of the most popular themes in native songs. In North Carolina, for example, murder tunes depicting the killing of women were more common than tunes about wrecks, storms, and moonshining. They were more popular even than songs concerning one of the most historically important events in North Carolina's history, the Regulator Movement. Although there are many such tunes, "Omie Wise" is typical. In fact, this song, based on an actual event, was one of the most prevalent in the entire South and found in every southern state. It described the early nineteenth-century murder of Naomi Wise by Jonathan Lewis. According to court records and oral sources, Lewis, a man from a prominent family, promised in 1808 to marry Wise, an orphaned field hand pregnant with his child; but Lewis's mother wanted him to marry the more affluent Hattie Elliott. When word circulated about Wise's pregnancy and engagement, Lewis told her that they would immediately wed. Instead of going to the magistrate, however, he took her to Deep River and "tied her dress above her head, and then held her beneath [the water with] his foot" until she died. Lewis was arrested for the crime but eventually escaped from jail. Although recaptured a few years later, he was acquitted of the murder.[19]

The tunes and oral histories that surround this murder are particularly interesting because they reveal the "'good girl" versus "bad girl" duality. In addition, several versions impart the message that bad things happen to "good girls'" when they turn into "bad girls." Oral sources, for example, pointed out that Lewis "ruin[ed]" Wise's "fair name" by getting her pregnant. She had been a decent, moral woman until she had premarital sex with Lewis, which "disgrace[d]" her. This attitude emerged in most versions of the tune. Several songsters explained that Lewis promised to marry Wise so that there would be "no disgrace." One balladeer pointed out, for example, that Lewis had "shame[d] and disgrace[d]" Wise. In fact, the singer made clear that he thought that Wise had been immoral, claiming that Wise begged for her life and said, "Don't kill me, let me live, full of shame." In addition, moral lessons emerged in some versions. One threatened all "Young people, oh, take warning" and be not, fooled into having premarital sex, or "you are sure to meet Naomi's fate." Likewise, another songster warned "young ladies" not to be "ruined" by such men. These songs plus the oral statements given by area residents are indications that unwed mothers were viewed as disreputable persons. Women were held to a higher sexual standard than men. Unlike a man, whose "infidelity" *[sic]* was viewed by area residents as "a natural sort of thing," an unmarried woman who lost her virginity was "ruined." Both Wise and Hattie Elliott had been "good girls" before they met Lewis, but unlike Wise, Elliott "baffled" Lewis when he tried to seduce her. In the end, however, Lewis chose to marry the virgin and kill the "ruined" Wise. The moral message was clear: women had to be "good" or be prepared to face ominous consequences.[20]

Women were almost always innocent victims; that is, they did not provoke their attacker in any way. In the popular southern version of an imported ballad, "Bo Lamkin," for example, a woman and her newborn were killed because her husband had not paid the stone mason he had hired to build his manor.[21]

In several songs, including "The Noel Girl," "Omie Wise," and "Bad Lee Brown," the killers are not executed for their crimes. In fact, Brown could not understand why he must be punished at all for killing his wife: "Forty-nine years in prison for life,/All I ever done was kill my wife." In "There Was a Rich Old Farmer," the killer was punished by his conscience, not the authorities. Moreover, the murderer often did not believe such brutal treatment of women would be punished. In "Rose Conoley" for example, the murderer's father led him to believe nothing would be done if he killed the pregnant Conoley, as is shown by the line, " My daddy often told me that money would set me free/If I should murder that dear, little girl."[22]

In some locations the murderers were not executed in 40 percent of the murder ballads involving the death of young women. These lyrics reflect the almost total lack of judicial interest in such cases, reinforcing scholarship on the colonial era showing no southern settlement had laws against wife abuse, unlike New England. Even as late as the Civil War there were "virtually no initiatives by the criminal justice system to control domestic violence, and a legislative 'vacuum' existed." In fact, in the early 1800s on the rare occasion when a man was finally brought to court for severely beating his wife, judges routinely dismissed the case. Moreover, although in the late nineteenth century some states adopted anti-wife-beating laws, no real enforcement policies existed. Historically, the legal system has taken the killing of certain types of females, such as adulterers, lesbians, and prostitutes, less seriously. A murdered female who did not fit one of these categories was in practice often "monitored for the extent to which she provoked her own demise." If the court found that provocation as great, as in adultery cases, sentences were frequently lenient or nonexistent and if the provocation was considered low, such as the charge of continual taunting, the male could be charged with manslaughter, which was not a capital offense, thus validating the lyrical evidence. When a male judge sentenced Bad Lee Brown to 49 years in prison for killing his wife,

Brown had every reason to be shocked because, as music reflected, historical practice has allowed men to "walk away free or to serve only token sentences" for killing their wives.[23]

Sometimes folksongs portrayed such men in a sympathetic light. Similar to the mass media of the late twentieth century, some folksongs turned them into tragic heroes—brave but misguided characters—not brutal villains. On the scaffold, for example, they typically accepted their fate "like a man." Often they gave heart-wrenching confessions in which they blamed whiskey or the victims themselves for their downfall. By allowing southern males to shift responsibility for their abusive behavior, the culture trivialized femicide, because the murders were slighted or glossed over.[24]

Southern society as revealed in its folksongs considered violence a proper method of gender control. Plantation masters customarily used the lash on female slaves. According to Edward L. Ayers, the lash was also used not only to control urban slaves but also the free African-American population. In the post-Civil War era white southerners used various forms of violence, including lynching and burnings, as control mechanisms. When African Americans or whites friendly to their cause were accused of a crime, they could be lynched, and females of both races were not immune from this kind of brutality. Since the term "femicide" refers to the "misogynist killing of females" and since the murders of African Americans in this era were often motivated by racism, not every case of an African-American woman being killed constitutes a femicide. In order to be labeled as such, the killings had to be "accompanied by a sexist act—most commonly rape."[25]

Some southern whites liked tunes that broadcast brutality against African-American women. A Pine Bluff, Arkansas fiddler explained that the popular tune, "The Hickory Hornpipe," had so much "shrill squealing in it" because the melody imitated a "nigger being whipped." He added that in the past, "if a nigger wench didn't behave, they just fanned her ass with a hickory. A young yaller gal will holler and dance mighty lively, and that's what this here tune is about." Although a white man might be lynched by a white mob, burning someone to death was reserved for African Americans, and again females were not immune. After a white Georgia mob captured Mary Turner, a pregnant African-American woman who threatened to swear out warrants for the arrest for her husband's killers, they tied her upside down from a tree, soaked her dress in gasoline and motor oil, and set her on fire. One ruffian then took his pocket knife and cut the fetus out of Turner's abdomen, and stomped it into the dirt. Not only did the males laugh as Turner burned and helplessly screamed, but a few days after they had completed their grisly task, one man also bragged, "Mister, you ought to've heard the nigger wench howl!" Besides, being a femicide (the sexist act being the crude Cesarean), these kinds of brutal acts were also control mechanisms. They not only stopped one person from contacting the authorities but also sent fear throughout the African-American community.[26]

The use of violence for gender control in both African-American and Caucasian tunes is evident from the careful planning of femicides. Sometimes, for example, graves were pre-dug. These songs show that southern men of both races believed that they were justified in using physical force to control women. An African-American songster, for example, advised males to take a gun and shoot their women "through an' through" if they ever tried to "bully" them around. Similarly, when a woman rejected a marriage proposal it was not uncommon for the jilted man to state that "since I cannot have you no one else can." In the popular African-American tune, "Delia Holmes," a woman is shot with a forty-four by a man she refused to marry. "When the time come for marriage/She refuse' to go./'If you don't marry me/You cannot live no mo'." In "Fair Fanny Moore," a man also kills a woman who would not marry him. "O Fanny, O Fanny, beware your fate!/Accept of my offer before it is too late/For I have come here to secure/The hand or the life of the fair Fanny Moore."[27]

Many songs demonstrate the existence of a paternalistic society in the South and provide evidence of the culture's acceptance of violence as method to control women, but adultery songs are the best examples. Southern states have had unwritten laws (laws which are sometimes honored even today) that allow a man to kill his unfaithful wife and her lover. Sociologist John Shelton Reed argues that, although such laws were unwritten, everyone understood them. Even in the modern South juries have "often been inclined to acquit" such murderers. Moreover, at times southern states have even written such laws into their judicial codes. In the eighteenth century, for example, Louisiana had a law stating that if a married woman was caught committing adultery, she and her lover were to be "turned over to the aggravated husband for punishment." The husband could do whatever he wanted to them; however, if he killed one individual, the law stipulated that he had to kill the other person. In fact, until 1974 a Texas law (Texas Penal Code 1925, article 1220) allowed a husband to murder his wife and her lover. This was not considered a criminal act, thus, the husband received no penalty if he found the couple in "flagrante delicto" and if the murder took place promptly. The state assumed that under those circumstances, the grief-stricken husband could be presumed to be acting on an "irresistible impulse."[28]

Adultery songs show how a southern male believed killing his wife and her lover was justifiable homicide. Yet rarely, if ever, did a song discuss a woman killing her unfaithful mate and his lover. Studies have own that, unlike a man, a woman who kills her unfaithful husband cannot depend upon the courts for forgiveness. The ballad "Arch and Gordon" relates the 1895 killing of Arch Brown and Nellie Gordon in western Kentucky by her husband, Archibald Dixon Gordon. By examining several versions of this song, the actual history of the murder, and the aspects of the case, the use of violence as a culturally approved means of controlling women becomes clear. First, although both victims were killed in cold blood, the coroner's jury ruled the murders justifiable homicide. The unwritten law was being enforced. When Gordon was taken to jail, "a hundred men were ready to go his bail." The singer informed the listeners that Arch had known that such behavior would get him killed. These and other stanzas indicate that males in the community were more than willing to uphold this kind of brutal behavior. Indeed, gender privilege was stronger than class and status. The singer told Brown's father, Governor John Young Brown, to stop crying because "you know your [only] son Arch has to die." The final stanza warns others that this type of behavior will get them killed no matter how influential their family might be.[29] In Lawrence County, Kentucky, during the late 1890s, a similar murder occurred when Lucy Adams was shot and killed by her husband when he found her with another man. Not only was her husband acquitted in court, but an interesting song of the events was written. In this tune the community where the killing occurred maintained that the lover "must die." Although the singer did not agree, because he thought that law and order should triumph, he understood the community's point of view. In fact, the song absolved the citizenry of any guilt in forgetting the law and falling back on cultural norms.[30]

Traditional British ballads which illuminated the brutal consequences of adultery were common in the South. In "Little Musgrave and Lady Barnard," for example, a husband finds out his wife is cheating on him. He kills the man and then "seized [his wife] by her little white hand/And cut her head away." Comparably, in "The Demon Lover," a woman who is persuaded to leave her husband and sail away with her former lover is doomed. Once on board the ship, she realized that he was a demon when she "spied his cloven foot." Although she pleads for her life, he sinks the ship and takes her to the "mountain of Hell."[31]

The brutal treatment of unfaithful women and their male lovers was not an artifact of white culture only. Tunes related instances of African-American women running away from their husbands, then begging to be reunited, only to be beaten. Other African-American women were not as fortunate—they were slaughtered. In the "'Coon-Can Game," (named for a common card game African Americans played in the nineteen century) a man shot his old lover who ran away with another man. "I Went To The Hop-Joint" is another example where an African-American man killed his female lover when she deserted him. In an untitled ditty, another man made clear what he would do to his wife's lover when he sang that he would "start a little graveyard of my own,/If you don't, ole nigger, let my woman alone." Another man boasted that he was going to buy a pistol and "kill the first fellow/Fooling with my long-haired girl." In some songs African-American women themselves cautioned their lovers that their husbands would kill them. One woman warned her lover not to let her husband "catch you here—/He'll kill you dead just' sho's you born."[32]

Even though some of these songs, such as "The Demon Lover," were obviously wishful thinking, the message is still clear. Both African-American and white women were being warned that adultery caused physical and/or spiritual destruction. These songs reveal that when culturally unacceptable events provoked southern males to commit murder, the community forgave the killer and chastised the victim. Although each song had its own particular twist, one thing always remained the same, women who cheated on or abandoned their husbands invariably died, or were at the least savagely beaten.

These tunes are also important in showing how the culture perceived males. While southern men who shot their adulterous wives were glamorized in the music, men who did nothing about such relationships were depicted as cultural outcasts. In one song, "May I Sleep In Your Barn Tonight, Mister?," a man who did not punish his adulterous wife became a "tramp" looking for pity and a place to stay on a stormy night.[33] In many southern songs murdering males were romanticized, while less aggressive men were scorned. These songs also illustrate that southern society had no room for males it considered weak. Likewise, they demonstrate that women were considered the property of men.

Moreover, these types of songs reflect how society attempted to control the behavior of women in ways more subtle than threatening death. In "Jesse Adams," the adulterous woman had two children who would suffer because of her actions. In the last stanza, the balladeer expressed the hope that the children would die, because the "stigma of their mother's behavior" would follow them throughout their lives and either make them "wicked, or at least so miserable that they will wish they had died."[34] Not only were women threatened with death for engaging in extramarital sex, but these tunes implied that their children would also endure the community's wrath. Even if a woman felt she might be able to run away thus, avoid physical punishment, the threat to her children's future as meant to be a deterrent. Such strategies continue today. Organizations that work with abused women report that it is not uncommon for males, or society in general, to use children as bargaining chips in their dealings with women. A man will, for instance, tell a woman that their children are solely her responsibility; thus, he will not allow her to work outside the home. Or if a woman tries to leave her husband, he will warn her that she will never see the children again. Similarly, these women are told that their children's friends or teachers will scorn them because of her actions.

Not only were women threatened by these cultural norms but also men. Men killing other men over women was not limited to adultery tunes. A Hat Hollow, Kentucky, resident claimed that Appalachian fathers "would blow your head clean off your shoulders for fooling with their girls." In fact, in both music and in real life, seldom was anyone punished when such killings occurred. In the Virginia version of "The Twa Brothers," a man killed his own brother because a woman refused his advances, preferring his brother instead; yet the murderer was not punished. In a popular Ozark version, "The Jealous Brothers," two brothers killed the man their sister wanted to marry. The same theme also appears in "The Bramble Brier." In this tune a group of brothers killed their sister's fiancé and threw him in a "patch of briers." Although in both of these songs the guilty parties perished, they died of natural causes. Similarly, in "Lovely William," a father killed his daughter's boyfriend but was never punished. The lyrics explain that he murdered the boyfriend before the "feared . . . deed would prove true," in an attempt to control his daughter's sexuality. In "Young Edwin in the Lowlands Low," a father kills his daughter's boyfriend. Even though the daughter told her father that he would be executed, the song does not mention any punishment.[35]

Finally, the ballads "Charming Beauty Bright," "The Drowsy Sleeper," "I Dreamt Last Night of My True Love," and "Rainbow Willow," all popular southern tunes, male opposition to a female's choice of a lover is illustrated. In "Charming Beauty Bright," for example, a father locked his daughter away, and "treated her so 'vere [severe]," when her lover asked to marry her that she died. As in so many other tunes, the father was not punished for his cruelty. In many cases, male relatives simply did what they wanted, and no one questioned their right to dictate to their female relatives, indicating that they thought of women as reproductive and/or sexual property that they owned and could exchange. This music reflects this "proprietary" character of gender relations.[36] The fact that adulterous males were also killed demonstrates not only a powerful fundamentalist morality in force in the rural South but also as feminist scholars maintain, that "same complex of control and male authority is involved when men kill men because of jealousy and possessiveness."[37]

Not only did southern culture provide balladeers ample material for Murder tunes concerning women, the description of these deaths is important to understanding rural southern culture. They narrated the vivid and gory details of murders, whether by beheading, stabbing, drowning, beating, or shooting. In the popular tune, "Pretty Polly," the balladeer who sang of the killing of Polly Aldridge by William Chapman at Buck Creek in Warfield, Kentucky, described how Chapman viciously cut open her abdomen, filled the empty cavity with rocks, and tossed the weighted corpse in Sug River. Although these types of tunes are numerous, it will suffice to mention two others, "There was a Rich Old Farmer" and a version of "Pearl Bryant." In the former an unsuspecting female was struck in the face with an eight-foot-long club, grabbed by her curly hair and lifted to her feet, before she was thrown into a deep river to drown. In the latter, the woman was viciously stabbed and beheaded.[38]

Such sadistic lyrics demonstrate that southern men could be extremely brutal towards women. Second, they reflect the society's thirst for gore. Scholars have shown that rural southerners, more than other Americans, like to witness and graphically discuss bloody events. Rural southerners, for example, are more inclined to rush to accident scenes, to take part in bear-baiting events, and to attend dog or cock fights. Similarly, after someone was killed in the South, men, women, and children all visited the crime scene. According to a Tennessee female, when locals heard of a homicide "they'd flock to the place like a bunch of buzzards . . . I went to one or two murders myself." In the same vein rural southerners clamored to hear the bloodier and more vicious tunes. As one balladeer stated, southerners would purchase a song "about killin' a heap quicker than a hymn-tune." According to criminologists, the use of excessive violence indicates that the males consciously determined to kill their victims. On a deeper psychological level, these songs described excessive violence in order to intimidate women. According to Kate Millett, patriarchal societies use violence and the threat of it to maintain control. In case the threat of being murdered was not enough to deter southern women from breaking cultural norms, the songs stressed that torture or mutilation of the corpse could occur.[39]

Folksongs indicate that murder was not the only form of violence men faced. The beating of women, especially wives, was a familiar theme. In many southern collections several versions of "The Wife Wrapped In Wether's Skin" appear. In this tune a farmer whose wife would not obey him placed a sheep's skin on his wife's back and made his "hickory go whickety-whack." Although the song did not directly instruct everyone to undertake such behavior, it did claim that such beatings made a wife obey her husband. In the tune, "If I Had A Scolding Wife," popular with both African Americans and whites, a man tells everyone what he would do to a woman who attempted to reprimand him. In the African-American version, the husband would "whoop 'er sho's you born,/Hitch her to a double plow/And make her plow my corn. In the white version man stated, "If I had a scolding wife/I'd whip her, sho as you born./I'd take her down to the still-house/And swap her off for corn."[40] Similarly, in "The Dumb Wife," a doctor told a man that in order to "make a scolding wife hold her tongue," he should use "the oil of hickory" and "just anoint her body round until the rooms begin to sound." in other words, he should beat her with a hickory stick until her screams echoed off the walls. In a folksong popular with both races, "When I Was A Bachelor," when a man finds out that his new bride was a "scolding Jane,'" he went to the woods and cut a green hickory switch, and "whipped her well,/Whipped her more than tongue could tell;/[and] Told her if she didn't prove better to be/The devils might come and take, her 'way from me." In a similar tune entitled "The Holly Twig," a man cuts the "toughest" stick he could find so that he could beat his wife. In fact, after he had "lammed" her, he "kicked her and cuffed her to the lowest pits of hell." This, woman was beaten so severely only because she had "scolded" her husband. In a popular Ozark tune, "Dick German The Cobbler," a man complains that his wife was always "scolding" him; therefore, he "ducked her three times in the river," and deserted her. In a North Carolina tune, "The Wee Cooper Fife," if a man's wife would not bake, brew, card, or spin for him, he simply "thrash[ed]" her to make her obey. One African-American songster claimed that if his wife did not treat him right he simply "knock[ed] her teeth down her throat." In a similar situation, another man advised males to pick up a big stick and beat her [with] all you might." Another African American sang that if his wife drank whiskey, he simply picked up a "stick and beat dat heifer to death."[41]

Even though wives and fiancées received the majority of psychological, verbal, and physical abuse, other female relatives, such as sisters, mothers, and grandmothers, were also vulnerable. In "The Mother-in-Law Song," for instance, a man hates his mother-in-law primarily because she stated her opinion when he stated his; he considers her too outspoken and ugly: "In Pridemore city they do good shooting/There's never a shoot but what it's a draw./I got seventeen dollars to give anybody/That'll take good aim at my mother-in-law."[42]

The popularity of such tunes demonstrates a tendency that Evan Stark finds prevalent today, that is, men assault women when they attempt to overstep the boundaries of gender stereotyping and become more self-expressive. What the nineteenth-century rural South considered just motivation for abuse, a wife who could not bake or a woman who chided a man, demonstrates that southern society's gender norms required women to stay home and listen to their male relatives.[43] Although this type of music shows that women were beaten and killed, it also demonstrates that southern men felt women were to blame for their being harmed. In one tune, "Little Birdie," a folk singer blamed his "little woman" for making him "do wrong" and said he would "rather drink muddy water/And sleep in a hollow log/Than to live with any woman/And be treated like a dog." More importantly none of these tunes depicted men as naggers or at fault for beating their wives. Even when men did not blame their victims, they never took total responsibility for their violent actions, generally blaming both whiskey and women for their abuse. In "Ye Sons of Columbia," for instance, the singer declared that "for whiskey and women are the downfall of all men,/Since old Adam was beguiled by old Eve." As modern researchers have shown, this is still a frequent excuse.[44]

The double standard in sexual relations found in adultery tunes is also prevalent in songs detailing murders of pregnant women. Folklorist Michael E. Bush found that a majority of the southern, murder tunes that detailed the deaths of young girls dealt with out-of-wedlock pregnancies. In addition to those tunes, other southern ballads involve the killing of pregnant women. In fact, some, such as "Jellon Grame'," are found only in the South. Even though these types of songs are numerous, none portray a pregnant woman killing her lover. The closest example was an 1824 tune entitled "Jeremiah Beechum" in which a woman had her new lover kill an old lover for getting her pregnant and leaving her.[45] Bush maintains that males who murdered pregnant females were hanged because they, too, had broken a significant biblical commandment, "Thou shall not kill." Therefore, both the murder of the female and the execution of the murdering male signified that community standards were restored. More significant, however, instead of blaming the victim's death on her premarital pregnancy, these ballads clarify the double sexual standards in the rural South: women had only to engage in premarital sex to be killed, whereas men had to murder in order to be executed. Not all unmarried pregnant women were killed. The significance of these tunes is that they intimidated white women with the threat of violence if they did not maintain their virginity before marriage.[46]

Although the songs dealing with the abuse of pregnant women constitute a form of social control, they also depict a pattern of behavior see by today's professional organizations concerned with these issues. During pregnancy family stress is higher and men resent the lack of attention they receive. Likewise, pregnant women are more physically vulnerable. Males beat pregnant women because they see themselves losing control over their mates. When a woman becomes pregnant, doctors, neighbors, or church members take more interest in her well-being. This was especially true before childbirth moved into hospitals. According to Judith Walzer Leavitt, until the twentieth century, "most women gave birth at home with the help of their female friends and relatives. . . . When possible, sisters and cousins and mothers came to help the parturient through the ordeal of labor and delivery, and close friends and neighbors joined in around the birthing bed." In this atmosphere, which could last for several months, women gained control and influenced events. As the rural Arkansan Nannie Jackson indicated in her diary, southern husbands sometimes got angry when their pregnant wives depended upon others for emotional support. On the 27th of June 1890, Jackson, who was eight months pregnant, visited her best friend and neighbor Fannie Morgan on three separate occasions. Jackson, whose marriage was "complicated and difficult," told Morgan her "troubles because it seems to help me to bear it better when she knows about it." William T. Jackson, reportedly a heavy drinker and illiterate ruffian, hated these visits and accused his wife of "working for nothing but to get him & Mr. Morgan in a row, & to make trouble between them." Jackson made it clear that he did not want his wife to have any outside contacts. No one knows for sure what else this man did or said that night, but his sobbing wife related, "I would rather he had treated me with silent contempt for 6 months than to talk to me as he did this evening . . . I can never get over what he said."[47] A domineering husband must always dictate who his wife sees, who she talks to and where she goes. Such a man will do all he can to limit his wife's involvement in outside activities, because isolation is the key to his control. Although they might need the extra help, these men are "fearful of the pregnant woman's increased contacts outside the home." Therefore, they do not care if the helpers are family members or health care providers; they simply view the outsiders as adversaries. In an attempt to regain the control he thinks he has lost, this type of man may resort to brutality.[48]

Nineteenth-century southern folk tunes also provide a valuable insight into the reasons southern society disapproved of women fighting back when their husbands or lovers beat or killed them. In one of the few southern songs that depicted a woman murdering a man, "Frankie Silver," non-ballad evidence indicates that the woman killed her husband in 1831 to protect herself from his brutality. Instead of incorporating this information into the song, balladeers made an important cultural statement omitting this detail. In many versions Silver killed her husband out of sheer jealousy. These songs reinforce studies that trace the cultural history of violence. In fact, studies have shown that even lawyers, who defended women who fought back, historically concealed the abuse.[49]

Southern folksongs reinforced the belief that women should not be aggressive under any circumstances. While men brawled with their would-be killers, women did not physically fight back. In 70 percent of the murder ballads Bush analyzed, the women simply begged for mercy. Similarly, in the Virginia version of "Jellon Grame'," the woman "pled upon her knee . . . oh, please have mercy." Moreover, when Pearl Bryan is about to be killed, she cries out, "I have always loved you" and she then falls "down on here [sic] knees before Him/She Pleaded for Her Life/When Deep in to Her Bosom/He plunged the fatle [sic] knife." Finally in the ballad "Jesse Adams," Lucy Adams is first shot in the arm as she tries to escape, then she "threw her hand upon her arm [and said] 'Lord a Mercy'" before being "shot through the head." In almost all of these songs the outcome is the same. The pleading does no good, and the woman is brutally killed. This pleading indicates that southern women had few alternatives. The culture placed women in a helpless position for neither society, the courts, nor law enforcement agencies helped abused women.[50]

Instead of stressing the idea that women should avenge themselves, these songs reinforced the cultural notion that men must protect women. Jeremiah Beechum, the man who killed his wife's ex-lover who had gotten her pregnant before abandoning her, was glamorized in novels, poems, ballads, and on stage for protecting "womanhood." In one ballad Beechum, the hero, states: "To kill the man that injured you/I surely shall feel free. . . . [for killing] Colonel Sharp/Who injured my poor wife/I always will protect her,/As long as I have life."[51]

According to numerous studies, males were accustomed to fighting in the South. In 1804, for instance, a traveler to the back country of North Carolina noted in his diary that gouging was common. These were brutal bouts in which combatants tried to scoop out an opponent's eye with their thumb nail. Although the eyes were the favorite targets, noses, fingers, and toes were routinely bitten off in these bloody brawls. These kinds of skirmishes were not uncommon in backwoods locations; thus, travelers reported that in Virginia "every third or forth [sic] man appears with one eye." These men were "like dogs and bears, they use their teeth and feet, with the most savage ferocity, upon each other." In fact, one man, John Stanley of Bertie County, North Carolina, took matters to the extreme and "sharpened his teeth for his opponents' noses and ears." When southern music showed women not responding aggressively to male violence, it reflected cultural realities. A female simply had no satisfactory alternative to taking the abuse. If she killed her tormentor, for example, society overlooked the male abuse and executed her.[52]

Although there are several factors which cause women to be more "susceptible to the development of a learned helpless response to violence," one stands out in the music of the time period. That is, helplessness is a result of "rigid adherence to traditional sex role stereotypes in the home." This is not a form of victim blaming, because it places the blame on the society which has conditioned a woman into believing she had no alternative. The music of the common people reinforced the idea of stereotypical helplessness all over the rural South.[53]

An examination of songs in which women were not harmed also throws light on the physical abuse of the times. When analyzing southern songs, it becomes apparent that women were not highly regarded. Numerous songs from both races indicate the subordinate position of women in society. Women were often the subject of African-American folktunes; yet "few exalted opinions of women" were exhibited. Instead, sex, jealousy, and physical characteristics predominated. The same can be said of white tunes. One, for example, suggested that a woman was only good for carrying a man home after a hard night of drinking. In another, a man's wife died, but he only seemed to miss her good cooking. In fact, he called her a fool for dying. Other songs typecast African-American women as "being of questionable quality." In one popular song, for example, a male stated that no man should ever "let yo' woman have her way;/Keep you in trouble all yo' day." Finally, women were often simply used for sexual pleasure. A typical example is a song in which a man claimed that "I got a woman an' sweetheart too;/Woman don't love me, sweetheart do."[54]

Moreover, in both African-American and white music, women were objectified. Looks, for example, were seen as essential to her worth as in the popular white tune "The Burglar Man." When a thief hiding under a bed sees an old woman remove her teeth, wig, and glass eye, he becomes "a total wreck" and is discovered. The woman then grabs a gun and tells man to either marry her or "I'll blow off the top of your head." In reply, the robber, who could not get away, stated "for Lord's sake shoot!"[55] In an untitled white ditty collected in Tennessee, a man claimed he would never marry any "old maid," because "her neck's too long and stringy/I'm afraid she'd never die." African-American males also sang similar lyrics. There are many African-American folktunes that pointed out what a "good-looking" woman could do. One song claimed that "A good-looking woman/Will make a bull dog join the church." On the other hand, one man claimed that he would never marry a "'black gal," because her hair was too "kinky." Others chanted they would never marry a "yaller nigger gal," because her "neck's drawn out so stringy an' long,/I'se afraid she 'ould never die." In eastern Tennessee African-American males sang that they wished their wives were dead so that they could go out with prettier women. Other songs also showed that unattractive women were left to their own protection, while young and beautiful would be protected by males. Finally, many white songs discussed the "lily white" hands, the delicate appearance, and the childlike behavior of white women. In contrast, independent women were unattractive and manly.[56]

The objectification of women is most blatant in "swap songs" such "When I Was A Little Boy." Northern versions of such swap songs where a man loses out every time he makes a trade often begins with the trading of a horse. In this particular North Carolina version, however, the man first "buy[s]" a wife. He then attempts to carry her home in a wheelbarrow but it breaks, so, he "sells" his wife and "buys" a cow. Trades continue until he has swapped for a cow, a calf, a cat, a hat, and a mouse. The implication that material goods were more important than women can also be seen in the song "Thimble Buried His Wife At Night," which was only found in Virginia and North Carolina. Instead of mourning the death of his wife, a man grieved because he could not get a diamond ring off of her finger before she was buried.[57]

A further look at nonviolent folksongs underlines the insistence on male dominance. It was culturally unacceptable for women to make decisions. For example, in "Father, Father, I Am Married," a newly married man complains to his father that his wife will not obey him. Finally, he tells her, "O wife, make no objection;/You must live by my direction./Wife, O Wife, I do declare/That the Britches I will wear!" In "The Scolding Wife," young men were warned that it would be better to marry a woman "blind, deaf, and dumb." Kelly Combs, a popular Kentucky ballad singer, sang "Adam" and "Johnny Buck," emphasizing a belief "common among mountain people" that husbands should rule their wives. The last stanza of "Adam" states that, "The woman was not taken/From Adam's head we, know/And she must not rule o'er him/It is mighty certain so." This theme also appeared in nonviolent African-American tunes. One man maintained, for example, that he would be happy if he had his "weight in gold," because he would then "have the women under my control."[58]

In conclusion, folk music of the nineteenth-century rural South both reflected and influenced societal views of women. Although such cultural norms were common both in Europe and the United States, they existed in the rural South in stark form. Although these songs demonstrate several things about gender relations, one thing stands out. The music shows that domestic violence was a serious problem in the nineteenth-century rural South. Southern folk music reinforced existing attitudes and values relating to gender and in so doing contributed to violence against women in the rural South by legitimating it.

Notes

1. Over the past century there have been many scholarly works dealing with southern male's penchant for violence. A few of the best include, Edward L. Ayers, *Vengeance and Justice: Crime and Punishment in the Nineteenth-Century American South* (New York: Oxford University Press, 1984); William B. Bankston and H. David Allen, "Rural Social Areas and Patterns of Homicide: An Analysis of Lethal Violence in Louisiana," *Rural Sociology* 45 (1980): 223–227; Richard M. Brown, "Southern Violence—Regional Problem or National Nemesis? Legal Attitudes toward Southern Homicide in Historical Perspective," *Vanderbilt Law Review* 32 (1979): 225–250; Dickerson D. Bruce, Jr., *Violence and Culture in the Antebellum South* (Austin: University of Texas Press, 1979); Wilber J. Cash, *The Mind of the South* (New York: Knopf, 1941); Raymond D. Gastil, "Homicide and a Regional Culture of Violence," *American Sociological Review* 36 (1971): 412–427; William Lynwood Montell, *Killings: Folk Justice in the Upper South* (Lexington: The University Press of Kentucky, 1986); John S. Reed, "Below the Smith and Wesson Line: Southern Violence," in *One South: An Ethnic Approach to Regional Culture* (Baton Rouge: Louisiana State University Press, 1982); John S. Reed, "To Live-and-Die-in Dixie: A contribution to the Study of Southern Violence," *Political Science Quarterly* 86 (1971): 429–443; Bertram Wyatt-Brown, *Southern Honor: Ethics and Behavior in the Old South* (New York: Oxford University Press, 1982). In a complete run of the Federal Bureau of Investigation's *Uniform Crime Reports,* I discovered, for example, that from 1920 to 1925 the southern homicide rate was two and a half times the national average. See also, Montell, *Killings,* 163. In fact, in the 1880s and 1890s southern homicides and prison populations both soared to the high levels of the Reconstruction Era; see Ayers, *Vengeance and Justice,* 250; Bruce, *Violence and Culture,* 7. The Mississippi law stated that a husband could "exercise the right of moderate chastisement in cases of great emergency and use salutary restraint in every case of misbehavior, without subjecting himself to vexatious prosecution, resulting in the discredit and shame of all parties." Similarly,

when North Carolina finally outlawed the practice in 1874 the state maintained "domestic discipline" by stating the court could not intervene in abuse cases "if no permanent injury has been inflicted, nor malice nor dangerous violence shown by the husband, it is better to draw the curtain, shut out the public gaze, and leave the parties to forget and forgive," quoted in Terry Davidson, "Wife Beating: A Recurring Phenomenon Throughout History," in *Battered Women: A Physchosociological Study of Domestic Violence,* ed. Maria Roy (New York: Van Nostrand Reinhold Company, 1977), 19; Diana E. H. Russell, "Femicidal Lynching in the United States," in *Femicide: The Politics of Woman-Killing,* ed. Jill Radford and Diana E. H. Russell (New York: Twayne Publisher, 1992), 53. It was not until the emergence of the women's movement in the late 1960s and early 1970s that social scientists and other scholars considered the abuse of women an important field of study. See Michele Bograd, "Introduction" in *Feminist Perspectives on Wife Abuse,* eds. Kersti Yllo and Michele Bograd (London: Sage Publication, 1988), 11; for an understanding of the historical perspective of wife abuse, see Davidson, "Wife Beating: A Recurring Phenomenon Throughout History," 2–21. Other forms of family violence, such as child abuse, are not dealt with in this paper because they "obscure the dimensions gender and power that are fundamental to understanding wife abuse"; see Bograd, "Introduction," *Feminist Perspectives on Wife Abuse,* 13.

2. Bruce, *Violence and Culture,* 99–100; Arthur Palmer Hudson, *Folksongs of Mississippi and their Background* (Chapel Hill: University of North Carolina Press, 1936), 254, Ruth Ann Musick, "Murderers and Cut-Throats In Song," *Tennessee Folklore Society Bulletin* 19 (June 1953): 31; see Alfred M. Williams, "Folk-Songs of the Civil War," *Journal* 5,265 ff; Bruce, *Violence and Culture,* 100; Bruce, *Violence and Culture* , 100–101. To be included in this manuscript, a song had to have been popular in the nineteenth-century South. That, however, does not mean that every song listed was written in the nineteenth century. Similarly, although many of the collections I consulted were completed in the early twentieth century, I included particular songs because translators and/or songsters pointed out that the tunes had been in the oral tradition for many years, typically for several generations. Although no folksong collection, no matter how good, contains every possible rendering of a particular song (an impossible task), historical judgements still can be made. For example, I was often able to find several similar versions of a particular song in various southern collections and locations which indicated that the versions were both widespread and popular. When words such as "tune," "song," "ditty," and melody" are used in this article, they refer to lyrics, not musical arrangements. Finally, even though some of the tunes mentioned could also be found outside the region, this does not invalidate their impact on the nineteenth-century South.

3. The study of culture through music is a new field. Analysis is largely based on three theories. First, the Marxist theory holds that the "ruling class controls the media and utilizes it to advance hegemonic ideas." I reject this view that the media controls the culture, because the music examined in this study was neither written nor approved by elites. The second theory views the media as only a reflection of culture, and therefore has no effect on society. I also reject this theory because modern psychological studies clearly indicate otherwise. The final theory concerning music and culture "envisions their relationships as reciprocal," an idea I find more compelling, given the evidence presented by psychologists and feminist scholars. For an examination of the various theories, see Dawn Renae Stiemsma, "Gender and Popular Music" (Master's thesis, Iowa State University, 1991); Stiemsma, "Gender and Popular Music," 4–5.

4. Walker points to studies conducted by Sonkin and Durphy, see Lenore E. Auerbach Walker and Angela Browne, "Gender and Victimization by Intimates," *Journal of Personality* 53 (June 1985): 182 179.

5. David P. Phillips and John E. Hensley, "When Violence is Rewarded or Punished: The Impact of Mass Media Stories on Homicide," *Journal of Communication* 34 (Summer 1984): 101, 103. Early studies of the effects of media violence on behavior include the following: A. Bandura, "Influences of Models, Reinforcement Contingencies on the Acquisition of Imitative Response," *Journal of Personality and Social Psychology* 1 (1965): 589–595; A. Bandura, D. Ross, and S. A. Ross, "Vicarious Reinforcement and Imitative Learning," *Journal of Abnormal and Social Psychology* 66 (1963): 601–607; L. Berkowitz and E. Rawlings, "Effects of Film Violence on Inhibitions Against Subsequent Aggression," *Journal of Abnormal*

and Social Psychology 66 (1963): 405–412; T. P. Meyer, "Effects of Viewing Justified and Unjustified Real Film Violence on Aggressive Behavior," *Journal of Personality and Social Psychology* 23 (1972): 21–29; I. Berkowitz and R. G. Geen, "Film Violence and the Cue properties of Available Targets," *Journal of Personality and Social Psychology* 3 (1966): 525–530; I. Berkowitz and J. T. Alioto, "The Meaning of an Observed Event as a Determinant of its Aggressive Consequences," *Journal of Personality and Social Psychology* 28 (1973): 206–217; S. Feshbach, "Reality and Fantasy in Filmed Violence," in *Television and Social Behavior* vol. 2, *Television and Social Learning,* eds. J. P. Murry, E. A. Rubinstein, and G. A. Comstock (Washington, D.C.: Government Printing Office, 1972), 318–345; R. G. Geen and D. Stonner, "Context Effects in Observed Violence," *Journal of Personality and Social Psychology* 25 (1972): 145–150; H. M. Lefcourt, K. Barnes, R. Parke, and F. Schwartz, "Anticipated Social Censure and Aggression-Conflict as Mediators of Response to Aggression Induction," *Journal of Social Psychology* 70 (1966): 251–263. For a list and use of such sources see George Comstock, "Types of Portrayal and Aggressive Behavior," *Journal of Communication* 27 (Summer 1977): 189–199; Comstock, "Types of Portrayal and Aggresive Behavior," 194.

6. Comstock, "Types of Portrayal and Aggressive Behavior," 192; Neil M. Malamuth and James V. P. Check, "The Effects of Mass Media Exposure on Acceptance of Violence Against Women: A Field Experiment," *Journal of Research in Personality* 15 (1981): 442.

7. G. Malcolm Laws, Jr., *Native American Balladry* (Philadelphia: Publications of the American Folklore Society 1964), 1; for example, in the late nineteenth century when James Reuben Broyles leaned "back in the old split-hickory-bottom chair" and started to perform the tune "The Little Ship," he would sing as if the dying child was his very own, usually bringing tears to someone in the audience. Loman D. Cansler, "Boyhood Songs of my Grandfather," *Southern Folklore Quarterly* 18 (September 1954): 181.

8. Robert Leslie Mason, "Ten Old English Ballads In Middle Tennessee," *Southern Folklore Quarterly* 11 (June 1947): 119; Cansler, "Boyhood Songs of my Grandfather," 177; George W. Boswell, "Songs To Sing—'There Was an Old Lady,'" *Kentucky Folklore Record* 15 (1969): 66.

9. *The Frank C. Brown Collection of North Carolina Folklore,* ed. Newman Ivey White, vol. 2, *Folk Ballads from North Carolina,* ed. Henry M. Belden and Arthur Palmer Hudson (Durham, N.C.,: Duke University Press, 1952), 452–454.

10. Daniel Linz, Edward Donnersteirn, and Steven Penrod, "The Effects of Multiple Exposures to Filmed Violence Against Women," *Journal Of Communication* 34 (Summer 1984): 1; Comstock, "Types of Portrayal and Aggressive Behavior," 191–192.

11. Dena L. Peterson and Karen S. Pfost, "Influence of Rock Videos on Attitudes of Violence Against Women," *Psychological Reports* 64 (1989): 321; Janet S. St. Lawrence and Doris J. Joyner, "The Effects of Sexually Violent Rock Music on Males' Acceptance of Violence Against Women," *Psychology of Women Quarterly* 15 (1991): 49–50; Malamuth, "The Effects of Mass Media Exposure on Acceptance of Violence Against Women," 437.

12. Because of the widespread nineteenth-century popularity of folktunes, modem psychological experiments are suggestive for analysis; John Q. Wolfe, "A Country Dance in the Ozarks in 1874," *Southern Folklore Quarterly* 19 (December 1955): 319.

13. O. J. Wilson, "In Search of a Ballad," *Kentucky Folklore Record* 12 (1966): 111; Karen A. Saucier, "Healers and Heartbreakers: Images of Women and Men in Country Music," *Journal of Popular Culture* 20 (Winter 1986): 147; Stiemsma "Gender and Popular Music," 1; Virginia W. Cooper, "Women in Popular Music: A Quantitative Analysis of Feminine Images Over Time," *Sex Roles* 13, n.s., 9/10 (1985): 504. Oral history sources also indicated the popularity of murder ballads in the nineteenth-century rural South. In fact, one balladeer, who specialized in writing and selling homicide ballads, pointed out that at hangings "men and boys hovered around me like bees to buy" the ballad of the condemned man. As other eyewitnesses have attested, this type of behavior was not an isolated experience. W. E. Boggs, an eyewitness to the 1884 hanging of William Neal, for example, maintained that "Lige Adams had a stack of ballads on the day of the hanging, stood on a big rock, and sold them as fast as three men could hand

them out." Southern people enjoyed violent songs to such an extent that even religious tunes could not supersede their popularity. See Jean Thomas, *Ballad Makin' in the Mountains of Kentucky* (New York: Oak Publications, 1964), 138. See John Harrington Cox, *Folk-Songs of the South: Collected Under the Auspices of the West Virginia Folk-Lore Society* (Cambridge, Mass.: Harvard University Press, 1925), 189.

14. To determine if European ballads which dealt with the murder of women were more popular in the South than in other parts of the United States, I examined the Frank C. Brown Collection, the most complete southern state collection. First, I classified the female murder tunes. Second, through an examination of other sources such as additional regional collections and articles, I compiled a list of the North American sites where these songs have been documented. Although in most southern states, unlike northern states, a particular tune could be found in several different locales, states were given only one credit for each song. By comparing the number of southern and northern states, some striking observations were apparent. First, 54 percent of the total number of sites were southern states. Moreover, of all the locations, only 23 percent were northern states. In fact, some tunes were only found in the South. I did not count the border states as northern because of extensive southern migration to the region. Although it would be impossible to state that all of the songs found in the border region were transported by southerners, many examples can be given. Mrs. Ernest Shope, for instance, was a "fine local singer of traditional ballads and songs" in Jeffersonville, Indiana, but she was not originally from Indiana but Campbellsville, Kentucky, where she learned the three murder ballads she sang for the interviewers. These tunes were "The Two Sisters," "The Cruel Mother," and "The Two Brothers." See Margaret Sweeney, "Mrs. Ernest Shope: A Memorable Informant," *Kentucky Folklore Record* 11 (1965): 17–24; Kentucky songs spread throughout both the North and South. For example, George W. Boswell maintained that of the 700 song variants in his Tennessee collection "no fewer than 128 were learned in Kentucky." Boswell, "Kentucky Folksongs in the Tennessee Archives," 115.

15. When dealing with the abuse of women it is not enough to simply list songs and make statistical comparisons. To obtain a clearer picture of the culture, historians must analyze why these women were killed. Men killed men, and men killed women, but women rarely killed men or even other women. Further, unlike females, males were not killed for engaging in premarital sex. In addition, women were more apt to be killed when caught in adultery. Nor were males killed for refusing marriage proposals. When males killed each other they were usually fighting; when they killed women, however, this was seldom the case. In fact, often no one seemed mad and nothing appeared out of the ordinary. Unlike males, women also usually trusted their assailants. In "Jellon Grame'," for instance, when told that Green wanted to see her, the victim said that Jellon was the "man I most desire to see on earth." In fact, many victims were to be married to their killers. In the ballad "Banks of the Ohio," when a woman told an acquaintance she would not marry him, he stabbed her and threw her into the Ohio River to drown. In many of these ballads, complete trust is often maintained, and the males involved were able to deceive their victims until the final moments. Males, however, were rarely deceived in such a manner. In versions of "There was a Rich Old Farmer," a variant of "The Wexford Girl" and "The Knoxville Girl," the victim and her assassin "walked and walked all hand in hand" until he killed her by striking her in the face with an eight-foot club before drowning her. The implied lied motive was premarital pregnancy. Conversely, a woman rarely, if ever, killed her fiancé for any reason. For the tunes mentioned above, see Arthur Kyle Davis, Jr. and Paul Clayton Worthington, "Another New Traditional Ballad From Virginia: 'Jellon Grame'," *Southern Folklore Quarterly* 22 (December 1958): 171. George W. Boswell, "A Song to Sing—'There Was a Rich Old Farmer," *Kentucky Folklore Record* 18 (1972): 75–76. Michael E. Bush, "Murder Ballads in Appalachia" (Master's thesis, Marshall University 1977), 40–46; I have only listed the major books and collections, but others could be mentioned. See George W. Boswell, "Kentucky Folksongs in the Tennessee Archives," *Kentucky Folklore Record* 4 (1958): 115–121; Newman Ivey White, ed., *The Frank C. Brown Collection of North Carolina Folklore* 8 vols. (Durham, N.C.: Duke University Press, 1952); Cox, *Folk-Songs of the South;* Arthur Kyle Davis, Jr., *Traditional Ballads of Virginia: Collected Under the Auspices of the Virginia Folk-Lore Society* (Cambridge, Mass.: Harvard University Press, 1929); Vance Randolph, *Ozark Folksongs* 4 vols. (Columbia, Missouri: The State Historical Society of Missouri, 1950); Oliver Dame Campbell and Cecil J. Sharp, *English Folk Songs from the Southern Appalachians* (New York: G. P. Putnam's Sons, 1917).

16. Twenty-three versions of "The Jealous Lover" were found in North Carolina alone. Belden and Hudson, *Folk Ballads From North Carolina,* 578–589; John Harrington Cox, *Traditional Ballads and Folk-Songs Mainly from West Virginia, in American Folk-Song Publications #3,* publication no. 75-S, ed. George Herzog and Herbert Halpert (Washington, D.C.: Works Progress Administration Federal Theater Project National Service Bureau, March 1939), xv, 105.

17. For instance, see Bush's interpretation and the various versions of the 1744 English ballad "The Wexford Girl," which was popular in the South. Bush, "Murder Ballads in Appalachia," 40–46; Davis and Worthington, "Another New Traditional Ballad From Virginia: 'Jellon Grame'," 166–168; Capers Edwin Kirkland and Mary Neal Kirkland, "Popular Ballads Recorded in Knoxville, Tennessee," *Southern Folklore Quarterly* 2 (June 1938): 72–74.

18. This was determined by an examination of the Brown Collection.

19. Belden and Hudson, *Folk Ballads From North Carolina,* 690–698.

20. *Ibid.,* 691–692, 694, 698.

21. I have found exceptions to this rule, but they are extremely rare. In the imported ballad "Lord Thomas," for example, a man's rich girlfriend kills his new bride. Upon seeing this, Lord Thomas decapitates the assailant, throws the head against the wall, and then kills himself. See Mason, "Ten Old English Ballads In Middle Tennessee," 120–123; the same situation prevails in the late twentieth century. Seventy members. Evan Stark, "Rethinking Homicide: Violence, Race, And the Politics of Gender," *International Journal of Health Services* 20 (1990): 19; Mellinger Edward Henry and Maurice Matteson, "Songs From North Carolina, Bo Lamkin," *Southern Folklore Quarterly* 4 (September 1941): 137–138.

22. "Bad Lee Brown" was found in several southern locations, and it was popular with both African Americans and whites. Randolph, *Ozark Folksongs,* vol. 2, 117–118; Boswell, "There Was a Rich Old Farmer," 75–76; Bush, "Murder Ballads in Appalachia," 6. The song "Rose Conoley" has been found in Wisconsin and Nebraska, but it was more popular in the South, with versions appearing in West Virginia, Virginia, North Carolina, Kentucky, and Missouri. More importantly, Lomax felt it originated in the South. See Bush, "Murder Ballads in Appalachia," 53. In some songs, such as "Pretty Polly" not even a sentiment of guilt is evident. Polly is killed by her lover who had been digging her grave all night. Once he tricks her into following him to the isolated gravesite, he stabs her and throws her in the grave. The killer's lack of concern is evident when he does not mourn but instead only unceremoniously "shoveled some dirt over her and turned to go home." See George W. Boswell, "A Song To Sing—Pretty Polly'," *Kentucky Folklore Record* 19 (1973): 87–88.

23. Eve S. Buzawa and Carl G. Buzawa, *Domestic Violence: The Criminal Justice Response* (London: Sage Publications, 1990), 24, 25; Jill Radford, introduction *Femicide: The Politics of Woman-Killing,* 5; Susan S. M. Edwards, "'Provoking Her Own Demise': From Common Assault to Homicide," in *Women, Violence and Social Control,* ed. Jalna Hanmer and Mary Maynard (London: Macmillan Press, 1987), 161, 165. For an examination of men killing women and being treated differently than when women killed males, and for an understanding of the provocation defense, see Sue Lee, "Naggers, Whores, and Libbers: Provoking Men To Kill," in, *Femicide: The Politics of Woman-Killing,* 267–288.

24. For a discussion of how the media of the late twentieth century romanticizes males who kill females, see Sandra McNeill, "Woman Killer as Tragic Hero," in *Femicide: The Politics of Woman-Killing,* 178–183.

25. Ayers, *Vengeance and Justice,* 102; Russell, "Femicidal Lynching in the United States," 53–54; Ayers, *Vengeance and Justice,* 238. This kind of violence also surfaces in southern music. In 1898, racial strife was rife in North Carolina, especially in Wilmington, because African Americans had returned to politics. As a consequence, lynching tunes emerged. See Belden and Hudson, *Folk Ballads From North Carolina,* 684–688; Chris Domingo, "What the White Man Won't Tell Us: Report from the Berkeley Clearinghouse on Femicide," in *Femicide: The Politics of Woman-Killing,* 200–201; Russell, "Femicidal Lynching in the United States," 53–54.

26. Vance Randolph, "Ribaldry at Ozark Dances," *Mid-South Folklore* 17 (Spring 1989): 11; Brundage,

Lynching in the New South, 92. The mob also added insult to injury by making an empty whiskey bottle with a half-smoked cigar stuck in its neck Turner's headstone. Russell, "Femicidal Lynching in the United States," 55; Walter F. Lackey, *History of Newton County, Arkansas* (Independence, Mo.: Zion's Printing and Publishing Co., 1950), 296. In such an environment African-American musicians also had to worry. No southern city offered a safe haven for them or their audiences. One scholar compared the first post-Civil War generation of African-American instrumentalists to "quails flushed from a thicket." In an age of lynchings, African-American performers, both male and female, literally risked their necks when they traveled into unknown territory, rural or urban. Not only did they have to worry about being lynched, but homicides were common in the juke joints, both black and white, in which they performed. In fact, the home of the blues, Memphis, was known for its deadly nightclub scene. Murder was so routine at the city's Monarch Cafe, locals labeled it "The Castle of Missing Men." At Memphis taverns, dead bodies were simply dumped outside so undertakers could collect them on their nightly runs. See Ronald L. Morris, *Wait Until Dark: Jazz and the Underworld* 1880–1940 (Bowling Green, Ohio: Bowling Green University Popular Press, 1980), 68, 71–73, 149.

27. Newman I. White, *American Negro Folk-Songs* (Cambridge, Mass.: Harvard University Press, 1928), 329; Chapman J. Milling, "Delia Holmes—A Neglected Negro Ballad," *Southern Folklore Quarterly* 1 (December 1937): 3–8; Cox, *Folk-Songs of the South,* 441.

28. Reed, *One South,* 142; Margo Wilson and Martin Daly, "Till Death Us Do Part," in *Femicide: The Politics of Woman-Killing,* 84.

29. Edwards, "'Provoking Her Own Demise'," 152–168; D. K. Wilgus, "Local Ballads: 'Arch and Gordon'," *Kentucky Folklore Record* 6 (1960): 51–56.

30. Cratis D. Williams, "Local Ballads: 'Jesse Adams'," *Kentucky Folklore Record* 8 (1962): 19–20.

31. Davis, *Traditional Ballads of Virginia,* 291; George W. Boswell, "A Song To Sing—'The Demon Lover'," *Kentucky Folklore Record* 18 (1972): 41–43.

32. Howard W. Odum and Guy B. Johnson, *The Negro And His Songs: A Study of Typical Negro Songs In The South* (Chapel Hill: The University of North Carolina Press, 1925), 186, 188, 161; Dorothy Scarborough, *On the Trail of Negro Folk-Songs* (Cambridge, Mass.: Harvard University Press, 1925; Hatboro, Pa.: Folklore Associates, Inc., 1963), 87–91.

33. Don Carlos Amburgey, "Folk Songs," *Kentucky Folklore Record* 9 (1963): 13–14.

34. Williams, "Local Ballads: 'Jesse Adams'," 19–20.

35. Montell, *Killings,* 29; Davis, *Traditional Ballads of Virginia,* 155; Randolph, *Ozark Folksongs,* vol. 1, 380–382, 417–418; Belden and Hudson, *Folk Ballads From North Carolina,* 229–231, 266–269.

36. W. K. McNeil, *Southern Folk Ballads,* vol. 1 (Little Rock, Ark.: August House, Publishers, 1987), 70–76. According to McNeil, many of these tunes were not only well-liked in the region, but were also found predominately in the South. In "The Drowsy Sleeper," a father refused to allow his daughter to marry a man, so the couple killed themselves. In "Rainbow Willow," a man had to kill his fiancée's uncle (who had locked her in a cell) before he could marry her. Similarly, in "I Dreamt Last Night of My True Love," an uncle also locked his niece away in a cell to stop her from marrying a man he did not like. In this case the couple married but the uncle was never punished for his cruelty. For a definition of the term "sexually proprietary," see Wilson and Daly, "Till Death Us Do Part," 85.

37. Stark, "Rethinking Homicide," 19–20.

38. Gory descriptions of death were found in all the songs mentioned by Bush, including "Pretty Polly," "The Wexford Girl," "Willy Guseman," "Rose Conoley," "Flo Ellen," "Pearl Bryan," "Omie Wise," "Banks of the Ohio" "Joe and Mary," and "Hindside Afore." In the "Wexford Girl," for example, the murderer stated that "I heeded not this fair maid's cries, I beat her o'er and o'er. I beat her till her body lie ableeding in a gore." Bush, "Murder Ballads in Appalachia," 9; Cox, *Traditional Ballads and Folk-Songs Mainly from West Virginia,* 76; Boswell, "There Was a Rich Old Farmer," 75–76; Frances D. Perdue, "Folksong Repertoire of Beulah C. Moody," *Kentucky Folklore Record* 22 (1976): 16–18.

39. Montell, *Killings*, 35; Bush, "Murder Ballads in Appalachia," 18; Bush Reed, Cash, Montell, Ayers and several other scholars of the South, have detailed acts that indicate a love of gore. Reed, for example, pointed out that southerners participate in more blood sports than other Americans. Southern urbanites, instance, hunt more than non-southern rural people. Moreover, the resurrection of modern dog-fighting is centered in the South, as is bear baiting and cock fights. Reed, *One South*, 155. In the past, lynching was also a sport. In 1893 E. L. Godkin of *The Nation* wrote that southern lynching parties were composed of men who go "nigger-hunting" just as they go to a "cockfight . . . for the gratification of the lowest and most degraded instincts of humanity. . . . They do not care a straw about seeing justice." In fact, after someone was lynched it was a common southern practice to riddle the body with bullets. See Ayers, *Vengeance and Justice*, 249; Thomas, *Ballad Makin'*, 138; Cox, *Folk-Songs of the South*, 189; Jacquelyn C. Campbell, "If I Can't Have You, No One Can," in *Femicide: The Politics of Woman-Killing*, 103; Kate Millett, *Sexual Politics* (Garden City, New York: Doubleday Books, 1970), 44–45.

40. The abuse of women in lyrics such as these is reinforced by court cases of the times. Robert Mason maintains that "The Wife Wrapped In Wether's Skin" is derived from Hazlitt's "The Wife Lapped in Morrel's Skin" about how a domineering wife is taken to a cellar by her husband, where he places an old horse hide on her back and beats her with sticks until she faints. When the woman recovers she is "perfectly reformed." For an interesting version of this song and the ballad, "The Farmer's Curst Wife," mixed together, see Mason, "Ten Old English Ballads In Middle Tennessee," 134–136; Belden and Hudson, *Folk Ballads From North Carolina*, 478–479. For other versions see Cox, *Traditional Ballads and Folk-Songs Mainly from West Virginia*, 57–60.

41. Belden and Hudson, *Folk Ballads From North Carolina*, 452–456; Campbell, *English Folk Songs from the Southern Appalachians*, 165–166; Randolph, *Ozark Folksongs*, vol. 1, 385–386; Arthur Lief, arr., "The Wee Cooper of Fife," in *Ballads and Folk Songs of America From the Repertoire of the Margaret Dodd Singers Series*, no. 5 (New York: Music Press, Inc., 1947) 1; White, *American Negro Folk-Songs*, 329.

42. George B. Boswell, "Songs to Sing—'The Mother-In-Law Song'," *Kentucky Folklore Record* 15 (1969): 22–23.

43. Stark, "Rethinking Homicide," 22.

44. Amburgey, "Folk Songs," 11; Cox, *Folk-Songs of the South*, 217.

45. Bush, "Murder Ballads in Appalachia," 17–18; Ann Scott Wilson maintains that Pearl Bryan was killed, not because of an abortion attempt gone wrong, but because the murderer wanted to conceal the fact that he had gotten her pregnant. This version does not negate my interpretation, since in this version the murder victim simply broke a different cultural taboo. Ann Scott Wilson, "Pearl Bryan," *Southern Folklore Quarterly* 3 (March 1939): 16. Bush did not discuss *all* such tunes Popular in the South; rather he examined a particular geographic region of the mountain South. "Jellon Grame'" was only found in Virginia. Davis and Worthington, "Another New Traditional Ballad From Virginia: 'Jellon Grame'," 163–172; Leonard Roberts, "Beauchamp and Sharp: A Kentucky Tragedy," *Kentucky Folklore Record* 14 (1968): 14–19.

46. Bush, "Murder Ballads in Appalachia," 18. It is interesting to note that younger, not older, women were generally the murder victims in all types of folktunes. Like today, in the nineteenth century young women were at a greater risk of being murdered. For an understanding of why younger women face greater risks, see Wilson and Daly, "Till Death Us Do Part," 94.

47. Teresa Gray, Iowa Family Violence Center and Health Coordinator, telephone interview with author, October 7, 1993. Margaret Kukreja, Outreach Director, House of Ruth, an organization that assists families victimized by domestic violence, Claremont, Calif., telephone interview with author, October 8, 1993; Judith Walzer Leavitt, "Under the Shadow of Maternity," in *Women's America: Refocusing the Past* 3rd ed., 203–204; Margaret Jones Bolsterli, ed., *Vinegar Pie And Chicken Bread: A Woman's Diary of Life in the Rural South, 1890–1891* (Fayetteville: The University of Arkansas Press, 1982), 12, 34–35.

48. Informational pamphlets, House of Ruth.

49. Belden and Hudson, *Folk Ballads From North Carolina,* 699; Stark, "Rethinking Homicide," 17.

50. Bush, "Murder Ballads in Appalachia," 6; Davis and Worthington, "Another New Traditional Ballad From Virginia: 'Jellon Grame'," 171; Faye Scott Anderson, "Another Version Of 'Pearl Bryan' / 'The jealous Lover'," *Kentucky Folklore Record* 21 (1975): 119–120. I have found this particular ballad in several different southern collections. For another version of this popular song consult Perdue, "Folksong Repertoire of Beulah C. Moody," 16–18; Williams, "Local Ballads: 'Jesse Adams'," 19–20.

51. Roberts, "Beauchamp and Sharp," 14, 17–18.

52. Charles William Janson, "The Stranger in America. Containing Observations Made During a Long Residence in that Country, on the Genius, Manners and Customs of the People of the United States; With Biographical Particulars of Public Characters; Hints and Facts Relative to the Arts, Science, Commerce, Agriculture, Manufacturing, Emigration, and the Slave Trade," in *Travels in the Old South,* vol. 2, *The Expanding South, 1750–1825: The Ohio Valley and the Cotton Frontier* (Norman: University of Oklahoma Press, 1956), 115; Ayers, Vengeance and Justice, 9; Janson, "The Stranger in America," 115.

53. Walker, "Gender and Victimization by Intimates," 179–193; Wini Breines and Linda Gordon, "The New Scholarship on Family Violence," *Signs* 8 (Spring 1983): 519.

54. Odum and Johnson, *The Negro And His Songs,* 160–161, 180, 283; White, *American Negro Folk-Songs,* 316.

55. Belden and Hudson, *Folk Ballads From North Carolina,* 465. In a Johnson County, Kentucky version the man's hair turns gray at the ugly sight of the woman. George W. Boswell, "Songs To Sing— 'Burglar Man'," *Kentucky Folklore Record* 14 (1968): 92–93.

56. "Collecting Ballads and Folk Songs in Tennessee: A Paper Presented at Second Annual Meeting of the Tennessee Folklore Society, November 9, 1935," *Tennessee Folklore Society* 2 (March 1936): 11; White, *American Negro Folk-Songs,* 313, 335; Odum and Johnson, *The Negro And His Songs,* 191.

57. Belden and Hudson, *Folk Ballads From North Carolina,* 473. Likewise, see "If I Had A Scolding Wife," where the man said he would trade her for corn. Belden and Hudson, 478, 484–485.

58. *Ibid.,* 478–479; Marie Campbell, "Adam," *Kentucky Folklore Record* 3 (April–June 1962): 136; Odum and Johnson, *The Negro And His Songs,* 283.

Reading 10

The Progressive Movement and the Negro

Dewey W. Grantham, Jr.

The progressive movement in the United States affected the whole of American life during the two decades before World War I. Walter E. Weyl noted that "Men in the Middle West, in the Far West, in the East and South; men in the factory and on the farm; men, and also women . . . are looking at America with new eyes, as though it were the morning of the first day." William Allen White, himself one of the Progressives, remembered that reform was everywhere:

> A sudden new interest in the under dog was manifest in the land. . . . Some way, into the hearts of the dominant middle class of this country, had come a sense that their civilization needed recasting, that their government had fallen into the hands of self-seekers, that a new relation should be established between the haves and the have-nots . . . because we felt that to bathe and feed the under dog would release the burden of injustice on our conscience.

Yet despite the comprehensive nature of their proposed reforms, American liberals of the Progressive era gave little attention to the status of the Negro, which all agreed represented one of the nation's social and political problems. This omission in the Progressive program poses the provocative question of why. By such indices as ownership of property, rate of literacy, entry into new occupations, and development of social and cultural institutions American Negroes made substantial advances during the four decades following Appomattox. The material progress and industrial leadership epitomized by the Atlanta Compromise and the efforts of Booker T. Washington won increasing endorsement of whites both North and South and apparently improved the relations between the two races. But the progress, particularly after 1877, was exasperatingly slow and painful, and Negroes remained in large part landless, uneducated, and diseased—the downtrodden bottom rail.

As the new century opened, the difficulty of reconciling the American ideals of democracy and legal processes with the prejudices of the dominant groups was outlined in sharp relief. The heavy lynching tolls of the 1890's continued into the twentieth century, and Negroes were often victims of antiquated convict leasing and chain-gang practices, of peonage, and of inferior accommodations on public carriers and in public places. Furthermore, the process of legal disfranchisement by the Southern states was well on the way to completion, and even where the Negro retained the right to vote, he could not participate in the Democratic primaries that really controlled Southern elections. In many ways the thirty-year period after 1877 was an era of retrogression for the Negro. Walter Hines Page wrote of the Southern Negro in 1907, "I'm afraid he's a 'goner.'" To liberals the Negro problem posed a challenge, but a challenge that might be rationalized and explained away or evaded.

Generalization about the nature of Progressivism is not without hazards. The Progressives were reformers, but reform could mean "all sorts of things"; Ralph H. Gabriel has called it "a potpourri of social theories and beliefs." A writer in 1912 observed that Progressivism was "inchoate and speaks with may voices. To many men it means many things." Whatever the regional and individual variations among Progressives, they were optimists who held fast to the idea of progress. The evils and imperfections that had come with the powerful economic tides of a changing America could be removed through the agency of the state. The rules must be changed somewhat, but not radically; economic power must be responsible to the government, and "new weapons of democracy" must make the government responsible to the people. There must be legislation to improve the lot of the working man, to restrain monopoly and abolish special privilege, to widen the electoral franchise and direct democracy. Man was fundamentally good and rational if dealt with fairly he would deal justly with his fellow men. The Progressives believed, as William Allen White wrote, that if the underdog were given "a decent kennel, wholesome food, regular baths, properly directed exercise, [and if someone would] cure his mange and abolish his fleas, and put him in the blue-ribbon class, all would be well."

If Progressives were convinced of the possibility of progress, if they advocated the abandonment of laissez faire and the use of positive government to promote that progress, if they desired to help the depressed elements in the nation's population and to answer "the simple demand for fair dealing, [and] for exact justice between man and man," it is pertinent to ask what they did about the nation's major minority problem. As individuals and as members of philanthropic groups, many Progressives considered the Negro question at some length and made significant contributions to the amelioration of the conditions that created the problem. To answer the question What did American liberals do about the Negro in a political way? requires a longer examination.

Progressive reformers appeared first on the municipal level; their attention was largely focused on breaking the control of the political machines, on effecting tax reforms, and on establishing a more wholesome relationship between public utilities and city governments. Mark Fagan and George L. Record, for instance, strove to improve the educational, health, and recreational facilities of Jersey City, but they fought their most vigorous battles for tax reform and control of public utilities. Tom Johnson made Cleveland "the best governed city in America," but his major efforts were to secure municipal ownership of street railways and to equalize the city's taxes. Joseph W. Folk flashed into the national limelight because of his sensational exposures of the corrupt alliance between business and government in St. Louis. In California the Los Angeles nonpartisan movement aimed at breaking the control of the Southern Pacific machine. Negroes as well as whites might benefit from reduced street railway fares, from tax reassessment, and from better school facilities, but the most reforms did not occur in the South, where most Negroes were concentrated, and when good government movements did reach Southern cities, Negroes seldom shared equally in such reforms. At any rate, the Negro question was incidental to other reforms supported on the city level during the Progressive period.

Much the same was true of Progressivism on the state level. Robert M. La Follette, of Wisconsin, was a democrat in the best sense of the word; he possessed a genuine concern for the rights and dignity of the individual and a keen desire to promote the welfare of the depressed man. La Follette, like most Progressives, felt that most political issues had a moral answer, but he saw that economic power was the keystone in the arch of American society. Therefore it was necessary to solve in some fashion the problem of the misuse of economic power, whether by aggregations of powerful business corporations, as in Wisconsin, or by strong organizations of labor, as in California. For this reason Progressives across the land concentrated their efforts toward handling the problem of the monopolization of economic forces; their belief in democracy led them to sponsor numerous democratic devices in an effort to make economic power responsible to political authority. There were state and regional variations, but in all states where Progressivism was strong Progressive leaders concentrated on the problem of dealing with powerful organizations of capital or labor and widening the base of a political democracy to nourish the state government.

The concern of political reformers on the state and local levels with the regulation of privilege and monopoly and their efforts to forge new "weapons of democracy" did not prevent them from attacking many specific problems involving social welfare. There were laws to abolish child labor, to regulate the working conditions of women, to provide for workmen's compensation, to increase the appropriations for public education, and to establish more adequate institutions for the care of the unfortunates. Negroes might benefit from all of these reforms, but the fact was there were relatively few Negroes outside of the South before the World War, and the Progressive movement was most effective in other regions. The Negro question for such non-Southern Progressives was thus a theoretical question or at most a national problem. Meanwhile, state and local Progressives focused their attention on their own pressing concerns.

There were reform governors and liberal leaders in the South during the Progressive period. Attempts were made there to regulate more effectively railroads and other corporations, to provide tax reforms, to abolish free passes and corrupt lobbying practices. Primary elections came into widespread use, the corrupt-practices legislation was enacted. The convict-leasing system was abolished, beginnings were made in the regulation of child labor, legislation to control of the liquor traffic was adopted, and increased appropriations were made for public education and health facilities, agricultural services, and state care of unfortunates. Negroes undoubtedly profited from much of this reform program despite the fact that most of its political sponsors were aiming at "Progressivism for whites only." But while the Negro might benefit from such reforms, their passage often cost his race a heavy price. This was true because the strongest group of Southern Progressives—those who sponsored the major reforms—were insurgent politicians who came to power not only because they denounced the corporations and sponsored a program of neo-Populism but also because many of them made the race issue their chief stock-in-trade and led such anti-Negro movements as that of disfranchisement. The strongest supporters of these political leaders were the most rabid Negrophobes. The Vardamans and Hoke Smiths might have represented "a genuine movement for a more democratic government in the South," as Ray Stannard Baker contended, but their democracy was for whites only and did great harm to the cause of the Negro and to good relations between blacks and whites.

Among another group of Southern liberals during the Progressive era were such men and women as Charles B. Aycock, Edwin A. Alderman, Walter Hines Page, Edgar Gardner Murphy, and Julia Tutwiler: men and women who worked for education, good government, the regulation of child labor, prohibition, and help for the Negroes. Believing that the South's hope lay in industrial and educational progress, they were more conciliatory toward the corporations than were the agrarian Progressives and less enthusiastic about vigorous government, although in their humanitarianism and middle-class approach they were similar to Progressives in other regions. Clearly, their restraint in dealing with the race question, their constructive work for education, and their espousal of such reforms as the abolition of child labor and of the convict-leasing system made a greater contribution to the progress of Negroes than did the work of the more radical agrarian leaders. But they were unwilling and unable to sponsor reforms for the Negro that would drastically change the relationship of the two races in the South. Furthermore, while their concern for social justice might be real, most of them were not in politics, and they were often opposed to the agrarian Progressives who were in power. Their interest in the advancement of the Negro might be genuine, but it was also paternalistic and philanthropic; their solution lay within the framework of white supremacy.

Thousands of people in the South wished the Negro well, but, as a contemporary Progressive noted, "The South is psychologically cramped." The ideology of white supremacy was all pervasive, and few were the Southerners who would answer in the affirmative Ray Stannard Baker's question, "Does democracy really include Negroes as well as white men?" Baker himself spoke of "a vigorous minority point of view," which he labeled the "broadest and freest thought" of the South: "a party of ideas, force, convictions, with a definite constructive programme." Yet the philosophy of this group rested on the maintenance of "racial integrity," the "gospel of industrial education," and disfranchisement. Charles H. Brough, professor of Economics and Sociology at the University of Arkansas, spoke for them when he declared: "As the sons of proud Anglo-Saxon sires, we of the South doubt seriously the wisdom of the enfranchisement of an inferior race." These "liberals" expressed their belief in progress for the Negroes, but, as Brough said: "I believe that by the recognition of the fact that in the Negro are to found the essential elements of human nature, capable of conscious evolution through education and economic and religious betterment, we will be led at last to a conception of a world of unity, whose Author and Finisher is God." Even Edgar Gardner Murphy, one of the Southerners most concerned with social justice, held Negroes to be a "backward and essentially unassimilable people," whom the "consciousness of kind" would forever set apart from the whites, whatever the race's advancement.

If the race problem was a national concern, as some people said it was, what were the attitudes of the national parties and political leaders as the twentieth century ushered in the Progressive period? Party pronouncements avoided the Negro question or at most had little to say on the subject. The Populist platform of 1896 condemned "the wholesale system of disfranchisement adopted in some States as unrepublican and undemocratic." The Socialist Labor platform in 1896 called for the equal right of suffrage without regard to color. The Republicans condemned lynching and termed "revolutionary" certain devices designed to overthrow the Fifteenth Amendment. In 1904 they called for a Congressional investigation to determine whether the vote had been unconstitutionally limited in any state and threatened proportionate reductions in representation if such restrictions were found to exist. In 1908 they asked for the enforcement of the Civil War amendments while reminding Negroes that the Republican party had been their "constant friend" for fifty years. These promises, it soon developed, were about as far as the party was willing to go on the Negro problem. The truth was that the Republicans had all but deserted the Negro. The Democratic position was well stated in the party's platform in 1904. While criticizing Republican imperialism for following one set of laws "at home" and another "in the colonies," the Democrats declared: "To revive the dead and hateful race and sectional animosities . . . means confusion, distraction of business, and the reopening of wounds now happily healed."

The literature of the muckrakers gave attention to the position of the Negro. Disfranchisement, sharecropping, peonage, racial segregation, the Negro's failure to obtain justice in the courts, lynchings, and race riots were seized upon as worthy materials by such writers as Richard Barry, Benjamin O. Flower, and William English Walling. Ray Stannard Baker's articles in the *American Magazine,* though perhaps not muckraking in the strict sense of the term, were widely read and were published in book form in 1908 under the title *Following the Color Line.* But Americans failed, somehow, to get very excited about muckraking materials on the Negro, and the Negro question proved a poor second to such topics as corporation evils and political corruption.

If the muckrakers failed to arouse widespread interest in the status of the American Negro, the same could not be said of President Theodore Roosevelt. Roosevelt expressed a deep concern for the Negroes, and his actions and his utterances stimulated avalanches of editorial copy. The President's closeness to Booker T. Washington, his denunciation of lynching and disfranchisement, and his announced determination to see that the Negro received his due generated a wave of hope among liberals on the race question and among the Negroes themselves. But what could Roosevelt do? As he wrote Albion W. Tourgée in the fall of 1901, "I have not been able to think out any solution of the terrible problem offered by the presence of the negro on this continent. . . ." He had decided, however, that "the only wise and honorable and Christian thing to do is to treat each black man and each white man strictly on his merits as a man." His objective for the Negro came to be "cautiously, temperately, and sanely, to raise him up."

In practice even this modest goal was beset with difficulties. Roosevelt might appoint only "reputable and upright colored men to office," as was his constant claim, but by doing so he alienated the whites in the South who were otherwise attracted to the Republican party. He was interested in building up the Republican party in the South and therefore anxious "not to shock southern sentiment," although as he wrote Lyman Abbott, it would be a serious mistake to let Southerners "think that they were blameless, or to let them cast the blame on anyone else." The mounting pressure on the part of white Republicans in the South for a lily-white party led Roosevelt to seek middle ground. His philosophy was well stated in a letter to Booker T. Washington in June, 1904: "The safety for the colored man in Louisiana is to have a white man's party which shall be responsible and honest, in which the colored man shall have representation but in which he shall not be the dominant force—a party in which, as is now the case in the Federal service under me, he shall hold a percentage of the offices but in which a majority of the offices shall be given to white men of high character who will protect the negro before the law." This was to remain essentially Roosevelt's position. He contended that his administration through the federal courts had accomplished a good deal to break up Negro peonage in the South and to secure equal facilities for Negroes on interstate carriers, but he saw little hope of federal action to enforce the Fifteenth Amendment, and in 1908 opposed including such a threat in the Republican platform. The principal hope of the Negro, he declared, must lie in the sense of justice and good will of Southerners, for the Northern people could do little for him. But Southerners, he found, continued to show a "wrong-headedness and folly" about the race question, while men like Oswald Garrison Villard and Charles Francis Adams, who had a genuine interest in promoting the Negro cause, had in the President's opinion "frittered away their influence" until they had no weight with either party.

Theodore Roosevelt's correspondence reveals the enigmatic quality of the Negro problem in his mind during the first dozen years of the century. Like his contemporaries, he never found an adequate solution, although he probably gave more thought to it than most other political leaders on the national scene. The "condition of violent chronic hysteria" on the subject in the South baffled him, and at times he felt that the region never made any progress on the race problem unless forced by outside pressure. Yet in the end he was not sure that his own efforts, which were certainly interpreted in the South as outside pressure, had been of much avail. He agreed with Owen Wister that the Negroes as a race and in the mass were "altogether inferior to the whites," and that the progress of the race would be slow and painful, but he did believe that progress was possible. After his action in the Brownsville affair, he became increasingly suspicious of the more radical Negro leaders and of what he called "shortsighted white sentimentalists." By the middle of his second administration, many Negroes and their white supporters had become convinced that they could expect little in the way of positive aid from Roosevelt. Nevertheless, the President was right when he wrote in 1908: ". . . I have stood as valiantly for the rights of the negro as any president since Lincoln . . ."

The election of William Howard Taft promised small encouragement for a positive program to advance the cause of Negroes. Taft was a peaceful man and refused to ruffle the political waters by making anything of the race question.

But, as the strong tides of Progressivism began to roll through the major parties on the national level, advocates of Negro progress began to experience a new optimism and a faith that Progressive ideals might also include the Negro. For a time the greatest expectations centered in the Progressive revolt in the Republican party and in Theodore Roosevelt's embryonic Progressive party with its liberal promises of positive federal action to promote the social welfare. Here, such leaders as W. E. Burghardt Du Bois felt, was "a splendid chance for a third party movement, on a broad platform of votes for Negroes and the democratization of industry." But when Roosevelt decided to endorse the organization of the new party on a lily-white basis in the South, in the hope that a strong, permanent party might thus be established in that region, he lost the support of many Negroes, including such leaders as Du Bois. The former President attempted to straddle the perplexing issue by advocating one policy for the North, where it was possible "to bring the best colored men into the movement on the same terms as the white men," and another for the South, where "actual conditions and actual needs and feelings" dictated a traditionally Southern approach. Roosevelt still believed that the Negro's best hope lay with the "intelligent and benevolent" whites of the South. "We have made the Progressive issue a moral, not a racial issue," he declared.

With their hopes thus dashed, where could Progressive Negro leaders turn? The Republicans under Taft provided no hope for a Progressive era. With some misgivings, many of the more militant Negro leaders accepted the New Freedom of Woodrow Wilson, aware of the danger posed by the South's part in the Wilson movement and of Wilson's own background, but encouraged by the liberalism that he represented and by certain promises he was understood to have made. One Negro reminded Wilson in the summer of 1913, "We enlisted with the delight of children at play under your standard and fought a good fight. . . ." Having helped elect the new President, Negroes turned to his administration for a share of the patronage and for additional evidences of justice to their race. The editor of the New York *Age* expressed the attitude of many Negroes when he wrote: "The race, as a whole, is not so deeply concerned in the question of the appointment of Negroes to office as it is [in] the attitude President Wilson will assume—whether he will give a helping hand to a struggling people or whether he will co-operate with those who believe that it is humane and American to do all in their power to keep the Negro down, thereby hindering the progress of the Nation."

Negro leaders were soon disappointed by Woodrow Wilson's course. The new President's attitude toward the Negro, as Arthur S. Link has said, was characteristically Southern. While he abhorred Southern demagogues who made the race issue a bête noire, his feeling toward the Negro was at best one of tolerance and kindliness, strongly paternalistic. He soon found that it was difficult enough to carry the South with him in the enactment of his major program and that to make an issue of the race question would jeopardize measures which he considered much more important than a frontal attack on a difficult minority problem. Thus it was that he allowed racial segregation among federal employees in certain of the federal departments, refused to make many Negro appointments, and failed to appoint a federal commission to investigate the Negro situation as some people urged. Southerners in Washington, led by James K. Vardaman, were vociferous in their demands that no Negroes be appointed to federal positions. When the news of one Negro appointment spread, Thomas Dixon wrote to Wilson to say, "I am heartsick over the announcement that you have appointed a Negro to boss white girls as Register of the Treasury." The President's reply was reassuring to white Southerners: "We are handling the force of colored people who are now in the departments in just the way they ought to be handled. We are trying—and by degrees succeeding—a plan of concentration which will put them all together and will not in any one bureau mix the two races." Wilson explained his dilemma to Oswald Garrison Villard in August, 1913: "It would be hard to make any one understand the delicacy and difficulty of the situation I find existing here with regard to the colored people." Emphasizing such matters as the tariff and antitrust legislation, Wilson viewed the Negro problem as a peripheral issue and one that was increasingly irritating. He desired to avoid "a bitter agitation" and to hold things "at a just and cool equipoise."

The disillusionment on the part of Negro leaders was rapid and eventually complete. Booker T. Washington wrote in late summer, 1913: "I have recently spent several days in Washington, and I have never seen the colored people so discouraged and bitter. . . ." The Negro press, Negro leaders, and men like Villard protested, but the President remained aloof. By 1916 Du Bois felt that the political situation was hopeless.

Still, many of the more moderate Negro leaders, such as Robert R. Moton of Tuskegee, admired Wilson for his accomplishments and for the idealism that permeated his addresses. Moton wrote Wilson late in 1916, "I realize that it was embarrassing and perhaps unwise for you to make any reference to the race question as it might perhaps hazard in some way the other important policies of your administration, but now that your election is assured and your policies are pretty definitely established and accepted by the nation as a whole, I am wondering if you could refer in some way to the ten or eleven millions of Negroes in our country." The President promised to do his best, but he was not optimistic. ". . . the truth is," he wrote, "that I have not been able to form a confident judgment as to what would be effective and influential." Nor did he form such a judgment.

The East St. Louis riot of July, 1917, brought heated demands to the Wilson administration for action against such "unchecked savagery." The lynchings in 1918 and the discriminations against Negroes in the armed forces brought further protests, while the President's course on the race question at the Paris Peace Conference was also criticized by some Negro spokesmen. Wilson publicly announced his abhorrence of lynching and commended the valor of Negro soldiers, but he gave no indication that he considered the Negro problem of primary importance. It seems fair to say that he never conceived of the Negro question in a broad sense as a federal problem. At any rate, the more extreme Negro leaders would have echoed the statement of a Philadelphia Negro, James S. Stemons, who wrote Woodrow Wilson in November, 1920: "The verdict of the masses, regardless of race or creed or clan, has long been that while you were vigorously preaching one thing you were, when expediency demanded it, as vigorously practicing the direct opposite."

If sectionalism and racial prejudice frustrated any possibilities of direct action on the Negro question by Woodrow Wilson's New Freedom and Theodore Roosevelt's New Nationalism, the same was true even of the Socialist party in its consideration of the problem. Socialists in the South proved no more tolerant on the race question than non-Socialists, and this prejudice was not restricted to the South. Victor Berger, for instance, declared in 1902: "There can be no doubt that the negroes and mulattoes constitute a lower race—that the Caucasians and indeed even the Mongolians have the start on them in civilization by many thousand years—so that negroes will find it difficult ever to overtake them." About the best the Socialists could do was to advertise Socialism as exclusively an economic movement, having nothing to do with social equality. Indeed, moderate Socialists contended that the races did not want to live together and that capitalism was at fault, since it forced them to do so. Eugene Debs opposed all discrimination, and the left-wing Socialists urged that racial prejudice be wiped out. But the Socialist party in the period before World War I made no real opposition to Negro discriminations as such.

It will be helpful at this point to differentiate between certain practical considerations that entered into the failure of Progressives to deal with the race question and the more fundamental philosophical background that conditioned their attitudes toward the Negro. As for the practical considerations, the fact was that the Negro problem prior to the World War was still essentially sectional. A great majority of the Negroes were still concentrated in the South, and the leading Progressives, such as Robert M. La Follette, Hiram W. Johnson, and Albert B. Cummins, operated in other regions. They never really came in contact with the Negro question, at least in a situation where they could make a direct contribution to its solution. They could adopt academically a liberal position on the question, and they sometimes took an incidental stand in Congress, but that was all. Such matters as suffrage and the whole broad question of social legislation were still considered the primary responsibility of state and local governments, although the Progressives generally emphasized a more vigorous central government. Many of the Progressives, however, were averse to centralized power, as was true of supporters of Wilson's original program. Another consideration was the inability of Negro leaders and their most zealous white supporters to agree upon a positive program or upon the means necessary to advance their cause.

To explain the philosophical limitations of the Progressive movement in facing the Negro question in American democracy is more difficult. It would appear paradoxical that a philosophy which emphasized the worth and the dignity of man and which laid stress on the democratic process should reveal this blind spot in regard to what was really a complete refutation of its most sacred premises.

One of the keys to this apparent enigma is to be found in the attitude of Americans during the period between 1898 and 1918 toward imperialism and the so-called "backward" races that were the subjects of imperialism. Progressives were no more willing to accord equal civil and social rights to the people recently subjugated by the American republic than were the majority of Americans. Most of them agreed with the imperialistic views of Theodore Roosevelt and Albert J. Beveridge, although many of them were probably influenced on their views on the subject by the mastery Roosevelt held over them. Roosevelt was emphatic in stating his position: ". . . I have the impatient contempt that I suppose all practical men must have for the ridiculous theorists who decline to face facts and who wish to give even to the most utterly undeveloped races of mankind a degree of self-government which only the very highest races have been able to exercise with any advantage." If the Filipinos were inferior and entitled to the privileges of American democracy only after a long apprenticeship, was not the same true of Orientals on the West Coast and of Negroes in the South? There was, moreover, what Southerners described as the "dreadful episode of Reconstruction" to provide apparent documentation of the Negro's backwardness supplemented by the widely circulated accounts of his continued degradation in the post-Reconstruction years. Once having accepted the ideology of the new imperialism, it was difficult to escape the logic of the Southerners' position. As Benjamin R. Tillman said, chiding the Republicans for their imperialism: "Your slogans of the past—brotherhood of man and fatherhood of God—have gone glimmering down through the ages." The conquered, it seemed, had overcome the conquerors.

Fortunately for Republican and Progressive theoreticians, the new sciences or pseudo-sciences, with their theories of the multiple origin of the races and the notion of retarded races, seemed to provide a scientific explanation that would justify imperialism, while history itself seemed to prove the superiority of Western culture. As for the democratic concept that governmental authority rested on the consent of the governed, Senator Beveridge pointed out that this was true only where the governed were capable of self-government. Lyman Abbott said the important thing was not government by the "consent of the governed" but government for the "benefit of the governed." Thus American imperialism could be viewed as a crusade to free backward people from their antiquated overlords and to set them on the road of progress under the tutelage of a benign and liberal government.

At home there was powerful evidence that Negroes, retarded as was their race, were making headway. This evidence was particularly apparent in the Booker T. Washington School, the material gains of which could not be doubted. Here was progress, tangible and capable of being measured; more important perhaps, progress based on a philosophy that received the whole-hearted endorsement of the middle-class heart of America—and of Progressives. It emphasized philanthropy and practical education, and it sought to avoid conflict between employer and employee, between class and class, and between race and race. It eschewed politics and worked within a framework that received the enthusiastic approval of the Southern whites. Thus it provided an opening for the powerful Northern philanthropic organizations, which were eager to help the Negro and to work with the more moderate Southern white leaders. So pervasive was the Washington philosophy that it received widespread support throughout the country. A non-Southerner such as Bourke Cockran could appeal for justice for the Negro in one breath and advocate the repeal of the Fifteenth Amendment in the next, while Ray Stannard Baker could say some years later that the North, "wrongly or rightly, is today more than half convinced that the South is right in imposing some measure of limitation upon the franchise." In 1909, in the words of Hilary A. Herbert, "Intelligent public opinion at the north is at this writing so thoroughly with us that there is now no longer any danger of interference with us from Washington, either legislative or executive, so long as we do not, by harsh or unjust treatment of the negro, now at our mercy, alienate the sympathies of the majority section of our union." The Progressive *New Republic's* solution followed the course charted by Booker T. Washington. "The greatest service which can be rendered the Negro to-day," declared its editors in 1916, "is to be dispassionate about it. It is, after all, only a problem like any other. There is no need to keep alight the old fire upon the abolition altar, or to blow into flames smouldering embers upon the ruined hearth of the old South."

Another element in the Booker T. Washington philosophy was the idea of self-advancement, the belief that the Negro must make his own way and demonstrate his own abilities to get ahead in the contest of life. This idea found easy lodgement in the Progressive rationale. It was implicit in much of Theodore Roosevelt's writing. Even such a zealous believer in Negro rights as Moorfield Storey counseled "patience, courage, and faith." "The prejudice against you today," asserted Storey, "is no stronger than the prejudice which Jews and Irish have overcome." "You are all soldiers in a great army fighting for the future of your race. . . ." Negroes must now work out their own destiny, declared Charles Francis Adams in 1908. "It is for the Afro-Americans, as for the American descendant of the Celt, the Slav, or the Let, to shape his own future, accepting the common lot of mankind."

This was not as inconsistent with the Progressive philosophy as might appear at first glance. Despite its humanitarian outlook and its interest in moral issues, the Progressive movement aimed at "the equalizing of opportunity" by an approach that was essentially negative. As Herbert Croly wrote in *The Progressive Democracy* (1914): ". . . the expectation was that if the concentrated economic system could be checked and disintegrated, small local producers, both agricultural and industrial, would have a much better chance of prosperity." The Progressives, then, hoped to produce a condition in which men might be free to prove their merit. If the Negro could make his way on the economic front, political and civil rights would take care of themselves.

Such were the main philosophical components that influenced the attitude of Progressives toward the Negro problem. To this explanation might be added what Herbert Croly described as the "Promise of American Life," an apt phrase with which he summed up the American faith in progress and in the peculiar destiny of America. That is, Americans believed their nation to be progressive regardless of its shortcomings.

In *The New Democracy* (1912) Walter Weyl called the Negro question "the mortal spot of the new democracy." But he noted that Americans wanted to avoid the issue; to illustrate his point he discussed Negro suffrage: "To-day, millions of men, discouraged by the dwindling but still large residuum of Negro ignorance, discouraged by the passion which seeps like a torrid wind over every phase of the question, seek to avoid the question of Negro suffrage. . . ." In reality Northerners and Republicans—and Progressives as well—had adopted attitudes toward Negroes and other colored races not unlike those of the South. What George W. Cable had written about the Negro question a generation before still seemed apropos. "The popular mind in the old free States," he had written, "weary of strife at arm's length, bewildered by its complications, vexed by many a blunder, eager to turn to the cure of other evils, and even tinctured by that race feeling whose grosser excesses it would so gladly see suppressed, has retreated from its uncomfortable dictatorial attitude and thrown the whole matter over to the States of the South."

The Progressive movement had certainly touched a responsive chord in the ranks of American Negroes, although it was true, as Walter Weyl said, that "The race is too poor, weak, ignorant, and disunited to make effective protest." Negro leaders, however, did protest, and many of them were inspired to believe that the Progressives really intended to battle abuses and to urge democracy on all fronts. Negro leaders themselves were divided and uncertain. As Du Bois wrote, "We all believed in thrift, we all wanted the Negro to vote, we all wanted to abolish lynching, we all wanted assertion of our essential manhood; but how to get these things—there, of course, must be wide divergence of opinion."

The Progressive movement came to be associated by the more militant Negro leaders with the Booker T. Washington school of thought. The failure of Roosevelt and then of Wilson to include the Negroes in their agendas for progress, the death of Washington, and the frustration of Negro aspirations in the World War precipitated a new unity, among Negro leaders and an acceptance of the philosophy of the National Association for the Advancement of Colored People. In conclusion it may be said that the Progressive movement, or perhaps it would be more accurate to say the climate of Progressivism, did bring some advances for American Negroes. There were the indirect benefits of Progressive legislation and gains deriving from humanitarian agencies. But in a larger sense the Progressive movement passed over the Negro question and, ironically, by doing so helped to promote the militant approach to the problem that most Progressives would have abhorred.

Reading 11

The Flowering of Black Nationalism: Henry McNeal Turner and Marcus Garvey

Edwin S. Redkey

Afro-Americans have reacted in different ways to the problems they have faced in the United States. Quite understandably, many have tried to get along as best they can, eking out a living, trying to avoid trouble, never losing hope for a better day. Others have protested to whites, asking for fair treatment, civil rights, and integration into American life. And others have militantly called for separation from whites, unity and pride in the black community, and a new political arrangement in which they control their own destinies. This last approach, generally labeled "black nationalism," has taken a number of different forms through the years, but the basic elements of black separatism and solidarity, race pride and political independence, have always been recognizable.

Some black nationalists have called for all-black states, cities, or towns within the United States; others have wanted to carve a separate country out of American territory. Often black nationalists have proposed establishing ties with blacks in other parts of the New World and in Africa. Recently this has taken the form of a sophisticated cultural identification with black Africa, whose peoples have inspired Afro-Americans by gaining political, independence after a century of European domination. In earlier years, black nationalists urged that a significant number of Afro-Americans emigrate to their fatherland and establish there a powerful new nation. Twice between 1890 and 1925 this "Back to Africa" form of black nationalism generated widespread enthusiasm among black Americans. Although few blacks actually emigrated to Africa, the movement's stress on race pride and the rejection of White America was indelibly impressed in many minds and inspired a new generation of militant black nationalists.

Conditions in the South in 1890

Although the concept of emigration to Africa to establish a powerful new black nation had been formulated before the Civil War, most notably by Martin R. Delany, the idea was then limited to a few black intellectuals, mostly free blacks in the North. As a mass enthusiasm, black nationalism first flowered during the 1890's among the black peasants who farmed the cotton plantations of the South. It was clear to them that, even though it was twenty-five years after the end of the Civil War, most white Southerners intended to keep blacks as near slavery as possible. Having built up elaborate intellectual defenses for slavery during the early nineteenth century, the whites were not willing or able to change their concept of blacks as inferior, almost subhuman beings. Nor could they imagine for them any role in society other than that of the lowest class, possessing a minimum of rights, power, and status. When ex-slaves tried to assert their rights and privileges as citizens, whites used every possible means to keep them "in their place."

Violence had been a frequent tool of repression in the days of slavery, and it continued to be used during and after Reconstruction. Lynching was a particularly terrifying means of social control, for it deprived its victims of any chance to prove themselves innocent of whatever charges were made against them; frequently they were brutally tortured and humiliated before being hanged, shot, or burned to death. The rate of lynchings increased rapidly during the 1880's and reached a peak in 1892.

Whatever political power blacks had gained during Reconstruction, Southern whites now whittled away through violence, fraud, and deceit. By 1890 it had become evident that Northern whites, who had supported the blacks for political reasons, had grown tired of their efforts and were no longer going to interfere in Southern racial politics. White Southerners quickly took advantage of this development and began formally and legally to strip away what little political power remained to the blacks. Mississippi led the way in 1890 with the passage of a new state constitution that effectively stopped blacks from voting. During the next eighteen years most Southern states followed Mississippi's example. Though legally free, blacks could not use politics to protect their freedom.

The economic life of blacks was also restricted by whites, who, as they had before the Civil War, still owned the land and controlled the economy. Blacks worked the farms and paid a large share of their crop to the white landowners as rent. And the portion of the crop retained by the sharecropper was probably already mortgaged to the white storekeepers for food and supplies. Therefore, after the merchants and landowners were paid off, the farmer was left with little or no profit from the harvest and usually remained in debt. When cotton prices declined, as they did in the late 1880's, or when a general depression gripped the nation, as it did during most of the 1890's, the black farmer could see little improvement in his situation since slavery.

Reactions to this social, political, and economic oppression took several forms. Undoubtedly, most blacks, unsophisticated in business and politics and dominated by the landowner, the merchant, and the sheriff, simply endured the hardships and made the best of a bad deal, no matter what dreams of escape they may have had. The spokesman for this group was Booker T. Washington, who made "accommodation" an ideology. He urged his people to work hard, live clean, quiet lives, save money, and demonstrate their worthiness so that whites would someday recognize and honor their virtue and thrift. Others, mainly intellectuals and middle-class Northern blacks, protested and appealed to the conscience of the nation to grant them equality and integrate them into white American life. Frederick Douglass was the early spokesman for this viewpoint; others, including W. E. B. Du Bois, followed. But as conditions in the rural South worsened during the 1890's, a significant number of blacks began to despair of ever attaining the good life in the United States. Neither accommodation nor protest seemed to make life any better for the vast majority of black farmers and workers, who had little chance of earning enough or learning enough to reach the middle-class standard of living. For a time, in the late 1880's, some black farmers joined with their white counterparts in the Populist movement, which sought better economic conditions for all farmers. But racial prejudice soon split the Populists, and the blacks realized that the main reason for their hardships was their color, not their occupation. Many began to dream of establishing a nation of their own where they could be free of white oppression, own their own land, and control their political destiny. The black nation of their dreams would be a credit to the entire race and gain respect for blacks wherever they lived. The chief advocate of this brand of black nationalism during the years between the Civil War and World War I was Bishop Henry McNeal Turner.

Bishop Turner's Nationalist Vision

Turner was born a free man in South Carolina in 1834, but restrictions on his "freedom" irritated and challenged him. He sought advancement through the church, becoming a preacher first in the Methodist Episcopal Church and then, after moving North, in the all-black African Methodist Episcopal (AME) Church. A vocal and militant advocate of black emancipation and equality, he was appointed a chaplain in the Union army during the Civil War. When the war ended, his church assigned him to work in Georgia, where he had tremendous success in winning blacks away from their old, white-controlled churches to the AME Church. At the same time he actively organized blacks for the Republican party. He served in Georgia's Reconstruction constitutional convention (1868) and was elected to the legislature that same year. His hopes for black equality and participation in American life reached their highest point with that election. They were dashed soon afterwards when the white members of the legislature expelled Turner and all other blacks and reasserted white political control. Turner became embittered and denounced both Democrats and Republicans for betraying the freed slaves.

Bishop Turner had long been interested in Africa as a potential home for Afro-Americans, whom he wanted to evangelize and civilize their fatherland. He had known of the American Colonization Society (ACS) and its offspring in Africa, the Republic of Liberia, before the Civil War. Now with his increasing disillusionment with whites, the idea of building a powerful black nation in Africa took hold of him. In 1870 he began to advocate emigration by a select group of blacks skilled and resourceful enough to build a powerful modern nation. Their example would lend strength to black men everywhere by showing conclusively that blacks were not inferior to whites in ability, virtue, or power.

Turner never deviated from this black nationalist posture throughout the rest of his long life. With colorful rhetoric and persistent attacks on all who disagreed with him, he condemned white American racism and urged blacks to emigrate. Of the United States he wrote, "We were born here, raised here, fought, bled and died here, and have a thousand times more right here than hundreds of thousands of those who help to snub, proscribe and persecute us, and that is one of the reasons I almost despise the land of my birth."[1] When the response of his fellow blacks was less than enthusiastic, he blasted the "scullion coons" who would neither fight nor run from oppression. And middle-class blacks, most of whom opposed both Turner and his ideas, he accused of wanting to be white: they did "nothing day and night but cry: Glory, honor, dominion, and greatness to White."[2] Turner stressed race pride and even proclaimed that "God is a Negro: Even the heathen in Africa believed that they were 'created in God's image.' But American Africans believed that they resemble the devil and hence the contempt they have for themselves and for each other!" All the more reason, wrote the Bishop, for a "Negro nationality where black men can be taught to respect themselves."[3]

Before 1890 most Afro-Americans responded negatively to Turner's emigration propaganda. The articulate middle-class blacks had clearly progressed since the time of slavery, so despite their handicaps they had reason to believe in the American dream. The great masses of blacks, however, were still tied to the cotton plantations and clinging to what little security they had. Even though Turner spoke and wrote widely about his African dream, most blacks were reluctant to leave home and head for a still unfamiliar and uninviting "dark continent." Occasional bursts of "African fever" led to the departure of small groups for Africa, usually with the help of the old and impoverished ACS, which annually sent about a hundred settlers to Liberia. Although most blacks had long opposed the ACS, fearing that it wanted to deport them forcibly, Bishop Turner, an honorary vice-president of the society, urged his followers to write to the ACS for free passage to Africa. As the economic condition of blacks grew increasingly worse, and as political oppression and lynching increased in 1890 and 1891, the society received more and more letters. The idea of escaping to Africa was flourishing among Southern black peasants whose circumstances made the American dream seem a cruel hoax.

Bishop Turner, sensing both the increase in oppression and the rising interest in emigration, decided to seize this moment to promote his brand of black nationalism. Late in 1891 he visited West Africa for the first time. Although other Afro-American travelers and settlers had described Liberia as a death trap of malaria and poverty, Turner focused on the bright side. "One thing the black man has here," he wrote, "and that is manhood, freedom, and the fullest liberty." He wrote back glowing accounts of the prospects for building a great nation in Africa, accounts that received wide circulation in the black press. He advocated settlement by Afro-Americans both for their own salvation and as a way of saving Africa from the domination of the European powers who were then dividing the continent into colonies. "I get mad and sick," Turner wrote, "when I look at the possibilities God has placed within our reach, and to think that we are such block heads we cannot see and use them."[4]

The quick response among Southern blacks overwhelmed the ACS. Thousands applied for passage aboard a small ship scheduled to depart for Liberia in March 1892. All but 50 were informed the there was no room for them. Yet so eager were they to flee to a place where they could have land of their own and find economic and political independence that over 300 blacks, mostly from Arkansas and Oklahoma, arrived in New York expecting transportation to Africa. Most were penniless, ragged, and uneducated—typical of Southern black farmers—but like many others, they believed that life could only get worse in the United States.

The ACS, already faced with internal problems and lack of money, was unable to help these people, who were left stranded in New York. After 1892, reacting to adverse publicity and to attacks from both whites and blacks, the society stopped sending settlers to Liberia. However, the ACS remained in existence for another twenty years, hoping that someday it could aid a black exodus from the United States.

After the effective collapse of the ACS, Bishop Turner launched an intensive campaign to secure other means for black emigration. First, he tried to get the federal government to pay reparations to blacks for their years in slavery; he asserted that whites owed blacks some forty billion dollars, "estimating one hundred dollars a year for two million of us for two hundred years."[5] The money, according to Turner, should be used to finance emigration to Africa. He and his followers sent such petitions to the government for many years, and emigration bills occasionally came before Congress, but all to no avail. Next, Turner urged businessmen, both white and black, to take part in the growing trade with Africa, a trade that was bringing new wealth to European nations. He maintained that every ship bound from America to Africa would be crowded with Afro-Americans seeking new homes. But that scheme also failed, for American shippers and merchants had more profitable interests in Latin America and the Orient.

Finally, Turner urged black people themselves to band together to finance their own migration. That was a difficult task, however, for black farmers seldom saw much cash. In addition, they suffered with the rest of the nation the effects of the economic depression during most of the 1890's. Further complicating the picture was the fact that a number of fraudulent ticket-to-Africa-for-a-dollar schemes had duped many blacks eager to leave the United States. There were numerous reports of groups who had sold or given away their possessions and camped by the railroad tracks waiting for trains to take them to nonexistent ships bound for Africa.

Despite these obstacles, in 1892 the Afro-American Steamship Company was started with Turner's support. Stock was to be sold at a dollar a month to "ship club" members throughout the country; the ships thus financed would earn profits by taking cargo and passengers to Africa. There was plenty of interest in the plan, and ship clubs sprang up in many places. But depression dollars were scarce and members could not afford to keep up the payments. By mid-1893 the company and its clubs collapsed, having purchased no ships and transported no emigrants.

Turner, though disappointed, once more pressed on with his efforts to create a powerful black nation led by Afro-Americans. Early in 1893 he started a monthly newspaper, *the Voice of Missions*, which advocated both evangelism and nationalism. Its wide circulation among preachers meant that the Bishop's propaganda reached into the entire South and everywhere else that black people lived. Turner made a second visit to West Africa in the summer of 1893. Again his many letters and reports painted a glowing picture of Africa and the progress being made by Liberia. These reports the excited interest of many a black peasant who longed for some land of his own, a chance to control his life, and independence from whites.

But peasants were not the kind of settlers needed by Liberia, nor could they finance either emigration or nation building. So Turner tried to persuade middle-class blacks to support his schemes. Late in 1893 he assembled a national convention at Cincinnati, Ohio, where he tried to convince the educated, middle-class delegates that the only practical response to the oppression facing them in the United States was emigration. Although the black laborers and farmers in the galleries cheered the Bishop's eloquent attacks on American racism, the delegates refused to endorse black nationalism or to support emigration to Africa, Mexico, Canada, or anywhere else. One black newspaper observed that "all the radical propositions bearing upon the future welfare of the race were talked to death. . . . The Afro-American went to down the would-be African, and so far as the convention is concerned, he succeeded. But he did nothing else. [The convention] was passive when it should have been radical. It was cowardly when it should have been heroic."[6]

Despite the failure of the convention, Turner was still convinced that if only transportation could be arranged, hundreds of thousands of lower-class blacks would leave the United States. Since the ACS no longer sent settlers to Liberia, and since the black elite refused to finance the movement, the Bishop turned to whites for help. As a result, a group of Birmingham, Alabama, businessmen, organized the International Migration Society (IMS) early in 1894 to recruit emigrants, sell them passage at moderate prices, transport them to Liberia, and help them get established there. The backers of the IMS planned to make a profit by doing a large volume of business with the thousands of blacks who Turner had said were ready to go. The IMS also profited from defaults on the monthly payments on the passage contracts, but its operations were basically honest.

Cheering the new organization, Bishop Turner publicized its operations in the *Voice of Missions*. Black local representatives of the IMS signed up would-be emigrants throughout the South. Although the depression still made dollars scarce, hundreds of black farmers nevertheless started paying on the $42 contracts. But by November only thirteen people had paid the full sum. The society sent them to Africa by way of Europe, hoping thereby to generate enough new excitement and payments to warrant chartering a ship to sail directly to Liberia.

The publicity, aided by Turner's steady barrage of propaganda, succeeded. Early in March 1895 a train carrying some 200 blacks from Arkansas, Mississippi, Alabama, Tennessee, and Texas pulled into Savannah. After a few days' delay they sailed for new homes in Africa. Despite some mismanagement by the IMS both in the United States and in Africa, Bishop Turner, then on his third visit to West Africa, reported the new settlers comfortably settled and at work clearing their land and building new homes.

Again the successful departure of emigrants generated new enthusiasm among rural Southern blacks. Dollars were still scarce, so it took another year to generate a third IMS "colony." But in March 1896 another ship carrying 321 emigrants left Savannah for Monrovia. The fate of this group, however, was not so fortunate. When the ship arrived in Liberia the officials of the IMS did not provide the food and care they had promised, and before many weeks had passed a number of the newcomers died of malaria and other diseases. Most others wanted to return to the United States, claiming they had been misled by false descriptions of easy wealth in Africa.

The adverse publicity hurt the recruiting operations of the IMS in the South. Furthermore, the American economy began to improve in 1897. Although the legal and social oppression of blacks continued, their economic condition improved somewhat as the price of cotton rose. At the same time, the threat of war with Spain began to generate a new patriotic enthusiasm among both whites and blacks. Bishop Turner sensed this threat to his nationalist dream and condemned the United States for planning to help Cuban rebels against Spain. He warned that once they realized that most of the Cuban rebels were black, white Americans would lose their zeal for "liberty from Spain." "We hope no Negro in this country will allow himself to be beguiled with [patriotic] sophistry," he wrote. "If the United States gets into war with Spain we shall stump the country against the black man taking up a gun."[7]

But the coming of the war and the increased prosperity of the economy proved too great a challenge to Turner's plans. Furthermore, in 1895, Booker T. Washington began increasingly to overshadow Bishop Turner and other black leaders as a result of his "Atlanta Compromise" address. Payments to the IMS fell off and few people went to Africa. The first mass flowering of black nationalism had come to an end. It is impossible to tell how many people had endorsed Turner's ideas, but signs of emigrationism had appeared in all the states of the Deep South and the Southwest, where over 90 percent of Afro-Americans lived. Thousands were directly caught up in one or more of the emigration schemes that sprang up during this period. Although only about a thousand people actually went to Africa, many other blacks seem to have shared Turner's pessimism about the United States.

Although mass enthusiasm for emigration collapsed after 1897, the idea of going to Africa to build a new nation was by no means at an end. The nationalist dream of a modern black state that would generate pride and independence among blacks everywhere continued to stir a few Afro-Americans. Bishop Turner, in particular, predicted that the black man must "emigrate or perish." During the years before World War I he encouraged a number of small, again unsuccessful Back to Africa organizations. The most significant of these was the Colored National Emigration Association, organized in 1901 by Turner himself. For five years the association struggled in vain to raise money for a ship, while the Bishop continued to publicize Africa and condemn the United States. He drew national attention in 1906 when he reportedly proclaimed that "to the Negro in this country the American flag is a dirty and contemptible rag. Not a star in it can the colored man claim, for it is no longer the symbol of our manhood rights and liberty."[8] Turner kept up his attacks until his death in 1915, but he was never able to launch a successful emigration plan, even though individuals and small groups occasionally migrated to Africa. Nevertheless, his efforts kept alive the dream of a strong African nation as a goal for Afro-Americans.

In 1913 an isolated African emigration was launched in Oklahoma by Chief Alfred C. Sam, reportedly of the Gold Coast, West Africa. Drawing on the residue of interest created by Turner and the despair caused by political oppression and another drop in cotton prices, Chief Sam managed to collect enough money from disillusioned black farmers to purchase a ship. With about sixty emigrants and a black crew, he and his ship sailed for the Gold Coast from Galveston, Texas, in August 1914, leaving behind hundreds more who planned to sail on the next trip. But diplomatic, political, and financial troubles cost Chief Sam his ship, and most of the emigrants eventually returned to the United States. Like the others before it, Chief Sam's effort did little more than demonstrate that many Afro-Americans, particularly farmers and laborers, were sufficiently unhappy with American conditions to want to flee the country.

Black nationalism had flowered during the 1890's, but it had not borne much fruit. Nevertheless, it proved to be a hardy plant that could wait another generation before flowering again, when disillusionment with the United States, and another vigorous nationalist spokesman led masses of blacks to work for African nationhood. Those conditions came with the end of World War I and the arrival in New York of Marcus Garvey.

Urban Blacks and Marcus Garvey

During the war years 1914–1918, the general situation of hundreds of thousands of blacks changed radically. Ever since the days of slavery blacks had looked upon the North as a kind of promised land of political and social freedom. But after Emancipation the economics of cotton farming had kept 90 percent of them in the South. Bishop Turner, among others, realized and publicized the fact that there was much prejudice and racism in the North, especially among recent immigrants from Europe who were competing with blacks for jobs. Nevertheless, a small but steady stream of blacks, mostly from Virginia and Kentucky, migrated to the industrial cities of the North and founded communities there.

With the coming of World War I, however, the labor situation in the North changed dramatically. Immigration from Europe was drastically reduced, while the demand for manufactured goods expanded. Industrialists in Chicago, Detroit, Cleveland, New York, Philadelphia, and other cities were crying for unskilled labor and began sending agents into the South to recruit blacks. Afro-American newspapers also summoned Southern blacks to the new bonanza, while letters home from early arrivals lured still others away from their cotton farms. In 1915 and 1916 those cotton farms were having hard times anyway, as the boll weevil marched across the South, destroying crops and making life even more difficult than usual for blacks.

The result of these forces was a sudden, dramatic spurt in the migration of blacks from the Deep South to the cities of the North. Almost overnight major cities gained large black populations. Attracted by jobs that paid in dollars instead of credit at the local store, by the growing all-black communities inside the cities, and by the relative political and social freedom in the North, nearly half a million black migrants had moved into the Northern cities by 1920, and the tide was to continue for several decades to come.

But the North was hardly a paradise for blacks. Friction over jobs, housing, and life styles quickly arose. And when the war ended, returning soldiers and new European immigrants displaced many of the black workers. Furthermore, the infamous Ku Klux Klan, with all its virulent racism, was revived and began to reach into the North as well as the South. The expanding black settlements spread from block to block in the major cities, displacing whites, changing neighborhoods, and altering political patterns. To these friction-generating changes were further added 400,000 black soldiers who had been away helping to "make the world safe for democracy," but who came home from Europe to find the same old racial oppression in the United States.

The result was a long series of race riots, many in Northern cities, in which blacks invariably suffered the most. During the economic recession that followed the war, urban blacks, who had been "last hired," found themselves "first fired" and frequently out of work. Although the North still offered more opportunities than the South, and despite the fact that blacks continued to pour into the cities, it became clear that even in the "promised land" black people were oppressed. Uprooted from familiar surroundings, crowded into small quarters in expanding ghettos, shunned by whites and restricted to the lowest levels of society, some blacks began to recall Bishop Turner's African dream of a free and powerful black nation outside the United States. Into this urban scene of black newcomers with new homes, new jobs, and new problems stepped Marcus Moziah Garvey, the man who was to mobilize them in the second mass flowering of black nationalism.

Garvey was born in the West Indian island of Jamaica in 1887; there he grew to manhood and learned the trade of printing. He tried his hand at labor organizing and newspaper publishing, first in Jamaica and then in various other Caribbean countries where black Jamaicans worked on sugar and banana plantations. Dismayed at the miserable living conditions of the workers and their exploitation by white or mulatto overseers, Garvey tried in vain to persuade Jamaican officials to intervene. In 1912 he went to London to carry his appeals to the British people and to learn about conditions of black people in other parts of the world. While in London he met Duse Mohammed, a black Egyptian who was promoting the defeat of European colonialism everywhere. He worked on Mohammed's magazine, *African Times and Orient Review*, met Africans, studied about Africa, and caught Mohammed's zeal for African nationalism.

Garvey also read Booker T. Washington's autobiography, *Up From Slavery*, and suddenly perceived that his own life work was to be a leader of the black race. Returning to Jamaica in 1914, he set about building an organization that would "unite the 400,000,000 Negroes of the world for the purpose of building a civilization of their own."[9] He called the organization the Universal Negro Improvement Association and African Communities League (UNIA) and began work among the black peasants of his home island. Among his goals was the creation of industrial schools to teach trades and skills—schools patterned after Booker T. Washington's Tuskegee Institute.

Garvey moved to New York in 1916 and took up residence in Harlem, then a fast-growing black ghetto. He began recruiting members for the UNIA, but his success was small in the booming war years. Not only were the newly arrived Southerners doing well, but Garvey's West Indian accent and style were foreign to them. However, with the end of the war, the collapse of the boom, and the beginning of the race riots in 1919, the message of the UNIA suddenly made sense. By the end of 1919, aided by his newspaper, the *Negro World,* and by his sometimes sensational publicity in the general press, Garvey reported that he had two million members in thirty chapters scattered across the United States and the West Indies. The second mass flowering of black nationalism was under way.

Central to Garvey's philosophy was the need to unite all black people and to give them a racial self-confidence that would enable them to throw off white oppression. Like Bishop Turner a generation earlier, Garvey hoped to stimulate race pride both by direct propaganda and by the establishment of a powerful black nation in Africa. Whenever he spoke, he urged Afro-Americans to shed the old thinking that "white was right" and that blacks were powerless. "Up you mighty Race! You can accomplish what you will!" was one of his mottoes. To the thousands of blacks who were caught in the anonymity of the big cities and who felt as helpless under the grinding wheels of Northern society as they had under the oppression of white Southerners, those words held out new hope.

To help stimulate pride and independence, Garvey demanded racial purity. He was himself of unmixed African descent, and, reflecting the three-way split in West Indian society, he despised mulattoes. Such distinctions between brown and black, however, were not as important in the United States. But Garvey's stress on the glories of the African heritage helped many Afro-Americans, both brown and black, to find new confidence in themselves and in one another. Garvey advised them not to be too concerned with political rights and social equality in the United States, but rather to become as independent as possible in the white man's country. He organized his followers into marching units of uniformed African Legions and Black Cross Nurses whose colorful parades inspired thousands of Harlem residents.

Economic independence was another factor in the UNIA plan. Garvey urged his followers to "buy black"—to patronize their own businessmen. Following Booker T. Washington's stress on self-sufficiency, the UNIA opened several business projects, including the Negro Factories Corporation, to assist black businesses. More important, Garvey founded the Black Star Steamship Line to serve as a commercial and spiritual tie among blacks wherever its ships traveled. Like Bishop Turner's shipping attempts, the Black Star Line was intended to carry freight as well as passengers. But contrary to popular belief, carrying emigrants to Africa was not one of the original motives of Garvey's enterprise. Black Star Line stocks were sold to blacks only, and Garvey promised stock buyers that they would not only be helping their race but might also make a handsome profit. To the surprise of his critics, Garvey collected enough money between 1919 and 1925 to buy four second-hand ships and to begin trade with the Caribbean.

For Garvey, the major path to black pride and economic independence was the redemption of "Africa for the Africans." "The only wise thing for us ambitious Negroes to do," he wrote, "is to organize the world over and build up for the race a mighty nation of our own in Africa."[10] It would be "strong enough to lend protection to the members of the race scattered over the world, and to compel the respect of the nations and races of earth."[11] He believed that "power is the only argument that satisfies man," and that "it is advisable for the Negro to get power of every kind . . . that will stand out signally, so that other races and nations can see, and if they will not see, then FEEL."[12]

The Garvey movement reached a peak in August 1920 at a month-long convention held in New York City. At least 25,000 people attended the many meetings, at which Garvey used all of his oratorical power to proclaim black nationalism. The emphasis was on the redemption of Africa. "The other races have countries of their own and it is time for the 400,000,000 Negroes to claim Africa for themselves," he announced, "and we mean to retake every square inch of the 12,000,000 square miles of African territory belonging to us by right divine."[13] Garvey was designated "Provisional President of the African Republic"; other officials of the UNIA were given similar titles. The convention adopted a long "Declaration of the Rights of the Negro Peoples of the World," which embodied most of Garvey's philosophy. A truly impressive affair in its magnitude and splendor, the convention brought Garvey to the attention of the world. He had managed to do what Bishop Turner and many other black leaders had failed to do: he had mobilized the black masses. Thousands of urban blacks were drawn to the red, black, and green flag of black nationalism. Many more read the *Negro World* and responded eagerly to the agents of the Black Star Line who circulated among them selling stock.

Garvey was aware that many difficulties stood in the way of the redemption of Africa. European imperialists controlled most of Africa by military force. Furthermore, the Africans themselves would need help in learning to cope with the powers and problems of the twentieth century. Garvey therefore proposed sending a limited number of Afro-Americans with skills, professions, and capital (twenty or thirty thousand families to begin with) to settle in Liberia. Liberia was at that time the only independent West African nation, and it was governed by an elite group of descendants of earlier Afro-American settlers who ruled the indigenous Africans. After 1920 several teams of Garvey's representatives visited Liberia to lay the groundwork for the newcomers. But the UNIA seemed a threat to these Americo-Liberian rulers, especially after they discovered Garvey's secret plan to take over the country. With the approval of the European colonial powers, which also felt threatened by Garvey's "Africa for the Africans" policy, Liberia broke off negotiations and refused to allow any UNIA members to settle there.

Thus ended Garvey's only real attempt to repatriate the descendants of Africa. The enormous appeal he had for Afro-Americans, however, was not based solely on the Back to Africa idea. Although he maintained that "the future of the Negro . . . outside of Africa, spells ruin and disaster," he did not actually call for mass emigration of American blacks. But mass emigration to escape oppression in the United States was an appealing concept to many of Garvey's working-class followers, and he did little to discourage that popular misinterpretation of his plans.

It was not only the Liberian government and the European colonial powers that were alarmed at Garvey's promises to redeem Africa through his African Legion and Black Flying Eagles; many Afro-Americans also opposed the UNIA leader. The black elite of businessmen and intellectuals resented Garvey just as they had resented Bishop Turner. Labor leader A. Philip Randolph, of the socialist journal *Messenger*, thought Garvey's Africa would be a reactionary dictatorship, not a democracy. Robert Abbott, of the influential *Chicago Defender,* arranged to have Garvey harassed for selling stock in Illinois without a license. Black churchmen resented Garvey's establishment of an African Orthodox Church, which threatened to win the allegiance of black Christians to a black God. W. E. B. Du Bois, editor of the NAACP magazine the *Crisis,* accused Garvey of being the worst enemy of the black race. Du Bois was then involved in a series of pan-African conferences which tried to bring together intellectual and upper-class blacks in an organization aimed at pressing for independence for colonial Africa. Although the Pan-African movement shared some basic goals with the UNIA, its style was quite different and its membership much smaller than that of the UNIA; Garvey despised Du Bois. The black elite, or "talented tenth," as Du Bois called them, not only opposed Garvey's black nationalism but also criticized the man himself for being uneducated, a foreigner, and a "demagogue." Many whites, including federal government officials, also viewed the UNIA as a dangerous "anti-American" movement.

At first, such opposition did little to dim Garvey's popularity with the black masses, but the Jamaican also had to take his "friends" into account. Although the UNIA was far-flung, its organization rested chiefly on Garvey himself rather than on strong local leaders. Nevertheless, the UNIA attracted a number of men who saw in it an opportunity to gain personal power or profit. At first Garvey was too trusting of his associates and allowed them to make decisions that later hurt the movement, especially their financial decisions for the Black Star Line. Despite the fact that millions of dollars had apparently been collected from UNIA members, most of it was never accounted for. And although the organization eventually bought four ships, they either turned out to be unseaworthy or were lost because of debt. The other financial affairs of the movement were also apparently mismanaged, so much so that Garvey's opponents, including some defectors from the UNIA and some disgruntled stock owners, alerted the United States government and charged that the Black Star Line was making false claims about its finances.

In February 1922 Garvey and three of his lieutenants were indicted by the federal government for using the United States mails to sell fraudulent stocks to subordinates who had betrayed him. His opponents rejoiced at his impending downfall, but the masses of the UNIA rallied behind their leader and the trial was delayed until May 1923. Now distrustful of most of his friends, Garvey dismissed his attorney and tried in vain to defend himself. The court record attests to the shabby financial procedures of the Black Star Line, although it seems clear that Garvey himself had no intention of defrauding his supporters. In spite of such evidence, his three subordinates were found not guilty. The fact that Garvey himself was found guilty suggests that the jury have been more alarmed by his black nationalism than by his business practices. He was sentenced to five years in prison; but after serving two years, he was released in 1927 and deported as an "undesirable alien."

Garvey's opponents were delighted, of course, and they published the details of how the UNIA members and Black Star Line investors had lost their money. They expected the movement to quickly collapse. During Garvey's two years in prison there was indeed a decline in the activities of the UNIA, for it had been held together primarily by the personality of Garvey himself. Nevertheless, some local chapters continued to function, waiting for the day when their leader would again rally them to the cause of black nationalism. But when Garvey was released from prison and tried to rekindle the old enthusiasm from a distance in Jamaica, he had little success. Even though there was a temporary rally, particularly in the West Indies, the damage had been done. Vestiges of the UNIA lingered on in the United States, but it was torn by factionalism, dissension, and bankruptcy. By 1930 it had ceased to be a major organization in Afro-American life. Garvey died in London in 1940, still clinging to the dream of a powerful African nation that would unite the descendants of Africa scattered around the world. But this second flowering of mass black nationalism in the United States had withered. Yet another generation would pass before such ideas again stirred American blacks.

Turner and Garvey in Perspective

Garvey's UNIA, of course, received much more public recognition than had Bishop Turner's movement. The reasons lie in the differences between their followers. Turner lived and worked in the South, where most blacks were farmers and where white oppression was much more personal and pervasive. Garvey, on the other hand, worked primarily in the large cities, where communications were better, leisure time more plentiful, white oppression less personal, and mass meetings more feasible. Furthermore, Turner's followers rarely saw much cash, whereas the urban blacks, though underpaid and underemployed, were paid cash wages. This made it easier for Garvey to raise money for his operations. In addition, many UNIA members, having recently moved to the North, found it easy to think of moving to yet another "promised land." These factors partially explain why Garvey, rather than Turner, succeeded in creating a large, visible nationalist organization.

However, Garvey and Turner shared not only a dream of African redemption and black pride but also certain personal qualities that influenced their activities. Although neither was superhuman and each had his glaring weaknesses, both possessed an overwhelming desire to see the black race achieve honor and equality with whites. They shared a vision of African power. Both were impressive speakers with a flair for the dramatic and a willingness to speak bluntly about white racism, and to speak it in the language of the masses. But, although Garvey and Turner were competent organizers on a surface level, neither possessed the shrewdness or ability to mobilize his followers efficiently and fend off attacks both by whites and by other blacks.

In contrast, Booker T. Washington, the dominant black leader in the years between Turner's and Garvey's heydays, was able to use people, publicity, politics, and personality to maintain his own power for almost twenty years. Of course, Washington paid a price for that power—namely, the humiliation of Southern blacks in their own eyes and in the eyes of whites in return for telling white businessmen what they wanted to hear about "happy, docile blacks." And although Washington's power gained him the respect of many blacks, he commanded little enthusiasm among the black lower class because he had no great, militant vision of the future of Afro-Americans. But he was a shrewd and capable organizer and manipulator of ideas and men. In the final analysis he was the most powerful black man in American history.

Had either Bishop Turner or Marcus Garvey combined Washington's organizational ability with their black nationalist understanding of what had to be done, the outcome might have been different. Although Turner fought for African redemption and Afro-American emigration throughout most of his long life, he had other interests, particularly church affairs, and so did not give his wholehearted attention to black nationalist agitation. Garvey had only one consuming passion, but his fatal weakness was his failure to select competent and loyal assistants.

There were other reasons why neither Turner nor Garvey was able to achieve ultimate success. Each had active opponents and, in the end, was overwhelmed by them. For, just as Turner's propaganda was taking effect in the mid-1890's, Booker T. Washington gained national attention and soon dominated black leadership. Garvey was overwhelmed, not by a new leader with new ideas, but by a concerted attack from his opponents, who succeeded in physically removing him from the scene. Both Turner and Garvey failed to get substantial support from the black upper class—the small but influential elite who had skilled jobs, professions, or college educations and who yearned for stability and integration more than race pride. Although Garvey was much more successful in getting money and ships, in the end neither he nor Turner was able to arrange a strong settlement of Afro-Americans in Africa or otherwise create a powerful black nation. Each man was so aware of the pervasive reality of white oppression and the powerfulness of blacks around the world that he ignored the necessary details of organization and nation building.

It was the concept of black nationalism rather than its organization that fired the imaginations of Turner's oppressed Southern followers and Garvey's Northern urban admirers. To be sure, there was a major element of escapism in the popular interpretation of black nationalism. That escapism forced both leaders to include mass emigration in their thinking, even though both maintained that a full exodus was both impractical and unnecessary for the establishment of a free black nation in Africa. But blacks seemed to want a nation of their own that would command the respect of the world, an idea they clearly adopted from whites; both the 1890's and 1920's were times of intense nationalism in both Europe and the United States. Southern and Northern whites proclaimed that this was a "white man's country." The ideas and arguments employed by Turner and Garvey were learned from these whites.

Central to the concept of black nationalism was the unity of all blacks in all parts of the world. Unity meant more than strength in numbers; the international approach reinforced the nationalists' awareness that the root of their problems lay not in racial inferiority, personal traits, or bad luck, but in white oppression. This was true not only in the United States and the Caribbean but in Africa as well. Bishop Turner watched in alarm as the European powers established their imperial control over the homeland during his lifetime. Both he and Garvey were early contributors to the small but growing movement for African nationalism among the Africans themselves, a movement that eventually led to their independence.

For Turner, Garvey, and their followers, Africa became a symbol more powerful than reality. As the home of their ancestors, it had a strong appeal to Afro-Americans, whose knowledge of Africa was clouded by generations of separation and years of brainwashing. New World blacks easily romanticized Africa and ignored its difficult problems—first of European control, second of economic growth in societies that had not yet begun to industrialize, and third of nation building on a continent containing hundreds of different ethnic groups. Both Turner and Garvey tried to learn about Africa, however, and their visions of an independent, powerful African nation were more than empty dreams.

The primary impact of both Turner and Garvey, of course, was on American blacks. Black nationalism gave Afro-Americans a feeling of independence and power in the face of suffocating, ever present white oppression. It also gave them a sense of working toward the day when black men would indeed have their own nations and be respected in the councils of the world. This sense of purpose drew together a people who had been lost in an American society supposedly very individualistic but actually very group-oriented, especially where race was involved. It got some of them—for a time, at least—to work together, to dream, to build, and brought a self-pride that mere rhetoric could never have produced.

The flowerings of black nationalism under Bishop Turner and Marcus Garvey left seeds that are still growing. First, the promise of African freedom inspired Africans to work for independence from Europe. Second, the stress on black accomplishments built a new pride in the Afro-American lower class that would one day blossom into a new black power and independence.

Notes

1. Henry McNeal Turner, letter to the editor, *Christian Recorder,* 22 February 1883.

2. Henry McNeal Turner, *A.M.E. Church Review* 1 (January 1885): 246.

3. Henry McNeal Turner, *Voice of Missions,* November 1895.

4. Turner's letters from Africa were collected in the *A.M.E. Church Review* 8 (April 1892): 446–98.

5. Turner, letter to the editor, *Christian Recorder,* 22 February 1883.

6. Editorial, *Denver Statesman,* 9 December 1893.

7. Henry McNeal Turner, *Voice of Missions,* April 1896.

8. Henry McNeal Turner, *Atlantic Constitution,* 24 February 1906.

9. Amy Jacques Garvey, ed., *The Philosophy and Opinions of Marcus Garvey,* 2 vols. (New York: Universal Publishing House, 1923, 1925), 2:95.

10. Garvey, *Philosophy of Marcus Garvey,* 1:58.

11. Ibid., 1:52.

12. Ibid., 1:21, 22.

13. Ibid.

Reading 12

Reckoning with Violence: W. E. B. Du Bois and the 1906 Atlanta Race Riot

Dominic J. Capeci Jr. and Jack C. Knight

While much has been written about the years that W. E. B. Du Bois spent in Atlanta (1897–1910), scholars view his southern sojourn a time of national leadership rather than regional influence or personal travail. They emphasize Du Bois's challenge to Booker T. Washington and view Du Bois's endeavors, from the publication of *The Souls of Black Folk* in 1903 to the founding of the National Association for the Advancement of Colored People (NAACP) in 1909, as a seamless series of achievements in the triumph of radical protest over conservative accommodation. Although historians describe Du Bois's response to the lynching of Sam Hose (1899) and the race riot of Atlanta (1906), they tend to overlook the enormous effect of these acts of violence on his thought, self-perception, and, consequently, his militant strategies. Only David Levering Lewis, Du Bois's most recent biographer, likens his life in the New South to a Theban tale, wherein a curse thwarts manful effort and lessons are learned from behind a bloodstained "veil." Indeed Lewis portrays a tragic Du Bois, so stunned by Hose's execution and, in a few weeks, his own son's death that he was led to his first realization of the overwhelming adversity confronting African Americans in Atlanta.[1]

Yet, more than any of his biographers, Du Bois revealed the devastating impact of the Atlanta riot on himself. In coded language, classical idiom, and religious imagery, he disclosed that southern racism inflicted massive damage on his own double consciousness—that troublesome intersection of racial identity and national citizenship in a white supremacist country that he described so poignantly in Souls. His writings of this period reveal a race leader unsettled by tragedy, found wanting in the riot, and shamed by his own withdrawal from public action. Thus, in the fall of 1906, after the riot, Du Bois jettisoned caste mannerisms for a self "more broadly human," underwent a "great spiritual upturning," and questioned several long-held ideals.[2] He confronted personal failings and contradictions of principle; he also laid the groundwork for new religious, sociological, and philosophical tenets in the struggle for racial equality that later fostered Marxian explanation and, more significantly, American pragmatism.

Du Bois had approached the South naively, though not uncritically. Twenty-nine years old, he arrived at Atlanta University in 1897 convinced that superior intelligence, scientific investigation, and collegial effort would solve the race problem. Four years earlier in Berlin, on his twenty-fifth birthday, he had pledged himself—before candle and altar in the epiphanic style of seventeenth-century philosopher/mathematician René Descartes—to a life's mission of racial advancement. In the verse of the classical poet Horace, Du Bois had seized the day and proclaimed himself a man of science and race.[3] He championed his black ancestry early in life because of a deep sensitivity for the human spirit and an even deeper love for his mother, who doubtless he had in mind years later when describing the "strength of character, cleanness of soul, and unselfish devotion" of all black women. He felt his blackness viscerally in the childhood snub of a classmate who refused his personal visiting card. He embraced his blackness more fully in his undergraduate days among fellow students at Fisk University and, in the summers, among his students, the children of nearby farm families of every shade of black, brown, and yellow, who shared "a half-awakened common consciousness" with their Cambridge-bound teacher.[4] Following his studies at Harvard University and the University of Berlin, Du Bois's personal understanding of the everyday trials of black people advanced during his fieldwork for *The Philadelphia Negro: A Social Study* (1899). Indeed, prior to entering the South, he elevated his personal pledge of racial identity to a creed for the American Negro Academy asserting that "the race idea" was the "most ingenious invention for human progress."[5]

Paradoxically, Du Bois had lived in several different racial environments and brought a decided class bias with him to Georgia. Such contradiction was possible because Du Bois viewed himself through Hegelianism and science, combining the spiritual strivings of black folk with the cultural standards of his white mentors. In fact, philosophy and research provided the key to his self-perception and, consequently, his strategies—southern and northern—for black advancement, white understanding, and social progress. Seemingly, Du Bois identified himself as a dark messiah groomed for heroic leadership. He appropriated Georg W. F. Hegel's belief that race progress derived from group self-realization and the exercise of will and reason. Conceding that slave trading and slavery rendered blacks underdeveloped as a race, Du Bois strived as a "world historical" man to establish African American self-understanding through an ideation that reached back in time and required separatism and revitalization. Hence he endeavored with others to consolidate and articulate the race within a nation's beliefs and folk culture, first to itself in writings like *Souls* and then to white society in scientific tracts and formal organizations. Herein lay the raison d'être of The Talented Tenth—intellectual "yeast" that would enable blacks to rise collectively.[6]

In that respect, Du Bois regarded his own heritage as a source of second sight that enabled him to see race relations along Hegelian lines. A northern-born mulatto, he envisioned himself as a conduit for the racially divided worlds of his own ancestry, promoting among blacks the lyric poetry of Aristophanes and revealing to whites the lack of African spirituality in their heroes.[7] His light skin presented him with modern educational opportunities, while his race heritage enabled him to see much deeper into the past. Doubtless, as a sociologist, he understood that the "looking-glass self" of a marginal man produced conflicting images of black and white, while it also triggered a full range of positive to negative feelings. Nevertheless, his allusion to blacks having been "born with a veil" related to the African belief that an individual born with a caul over the face possessed two spirits, one that remained in his body and one that went about aiding him. And—true to black folklore—he believed that the gift of vision carried for race savants like himself a curse of "contradiction": satisfying "two unreconciled strivings," one for blacks, the other for whites.[8] Essentially, he combined aspects of European philosophy and African religion that required personal sacrifice at the hands of both races and prompted him to confide on the date of his ritualistic pledge to blackness, "if I perish—*I Perish.*"[9]

Moreover, Du Bois came of age when race relations were undergoing a "grand changeover" as the attitudes of white elites were transformed from grudging acceptance of mulattoes to complete rejection. Finding himself in a white world whose culture he admired but whose racism he despised, he sought achievement according to white standards yet identified with black struggles. Ultimately, he employed scientific inquiry to question the white supremacist belief that one drop of black blood defined an individual and that mulattoes were either "degenerates," further debased than either race, or achievers, "by reason of their white blood."[10] He denied the superiority of mulattoes and admired all race men who excelled, regardless of their hue; he realized that mulattoes dominated The Talented Tenth and, almost exclusively, the power of second sight, but did not ascribe their elevated position to the racial mixture, as certainly Hegel himself would have.[11]

Thus Du Bois entered the South "a Negro and an American," envisioning the preservation of each in the other through Hegelian synthesis.[12] Shortly before going to Atlanta, he had spoken of blacks in the third person and compared the examination of race to research on aborigines; and after he arrived, he even thought himself capable of inducing southern whites to reward deserving blacks.[13] Small wonder that initially he embraced several of Booker T. Washington's precepts and veered his distance from both the black masses and the humiliations of a Jim Crow society, for example by walking downtown rather than riding segregated streetcars. Yet residing in the West End, a suburb of Atlanta, surrounded by the worst slums of the city, Du Bois was daily reminded of his own blackness and lone academic appointment among white colleagues. His "little spot of Puritan New England in the midst of black Georgia"—in the appropriated description Richard R. Wright— was more imagined than real.[14]

Du Bois was soon confronted by southern terrorism and personal tragedy. In April 1899 Sam Hose was lynched. The horror of Hose's death was unprecedented, even in Georgia, where 115 racial killings had been recorded during the previous decade. This blood-lust orgy violently underscored the color line's harsh realities and, when followed in May by the death from diphtheria of his and Nina Gomer Du Bois's eighteen-month-old son, Burghardt, drove Du Bois even deeper into himself and his mission.[15]

Like other Atlantans, Du Bois had read that Hose murdered Alfred Cranford, his white employer, near the farm community of Palmetto. Mrs. Cranford claimed that Hose killed her husband with an ax, raped her, terrorized their small children, robbed the premises, and fled uttering "let them kill me if they can."[16] Thereafter, hundreds of people searched the countryside while rumors heightened the drama of the chase and fed public hysteria, as did sensational press coverage by Atlanta's five dailies.[17] The Atlanta *Constitution*, for example, circulated Hose's description, justified conditions for mob vengeance, and matched Governor Allen Candler's offer of a five-hundred-dollar reward for Hose's capture. The paper also manipulated racial opinion by coaxing black leaders to condemn black crime and by misrepresenting Booker T. Washington's initial refusal to comment on the Hose case.[18]

Determined to correct the record, Du Bois set out for the offices of the *Constitution* with a written statement. In passionless language he characterized Hose as an object lesson for the evils of race separation, convict-leasing, southern courts, and mob violence. Without defending Hose—whom he thought guilty of murder—Du Bois blamed white society for black crime.[19] He did not deliver his statement, however; learning that Hose had been captured and lynched, his knuckles on display at a nearby grocery like a trophy from a successful hunt, Du Bois returned to the campus of Atlanta University.[20]

That day, "something died in me," Du Bois wrote later.[21] A pacifist who as a child had recoiled even at the thought of hunting for food, he was "startled" by the festive capture and ghoulish torture that ended in castration and incineration, with strips of Hose's liver cooked and sold for ten cents. The message to all blacks was that they, too, could be sexually mutilated, reduced to meat, and consumed—exorcised in cannibal meaning and act.[22]

Nevertheless, Du Bois responded decisively. He joined other prominent blacks in calling on Governor Candler to protect the race, only to hear Georgia's highest official admonish them to raise the moral level of "their own people" and trace Hose's lynching directly to black participation in politics.[23] Thereafter, Du Bois and his allies mobilized to challenge the Hardwick bill, which sought the disfranchisement of blacks statewide. He acted the race leader publicly, cooperated with Booker T. Washington, who uncharacteristically entered the fray, and presented white officials with a November petition of black signatories supporting limited suffrage.[24]

Having stepped forward on the racial front, Du Bois still held firm to his class bias and cleaved to accommodation. He—like Washington—blamed lynching on riffraff and emphasized the difference between blacks like Paul Laurence Dunbar and those like Sam Hose.[25] Du Bois's reassertion of Chandler's racist stereotype stemmed partly from his accepting the accuracy of deliberate journalistic misrepresentations. Southern newsmen transmogrified Hose from an honest laborer who killed his employer, Alfred Cranford, in self-defense (but did not touch Mrs. Cranford) to a black beast who attacked both Cranfords in a fit of irrepressible African savagery. By distorting the lynching victim, Atlanta newspapers placed whites in a morally superior position and blacks, especially elites like Du Bois, in a wholly untenable one.[26]

In part, too, Du Bois clung to past beliefs because he suffered emotional trauma for some time after the deaths of his son Burghardt and Sam Hose. Such beliefs seem to have provided philosophical amid personal torment as bereavement became complicated by marital estrangement: Nina held him responsible for the loss of their son. Du Bois's incomplete mourning evolved slowly from "philosophical reflection"—that is, identifying with Hose's "crucifixion" and his own son's fictive ascension "above the Veil"—to political statement.[27] Indeed, in 1903 he joined William Monroe Trotter's radical challenge to Washington following his own criticism of the Tuskegeean in *Souls*.[28]

Ironically, in 1903 and 1904 Du Bois cooperated with Washington in a failed effort to forge an organization of organizations to coordinate the efforts of both accommodationists and radicals. Or, so he thought when initially responding to the latter's initiative in October 1903 and, despite his instincts, submitting recommendations aimed at broadening the membership, program, and scope of what would, in March 1904, become the Committee of Twelve. Du Bois resigned in disgust that August, correctly believing that the Tuskegeean was more interested in consolidating his power and checking his opponents than in advancing the racial struggle. Nonetheless, in calling for "Concerted and Systematic Effort for Negroes of the Whole Country" to establish "committees of correspondence," connections to "the rank and file," and programs for sociopolitical redress, Du Bois outlined plans for what would come the Niagara Movement and, though unforeseen, the NAACP.[29]

Washington's secretary, Emmett Jay Scott, later noted the link between Du Bois's position paper and his impending Niagara Movement but did not mention that the Niagara Movement would contain a southern strategy.[30] Scott, like most everyone else, seemed aware only of Du Bois's northern loyalties and scholarship, but Du Bois had spoken earlier of a "southward" excursion by "the broadly trained University man" in order to correct an economic system that depended on black industrial laborers yet refused to grant them political franchise. Indeed, once in Atlanta, his research often focused on the rural South, including communities in Virginia (1897), Georgia (1899/1901), and Alabama (1906). These studies for the Department of Labor and Du Bois's own demographic inquiries verified census data demonstrating that the great mass of blacks remained in the South, which also had become the "magnet" for mulattoes during the changeover period of race relations when northern whites began to reject them. The existence of statistics indicating that the "heartland of Negro life" centered in the Deep South was reason enough for a visionary of Du Bois's gift to begin the nationally conceived racial program in that region.[31] Neither northerner nor Southerner, he stood marginal and cosmopolitan, viewing the country as a laboratory in which to solve the race problem, which was itself an intellectual construct.

Had Washington's Atlanta Compromise of 1895 been effective, Du Bois might have continued to concentrate on a scientific approach to solving the nation's racial riddle. Conceivably, if white southerners had given black southerners "a man's chance" of economic opportunities and moved, however slowly, in the direction of political rights, he would have welcomed the space provided by segregation to develop the race along Hegelian concepts of progress—movement toward freedom and equality. To this extent, Du Bois had been an accommodationist.[32] But compromise had become capitulation, sacrificing the very manhood that he deemed necessary for African Americans to attain their potential as a people beautiful, learned, and respected. And Du Bois became convinced that the Tuskegeean's article of faith had failed as a vehicle for racial progress, mutual or otherwise, and that the Committee of Twelve simply continued on a course of defeat for blacks in their individual lives and collective destiny. Instead of standing in place like Washington, Du Bois stepped forward (almost literally on the seventh anniversary of Burghardt's birth) to advance his "Credo"; in millennial and personal language, unmistakable in its antipathy toward suffocating accommodationism and white supremacy, he "believe[d] in Liberty for all men; the space to stretch their arms and their souls . . . ."[33]

By October 1904 Du Bois had come increasingly to downplay individual accomplishment and science, question Hegelian inevitability, and rely on "propaganda"—poetry and polemics—as he moved toward political action.[34] The following June he promoted his own protest leadership, organizing the radicals—elites all—to counter Washington, his philosophy, and his machine. Neo-abolitionist in outlook, Du Bois's Niagara Movement advocated federal school subsidies, economic reconstruction, and black suffrage and repudiated racial subservience and religious hypocrisy.[35] It organized annual state conventions and local projects, calling for civil rights litigation, party politics, and public protest.[36] And, despite meeting in Canada and having northern support, it implemented Du Bois's vision for "The Committee of Twelve" and evinced strategies for "Negroes of the Whole Country." In fact, of fifty-nine individuals signing the call for the Ontario conference, nine—15 percent—came from the South, including five prominent Georgians: Du Bois, John Hope, Dr. Loring B. Palmer, George A. Towns, and Monroe N. Work. And, of twenty-nine men who attended the conference, six—nearly 21 percent—represented three southern states: Du Bois, J. Max Barber, and Alonzo F. Herndon from Georgia; J. L. R. Diggs and F. H. M. Murray from Virginia; and Richard Hill from Tennessee.[37]

Du Bois's plan for a "southern movement" within the national protest was completely serious.[38] He moved quickly to implement one of the major conference decisions, a Thanksgiving Day celebration of William Lloyd Garrison's one-hundredth birthday for the purpose of demonstrating Niagaran strength, expounding its principles, and reminding black people of white friends who gave their lives "to the cause of our uplift."[39] The celebration was held in twenty-five cities, including Washington, D.C., Wilmington, Delaware, Raleigh, and Savannah, and Du Bois personally secured the Wheat Street Baptist Church for the observance of November 30, 1905, in Atlanta.[40] There he attracted the participation of several prominent citizens who questioned Washingtonian principles or desired a closer look at the Du Boisian alternative: most notably, the Reverend Peter Bryant, pastor of Wheat Street Baptist, whose church—according to Benjamin J. Davis, the editor of the Atlanta *Independent*—was the only place that a movement in the midst of being born, and with no titular head, could have had an audience; the Reverend Henry H. Proctor of the First Congregational Church, a Washingtonian who had earlier joined Du Bois to challenge local discrimination; and Collector of Internal Revenue Henry L. Rucker, one of three Georgia Republicans backed by the Tuskegeean. Politically more astute than he was given credit for, Du Bois had them joined on the platform by Niagaran John Hope and Adrienne Herndon, Alonzo Herndon's wife and an Atlanta University instructor. At the gathering Du Bois addressed issues beyond the Niagara principles, such as Rucker's endorsement for another term. In the process, Du Bois also found a kindred spirit in Dr. William J. White of Augusta, editor of the *Georgia Baptist,* who spoke at the special occasion.[41]

Du Bois eagerly accepted a reciprocal invitation from White to be part of a 1906 statewide gathering in Macon that would issue "good strong manly expressions" and thoughtful pleas for racial justice.[42] He did much more than merely participate, as indicated by Niagaran involvement in the 1906 Macon meeting—styled the Georgia Equal Rights Convention—which drew two hundred delegates: Du Bois was a "Call" signee; Towns, assistant secretary; Bryant, prelate; Du Bois, Bryant, Hope, Barber, Henry M. Porter, and Judson W. Lyons, among the seventeen signatories of the "Address," which criticized discrimination statewide. While acknowledging that black residents were partly responsible for their own ignorance, the signers intended to protest, in unmistakable Du Boisian language "against the invasion of our manhood rights . . . ." They condemned—without naming Sam Hose—black criminals and white lynchers and proffered peaceful coexistence with law-abiding whites—"as man and man, equal in the sight of God and in the eye of the law . . ."[43] In fact, the words were penned by "a Niagaran man"—Du Bois himself.[44]

Essentially Du Bois implemented the movement's strategy of cooperating with local and, in this case, state efforts, simultaneously advancing the Georgia Equal Rights Convention and, in his own phrase, "the Georgia Niagara Movement."[45] White saw the arrangement in the wanting to discuss matters with Du Bois after the convention and "then go to work" extending its influence throughout the state: "Our men are ready to follow as we wisely lead."[46] More than respected local leader and national consultant engaged in a singular experience, White pledged himself and his delegates to the Niagaran fight; Du Bois, again demonstrating political acumen, sparked new hope among some black Southerners, struck a militancy where supposedly none existed, and staked his protest movement deep in Washington's turf.

Against these southern triumphs, Du Bois also succeeded in the North where he established association with Constitutional League members, among others, and demonstrated his desire to influence rather than dominate protest leaders and organizations. Thus he brought the Niagara Movement to full stride at its second annual meeting, in West Virginia.[47] On August 17, 1906, conferees celebrated the spirit of John Brown by tramping barefooted, following Du Bois, to the fort at Harpers Ferry, where the revolutionary had consecrated followers prior to their fateful insurrection in 1859.[48] Niagarans committed themselves—as Du Bois had committed himself in Berlin—to a life's crusade of protest for equal rights, vowing that "the trump of doom [will] find us still fighting."[49]

And "us" included many new southern members, such as William Pickens, who was the secretary for the Alabama Niagara Movement. They came from all eleven former Confederate states (as compared to four at the Ontario meeting). Professor John B. Watson of Atlanta Baptist College, Dr. William F. Penn of Atlanta, and Judson W. Lyons, an Augusta Republican, were also new members, which signified that southern heart of Du Bois's movement was his own city and state. There, as elsewhere, membership was inclusive and determined by a commitment to principle, not by collegiality. Hence in one year's time, Du Bois's home-grown effort—greatly stimulated by the Macon conference—had produced significant results, threatening both Washingtonians and white conservatives.[50]

Du Bois returned to Atlanta buoyed by the expectation that well-placed complaint could bring change. Instead, he encountered the climax of an eighteen-month-long gubernatorial election campaign in which major candidates played on white fears of black domination.[51] The eventual winner, race-baiting Hoke Smith, might have conspired with ruffians who masqueraded as blacks and assaulted white girls, while Atlanta editors published unsubstantiated accounts of black beasts raping white women.[52] The *Evening News* even misrepresented Washington's denunciation of black misconduct as a "call for a thousand men to hunt the Negro criminal."[53]

In this charged atmosphere of early September, Du Bois left the city to complete a federally commissioned study of peonage in Lowndes County, Alabama. He seemed torn between class myths that said law-abiding black neighborhoods were beyond the reach of white toughs and racial realities that marked all persons of color, including mulattoes, for violence. In truth, he rehearsed his young daughter Yolande in a protective drill in which she dressed in black and hid in the closet at the first sign of danger.[54] Du Bois's disquietude became deep-seated fear for his wife and daughter when he learned in Alabama that the worst rioting in Georgia's history had erupted in downtown Atlanta at 8:30 P.M. on Saturday, September 22, 1906.

Precipitated by four extra editions of the *Evening News* trumpeting successive cases of alleged black rape, frenzied whites—who by 10:30 P.M. numbered ten thousand men, women, and children of all classes—killed or beat every black in sight. Before the five-hour massacre ended in the face of sheer exhaustion and a fortuitous downpour, the mob had attacked juke joints, pool halls, stores, and streetcars and had committed unspeakable atrocities—using a small black child for target practice and beating to death two barbers who worked in Alonzo Herndon's shop.[55] Rioters crucified several bodies on utility poles and expressed contempt for the New South's concession to racial progress by laying three corpses at the monument to Henry W. Grady, Atlanta's leading architect of racial reform. They also chased blacks into traditional refuges: homes of paternalistic whites, recreation areas, suburbs, and campuses of black schools.[56]

Learning of this terror, Du Bois boarded a train for Atlanta. He rode toward the still unfinished pogrom, hearing death cries, seeing blood lust, and penning the "Litany of Atlanta." In lengthy self-dialogue that lay bare religious belief in the collective salvation of all black people and personal doubt about his own optimism, he called upon God to show Himself and deliver His suffering servants: "Bewildered we are . . . What meaneth this?/Keep not Thou silent, O God!" Du Bois pondered whether God was, after all, white, sought immediate forgiveness for such blasphemy, if not racial apostasy, and begged for direction: "point us the path!" He also beseeched vengeance on the rioters. And, once in the city, he armed himself with a shotgun, lest prayer failed.[57]

Before Du Bois's arrival in Atlanta, violence erupted anew on Monday evening. Fearing retaliation for the earlier massacre, county police undertook to disarm blacks in the Brownsville area near Clark University. The police were ambushed, and a deputy sheriff was killed by frightened residents. The following day, a well-armed militia invaded Brownsville, disarmed everyone, and, in cold blood, killed four people—a store owner, a Union army veteran, a mason, and a carpenter—none of whom fit the profile of an outlaw or had provoked violence. The militia also raided nearby Gammon Theological School, assaulted its president, Dr. John W. E. Bowen, and marched three hundred citizens toward Atlanta for the murder of the slain policeman.[58]

Later in the morning, with calm hardly restored to Brownsville, a handful of black leaders, including Proctor and Herndon, met with Atlanta's mayor, chief of police, and area troop commander. They were joined at city hall by ten black ministers, who requited white pledges of protection with promises of lawfulness. Within hours, one thousand mostly white Atlantans attended a Chamber of Commerce meeting to coax laborers back to work and restore credibility with northern capitalists. They also addressed compensation for victims, safety for blacks, and justice for rioters. Charles T. Hopkins, attorney for Atlanta University, inspired private relief donations of $4,423 and led white reformers, who established a recovery committee and passed resolutions condemning the riot.

White goodwill carried over in the formation of a Civic League that five thousand Atlantans were invited to join, which was formed by Hopkins on Thanksgiving Day, 1906. It continued post-riot efforts by image-conscious white businessmen and prominent black leaders who influenced the closing of most black saloons, prosecuting some white rioters, and dismissing several policemen, while also inducing promises of better racial treatment on streetcars. It gained further currency by aiding in the release of blacks indicted for conspiracy in the riot and commissioning an adjunct "Coloured Cooperative Civic League" chaired by Proctor. That winter it also provided legal counsel to poor blacks, helped clear Joe Glenn of sexual assault against a white woman, and created the atmosphere for the arrest of two patrolmen for harassing a Brownsville victim's widow.[59]

In addition to these progressive achievements, former governor William J. Northen, already popular among blacks for having advocated equal suffrage and spoken against lynching during his term, undertook a biracial alliance of southern churchmen to ensure "absolute justice" for blacks.[60] This alliance, called the Christian League, endeavored to unite "the good men of both races to put down the bad of both" and denounced mob violence through a statewide organization of local committees. Northen's activity, like that of Hopkins, led many participants of Proctor's caliber to envision a "rainbow of racial cooperation . . . destined to span the South."[61]

Black leaders played to this paternalism almost immediately and, as the price for racial peace, validated black crime as the primary cause for upheaval and segregation. Indeed, many followed the lead of Dr. William F. Penn, who had stated at the Chamber of Commerce meeting that black

Atlantans should protect white women from the "criminal negro classes." Thereafter, Benjamin J. Davis of the Atlanta *Independent* urged "decent Negroes" to "remove the only excuse for mob violence"— black dives. And as late as November, Proctor stated that "one good result" of the disorder was that it unified "better elements" in both races for the purpose of restraining lower elements—black and white.[62]

In this atmosphere, Booker T. Washington seized the opportunity to promote himself, while deliberately maligning Du Bois, whose recent challenge was proving effective. Shortly before the riot, Washington had chided Lyman Abbott for giving "too much serious attention to Dr. Du Bois and his movement" and informed a follower that "the little crowd" sought "notoriety," acted out of "jealousy," and passed resolutions that hurt the race.[63] Unlike his silence and inaction in response to the 1898 Wilmington, North Carolina, riot, Washington spoke and acted dramatically in Atlanta. In 1898 northern protest against racial violence was, in the words of supporter T. Thomas Fortune, "altogether foreign to Prof. Washington's work"; in 1906 Washington's public demonstration of concern, if not complaint, was altogether imperative if his work was to have any chance of surviving in the South.[64]

Consequently, Washington publicly urged the best elements of both races to "come together" and, six days later, ventured into Atlanta, where he participated in the evolving interracial accommodation—the upheaval's silver lining." He also permitted the circulation of an editorial written by his secretary, Emmett Jay Scott, that compared Washington's heroic reaction to the violence with Du Bois's supposed cowardly absence from the city.[65] Thereafter, Washington sniped at Du Bois and his followers, most pointedly before an October meeting of the Afro-American Council in New York City; "the Negro in the North," he asserted, should advise only "that which he himself would be willing to take into the heart of the South. . . ."[66] He returned to Atlanta and continued to court black and white Atlantans, such as Proctor and Clark Howell, editor of the Atlanta *Constitution*. On December 9, the date previously appointed by Niagarans to honor abolitionists but after the riot set aside for sermons on law and order, Washington praised the accomplishments of the Christian and Civic Leagues and warned of "agitators among both races" who sought to attract "attention to themselves."[67]

Washington, in short, framed his response to the riot in the context of his ideological war with Du Bois, believing—as he had to believe—that the Atlanta Compromise survived the bloodshed and that the conservatives of both races remained in command to advance his philosophy and leadership throughout the South.[68] Such required that he blame disorder on the riffraff of both races and, primarily, on black radicals whose quest for "social equality" and "artificial forcing" of political rights wrought much more than the "extremist folly" predicted in his Atlanta address eleven years earlier.[69] Only by seeing the violence as an aberration in race relations could Washington save the compromise between black and white southerners; only by seeing himself as indispensable peacemaker could he preserve his personal covenant with white conservatives.

Ultimately, Washington succeeded only in preserving his reputation and covenant, for the riot demonstrated the failure of his compromise with the New South. Southern conservatives proved incapable of enforcing its most basic tenet. Washington had implied in his address of 1895 that, in return for their subservience to whites in social matters, blacks would be assured of economic opportunity, civil treatment, and ultimately "absolute justice." Four years later, in his response to Hose's lynching, Washington stated forcefully that, in return for noninterference by northerners and federal officials in regional racial matters, white southerners accepted a "sacred trust" to guarantee the personal safety of black citizens. Indeed, peaceful coexistence was at the center of accommodation—and the center had failed to hold.[70]

Nor were white conservatives guiltless for the bloodshed that had claimed 25 dead and 150 wounded and had caused over 1,000 people, mostly blacks, to emigrate from the South.[71] Several well-known conservatives were closely associated with the Atlanta newspapers that for weeks preceding the riot had whipped whites into a frenzy over allegations of black rape and, in the case of the *Evening News,* had printed the extra editions that precipitated the bloodshed on September 22.[72] They included editor Howell of the *Constitution,* editor John Temple Graves of the *Georgian,* business manager John S. Cohen of the *Journal,* and board members Charles T. Hopkins and James W. English of the *Evening News.*[73] In fact, even though they participated in the post-riot meetings called by the Chamber of Commerce, some of them—like Howell, Hopkins, and English, who emerged as chairman of the Civic League's Citizens Committee—combined with other conservatives who welcomed—if they did not incite—the riot.[74]

Together, white conservatives used the riot to protect the compromise from the militancy sparked by Du Bois's southern strategy and, significantly, to reshape it into a more inclusive and modern concept for white solidarity across class lines.[75] Following the Georgia Equal Rights Convention of the previous winter, Dr. William J. White had informed Du Bois that Georgia whites were "in a quandary" and "afraid to talk about our Macon meeting." They knew, continued White, neither "how to take it" nor "the people they live among."[76] To the contrary, whites probably understood all too well the public address given at the Equal Rights Conventions calling upon blacks to "agitate, complain, protest . . . and above all organize these million . . . into one great fist . . . to pound at the gates of Opportunity until they fly open."[77] Such assertiveness had precipitated backlash by whites, including white elites, in the bloodshed at Wilmington, North Carolina, in 1898 and in the race-baiting 1906 Georgia gubernatorial campaign between regulars and radicals of the Democratic Party. During the campaign, conservative candidate Clark Howell—who in 1895 had praised Washington's exposition speech as a platform upon which both races could stand "with full justice toward each other"—presented educated blacks as "the fatal enemy which held the knife at Georgia's political throat." Radicals backing Hoke Smith, in turn, condemned black suffrage and highlighted black crime as if blacks were in the process of unilaterally breaking the compromise.[78]

Within this context of white supremacy, Dr. White's convention frightened both radical and conservative Georgians, who probably perceived Atlanta as the locus of racial militancy. Thus, it appeared more than coincidental that rioters assaulted Herndon's barber shop, Penn's home, Bowen's person—activists all—and moved on Brownsville and black colleges, sanctuaries of Bowen, Du Bois, Hope, and Watson, some of which had been threatened earlier in this era of expanding backlash.[79] Whites certainly intended to send the message that neither class nor skin color separated black people, for all were "niggers" who had better stay in their place—violence as social control.

Du Bois understood their point, though he escaped the worst effects of the four-day carnage. On the student-patrolled grounds of Atlanta University with other "namelessly afraid" residents and close enough to the attacks to hear screams and shots, he personalized the vulnerability felt daily by lower-class blacks.[80] He struggled with the profound impact of white brutality on his psyche and philosophy and avoided involvement in post-riot efforts to reconstruct the Atlanta Compromise.

In part, Du Bois remained inactive because he sensed Washington's post-riot role in J. W. E. Bowen's abandonment of "race men" principles. Bowen, who courageously defended his seminary from white militiamen during the violence, acted—in the words of one critic—"panic stricken" afterward. Within days of the bloodshed, he received assurances from Washington that he had not contributed to the mayhem and that good would come "from the present trials."[81] Thereafter, in the New York *World* of September 30, he identified the sources of racial harmony as home, church, school, and state, above all stressing the need to check "dangerous black harpies" who "attack white women" and "pluck . . . at the vitals of their own race." Never mentioning white rioters, he called for the hiring of black policemen and the seating of black jurors as the formula for peace: "Punish the guilty, protect the innocent."[82] In response to those who criticized him for these and similar pronouncements elsewhere, Bowen dissembled into accommodationism: "I am willing to take the penalty for it; viz., I serve, I suffer and I keep quiet."[83]

Even more troubling to Du Bois was Washington's exploitation of Max Barber's flight from Atlanta. Barber, the managing editor of the *Voice of the Negro,* a Niagara Movement charter member, and a witness to the violence who originally seemed bolstered by peace commitments of whites, soon feared for his life. Anonymously, he protested John Temple Graves's racist contention that the riot would rid Atlanta of black crime for the next five years. After being exposed as the New York *World* letter writer, "Colored Citizen," he was threatened by none other than white conservative leader James W. English—and he bolted for Chicago.[84]

Barber, Washington then informed the black press, was rumored to have fled in the midst of riot while other leaders "stood their ground." Continuing his manipulation of the disorder for political advantage, Washington added that he hoped Barber would avoid "the example of so many" fugitives who gave long-distance advice on how southern blacks should conduct themselves—an unmistakable reference to Niagarans, especially Du Bois.[85] Thus Washington's taunt that radical protest seemed plausible only from the safe distance of the North appeared to be justified by Du Bois's inactivity in post-riot Atlanta.

Furthermore, Washington implemented and benefited from the insistence of conservatives that blacks refrain from publicly criticizing the actions of whites during the riot. The lack of criticism enabled white conservatives to reclaim control of the race issue from the radicals, protect the city's reputation nationally, and advance a new race and class arrangement—a twentieth-century compromise turning on greater white control and solidarity.[86] Black conservatives were also able to regain black moderates and dampen the influence of militants, while holding out hope for a new, more lasting agreement.

Hence, while conservatives of both races cooperated to reconstruct their ever-fragile covenant, Du Bois kept a low profile. He arrived in Atlanta too late to participate in their initial meetings, and his only exposition on the riot was conspicuous for its lateness and lack of Niagaran bravado. In November, six weeks after the riot, in the *World Today*, a northern journal, he matter-of-factly corrected untruths about pre-riot reports of black crime and cited the gubernatorial campaign as the cause for violence. Predictably, he praised black self-defense during the riot, challenged accommodation in its aftermath, and advocated equality before the law and black enfranchisement in order to promote interracial peace. Yet Du Bois's tone lacked the missionary zeal and personal fury that he had demonstrated at the Niagara Movement meeting at Harpers Ferry and in "Litany." Lamely, he spoke of riot as a "distraction," argued in the abstract, and failed to deliver on his own comment of eight years earlier to educate citizens nationwide about conditions and attitudes underlying racial violence.[87]

Du Bois's return to Lowndes County, Alabama, a scant eight days after his arrival in Atlanta, revived the criticism of him by accommodationists.[88] That he had been portrayed as a coward in newspapers controlled by Washington's henchmen, who falsely said that he had run during the riot, now took on greater consequence.[89] His absence from Atlanta from early October to late November elicited the parodies appearing in Davis's *Independent* that ridiculed the "fesser's" lack of physical courage and posted a ten-dollar reward for knowledge of his whereabouts![90]

Perhaps in part to parry this criticism, Du Bois accepted Proctor's invitation to serve as a member of the executive committee of the Colored Civic League upon its formation in late November. However, he attended few committee meetings and retreated again—permanently—from further participation.[91] For example, early in 1907 he declined to speak on education at a mass meeting organized by R. D. Stinson of Morris Brown College, which featured white peacemaker James W. English, the banker who had sent Barber packing.[92] Surely, Du Bois found working with accommodationists and their conservative racist allies extremely repugnant. Doubtless, his reputation among other black leaders for "blunt" speech contributed to his obscurity during the conservative rebuilding.[93]

The riot and Washington's initiatives paralyzed Du Bois. While the blood lust forced him to rethink his scientific rejection of amoral fate and his reliance on rationality (both of which supposedly limited racist excesses), the Tuskegeean's masterful public and clandestine maneuvers discredited Du Bois and his Niagara Movement. Even though the upheaval dismantled Washington's Atlanta Compromise—after the riot, efforts at accommodation became simply "cosmetic reforms"—it demonstrated, as Washington himself conceded, the vulnerability of black militants and the limits of their protest in the South.[94] If the outburst revealed that Washington's accommodation required rational white people and striving black people for its success, it also demonstrated the same for Du Bois's southern strategy (and his belief in an Hegelian transformation). If the disorder brought into question Washington's covenant with conservatives, it also demonstrated Du Bois's limitations as a leader of race men. Du Bois broke his unspoken agreement with blacks who followed him; he made no agreements with white Georgians—only Washington did that. Ironically, the Atlanta tumult also ended the most defining periods of each man's life, though Washington was less emotionally affected and his ideological course was less diverted. The experience with violence for Du Bois, in contrast, served to close thirteen years of intellectual and political maturation that had opened with his twenty-fifth birthday pledge.

Reeling from the spilled blood and the loss of his mission, Du Bois flinched badly. He had arrived in Atlanta as the bloodshed petered out, checked on his family, and returned quickly to Lowndes County. His departure reflected both an obsessive, driven personality and a crisis response similar to that he had displayed at the time of Burghardt's death, when he displaced grief in work; in part, his leaving provided an escape, however unconscious, from the shambles of Atlanta and the savaging of his philosophy, organization, and dream in the face of triumphant accommodation.[95] Like Barber, Du Bois fled in a situation that offered little alternative for his personal independence and commitment to racial liberation; unlike Barber, he left his wife and daughter, an unthinking, perhaps even craven act, though necessary if he was to hold any hope—some would say illusion—for himself, his family, or his movement in Atlanta. Neither man was a coward, but Du Bois's flight seemed more than that of a wounded fugitive, momentarily in need of distance and catharsis. He immersed himself in the study of black oppression in Alabama—a less tormenting reality than the riot and the political reign of Washington, Proctor, Hopkins, and Northen in Atlanta.

Returning to the city in November, Du Bois slowly reconstructed his public world, coping defensively with the upheaval and its aftermath yet unable to resuscitate himself or his movement politically. He lacked enthusiasm and, one suspects, conviction that Niagaran principles—with Barber in exile, Bowen in conversion, and himself in retreat—would ever reign in the South. Rising expectations once generated by the Thanksgiving Day commemoration and the Georgia Equal Rights Convention gave way to crushing pessimism wrought by the Atlanta pogrom. The viability of his protest as an alternative to Washingtonian accommodation had been dashed, a fact that was recognized by those—like Proctor—who initially stepped toward Du Bois but in the face of brutal violence quickly retreated to the Tuskegeean. Thus, Du Bois proved incapable of working with Proctor's committee, for he found that Hopkins was condescending and that members of the committee were fronting—as Washington fronted—for the Civic and Christian Leagues. Du Bois could betray neither his intellect nor his principles, believing that tension could be assuaged only by granting blacks fair treatment. Adopting a strategy of passive resistance, he admitted his lack of faith in the accommodationist effort and his inability to tell white southerners what they wanted to hear.[96] Unable to speak freely in circumstances inimical, if not suicidal, for protest, Du Bois turned down Stinson's invitation to speak in January 1907 rather than appearing only to say what he did "not believe." Essentially, he did what was best for his own beliefs and safety, and for the first time since arriving in Atlanta he truly became "a lone wolf."[97]

Isolated, Du Bois also perceived himself to be in a philosophical bind. He complained, again behind closed doors, that often only he "was willing to speak out" and was then "bitterly opposed." He, like Washington, divided blacks into better and worse elements, including a lower class composed of "fairly good working men" who joined criminals during riots and committed "sins of which this whole middle class is judged."[98] Whatever his experience during the riot, in which all black people encountered indiscriminate terror, Du Bois failed to overcome his own class bias or to refute adequately the racist charge that black criminality triggered white violence.

Nevertheless, Du Bois endeavored to set the record of the riot straight. Hence his November exposition in the *World Today* and his much more elaborate January 1907 colloquy with the Reverend C. B. Wilmer, a white man who was rector of St. Luke's Episcopal Church in Atlanta, and journalist Ray Stannard Baker, who sought material for *Along the Color Line* (1908). Du Bois wanted to explain himself and to influence Baker's interpretation of the South to a national audience. Therefore, throughout his conversation with the accommodationist cleric and the northern progressive, Du Bois repeatedly questioned Washington's optimism about race relations and the truth of his expressions of "not what was actually the case" but what the Tuskegean wanted it to be.[99] Coming too late and lacking force, however, Bois's statements to Baker and Wilmer had little influence on Washington's domination of the aftermath of the riot.

In truth, Du Bois refused to act publicly, and ironically he delivered the death knell to his own southern strategy in Georgia. His failure to endorse the eight-month-long Savannah streetcar boycott betrayed the Niagaran pledge to protest "eternally" public discrimination.[100] Admittedly, he preferred legal recourse over the boycott method, yet other Niagarans practiced the latter tactic that he, too, had endorsed at the Georgia Equal Rights Conference.[101] Nor did he participate in the second equal rights conference at Macon, having accepted a speaking invitation in Chicago for that date, which was Lincoln's Birthday, 1907. He promised to provide "a rough draft of some proposed resolutions" but did not act as "invaluable planner," "indefatigable worker," and provider of statistics, as he had at the previous year's meeting. Furthermore, in comparison to efforts in nearby states, such as Florida, Du Bois's once-touted Georgia Niagara Movement seemed moribund.[102]

Similarly, Du Bois's writings disappointed his fellow Niagarans. In January 1907 he editorialized about the Belgian Congo in the first issue of *Horizon*, the official publication of the Niagara movement. Nor did he address the riot directly in the February issue of the monthly, utilizing indirect language, covert meaning, and the jeremiad as an alternative idiom.[103] In "The Song of the Smoke," he railed at wrongs committed by whites and affirmed Messianic justice for the oppressed. By evoking ritualized protest Du Bois identified with Frederick Douglass, who had employed angry prophecy as righteous truth-telling for the purpose of reviving his abolitionist followers and reorganizing principles during crises. Thus "Song" fantasized a powerful "Smoke King" who moved across the land righting wrongs: "swabbing Hell in White ..." By writing in the first person, Du Bois revealed his own helplessness, invisibility, and diminished stature. Indeed, he had succumbed to the slave strategy of "cajolery" and "deception" that he so openly decried in *Souls*. Alas, he expressed his "manliness ... and courage" through furtive Biblical allusions.[104]

Belatedly Du Bois sought to preserve his own image as race prophet and in March penned "The Value of Agitation" for Barber's relocated and retitled *Voice*. He reduced his own leadership—and the Niagara Movement's protest—to writing and speaking; agitation became the act of merely pointing out "evil." Mentioning the "lost ground" suffered by the race during the "last year"—a reference to the riot—his remedy, that blacks "stand up" and tell what they want, appeared flat and incomplete to those expecting leadership.[105]

Even his close friend Mary White Ovington puzzled over Du Bois's uncharacteristic silence and indirectness and in April asked "when are we going to see you in print in some of these magazines that are deep in the negro question?"[106] In May, Du Bois, struggling with his own retreat in the face of the riot, purged himself emotionally in "Nulla Dies," a poem that referred back to his twenty-fifth birthday consecration in Berlin. Fourteen years after that rite of passage and seven months after the ordeal of the riot, he amended Horace's "carpe diem" entreaty, which undergirded his own life's work and areligious nature. Du Bois confided to Horace—like himself the learned son of the lower caste—that, in truth, every commitment has boundaries: "Nulla dies [no day] is without its limits."[107] Central to the poem is Horace's confession of cowardice in throwing his shield to the ground during the battle at Phillipi and in retiring from youthful politics to a career of writing light-hearted "songs of wine."[108] Du Bois wondered if, again like himself, Horace had recognized the contradiction between the admonition to "seize the day" and the refusal to speak openly; and if, still again like himself, Horace had felt like throwing down his pen in self-disgust at the useless-ness of waging war with riddles.

> Horace tells us—Horace knows,
> Yet I wonder if hale Horace
> Ever sat in mortal throes
> With the "Dies" but the "linea"
> Of some flowing carmina vinea
> Flatly, furiously declining,
> Notwithstanding all his whining,
> >   To appear,
> >   Till the seer
> Threw his pen in deep disgust,
> With his ethics, in the dust
> >   As I
> >   >   do
> >   >   >   now?[109]

Essentially, Du Bois bared his ineffectiveness—as leader, propagandist, husband, and father—in the face of real violence and recriminated himself for masking unmanly cowardice in the rhymes of jeremiad wish-fulfillment. That he did so in the *Horizon* revealed the depths of his personal torment.

Du Bois held on through the summer, perhaps buoyed by prospects of the Niagara Move-ment's third conference in Boston, which quickly proved disastrous. He faced one setback after an-other, from financial problems to demoralized members, which culminated in his split with the Boston journalist Monroe Trotter and hastened the movement's "disintegration."[110] However, when interviewed by newsmen, he claimed that the movement had over four hundred members spread throughout nearly every state, played up "manhood" and suffrage as the twin imperatives for racial progress, and insisted on first-class citizenship, but not revolutionary activity, for blacks. He again discussed impact of the riot: the "massacre of blacks" cost Atlanta one million dollars, their disfran-chisement would dash all "hope of redress," and the "dominant sentiment in the South" opposed blacks—despite the sympathy of many whites toward them. Du Bois thus indicated his frustration with both acquiescent blacks and racist whites in the post-riot reconstruction and complained aloud that the man who becomes a Niagaran "takes his living in his hands."[111]

Returning to Georgia, Du Bois knew that he had failed in both the South and North. Indeed, his high-flying leadership at Harpers Ferry crashed in the wake of the riot, its flames spreading na-tionwide as witnessed by the loss of Niagaran momentum and "internal strain" at Boston. He later noted the difficulty, in the face of white opinion, of accomplishing much as "a Negro organization." Yet, in 1907, he reeled more from white violence and black dissension, the latter prompting him to consider resigning as executive secretary of the Niagara Movement in both September and December.[112]

These contemplated resignations were symptoms of emotional unraveling so extensive that Du Bois sought—significantly, during the month of the riot's first anniversary—psychiatric help from the Westborough Insane Hospital in Massachusetts.[113] Although he had been traumatized by the deaths of his son Burghardt and Sam Hose, he seemed even more paralyzed by the long-range ramifications of urban disorder on his philosophical beliefs and protest strategies. In 1899 he appeared to have been more deeply affected by the passing of his firstborn and its accompanying marital estrangement than by Hose's execution; one delivered a tortured pain that haunted his personal life forever, and the other signaled the limitations of his public theories for race advancement without forcing immediate changes in them. Simply put, Hose's killing gave Du Bois philosophical pause but failed to alter his thinking and actions outwardly, even after having been coupled with and accentuated by Burghardt's demise. Du Bois seemed to identify with each as a victim, sharing the grief—and guilt—of his son's death publicly (in "Of the Passing of the First-Born") without resolving it completely.[114]

Eight years later, as an insecure race leader rather than a grieving father and ostracized husband, however, Du Bois staggered under the weight of a southern, racist reality that for him began with riot and, unlike either Burghardt's death or Hose's lynching, intensified with geometric progression over the lengthy period of personal reconstruction. His emotional turmoil carried the added burden of delayed grief for the loss of his son, whom he had never properly mourned and whose decease—because of the riot—lost its redemptive quality; the deaths of twenty-five black Atlantans and of his own leadership rendered his son's passing purposeless.[115] Du Bois stood mute in the place that had bled black so profusely and awaited his chance to counterattack that spring at the Niagara Conference in Boston, only to find himself shorn of his southern strategy and unsure of his northern leadership—the titular head of a divided, dying movement. Returning in the fall to Atlanta, the scene of all his misery, Du Bois sensed his own failure and isolation, even to the point of being kinless and suspicious of accommodationist companions around him: feelings that triggered shame and self-doubt.[116] He sought medical treatment, suggesting that the "psychological punishment of the place," experienced in 1899, after his son and Sam Hose had died, had become overwhelming following collective violence in 1906 and, especially, its unforgiving aftermath.[117]

Du Bois, of course, did not resign as executive secretary of the Niagara Movement but once again flagellated white society and himself. His jeremiad reappeared in "The Burden of Black Women" (November 1907), wherein he fulminated "Valiant spoilers of women/And conquerors of unarmed men/I hate them, Christ!/As I hate Hell."[118] He vented more than prophesied, for his failure in the face of the riot undid the personal success with which he atoned for his mother's status, his wife's health, and his son's death. Finally, he conceded the fallacy of Hegelian destiny in the face of irrational violence. Angrily he lamented black submissiveness and embraced black retaliation, which, given his impotence, required further self-mockery. Therefore, Du Bois restyled the theme of "The Song of the Smoke." In "Death" (December 1907), he portrayed the failed rescue of a submissive "maid" by a hero with a "bold black face." Sadly, when the "World and Warrior, Maid and Mist" eventually "met and kissed," the warrior died "wrapped in rue."[119] Thus, Du Bois belittled his own "nerveless acquiescence" before Atlanta accommodationists and, admittedly more symbolically, Boston upstarts—the same cowardice that he had advised black victims of an earlier riot in Springfield, Ohio, never to embrace.[120] Published in *Horizon*, his poetry seemed even more cathartic than his Horatian Odes. Both were therapeutic bromides, however unintended as such.

Du Bois's concern for his personal identity was in much the same vein. Within a week of his December letter of resignation from the Niagara Movement, he became preoccupied with the genealogy of his father's family.[121] His inquiries to relatives in the North were part of an ongoing search for self that dated from childhood, but his sense of worthlessness stemming from the riot and its aftermath, including the debacle in Boston, invested it with additional meaning and new urgency.[122]

Into 1908 Du Bois continued to struggle, as he would time and again, with his twin failures—North and South. He kept silent during that year's debate over black suffrage, having decided previously not to join prominent black leaders, including Niagarans Herndon and Towns, in a petition protesting Georgia's disfranchisement amendment. He excused himself by citing the negative effect his involvement would have had on northern funding for Atlanta University, without noting Towns's similar affiliation with the institution or earlier censure by its trustees for having sided with Trotter in his 1903 confrontation with Washington.[123] And he stood aside as efforts to desegregate Savannah along Niagaran principles fell before "the rising tide of racism," which chased many, like his former Lowndes County research assistant, Monroe N. Work, into the Tuskegee camp.[124]

Perhaps because of these setbacks, Du Bois reprised the Horace theme in a commencement speech to Fisk University students in June 1908. He spoke of Galileo Galilei as a revolutionary whose fate paralleled that of contemporary rebels: when faced with "open war" for having upended the theological heavens, Galileo "hesitated," then "explained," "conciliated," and "argued," and finally made one of the "most uncompromising denials of what he knew to be the truth ever recorded." Such Du Bois criticized as a "cowardly lie" that retarded civilization and unleashed bigotry, simply because a "broken man" dared not "die for the glory of a great cause and make it . . . more glorious."[125]

In this disjointed, passionate history of a fellow visionary, Du Bois seemed personal and self-condemning. He, too, had hesitated in the face of conflict, explained to friends, and conceded to—if not conciliated—enemies in the wake of riot. He, too, through paralysis and silence, had given credence to accommodationist falsehoods and set back the cause of racial progress. He, too, had endeavored unsuccessfully to dodge the issue and now whispered—as he purported Galileo had whispered—that his behavior, if not his spoken word, was a lie. Yet, in chastising Galileo for cowardice, Du Bois better understood his own moment of weakness: permitting him to search for personal atonement and self-respect.

Of more lasting significance, Du Bois experienced permanent transformation from organizational leader to race propagandist. During 1908 and 1909, he found rationalizing his faintheartedness difficult in the wake of riot, for his manhood demanded hands-on action.[126] Nor did he excuse himself through comparison with Frederick Douglass, who had refused—through "discretion" or "cowardice"—to join John Brown's suicidal assault on Harpers Ferry.[127] Instead, Du Bois sought the meaning of his own failure to act by writing a study of Brown's life (1909), which revealingly he considered one of his best writings while most critics judged it his worst.[128] Reflecting his own postriot changes, Du Bois recast Brown as a modern, tragic hero, who was too radical by Niagaran standards.[129] Specifically, he made the curse of slavery America's equivalent to the curse of the lionheaded sphinx of Greek mythology, demanding a solution to its riddle and eliminating every wrong respondent. Brown also served as counterpart to Sophocles' Oedipus, and his Harpers Ferry raid as decisive reply to Theban oppression. Thus Brown's military defeat, rebuff by Garrison, and federal execution appeared inevitable and tragic and so did his heroic choices, themselves limited by the urgency and uncertainty of answering the riddle aright. Suspending expediency and conventional morality, Brown answered in blood—correctly, argued Du Bois—paid in life and reputation. Thus history rebuffed a hero of bold and guiltless action.[130]

Surely the parallel for Du Bois was unmistakable, for he, too, had sought most of his life to solve the riddle of American racism. Having traveled to Atlanta, as had Oedipus to Thebes, he confronted the modern Sphinx and paid dearly: the loss of his son, his wife, and his friends, and the ridicule of his enemies. And for such great personal sacrifice, his solution to the riddle had been shortsighted; he had grumbled in the right key but in the wrong place and at the wrong time. John Brown alone had the wisdom to respond in kind to southern racism. But, together, Du Bois and Brown had both felt more righteous victim than exultant hero.

Actually, Du Bois acted more in accordance with Douglass's "pragmatic politics of survival" and, again in line with Douglass, resolved his own divided mind by practicing fantasy denial, much the way he glossed his family's genealogy.[131] Thus Du Bois conceded that blacks should "fight with . . . eyes upon [their] bread and butter," knowing that armed resistance invited deadly retaliation. He believed that black violence was preferable to cowardice only when protest failed.[132] However, where Douglass successfully invented a heroic self-identity by falling back on his real-life struggle against slavery, Du Bois could only do so by writing exercises of literary and historical vengeance.

Nonetheless, the question of his true self was resurrected as Du Bois slowly wrote himself back to mental health. During a three-year span following the riot, he completed his first novel *The Quest of the Silver Fleece* (1909), depicting a conversion in the character of Bles that corresponded to his own. Early on, Bles instructs the untutored Zora in the meaning of "purity," telling her that she—and anyone else—is guiltless for moral infractions as long as she is "as good as a woman knows how" to be. Bles reneges on his abstract philosophy, however, when he discovers Zora's impure past. In time his love is rekindled and they rejoin, but only after Bles transforms himself.[133] Similarly, Du Bois's commitment to race and family before the riot been academic and perfunctory. Indeed, he was too assured by textbook ethics. Though he regarded the race as underdeveloped and his mother as tainted for having borne a child out of wedlock and given him a bigamist's name from a "runaway marriage," he remained loyal to both.[134]

In the guise of this redemptive story, Du Bois unburdened his shame for having treated the real-life concerns of African Americans hypothetically. He came to this point because Atlanta's violence overwhelmed his own double consciousness, forcing him to seek self-forgiveness and personal regeneration. It disabused him of relying on his own racially mixed heritage as a sign from God to arbitrate race relations: uplifting his black brothers to the standards of white brothers. For the first time, he embraced his mother's blackness—instead of his father's whiteness—and forgave her cultural backwardness, while repenting his own failings; for reasons of psychological survival, he came to identify himself as largely African, part French, and a little Dutch, but "thank God! no 'Anglo-Saxon'."[135]

From 1906 through 1909, then, Du Bois undertook a dark journey. In fact, his mood change, his feelings of worthlessness, powerlessness, and hopelessness, and his incapacity for action surfaced in the first line of the "Litany" and, in varying degrees, continued to the last stanza of "Death."[136] He spewed his anger outward, mostly onto God and white devils, and revealed his guilt as a sinner and failed leader.[137] He found self-expression in poetry and prose—compensation for his paralysis in the public arena and his lost creativity in more serious writing. For this reason, he took four years to complete *John Brown* despite goading from impatient publishers; he copied pages of what others had previously written about Brown before penning the original, highly personalized penultimate chapter, which solved the riddle of the Sphinx and offered a prescription for mental health.[138] In writing about Galileo, Brown, and Bles, Du Bois controlled his rage, regained his emotional footing, and understood his plight in realistic terms. Ultimately, he found the key to that personal truth in his intellect, campus haven, and life-affirming personality. In other words, Du Bois survived a major depressive episode, first blinding himself to what he found too painful to witness—losses of black lives and personal leadership—and later facing the true meaning of the riot and its fallout as a "whole man" rather than one viewing abstract principles.[139]

Having slowly shed inner defenses, Du Bois finally accepted the riot's personal meaning. Perhaps the most painful revelations were that he was "no natural leader of men" and that his organization was incapable of speaking "some of the plainest English" for southern black men.[140] In Atlanta, as Du Bois himself discovered, blacks—contrary to Niagara boastings—had to "pussy-foot" and ignore their own rights or face annihilation—as had those in September of 1906.[141] Moreover, Du Bois found himself trapped in the city where the racial hatred and bloodshed that he "had never dreamed of" crowded and cowed him at every turn.[142] Elsewhere his Niagara agenda had been discredited, and, thereafter, he led a puny organization that tilted at racist windmills and itself collapsed within a handful of years under the weight of internal conflicts and pressures from Booker T. Washington.

Although the carnage of the Atlanta riot silenced Du Bois and his movement, the riot in Springfield, Illinois, two years later precipitated his departure from the South.[143] He moved to New York to accept the job of Director of Publications and Research of the NAACP, which had been founded in response to the Springfield violence. Du Bois had participated in establishing the new organization, which doubtless reinforced the therapy of writing prose and explained why the next year he leaped at the offer to become its Director of Publications. Indeed, he accepted the neo-abolitionist role without assurances of a salary, later—and unconvincingly—emphasizing that he left Atlanta solely because his "radical beliefs" were creating financial difficulty for the university.[144] In 1912 he tried, and failed, to convince Atlanta University officials to move the *Atlanta University*

Studies, which he had directed, to New York. This failure completed his exodus from Atlanta. Over the next decade, he occasionally returned to Atlanta as a speaker, investigator, visitor, and even as recipient of the NAACP's Spingarn Medal, which was awarded to him for accomplishments largely achieved elsewhere.[145]

More than simply abandoning the historically significant Niagara Movement and his own equally significant life in the South, Du Bois found personal liberation in the NAACP and new hope for his "freedom now" philosophy in New York City.[146] Instead of continued silence in Atlanta, he spoke in New York without curbing his tongue and, over the next decade, found himself again face-to-face with the issue of mob violence. Initially and stoically, he argued—as had Douglass fifty years earlier—that a caste system and its violence deformed white souls as certainly as they crushed black lives.[147] When Europeans marched to war in 1914, however, he seemed less convinced of progress toward racial equality, yet buoyed by the possible liberation of Africans and Asians—and black Americans.[148] Three years later as racial bloodletting again stained the home front—in Houston, East St. Louis, Memphis, and elsewhere—Du Bois reconsidered his pacifism and the uses of violence. He advocated the enlistment of blacks in the war effort and their resistance to mob rule (at least rhetorically).[149]

In the face of postwar carnage in the United States, particularly during the Red Summer of 1919, and the Allies' suppression of African and Indian autonomy, Du Bois sought an even more comprehensible account of racial violence.[150] He had attributed racism to ignorance and meanness and had looked for its remedy in social uplift, moral argument, scientific study, and public protest, disagreeing with Washingtonians only in emphasis and strategy. The emergence of Marxism in revolutionary Russia, however, promoted his revision: racism emanated from flawed economics and its remedy existed in militant socialism.[151] Du Bois, who until this moment in his life had considered violence the roadblock to black progress, now—in the aftermath of global war and social upheaval—gave intellectual currency to blood revolution as necessary for the destruction of racism in America.

Ultimately, Du Bois deemed Marxism unrealistic for an African American minority amidst a white majority unwilling to forsake racial advantages for class solidarity.[152] For a while he considered grafting Gandhi's non-violent soul force onto Marxist doctrine. He abandoned the idea because it failed in India and because it, like Hegelian transformation and southern strategy, required conscience-stricken oppressors. No doubt recalling his Atlanta experience, Du Bois reasoned that southern whites would sooner kill boycotting blacks than rethink their own immorality.[153] He tempered his expectations, taught patience, and looked for Marxian successes in the third world.

The problem of racial reform remained insoluble for Du Bois.[154] At last, he realized nature's double cross: correct theory—democratic or socialistic—had no application for an oppressed race most in need of truth. Such pained him, for he was nothing if not a pragmatist in search of justice and a progressive in search of order. More consistent than paradoxical, Du Bois endeavored to rally blacks in common cause (much like his hero, Otto von Bismarck, "had made a nation out of a mass of bickering peoples").[155] Indeed, his activity on behalf of the Niagara Movement and the NAACP represented the organizational factor in a modern state.[156] Significantly, his life-long crusade collided with society's most profound irrationality: white violence. More than any other dimension of racism, it upended Du Bois's most thoughtful plans and dogged his every ideological turn. Every lynching "scar[red]" his soul, and none was more searing than that of Sam Hose; every riot laid heavily on his mind, and none was more pressing than Atlanta in 1906.[157]

Endeavoring to solve the riddle of the Sphinx, Du Bois had evolved from social scientist to neo-abolitionist before becoming the race's most effective propagandist. In the face of bloodshed, he stood naked, stripped of his honor in that city and of his leadership in northern centers. Thereafter, he struggled to keep personal and protest spirit alive and, finally in 1910, succeeded in healing, if not curing, himself and enhancing the NAACP drive toward Niagaran principles. In the process, he exposed much of himself in prose and poetry. But, despite Du Bois's jeremiads (and his later editorials exhorting violence in pursuit of black self-defense and liberation), he seemed unconvincing; his humanity and intelligence wretched at the message of Hose's lynching and Atlanta's riot that required one human being to deprive another of "identity and community."[158] For all the wrongs done African Americans, Du Bois could never accept such barbarism, much less a more modern concept of liberation by violence. His attraction to Marxism aside, Du Bois's human spirit always rose to smother the intellectual call to arms regardless of its theoretical appeal or socio-psychological underpinnings.[159]

Tragically, Du Bois, who taught African Americans about "double consciousness" and whose "dogged strength alone" kept him "from being torn asunder" in Atlanta, could not make it possible "for a man to be both a Negro and an American, without being cursed and spit upon. . . ." He personally attained "self-conscious manhood," but not by merging "his double self into a better and truer self" in the United States. Renouncing his citizenship and reaffirming his blackness, he became a Ghanaian and, in 1963, died some distance from, but still very much behind, the veil of racism—doubtless haunted by Hose and the "scream and shots" of the Atlanta riot.[160]

Notes

1. The violence of the Atlanta period does not figure prominently in Francis L. Broderick, *W. E. B. Du Bois: Negro Leader in a Time of Crisis* (Stanford, 1959); Elliott M. Rudwick, *W. E. B. Du Bois: Propagandist of the Negro Protest* (New York, 1968); August Meier, *Negro Thought in America, 1880–1915: Racial Ideology in the Age of Booker T. Washington* (Ann Arbor 1963); or Manning Marable, *W. E. B. Du Bois: Black Radical Democrat* (Boston, 1986). Du Bois's turn from scientific idealist to activist is acknowledged in Thomas C. Holt, "The Political Uses of Alienation: W. E. B. Du Bois on Politics, Race, and Culture, 1903–1940," *American Quarterly* XLII (June 1990), 301–23; and Cornel West, *The American Evasion of Philosophy: A Genealogy of Pragmatism* (Madison, 1989), 138–50, but these authors do not attribute Du Bois's transformation to violence specifically. William M. Tuttle Jr., ed., *W. E. B. Du Bois* (Englewood Cliffs, N. J., 1973), 10, discusses the Hose lynching but does not link it to the Atlanta riot or to the evolution of Du Bois's radicalism. David Levering Lewis, *W. E. B. Du Bois: Biography of a Race, 1868–1919* (New York, 1993), 226, 228, 333–37, 363–64, and 408, builds on Tuttle, stressing collective violence, in particular Hose's killing, as an explanation for Du Bois's transformation in Atlanta. Lewis's richly detailed descriptions of Du Bois's reactions and of his exposé of white southern pretensions, however, fail to indicate that the riot also upended Du Bois's southern strategy, Niagara Movement, and image as race leader, leaving him isolated personally and politically throughout the remainder of the decade.

2. W. E. B. Du Bois, *The Autobiography of W. E. B. Du Bois: A Soliloquy on Viewing My Life from the Last Decade of Its First Century* (New York, 1968), 213.

3. W. E. B. Du Bois, "Program for the celebration of my twenty-fifth birthday," in *The Papers of W. E. B. Du Bois* (microfilm ed.; Amherst, Mass., 1981), Reel 87, frames 468–73 (hereinafter cited as *Du Bois Papers* with the appropriate reel and frame numbers).

4. See W. E. B. Du Bois, *Darkwater: Voices From Within the Veil* (rpt; Millwood, N.Y., 1975), section entitled "Damnation of Women," 185 (first quotation) and 163; W. E. B. Du Bois, *The Souls of Black Folk: Essays and Sketches* (New York, 1989), 4, 57 (second quotation); and Lewis, *W. E. B. Du Bois,* 72, though Du Bois's racial self-discovery was more than "polemical contrivance," as claimed by Rayford Logan.

5. W. E. B. Du Bois, "The Conservation of Races," in Nathan Huggins, ed., *W. E. B. Du Bois: Writings* (New York, 1986), 815–26; and Alfred A. Moss Jr., *The American Negro Academy: Voice of the Talented Tenth* (Baton Rouge, 1981), 48–50.

6. Du Bois, "Conservation of Races," 816–18; Joel Williamson, "W. E. B. Du Bois as a Hegelian," in David G. Sansing, ed., *What Was Freedom's Price?* (Jackson, Miss., 1978), 32–42; Georg Wilhelm Fredrich Hegel, *The Philosophy of History,* translated by J. Sibree (New York, 1956), 30 (first quoted phrase);

Du Bois, Souls, 3–12; and W. E. B. Du Bois, "The Talented Tenth," in Booker T. Washington, *et al., The Negro Problem* (rpt.; Miami, 1969), 46 ("yeast"). According to Hegel, groups contributed to humanity through their specific, complementary gifts. Du Bois believed that, in America, the same held true for races. Thus, out of the clash of white society's advanced culture (thesis) with black society's soulful spirit (antithesis) would come impractical harmony (synthesis). He considered himself a historical man necessary for the promotion of African American self-realization, without which his people could never arrive at, much less contribute to, the Hegelian vision of world progress. See Hegel, *Philosophy of History,* 29–32.

7. Du Bois, *Souls*, 5; Houston A. Baker, Jr., *Long Black Song: Essays in Black American Literature and Culture* (Charlottesville, 1972), 98; and W. E. B. Du Bois, "Jefferson Davis as a Representative of Civilization," in Herbert Aptheker, ed., *Against Racism: Unpublished Essays, Papers, Addresses, 1887–1961* (Amherst, Mass., 1985), 14–16. Here we combine Joel Williamson's Hegelian interpretation with Du Bois's mulatto heritage to explain the advantage of second sight.

8. Everett V. Stonequist, *The Marginal Man: A Study in Personality and Culture Conflict* (rpt.; New York, 1961), 145 (first quotation); Du Bois, *Souls*, 5 (second and fifth quotations) and 6 (fourth quotation); Melville J. Herskovits, *The Myth of the Negro Past* (Boston, 1958), 190 (third quotation); and Charles Joyner, *Down by the Riverside: A South Carolina Slave Community* (Urbana and Chicago, 1984), 146.

9. *Du Bois Papers,* Reel 87, frame 472.

10. Joel Williamson, *New People: Miscegenation and Mulattoes in the United States* (New York, 1980), 61–62 (p. 61 for quoted phrase), discusses the changeover, which occurred between 1850 and 1915, and W. E. B. Du Bois, ed., "The Health and Physique of the Negro American," *Atlanta University Publications,* No. 11 (1906), 36 (which appears in Volume II of a two-volume set of *Atlanta University Publications,* reprinted in New York in 1968).

11. Edward Byron Reuter, *The Mulatto in the United States . . .* (rpt.; New York, 1969) 186 and 196 (Du Bois named only two blacks to the twenty-one members of The Talented Tenth.); and Lewis, *W. E. B. Du Bois,* 62.

12. Du Bois, *Souls*, 5.

13. Ray Stannard Baker, "A Colloquy on the Negro Problem," in *The Papers of Ray Stannard Baker* (microfilm ed., Washington D.C., 1982), Reel 47, frame 54; W. E. B. Du Bois, "The Study of the Negro Problems," *Annals of the American Academy of Political and Social Science,* XI (January 1898), 16; and the Reminiscences of W. E. B. Du Bois (1960), p. 146, in the Oral History Collection of Columbia University (hereinafter cited as Du Bois, OHC).

14. Du Bois, OHC, 138, 163, 167–68; and Richard R. Wright, *87 Years Behind the Black Curtain: An Autobiography* (Philadelphia, 1965), 29.

15. National Association for the Advancement of Colored People, *Thirty Years of Lynching in the United States: 1889–1918* (rpt.; New York, 1969), 56–58; and Lewis, *W. E. B. Du Bois,* 226–28.

16. Atlanta *Constitution* (hereinafter *Constitution*), April 13, 1899, p. 3, and April 14, 1899, p. 1; and Mary Louise Ellis, "'Rain Down Fire': The Lynching of Sam Hose" (Ph.D. dissertation, Florida State University, 1992), for the fullest account of Hose's execution.

17. *Constitution,* April 14, 1899, p. 2, and April 15, 1899, pp. 1–2.

18. *Ibid.,* April 14, 1899, p. 1, April 15, 1899, p. 2, April 16, 1899, p. 16, April 19, 1899, p. 4, April 21, 1899, p. 6, and April 23, 1899, p. 5. Louis R. Harlan, in *Booker T. Washington: The Making of a Black Leader, 1856–1901* (New York and Oxford, 1972), 262–64, discusses Washington's belated response, which was brought about by pressure from the more assertive Afro-American Council, and quips that "Washington stood firmly on both sides of the question" (p. 263).

19. Du Bois, *Autobiography*, 222; Du Bois to Albert Bushnell Hart, n. d., *Du Bois Papers,* Reel 2, frame 52; and W. E. B. Du Bois, "The Negro and Crime," *Independent,* LI (May 18, 1899), 1355–57.

20. Du Bois, *Autobiography*, 222.

21. W. E. B. Du Bois, "My Evolving Program for Negro Freedom," in Rayford W. Logan, ed., *What the Negro Wants* (Chapel Hill, 1944), 53 (quotation); and Paul Gilroy, *The Black Atlantic: Modernity and Double Consciousness* (New York, 1993), 118, and 240*n*12.

22. *Constitution*, April 29, 1899, p. 6; Du Bois, *Autobiography*, 286; W. E. B. Du Bois, *Dusk of Dawn* (rpt.; Millwood, N.Y., 1975), 67 (quoted word); and Du Bois, "My Evolving Program for Negro Freedom," 53. See Herbert C. Kelman, "Violence Without Moral Restraint: Reflections on the Dehumanization of Victims and Victimizers," in George M. Kren and Leon H. Rappoport, eds., *Varieties of Psychohistory* (New York, 1976), 282–314, for the theory that conditions weaken moral restraints in individuals and foster their participation in the level of violence that wrought Hose's complete annihilation.

23. *Constitution*, April 24, 1899, p. 1 (quotation); and W. Fitzhugh Brundage, *Lynching in the New South: Georgia and Virginia, 1880–1930* (Urbana and Chicago, 1993), 204.

24. "Georgia Negroes on the Hardwick Bill, 1899," in Herbert Aptheker, ed., *A Documentary History of the Negro People in the United States* (New York, 1951), 784–86; W. E. B. Du Bois, "The Suffrage Fight in Georgia," *Independent*, LI (November 30, 1899), 3226–28; and Lewis, *W. E. B. Du Bois*, 231–32.

25. Birmingham *Age-Herald*, April 26, 1899, p. 2; W. E. B. Du Bois, "The Relation of the Negroes to the Whites in the South," *Annals of the American Academy of Political and Social Science*, XVIII (July 1901.), 140.

26. Du Bois, OHC, 148; and Brundage, *Lynching in New South*, 82–85. Perhaps Du Bois later learned the truth about Hose from an investigation underwritten by Mary Church Terrell of the National Association of Colored Women, which was reported in Terrell, "Lynching from a Negro's Point of View," *North American Review*, CLXXVIII (June 1904), 859–60. The killing was caused by an argument over Hose's time off.

27. Lewis, *W. E. B. Du Bois*, 227 (first quotation) and 228–29; W. E. B. Du Bois, "Two Negro Conventions," *Independent*, LI (September 7, 1899), 24–25 (second quotation); Du Bois, *Souls*, 175 (third quotation); and Roderick J. Watts, "Racial Identity and Preferences for Social Change Strategies among African Americans," *Journal of Black Psychology*, XVIII (Spring 1992), 1–18.

28. Stephen R. Fox, *The Guardian of Boston: William Monroe Trotter* (New York, 1970). 58–64; and Du Bois, *Souls*, 36–50.

29. Lewis, *W. E. B. Du Bois*, 304–11; Harlan, *Booker T. Washington: The Wizard of Tuskegee, 1901–1915* (New York and Oxford, 1983), Chap. 3; Rudwick, *W. E. B. Du Bois*, 77–93; and W. E. B. Du Bois, "Committee of Twelve," [February 20], 1904, in *Du Bois Papers*, Reel 1, frame 655 (quotations). In this instance, Booker T. Washington's effort revealed him to be more an accomodationist than a constructionalist, a statesman transcending personal concerns to build the black community. Maceo Crenshaw Dailey, Jr., "Neither 'Uncle Tom' Nor 'Accomodationist': Booker T. Washington, Emmett Jay Scott, and Constructionalism," *Atlanta History*, XXXVIII (Winter 1995), 27–28.

30. Emmett Jay Scott to Washington, July 18, 1905, in Louis R. Harlan *et al.*, eds., *The Booker T. Washington Papers* (14 vols.; Urbana, Chicago, and London, 1972–1989), VIII, 329–30.

31. W. E. B. Du Bois, "Harvard and the South," in *Du Bois Papers*, Reel 87, frames 245–61 (first two quotations on frames 255 and 260); Lewis, *W. E. B. Du Bois*, 195–97; Du Bois, ed., "Health and Physique of the Negro American," 1–112; and Williamson, *New People*, 113–14 (last two quotations).

32. Booker T. Washington, "Up From Slavery," (1901), in Harlan *et al.*, eds., *Booker T. Washington Papers*, I, 331. See Evelyn Brooks Higginbotham, *Righteous Discontent: The Women's Movement in the Black Baptist Church, 1880–1920* (Cambridge, Mass. 1993), 8–81, for a discussion of segregation.

33. Lewis, *W. E. B. Du Bois*, 312–13, for the symbolism of Burghardt's death and, by inference, Hose's death; and W. E. B. Du Bois, "Credo," *Independent*, LVII (October 6, 1904), 787.

34. Du Bois, OHC, 147.

35. W. E. B. Du Bois, "The Niagara Movement," *Voice of the Negro*, II (September 1905), 619–22.

36. W. E. B. Du Bois, "Niagara Address of 1906," in Aptheker, ed., *Documentary History,* 907–10.

37. Du Bois, "Committee of Twelve," frame 655 (quotation); "Niagara Movement [Call]," n.d. [1905], *Du Bois Papers,* Reel 2, frame 839; and "N.M. [Niagara Movement] First Annual Meeting," n.d. [1905], *ibid.,* frame 847.

38. Du Bois, OHC, 148 (quotation); and William J. White to Du Bois, January 9, 1906, *Du Bois Papers,* Reel 1, frame 10 13.

39. Du Bois to State Secretaries, October 7, 1905, *Du Bois Papers,* Reel 2, frame 855.

40. Du Bois, "Growth of the Niagara Movement," *Voice of the Negro,* III (January 1906), 44.

41. B. J. Davis, "The Niagara or Headless Movement Has Accomplished Two Things," Atlanta *Independent,* December 2, 1905, p. 4; Penelope L. Bullock, "Profile of a Periodical," *Atlanta Historical Bulletin,* XXI (Spring 1977), 96, for Bryant; Gregory L. Mixon, "The Atlanta Riot of 1906" (Ph.D. dissertation, University of Cincinnati, 1989), II, 393–95, for Proctor; and John Dittmer, *Black Georgia in the Progressive Era, 1900–1920* (Urbana, Chicago, and London, 1977), 91–92, for Rucker.

42. White to Du Bois, January 9, 1906.

43. "Address of the First Meeting of the Georgia Equal Rights Convention," February 14, 1906, *Du Bois Papers,* Reel 1, frames 1021–23.

44. Du Bois to Dear Colleagues, February 26, 1906, *Du Bois Papers,* Reel 2, frame 863. See Lewis, *W. E. B. Du Bois,* 327, for Du Bois's authorship of the address.

45. Du Bois to Dear Colleagues, February 26, 1906, frame 863.

46. William J. White to Du Bois, March 2, 1906, *Du Bois Papers,* Reel 1, frame 1014.

47. See Du Bois to Colleagues, June 13, 1906, *Du Bois Papers,* Reel 2, frame 864, for summary of Niagara Movement activities during its first year of operation.

48. Editorial, *Moon Illustrated Weekly,* I (March 17, 1906), 12; J. Max Barber, "The Niagara Movement at Harpers Ferry," *Voice of the Negro,* III (October 1906), 402–11; Ridgely Torrence, *The Story of John Hope* (New York, 1948), 150–51; and Lewis, *W. E. B. Du Bois,* 329.

49. Du Bois, "Niagara Address of 1906," p. 909.

50. "Secretaries of the Niagara Movement," Secretaries and Committees of the Niagara Movement," and "Treasurer's Report, 1906," *Du Bois Papers,* Reel 2, frames 892, 896, 882–84. Fully one-third of all states boasting Niagara Movement chapters were located in the South, evidence anew of Du Bois's southern strategy.

51. Lewis, *W. E. B. Du Bois,* 334–35 and 337, Walter White, *A Man Called White* (New York, 1948), 6–7; and Charles Crowe, "Racial Violence and Social Reform—Origins of the Atlanta Riot of 1906," *Journal of Negro History,* LIII (July 1968), 236–48.

52. J. Max Barber, "The Atlanta Tragedy," *Voice of the Negro,* III (November 1906), 478. For a discussion of the attitude of southern whites toward interracial rape see W. J. Cash, *The Mind of the South* (New York, 1941), 116–20.

53. Mary White Ovington to Du Bois September 20, 1906, *Du Bois Papers,* Reel 2, frame 1100.

54. Mary White Ovington, *The Walls Came Tumbling Down* (rpt.; New York, 1969), 65.

55. *Constitution,* September 23, 1906, pp. 1–4, September 24, 1906, pp. 1–4, September 25, 1906, p. 1, and September 26, 1906, pp. 1–2; Charles Crowe, "Racial Massacre in Atlanta September 22, 1906," *Journal of Negro History,* LIV (April 1969), 150–73; Dittmer, *Black Georgia in the Progressive Era,* 125; and Joel Williamson, *The Crucible of Race: Black-White Relations in the American South Since Emancipation* (New York and Oxford, 1984), 215–23 for information in this and the next five paragraphs unless cited otherwise.

56. W. E. B. Du Bois, "Looking Seventy-five Years Backward," *Phylon,* III (2d Quarter, 1942), 245. For a discussion of Henry Grady and the failure of his "Atlanta Spirit" see Don H. Doyle, *New Men, New Cities, New South: Atlanta, Nashville, Charleston, Mobile, 1860–1910* (Chapel Hill and London, 1990), 157–58, 261–66, and 313–18.

57. W. E. B. Du Bois, "Litany at Atlanta," *Independent*, LXI (October 11, 1906), 857 (first quotation) and 858 (second quotation); Arnold Rampersad, *The Art and Imagination of W. E. B. Du Bois* (Cambridge, Mass., and London, 1976), 105; and Du Bois, *Autobiography*, 286.

58. The three hundred residents of Brownsville appeared to have been placed under military arrest and marched through the streets of Atlanta, in part to dissuade other blacks from taking up arms. Many returned to their neighborhood, confined to their homes. Ultimately, sixty individuals were indicted for the policeman's murder. New York *Times*, September 26, 1906, p. 5; and *Constitution*, October 6, 1906, p. 1A.

59. Brundage, *Lynching in the New South*, 212–15; Booker T. Washington, "Extracts from an Address in Atlanta, Georgia," December 9, 1906, in Harlan *et al.*, eds., *Booker T. Washington Papers*, IX, 158–61; Booker T. Washington, "The Golden Rule in Atlanta," *Outlook*, LXXXIV (December 15, 1906), 913–16; Editorial, Atlanta *Independent*, November 24, 1906, p. 4, and December 15, 1906, p. 6; and Ray Stannard Baker, *Following the Color Line: An Account of American Negro Citizenship in the American Democracy* (New York, 1908), 20–23.

60. Baker, *Following the Color Line,* 24.

61. Henry H. Proctor, "The Atlanta Riot: Fundamental Causes of Reactionary Results," *Southern Workman*, XXXVI (August 1907), 425–26.

62. *Constitution*, September 26, 1906, pp. 1 and 2 (Penn quotation); Editorial, Atlanta *Independent*, October 6, 1906, p. 4; and Henry H. Proctor, "An Explanation of Race Riots," *Southern Workman*, XXXV (November 1906), 580–81. For a discussion of class consciousness among turn-of-the-century blacks see Edward L. Ayers, *The Promise of the New South: Life After Reconstruction* (New York and Oxford, 1992), 158.

63. Washington to Lyman Abbott, September 2, 1906 (first quotation), Washington to Richard Carroll, September 5, 1906 (second, third, and fourth quotations), Washington to Oswald Garrison Villard, September 6, 1906, and Washington to the Editor of the New York *World*, September 25, 1906, all four in Harlan *et al.*, eds., *Booker T. Washington Papers,* IX, on pages 67, 69, 69–70, and 74–75, respectively.

64. H. Leon Prather, Sr., *We Have Taken a City* (Rutherford, N.J., and other cities, 1984), 185; and T. Thomas Fortune to Washington, November 30, 1898, in Harlan *et al.*, eds., *Booker T. Washington Papers,* IV, 524*n*1 (quotation).

65. Harlan, *Booker T. Washington: The Wizard of Tuskegee,* 299–300.

66. Booker T. Washington, "Extracts from an Address Before the Afro-American Council," October 11, 1906, in Harlan *et al.*, eds., *Booker T. Washington Papers,* IX, 95.

67. Harlan, *Booker T. Washington: The Wizard of Tuskegee,* 301; and Washington, "Extracts from an Address in Atlanta," December 9, 1906, p. 161.

68. See Washington, "Golden Rule in Atlanta."

69. Washington, "Up From Slavery," 333.

70. *Ibid.,* 334 (first quotation); and Booker T. Washington, "The Story of My Life," (1900), in Harlan *et al.*, eds., *Booker T. Washington Papers,* I, 150 (second quotation). See Harlan, *Booker T. Washington: The Making of a Black Leader,* 263, for the context of the lynching statement.

71. Crowe, "Racial Massacre in Atlanta, September 26, 1906," p. 168.

72. J. Max Barber, "Why Mr. Barber Left Atlanta," *Voice of the Negro,* III (November 1906), 470.

73. *Constitution*, September 26, 1906, p. 1; and Glenn Weddington Rainey, "The Race Riot of 1906 in Atlanta" (M.A. thesis, Emory University, 1929), Chap. 5, p. 2, for the newspaper associations of Cohen, Hopkins, and English.

74. *Constitution*, September 26, 1906, pp. 1 and 2.

75. Mixon, "Atlanta Riot of 1906," II, 761–71, for the riot thesis. See Roberta Senechal, *The Sociogenesis of a Race Riot: Springfield Illinois, in 1908* (Urbana, 1990), 194–99, for the significance of white class divisions in a northern riot.

76. White to Du Bois, March 2, 1906.

77. "Address of the First Meeting of the Georgia Equal Rights Convention," frame 1023.

78. Washington, "Up from Slavery," 334 (first quotation); Mixon, "Atlanta Riot of 1906," I, 334–40, *ibid.*, 359 (second quotation). For a discussion of the influence of the Wilmington riot on the Georgia gubernatorial campaign see *ibid.*, 371–73. Hoke Smith won a landslide primary victory over Clark Howell and three minor candidates. Howell raised the race issue by attacking Smith's plan for complete disfranchisement of blacks. The race issue greatly polarized the entire and contributed to the racial tension that exploded into riot.

79. David F. Godshalk, "In the Wake of Riot: Atlanta's Struggle for Order, 1899–1919" (Ph.D. dissertation, Yale University, 1992), 396; and Torrence, *Story of John Hope*, 153. John Hope's wife, Lugenia, recalled that rioters had threatened to burn all of Atlanta's West End black colleges, including Atlanta University. "Gangsters" camped outside Atlanta Baptist College's gates and charged nearby Spelman College. Du Bois's fear for his family is understandable in the face of the violence and threats of violence. For protection black residents smuggled munitions into the neighborhood in coffins, stationed armed defenders "prepared to die protecting," and patrolled area campuses. Jacqueline Anne Rouse, *Lugenia Burns Hope: Black Southern Reformer* (Athens and London, 1989), 43–44.

80. Du Bois, "Looking Seventy-five Years Backward," 245; and Torrence, *Story of John Hope*, 154. Like other heads of households, Du Bois stood armed guard over his residence during the riot. The gunfire Du Bois recalled might have been Tuesday's assault on Brownsville some three miles away; no shooting occurred in Du Bois's neighborhood during the riot, and the center city stood quiet after Sunday when "Darktowners" rebuffed rioters. Du Bois, *Autobiography*, 286.

81. "Backsliders—New Names," *Horizon*, II (July 1907), 23 (first quotation); Godshalk, "In the Wake of Riot," 399, for Bowen's courage during the riot; Editorial, "Has Dr. J. W. E. Bowen Gone Crazy?" *Horizon*, I (February 1907), 16 (second quotation); Washington to John Wesley Edward Bowen, September 26, 1906, in Harlan *et al.*, eds., *Booker T. Washington Papers*, IX, 79 (third quotation).

82. New York *World*, September 30, 1906, p. 1E.

83. Editorial, "Rev. J. W. E. Bowen, Again," *Horizon*, I (April 1907), 18. In January 1907 Bowen told the Mississippi Conference of the Methodist Episcopal Church that blacks could win their freedom only if whites evaluated them as honest people: "If the white people living in the south by your side for all these years think you are a bad people, you are bad." *Ibid.* See Godshalk, "In the Wake of Riot," 394–98, for a more positive interpretation of Bowen's post-riot activity—his "strategy of silence" (p. 398).

84. New York *World*, September 24, 1906, p. 2; and J. Max Barber, "Why Mr. Barber Left Atlanta," *Voice of the Negro*, III (November 1906), 470–72.

85. Washington to the Editor of the New York *Age*, October 1, 1906, in Harlan, *et al.*, eds., *Booker T. Washington Papers*, IX, 82. Most duplicitous, Washington circulated this rumor on the day that he told Oswald Garrison Villard how unsafe it was to send him wires regarding Atlanta because Barber himself "had gotten into serious trouble through a telegram sent to New York." Washington to Oswald Garrison Villard, October 1, 1906, *ibid.*, 81.

86. Godshalk, "In the Wake of Riot," 391–94; and Mixon, "Atlanta Riot of 1906," II, 761–71.

87. W. E. B. Du Bois, "The Tragedy of Atlanta," *World Today*, XI (November 1906), 1173–75; Du Bois, "Two Negro Conventions," 24–25; and W. E. B. Du Bois, "The Negroes of Wilmington, North Carolina," c. 1899, *Du Bois Papers*, Reel 82, frame 1260. See W. E. B. Du Bois, *The Black North in 1901* (New York, 1969), 44, for a one-sentence reference to the Wilmington riot's spurring black migration to Philadelphia. See Prather, *We Have Taken a City*, 158, for an overstatement of Du Bois's protest of the Wilmington riot.

88. Du Bois to Charles P. Neill, U. S. Commissioner of Labor, October 1, 1906, in *Du Bois Papers*, Reel 3, frame 406.

89. Washington rumored that Du Bois spent the four days of rioting "hiding at [Lowndes County's] Calhoun School." T. Thomas Fortune, editor of the New York *Age,* renewed in late 1910 the charge that Du Bois had run from the riot, causing a defensive Du Bois, newly arrived to New York City, to respond in the pages of the New York *Amsterdam News.* Robert E. Park, another Tuskegeean sympathizer, recorded in his diary a similar account, claiming that during the riot Du Bois "hid in a country farmhouse." The basis of fact in these accounts is that as late as Monday, September 24, Du Bois was in rural Lowndes County doing fieldwork. However, it is plausible that after having learned of the riot, most likely from the Montgomery Sunday paper, he "rushed back" to Atlanta, wrote "Litany" on the way, and arrived during the riot's waning hours, very late Monday night or possibly Tuesday morning. Washington to T. Thomas Fortune, January 20, 1911, in Harlan *et al.,* eds., *Booker T. Washington Papers,* X, 555 (first quotation in footnote and 556*n*1 (Fortune remarks); Winifred Raushenbush, *Robert E. Park: Biography of a Sociologist* (Durham, N.C., 1979), 47 Du Bois to Charles P. Neill, U. S. Commissioner of Labor, September 24, 1906, *Du Bois Papers,* Reel 3, frames 402–4; and Du Bois, *Autobiography,* 286.

90. Atlanta *Independent*, November 17, 1906, p. 4.

91. Baker, "Colloquy on the Negro Problem," 27–32.

92. R. D. Stinson to Du Bois, December 12, 1906, and Du Bois to Stinson, January 4, 1907, *Du Bois Papers,* Reel 1, frames 471–73.

93. Dorothy Cowser Yancy, "William Edward Burghardt Du Bois' Atlanta Years: The Human Side—A Study Based Upon Oral Sources," *Journal of Negro History*, LXIII (January 1978), 63 (quotation); and Willard B. Gatewood, *Aristocrats of Color: The Black Elite*, 1880–1920 (Bloomington, 1990), 310.

94. Harlan, *Booker T. Washington: The Wizard of Tuskegee,* 303.

95. Du Bois, *Souls*, 172; and the authors' interview with Dr. Clifford I. Whipple, professor emeritus of psychology at Southwest Missouri State University and a licensed clinical psychologist, Springfield, Missouri, April 5, 1994 (recording in authors' possession).

96. Baker, "Colloquy on the Negro Problem," 27–28, 30–32, 36–37, and 54, for information in this and the next paragraph unless cited otherwise.

97. Du Bois to R. D. Stinson, January 4, 1907 (first quotation), and Yancy, "Du Bois' Atlanta Years," 63 (second quotation). Mob violence caused Atlanta Niagarans to recast "manful" protest as silent stoicism that protected both pride and person. Thus, like Du Bois, John Hope refrained from speaking on issues that supported the "enemy" or falsified Niagaran doctrine. Nearly a decade later, George Towns's warning to Atlanta University students not to discuss the Leo Frank lynching epitomized the riot's long-term impact on Du Bois's supporters and his strategy the South. Godshalk, "In the Wake of Riot," 400–401.

98. Baker, "Colloquy on the Negro Problem," 11.

99. Perhaps, too, he knew that his close friend, the northern progressive Mary White Ovington, had recommended him to Baker and, like her, he wanted the black radical perspective to be told. Du Bois also endeavored to influence Baker afterward, sending him the names of others whom he might interview. So did Washington, who wanted the riot's causes exposed and his post-riot philosophy praised; shrewder than Du Bois, he also dined with Baker and read the draft of his first article on the riot. *Ibid.,* 35; and William M. Tuttle Jr., [ed.], "W. E. B. Du Bois' Confrontation with White Liberalism During the Progressive Era: A *Phylon* Document," *Phylon*, XXXV (September 1974), 241–58. See Harlan *et al.,* eds., *Booker T. Washington Papers,* IX, 134, 208, and 272, for the Washington-Baker correspondence.

100. August Meier and Elliott Rudwick, "The Boycott Movement Against Jim Crow Streetcars in the South, 1900–1906," *Journal of American History,* LV (March 1969), 774; and Du Bois, "Niagara Address of 1906," p. 907 (quotation).

101. Du Bois to Kelly Miller, February 25, 1903, in Herbert Aptheker, ed., *The Correspondence of W. E. B. Du Bois* (2 vols.; Amherst, Mass., 1973–76), I, 53; and Meier and Rudwick, "Boycott Movement Against Jim Crow Streetcars," 773.

102. Du Bois to William J. White, January 24, 1907, *Du Bois Papers*, Reel 1, frame 1025 (first quotation); "Our Monthly Review," *Voice of the Negro*, III (March 1906), 165 (second and third quotations); and "Remarks of Rev. Waldron of Florida," August 27, 1907, *Du Bois Papers*, Reel 2, frame 912.

103. "Congo," *Horizon*, I (January 1907), 6; and David Howard-Pitney, "The Enduring Black Jeremiad: The American Jeremiad and Black Protest Rhetoric, from Frederick Douglass to W. E. B. Du Bois, 1841–1919," *American Quarterly*, XXXVIII (No. 3, 1986), 487–49.

104. W. E. B. Du Bois, "The Song of the Smoke," *Horizon*, I (February 1907), 4–6; Du Bois, *Souls*, 166 (last three quotations); and St. Clair Drake, *The Redemption of Africa and Black Religion* (Chicago, 1970), 12–13.

105. W. E. B. Du Bois, "The Value of Agitation," *Voice*, IV (March 1907), 110.

106. Mary White Ovington to Du Bois, April 13, 1907, in Aptheker, ed., *Correspondence of W. E. B. Du Bois*, I, 132.

107. "Nulla Dies," *Horizon*, I (May 1907) 10. The poem Was originally titled "Ad Flaccum," meaning "To Horace," *Du Bois Papers*, Reel 88, frame 1523. Herbert Aptheker claimed wrongly that the poem's first verse quotes Horace; it is Du Bois's own composition. Aptheker, *Annotated Bibliography of the Published Writings of W. E. B. Du Bois* (Millwood, N.Y., 1973), 112.

108. Horace, "O saepe mecum," *Odes* ii, 7, in *Horace: The Complete Odes and Epodes with the Centennial Hymn*, translated by W. G. Shepherd (Penguin Classics, New York, 1983), 111:

> Oh my friend and oldest comrade . . .
> With you I knew
> the rout at Philippi and my shield,
> to my shame, left behind
> where manhood failed and words
> were eaten.

109. "Nulla Dies," 10.

110. Elliott Rudwick, "The Niagara Movement," in August Meier and Elliott Rudwick, eds., *The Making of Black America: Essays in Negro Life and History*. Volume II: *The Black Community in Modern America* (New York, 1969), 140–44 (quotation on p. 144); and Lewis, *W. E. B. Du Bois*, 376.

111. Springfield (Mass.) *Daily Republican*, August 29, 1907, p. 6.

112. Rudwick, "Niagara Movement," 141–47 (first quotation on p. 142); and Dittmer, *Black Georgia in the Progressive Era*, 174 (second quotation).

113. S. C. Fuller to Du Bois, September 25, 1907, *Du Bois Papers*, Reel 1, frame 995.

114. Lewis, *W. E. B. Du Bois*, 226–29; Whipple interview, April 5, 1994; Alberta B. Szalita, "Grief and Bereavement," in Silvano Arieti, ed., *American Handbook of Psychiatry*. Volume I (New York, 1974), 674; Reuben Fine, *The History of Psychoanalysis* (New York, 1990), 433, for Melanie Klein's theory that artistic creativity such as the essay in *Souls* serves as "reparation" for guilt over the loss of a loved one.

115. Lewis, *W. E. B. Du Bois*, 31, for the redemption parallel that allowed Du Bois's success to compensate for his mother's sacrifice.

116. Bertram Wyatt-Brown, "The Mask of Obedience: Male Slave Psychology in the Old South," *American Historical Review*, XCIII (December 1988), 1233, 1235, and 1246–47, for the theory of shame and self-doubt in another period of African American history that is insightful in analyzing Du Bois's post-riot mood; Baker, "Colloquy on the Negro Problem," 16. In all likelihood, Du Bois's marriage suffered even greater strain as the riot resurrected the ills of Atlanta that Nina blamed for Burghardt's death. By mid-January she was seeing a physician three times a week and spent mid-February to mid-April, with Yolande, at the Arlington Health Resort in Massachusetts. Perhaps Du Bois sent them away because he felt incapable of caring for them given his own stress. In any case, their estrangement and time apart in the critical year after the riot created long periods of his having been without kin. Arthur H. Ring to Du Bois, February 1, 1907, *Du Bois Papers*, Reel 2, frame 1281; and Mary White Ovington to Du Bois, April 13, 1907, *ibid.*, frame 132.

117. Lewis, *W. E. B. Du Bois,* 228. The issue of Du Bois's mental health is problematic and tenuous. Based on a medical report written in 1933, Lewis's account of Du Bois's psychological distress mentions it in one qualified sentence and assigns it to the Hose-Burghardt era: "The psychological punishment of the place was so severe at that time that Du Bois would claim years afterward that he had actually suffered a nervous breakdown." Certainly, Du Bois hurt greatly in 1899 and, as an accomplished social scientist, knew the clinical meaning of "a nervous breakdown"—major episode of depression—which he no doubt suffered. But, like other prominent leaders including his role model Frederick Douglass, he sometimes confused occurrences and, as demonstrated in his three autobiographies, reinvented them for personal and political reasons. Hence, it is more likely that he experienced uncomplicated bereavement over Burghardt's death, rather than a nervous breakdown, which—as indicated by his uncharacteristic, lengthy withdrawal from public activity in the face of the riot and by the letter from Dr. Fuller of the Westborough Insane Hospital responding to his call for help—occurred instead in 1907, as did a greeting from William Pickens, who trusted that Du Bois soon would be "turning in health and good cheer" toward his work. Certainly, the trauma of his son's death carried over and contributed to the psychological devastation of the riot, but Du Bois's public actions between the lynching of 1899 and the riot of 1907 exhibit little in the way of drastic behavioral change that accompanies a mental crack-up; in contrast, his reclusive habits and roman à clef writings of the period following the riot suggest that an activist normally known for his "iron self-control and intellectual purpose" was adrift and brooding. The possibility that Du Bois might have suffered successive breakdowns raises even more serious questions when interpreting his long-term leadership and its significance. In any case, much more information about Du Bois's medical history is needed for a comprehensive analysis of his mental health and its impact on his life and achievements. Lewis, *W. E. B. Du Bois,* 228 (quotation) and 632*n*39; David W. Blight, *Frederick Douglass's Civil War. Keeping Faith in Jubilee* (Baton Rouge, 1989), 73–74 and 74*n*28; Allison Davis, *Leadership, Love, and Aggression* (San Diego, New York, and London, 1983), 23–26, 29, and 36; Whipple interview, April 5, 1994; S. C. Fuller to Du Bois, September 25, 1907, *Du Bois Papers,* Reel 1, frame 995; and William Pickens to Du Bois, September 4, 1907, *ibid.,* Reel 2, frame 1189.

118. W. E. B. Du Bois, "The Burden of Black Women," *Horizon,* II (November 1907), 3–5 (quotations on p. 4).

119. "Death," *Horizon,* II (December 1907), 8.

120. Editorial, *Moon Illustrated Weekly,* I (June 23, 1906), 12; and Du Bois, "Niagara Movement," 621.

121. H. W. Beecher S. Bates to Du Bois, December 23, 1907, and Agubah Burghardt to Du Bois, January 10, 1908, both in *Du Bois Papers,* Reel 1, frames 342 and 484.

122. Lewis, *W. E. B. Du Bois,* 40–47.

123. Du Bois to William Hayes Ward, March 27, 1908, in Aptheker, ed., *Correspondence,* I, 141; and Horace Bumstead to George A. Towns, December 5, 1903, George A. Towns Papers (Division of Archives and Special Collections, Atlanta University Center Woodruff Library, Atlanta, Ga.)

124. Linda O. McMurry, *Recorder of the Black Experience: A Biography of Monroe Nathan Work* (Baton Rouge and London, 1985), 45–46 and 147 (quotation).

125. W. E. B. Du Bois, "Galileo Galilei," June, 1908, in *Du Bois Papers,* Reel 80, frames 164–71.

126. Richard Yarborough, "Race, Violence, and Manhood: The Masculine Ideal in Frederick Douglass's "The Heroic Slave'," in Eric J. Sundquist, ed., *Frederick Douglass: New Literary and Historical Essays* (Cambridge [England], 1990), 141–88.

127. Du Bois, *John Brown* (rpt.; New York, 1962), 344; and Frederick Douglass, *Life and Times of Frederick Douglass* (rpt.; New York, 1962), 320.

128. John Hope Franklin, *Three Negro Classics* (2d. ed.; New York, 1969), xviii.

129. Du Bois, *John Brown,* 338–64, and W. E. B. Du Bois, "John Brown," n. d., in *Du Bois Papers,* Reel 80, frames 201–2, for all of Du Bois's references to Brown in the paragraph.

130. Sidney Hook, *Pragmatism and the Tragic Sense of Life* (New York, 1974), 15, for a Similar analysis. Du Bois illustrated the dilemma of protest in a 1906 short story, "A Race Riot," written almost certainly during the weeks following the Atlanta riot. Depicting the "shout" of the mob as inevitable backlash to black agitation, Du Bois disclosed a growing understanding of the high stakes of provocation. The story was not finished, suggesting anew that in the wake of riot Du Bois was as much confounded by white violence's thwart of rational morality as he was overwhelmed by its sights and sounds. "A Race Riot," 1906, in *Du Bois Papers*, Reel 88, frames 1185–88; see also Mary Frances Berry and John W. Blassingame, *Long Memory: The Black Experience in America* (New York and Oxford, 1982), 277.

131. Waldo E. Martin, *The Mind of Frederick Douglass* (Chapel Hill, 1984), 202; Davis, *Leadership, Love, and Aggression,* 111; Lewis, *W. E. B. Du Bois*, 28; and Gatewood, *Aristocrats of Color,* 311.

132. W. E. B. Du Bois, "The Forward Movement," October 1910, in *Du Bois Papers*, Reel 80, frame 257.

133. W. E. B. Du Bois, *The Quest of the Silver Fleece: A Novel* (rpt.; Millwood, N.Y., 1972), quotation on p. 98.

134. Du Bois, "Conservation of Races," 824; Du Bois, *Dusk of Dawn,* 11–12; Du Bois, *Autobiography*, 65–72 (quotation on p. 72); and Lewis, *W. E. B. Du Bois,* 11, 22–24. See also Rampersad, *Art and Imagination of W. E. B. Du Bois,* 121 and 132, for another interpretation of *Quest of the Silver Fleece.*

135. Du Bois, *Darkwater,* 9 (quotation); Wilson Jeremiah Moses, *Black Messiahs and Uncle Toms: Social and Literary Manipulations of a Religious Myth* (University Park, Pa., 1982), 142; Vincent Harding, "W. E. B. Du Bois and the Black Messianic Vision," in John Henrik Clarke, Esther Jackson, Ernest Kaiser, and J. H. O'Dell, eds., *Black Titan: W. E. B. Du Bois* (Boston, 1970), 54; and John Dollard, *Caste and Class in a Southern Town* (New Haven, Conn., 1949), 154 and 156–57.

136. *Diagnostic and Statistical Manual of Mental Disorders* (3d ed.; Washington, D. C., 1987), 218–25; and Benjamin B. Wolman, ed., *Handbook of Clinical Psychology* (New York, 1965), 1035.

137. Whipple interview, April 5, 1994; and Dominic J. Capeci Jr. and Jack Knight, "'I Hate Them, Christ!'" W. E. B. Du Bois's Jermiad to Southern Violence," presented at the Conference on Representations of Love and Hate, Atlanta, Georgia, October 23, 1993.

138. Ellis R. Oberholtzer to Du Bois, September 29, 1908, and November 10, 1908, in *Du Bois Papers*, Reel 2, frames 261 and 262.

139. Rollo May, *Man's Search for Himself* (New York, 1953), 252 (quotation); and Whipple interview, April 19, 1994 (recording in authors' possession).

140. Du Bois, *Dusk of Dawn,* 89 (second quotation) and 94 (first quotation).

141. Du Bois, OHC, 153.

142. Du Bois, *Darkwater*, 21.

143. Charles Flint Kellogg, *NAACP: A History of The National Association for the Advancement of Colored People*. Volume I: *1909–1920* (Baltimore, 1967), Chap. 1.

144. Du Bois, *Darkwater*, 23 (quotation); and Ovington, *Walls Came Tumbling Down,* 107.

145. Lewis, *W. E. B. Du Bois,* 463; and *Du Bois Autobiography,* 255. Du Bois's addresses were thematic instead of political, he played down southern grievances, and he took no part in the formation of the Atlanta NAACP chapter in 1916, all of which suggest that he had removed himself from southern concerns. To be sure, the Spingarn ceremony at Atlanta University in 1920 signified Du Bois's national status, honoring him for Pan African efforts; but Georgia blacks could not miss the point of his absence from their struggles. Perhaps his visits served to rid himself of the trauma attached to the place of riot, if not the upheaval itself. *Crisis,* XX (July 1920), 133–34; Edgar A. Toppin, "Walter White and the Atlanta NAACP's Fight for Equal Schools, 1916–1917," *History of Education Quarterly,* VII (Spring 1967), 3–21; and Whipple interview of April 19, 1994, applying M. Scott Peck, *The Road Less Traveled.*

146. Rudwick, "Niagara Movement," 148; and Rudwick, *W. E. B. Du Bois,* 119 and 304.

147. W. E. B. Du Bois, "The Souls of White Folk," *Independent*, LXIX (August 18, 1910), 339–42.

148. W. E. B. Du Bois, "The African Roots of War," *Atlantic Monthly*, LXV (May 1915), 707–14.

149. *Crisis*, II (September 1911), 195, XII (October 1916), 270–71, and XVI (July 1918), 111.

150. Du Bois attributed the racial violence of the period to labor competition, increased black expectations, and wartime demographics. See, for a related analysis, the NAACP investigation conducted by Du Bois and Martha Gruening, "The Massacre of East St. Louis," *Crisis*, XIV (September 1917), 219–38.

151. *Crisis*, XXII (July 1921), 102–4, and XL (September 1931), 313–15; John Brown Childs, *Leadership, Conflict, and Cooperation in Afro-American Social Thought* (Philadelphia, 1989), 39–40.

152. Du Bois to George Streator, April 24, 1935, in Aptheker, ed., *Correspondence of W. E. B. Du Bois*, 11, 90–93.

153. *Crisis*, XVIII (September 1919), 231, XIX (November 1919), 335, and XXIII (April 1922), 251–52. Though Du Bois lived to witness the gains of the civil rights era, he remained skeptical that nonviolence would prevail over "pathological" southern racism. W. E. B. Du Bois, "Will the Great Gandhi Live Again?" *National Guardian*, IX (February 11, 1957), 8. See also Erik Erikson, "Psychoanalysis and Ongoing History: Problems of Identity, Hatred and Nonviolence," *American Journal of Psychiatry*, CXXII (September 1965), 241–50.

154. Du Bois summarized his misgiving late in life, just before leaving America for residence in Ghana: "I just cannot take any more of this country's treatment. . . . I set no date for return . . . Chin up, and fight on, but realize that American Negroes can't win." Du Bois to Grace Goens, September 13, 1961, in *Du Bois Papers*, Reel 75, frame 242.

155. Clarence E. Walker, *Deromanticizing Black History: Critical Essays and Reappraisals* (Knoxville, 1991), 104–7; Meier, *Negro Thought*, Chap. 11; and Du Bois, *Dusk of Dawn*, 32.

156. For a discussion of the organization in the modern state see Louis Galambos, "The Emerging Organizational Synthesis in Modern American History," *Business History Review*, LIV (Autumn 1970), 279–90.

157. Davis, *Leadership, Love, and Aggression*, 118; Du Bois, "Looking Seventy-five Years Backward," 244.

158. Kelman, "Violence Without Moral Restraint," 302. Late in life Du Bois called anew for educational programs to raise the cultural level of blacks and to change the racial attitudes of whites. See "A Program of Organization for Realizing Democracy: Statement by W. E. B. Du Bois," Conference on Race Relations, March 22, 1944. Box 46, Philleo Nash Papers (Harry S. Truman Library, Independence, Mo.).

159. See Frantz Fanon, *The Wretched of the Earth*, preface by Jean-Paul Sartre (New York, 1963), 21–22, 57–58, 71–72, and 309–10, for the theory of "man recreating himself" through violence against his oppressors. David Caute, *Frantz Fanon* (New York, 1970), 91–98 (quoted phrases on p. 93), discusses why Du Bois could never have embraced Fanon's concept of bloodshed as either a collective "existential necessity" or a personal "cleansing force": violence dehumanizes everyone, thus striking at the core of Du Bois's belief in humanity; violence requires a complete break from all things European, thus challenging Du Bois's intellectual faith in rationalism over emotionalism and his personal multi-racial heritage. Essentially, Du Bois's humanity, intellect, and identity would have dismissed Fanon's scorched-earth psychology as a solution for the race riddle. Certainly in the United States where whites outnumbered blacks and so easily annihilated them, his pragmatism would have questioned such a potentially suicidal and self-destructive creed.

160. Du Bois, *Souls*, 5; W. E. B. Du Bois, "The Negro and the Warsaw Ghetto," in Philip S. Foner, ed., *W. E. B. Du Bois Speaks, Speeches and Addresses, 1920–1963* (New York and London, 1970), 252.

Reading 13

The NAACP as a Reform Movement, 1909–1965: "To reach the conscience of America"

August Meier and John H. Bracey, Jr.

The history of the National Association for the Advancement of Colored People (NAACP) from its origins in the Progressive movement to the victories achieved in the passage of the Civil Rights Act of 1964 and the Voting Rights Act of 1965 illuminates the history of American reform in the twentieth century.[1] The focus of this essay will be on the development of the NAACP and its programs and the dynamics of their interrelationships with the changing social milieu in which the Association operated. Involved on the one hand are both the political and economic transformations that were taking place in U.S. society and the long-range shifts that were taking place in white attitudes toward racial minorities. On the other hand are the NAACP's responses to rivals and critics from within the black community. As in any organization there were also internal conflicts over program and strategy and intense rivalries between leading personalities. In contrast to the situation in many social movement organizations, however, these internal conflicts had scant impact on the basic direction of the NAACP's programs and goals.

The authors' interest in these particular issues stemmed from our attempts to address two broad questions. One was that posed some years ago by historians who were investigating the fate of the Progressive movement and the possible relationship of the Progressive movement to the New Deal. The other was the sociological one of how a reform organization interacts over time with its changing environment. Using this conceptual framework we have carried our analysis of the NAACP's history through to the climax of American liberalism and civil rights reform in the 1960s.

Born in 1909 on the fringes of Progressive Era reform, the Association single-mindedly kept to its original goal of securing the basic citizenship rights guaranteed by the Fourteenth and Fifteenth Amendments of the Constitution. However, the NAACP also proved to be a flexible organization, modifying its tactics and strategies to meet the challenges of the changing economic and political environment in which it operated. For example, beginning with the Great Depression and the New Deal, the NAACP was able to incorporate into its program new economic concerns without altering its basic goal. Amid the reform impulses unleashed during the depression and World War II, the NAACP flourished. The membership and staff grew to unprecedented size. Its legal arm, the NAACP Legal Defense and Educational Fund Inc., won a series of stunning victories before the Supreme

Court in the space of ten years: from *Smith v. Allwright,* which outlawed the white primary in 1944, to the *Brown* decision of 1954.[2] There then followed a decade of legislative successes culminating in the passage of the Civil Rights Act of 1964 and the Voting Rights Act of 1965, which together brought to a conclusion the struggle to achieve the original goals enunciated by the NAACP in 1909.

Given this long history and its relationship to American reform, it is interesting to note that the NAACP and its achievements are given scant attention in virtually all of the general studies of Progressivism and liberal reform. The early influential study of the Progressive movement, John Chamberlain's *Farewell to Reform: Being a History of the Rise, Life and Decay of the Progressive Mind in America* (1932), has no references to Negroes or to the NAACP. Twenty years later, another influential study, Richard Hofstadter's *The Age of Reform: From Bryan to F.D.R* (1956) has only seven incidental references. Scholars such as Eric F. Goldman in *Rendezvous with Destiny* (1952) and Allen F. Davis in *Spearheads for Reform: The Social Settlements and the Progressive Movement, 1890–1914* (1967) do pay significant attention to racial matters. In *An Encore for Reform: The Old Progressives and the New Deal* (1967), Otis L. Graham, Jr., exhibits an awareness that support for the NAACP was a significant indicator of Progressive sentiments but otherwise ignores the question. And in his later volume, *Toward a Planned Society: From Roosevelt to Nixon* (1976), there is no reference at all to racial matters.

It is indeed surprising that even after the shift in racial consciousness brought about in the late 1950s and 1960s, most of the books on liberal reform either have omitted or have given only passing attention to the NAACP. Thus for example a symposium published by the Lyndon B. Johnson School of Public Affairs and edited by Wilbur J. Cohen, entitled *The Roosevelt New Deal: A Program Assessment Fifty Years After* (1986), has chapters on the New Deal and Jews, the New Deal and women, and the New Deal and labor, but none on the New Deal and blacks![3]

A survey that does pay attention to race and to the NAACP is Arthur S. Link and Richard L. McCormick, *Progressivism* (1983). This is in sharp contrast to Link's seminal 1959 article, "What Happened to the Progressive Movement in the 1920's?" in which race is not mentioned at all. On the other hand, Alonzo L. Hamby's *Liberalism and Its Challengers: FDR to Reagan* (1985), while uneven, does devote a full chapter to Martin Luther King, Jr., and the civil rights movement of the 1960s, but its references to the NAACP are generally inaccurate. Significant exceptions are two studies of Americans for Democratic Action (ADA), the leading predominantly white liberal reform organization of the post–World War II era, which made civil rights one of its central concerns. Thus Clifton Brock in *Americans for Democratic Action: Its Role in National Politics* (1962) does address this matter. Oddly enough, while devoting much attention to the ADA's civil rights activities, Steven M. Gillon's more recent study, *Politics and Vision: The ADA and American Liberalism, 1947–1985* (1987), does not use the NAACP papers nor does it contain any mention of the NAACP's interactions with the ADA. Moreover, the index contains no references to such prominent NAACP leaders as Clarence Mitchell, Jr., Walter Francis White, or Roy Wilkins. From the NAACP's point of view, Denton L. Watson's *Lion in the Lobby: Clarence Mitchell, Jr.'s Struggle for the Passage of Civil Rights Laws* (1990) contains numerous references to the ADA and to Joseph L. Rauh, the ADA's most notable civil rights advocate.[4]

Given the extreme racism of the Progressive period, the discriminatory impact of some important Progressive reforms *(e.g.,* the way in which the new primary system served to disenfranchise black voters in the South) and the racist attitudes of many Progressive leaders and intellectuals from John R. Commons to Theodore Roosevelt, it is paradoxical that among the highly varied reform organizations originating at that time was one like the NAACP. Although some of its leaders were prominent in other reform activities (most notable perhaps was Oswald Garrison Villard, publisher of the New York *Evening Post* and editor of the *Nation,* whose interests ranged from pacifism to women's suffrage), the NAACP itself was marginal to the Progressive movement as a whole. But this is especially ironical in view of the NAACP's attempt to extend Progressive values, goals, and methods into the area of race relations. The Association's belief in investigation and exposure and in the importance of laws and of the state as a guarantor of social order, its faith in the assimilability of minority groups, its belief in progress and the essential rationality of human behavior, all reflect the ideas of mainstream Progressivism. But unlike most other Progressives who either ignored the race problem or considered blacks and Asians to be inferior, the NAACP was willing to carry the implications of Progressivism to their logical conclusions and in this regard was more progressive than most of the Progressives themselves. Above all the appeal of the NAACP like that of the Progressives was fundamentally a moral one, or as the NAACP said in its tenth annual report its goal was "to reach the conscience of America."

Like many of the organizations formed during the Progressive Era, the NAACP had links back to nineteenth-century reformism through the descendants of white abolitionists and a few veterans of the older black self-help organizations such as the Afro-American League.[5] The leading founders among both the whites and the blacks ranged ideologically from socialist intellectuals like W.E.B. Du Bois to politically conservative Republicans like Moorfield Storey of Boston (a past president of the American Bar Association), who were united by their intense dislike of imperialism and racism and their skepticism as to the efficacy of the strategies of Booker T. Washington. This group, resolutely interracial in its outlook, virtually adopted the program of Du Bois's Niagara Movement (1905–1910) as its own. Both the Niagara Movement and the NAACP were united in their opposition to Booker T. Washington's policies and in their program of militant protest and litigation against the denial of constitutional rights guaranteed to black Americans by the Fourteenth and Fifteenth Amendments. Like the Afro-American League, the Niagara Movement was all black. Given conditions at the turn of the century this mode of organizing appeared at least to its adherents to be the only viable option. Du Bois and most of his colleagues in the Niagara Movement acted with little hesitation when given the opportunity to forge effective alliances with sympathetic whites. In fact, it was largely through Du Bois's efforts that people like Villard became convinced of the bankruptcy of Washington's approach and were willing to ally with blacks in posing an alternative.[6]

This of course was a period of disfranchisement legislation, Jim Crow laws, sharecropping and debt peonage, lynchings and racial pogroms. Given these extreme manifestations of white racism, the indifference of even most enlightened northern opinion, and the reluctance of most black intellectuals to challenge the leadership of Booker T. Washington, the NAACP began as a frail organization. Except for Du Bois, the principal figures in the early years were leading white Progressives such as Villard and Joel Elias Spingarn, and for the first decade the executive secretaries of the NAACP were white reformers. Du Bois edited the *Crisis,* which served as an effective vehicle for keeping the organization's programs and activities before the black public. With its limited resources, the NAACP began its long-term strategy of undermining the legal foundations of the American race system by involving itself in court cases dealing with disfranchisement and residential segregation. In 1915 the Supreme Court declared Oklahoma's "grandfather clause" unconstitutional and two years later overturned the Louisville, Kentucky, municipal residential segregation ordinance. The Association also initiated public protests against Jim Crow arrangements being instituted in federal offices in Washington, D.C., and against showing D.W. Griffith's 1915 racist movie, *The Birth of a Nation.* In both the legal cases and the protests the NAACP achieved only limited results. Much more successful was its vigorous opposition to the rash of anti-Negro legislation that came before Congress and a number of northern state legislatures during Woodrow Wilson's presidency.[7]

From its founding until past the middle of the century what highlighted the NAACP's activities and dramatized its work were its efforts to secure the protection for black Americans of the basic rights to life and liberty. Both rights were threatened by mob violence (lynchings and race riots) and by gross mistreatment in the area of criminal justice on the part of law enforcement authorities and the courts. This mistreatment took place in the South and in the North. In addition to its intrinsic importance, the attention to lynchings and criminal justice was sound strategy that enabled the Association to rally the broadest possible range of support and garner maximum publicity for its programs.

For nearly thirty years the NAACP devoted immeasurable amounts of energy and large amounts of money in the ultimately futile effort to achieve the passage of a federal antilynching bill, although lynchings did almost come to a halt by 1940. Similarly the NAACP devoted considerable efforts to cases involving injustice before the courts, especially in the South. The NAACP was involved in attempts to protect the lives of individual blacks and/or to bring to justice whites guilty of mob violence in such cases as the Coatesville, Pennsylvania, lynching of 1912; the railroading of soldiers in the all-black Twenty-fourth Infantry Regiment of the U.S. Army to death sentences and long prison terms because of their alleged involvement in the Houston riot of 1917; the East St. Louis riot of the same year; the Elaine, Arkansas, and Chicago riots of 1919; the Tulsa, Oklahoma, riot of 1921; the Ossian Sweet case in Detroit in 1925; the Scottsboro case, which began in 1930; the Detroit riot of 1943; the blinding of World War II veteran Isaac Woodward by two white South Carolina policemen in 1946; the assassination of Harry T. Moore, NAACP state coordinator of branches for Florida, and his wife in 1951; and the Emmett Till and Mack Charles Parker lynchings in 1955 and 1959, respectively.[8] A striking and unusual case that illustrates the strengths and limitations of the NAACP's approach to mob violence was the Aiken, South Carolina, lynchings in October 1926. What we know about the lynchings is due to the efforts of Walter White, the NAACP's assistant secretary who, able to pass for white, undertook an investigation that included interviews with members of the mob and the compilation of vivid eyewitness accounts. White, using his contacts with the press, persuaded the New York *World* to do a lengthy series of articles spotlighting these South Carolina lynchings. The gist of this case was that in April 1925 a family of sharecroppers named Lowman was accused of making and selling illegal liquor. During the attempt to arrest Sam Lowman, the father and head of the family, who was away at the time, a gunfight occurred in which the white sheriff and Mrs. Annie Lowman were killed. The three children, the oldest of whom was thirteen, were seriously wounded. The Lowman children were arrested, charged, tried hastily, and convicted of murder. The two males were sentenced to death, and the female received a life sentence. The father was subsequently charged with possession of liquor and given a two-year sentence on a chain gang.

The injustice of these proceedings outraged N.J. Frederick of Columbia, South Carolina, the only black lawyer in the state who took civil rights cases and had previously handled NAACP cases. Frederick initiated an appeal of his own, retaining at his own expense a white lawyer who was willing to assist him. They were successful in securing from the South Carolina Supreme Court a reversal of the convictions, resulting in a directed verdict of "not guilty" for one defendant and jury trials for the remaining two. The youth who had been acquitted was immediately rearrested on new charges and sent back to jail. Late that same night a mob of two thousand people stormed the jail where the three black children were being held, took them away, told them to run, and then shot them from behind until they were dead. Despite a quite vigorous publicity campaign that caused some South Carolina newspapers to condemn the lynchings, no members of the mob were ever brought to justice. The NAACP's annual report for 1926 seized upon this situation to make yet another appeal for a federal antilynching law.[9]

Despite the unsatisfactory resolutions of many of the NAACP's legal cases, there were enough victories to warrant the observation by Ralph J. Bunche, a NAACP critic from Howard University, that in the first three decades of the NAACP's history "the most important of the tactics employed by the NAACP is that of legal redress. The outstanding victories of the Association have been in court."[10]

Meanwhile during and following World War I there were major changes in race relations that affected the workings—both internal and external—of the NAACP. These tumultuous years witnessed extensive migration of blacks to northern cities, antiblack riots, the revival of the Ku Klux Klan, the rise of Marcus Garvey, the onset of the Harlem Renaissance, the introduction of varieties of Marxist thought among black intellectuals, and the emergence of a new breed of black politician in northern cities (that would in 1928 lead to the election of Oscar De Priest of Chicago as the first black congressman from a northern district and the first black in Congress since 1901). In short, the general atmosphere was one of heightened racial consciousness on all fronts, epitomized by the widespread usage among blacks of the term "the New Negro."

In this context the NAACP, while holding on to its basic program of seeking legal redress and legislative reform, underwent important changes in internal organization. Due in large part to wartime prosperity and the shift in black population to northern cities where it was safer to join the organization, NAACP membership grew among blacks so rapidly that by 1920 membership fees from blacks were supplying most of the organization's income. This development masked the failure of the deliberate attempt to attract large numbers of white members. But perhaps the most important internal consequence was the transfer of administrative power to the black secretariat. In 1916 James Weldon Johnson was employed as field secretary. This was followed in 1918 by the appointment of Walter White as assistant executive secretary. In 1921 Johnson was promoted to executive secretary on a permanent basis, a post he held for the next decade. The same rise in race consciousness that led to the success of Marcus Garvey's nationalist appeal also had an impact on the NAACP. This consciousness coupled with the hiring of black staff led to the increase in black membership, which in turn reaffirmed the strategy of hiring black staff. The stature and talent of these new staff members were further affirmations; both Johnson and White as well as Robert W. Bagnall, the director of branches, were men of considerable organizational skills with extensive contacts among black fraternal orders, churches, and business and civic leaders.

As editor of the *Crisis,* W.E.B. Du Bois was at the center of much of the ideological controversy that characterized the postwar period. Even though Du Bois had been fostering his own version of Pan-Africanism since the beginning of the century, that did not prevent Marcus Garvey from attacking Du Bois from Garvey's own nationalist point of view. The NAACP's interracial makeup, its politics of integration and assimilation, and even Du Bois's light skin color were anathema to Garvey who, in his speeches and in his newspaper the *Negro World,* ridiculed the NAACP and called Du Bois "purely and simply a white man's nigger." Although Du Bois had considered himself a socialist for some time, he was also attacked from the left by socialists such as A. Philip Randolph, the militant editor of the *Messenger.* In Randolph's view Du Bois and the NAACP had sold out to bourgeois interests and were not at all concerned with the problems facing the black working class. Despite all the attention that these polemics received, there was no discernible effect on the NAACP's programs or direction. At the end of the decade the *Crisis* was still the preeminent black journal while Randolph's *Messenger* was defunct and Garvey's *Negro World* had lost most of its influence.[11]

The NAACP's relationship with the Harlem Renaissance can be best understood as "the politics of art," to use David Levering Lewis's phrase.[12] Characteristic of this renaissance was the intricate interaction of racial advancement organizations with art and artists. From the point of view of NAACP strategy there was a widespread assumption that the work of black artists was an aspect of the struggle to advance the status of black Americans. The positive images flowing from their art were widely recognized as a cultural force capable of both undermining notions of white supremacy and encouraging self-esteem among Negroes.

From its founding the NAACP had among its leaders creative writers and literary critics. The writings of Du Bois of course are well known. Less known are the writings of Du Bois's closest NAACP associates during this period, Joel Spingarn and Mary White Ovington, both white liberals. Spingarn, a poet, leading literary critic, and a founder of the "new criticism," served for many years as treasurer or chairman of the board of directors of the NAACP. Mary White Ovington, a founder who was active in the NAACP for almost four decades, was a novelist and playwright.[13]

When the NAACP began to expand the number of its black staff, the most prominent of its additions, James Weldon Johnson, had extensive literary and cultural interests and was appointed to the staff at Spingarn's insistence. It is easy to infer that one of the reasons that Spingarn found the multi-talented Johnson so attractive was the quality of his literary work. Walter White, who came from an insurance background, did not begin to write until well after he joined the NAACP staff. Perhaps influenced by the number of writers around him, White wrote both novels and nonfiction. Beginning in the late 1910s and 1920s the *Crisis,* like the Urban League's *Opportunity* magazine later on, encouraged young writers to publish in its pages and to compete for a literary prize named for Amy Spingarn, Joel's wife. Also joining the staff during this period were the novelist Jessie Redmon Fauset, literary editor of the *Crisis,* and William Pickens, field secretary from 1919 to 1938.[14]

Given this unparalleled collection of literary talent in one organization the NAACP was in an ideal position to exercise a major role in the creative flowering of the 1920s and to undertake a program of cultural advancement in conjunction with its legal and protest activities. The NAACP, in providing an outlet for some of the early writers of the Harlem Renaissance, both stimulated the cultural outpouring and benefited from this newly awakened consciousness.

During the 1920s, a period when Republicans dominated the White House and black voters remained overwhelmingly Republican, the black vote, such as it was, was essentially taken for granted. Conditions in the South were not improving for blacks, and conditions in the North in many respects were growing worse. The NAACP continued the fight for an antilynching bill and chipped away with minor successes against the white Democratic primaries in the South. The NAACP had less success opposing the restrictive covenants that hemmed the growing urban black populations into overcrowded ghettos.[15]

The 1920s was neatly bracketed by two important legal battles: the Arkansas riot case that arose in 1919 and the opposition to the nomination to the U.S. Supreme Court of Judge John J. Parker of North Carolina, who had endorsed black disfranchisement. The Arkansas riot case had arisen from an incident in 1919 when, as a result of a racial altercation, eighty-nine blacks were convicted for their alleged involvement; twelve were sentenced to death. The NAACP took the case all the way to the Supreme Court, and after five years of litigation the defendants were freed on the grounds that an impartial trial had not been possible because of mob intimidation of the community and court. Then in 1930, emboldened by the increasing black voting power in the North, the NAACP made significant contributions to mobilizing senators to vote against the confirmation of Judge Parker. This political effort challenged President Herbert C. Hoover's "lily-white" policies and his indifference to the black electorate. After campaigning vigorously against the reelection of four of the senators who had voted for Parker, the Association could take considerable credit for the defeat of two of them.[16]

Although the anti-Parker campaign was dramatic, it had no lasting impact on the NAACP. However, a tentative decision taken about the same time initiated a series of legal steps that would have an enormous impact on the NAACP's future course of litigation. By the end of the 1920s the Association was exploring the utility of exposing the blatant inequities between black and white schools in the South as an opening wedge in the long-range effort to overturn *Plessy v. Ferguson,* the 1896 court decision that based segregation on the doctrine of separate but equal facilities.[17]

Building on the legal work of the 1920s the NAACP program of litigation continued to expand, even during the Great Depression. The deaths in 1929 of both Louis Marshall and Moorfield Storey, two whites who were among the country's leading constitutional lawyers and who had worked for the NAACP for years on a pro bono basis, compelled the Association to consider whether to develop its own paid legal staff and what role black lawyers would play. After discussing these issues for several years and weighing pressures from the black bar association, the NAACP by mid-1935 had employed Charles Hamilton Houston as its full-time special counsel. This decision would prove to be the beginning of the development of a black legal staff.

Houston played a critical role in this process. First, the move to hire a black counsel was facilitated by the emergence of a small group of black lawyers who had studied constitutional law under Felix Frankfurter of the Harvard Law School. Two of the most prominent of them were Houston himself and his close friend William H. Hastie, both of whom were destined to play important roles in the future of the NAACP. Second, in its effort to improve black higher education in general, the Rockefeller Foundation's General Education Board decided to develop a first-rate law school at Howard University under Houston's leadership. Houston was committed to creating a cadre of skilled black lawyers who would be experts in civil rights law, and he firmly believed that such a cadre would then be able to undertake the litigation required to overturn discrimination in the South.

Houston was optimistic about what could be done through the use of the law, which he saw as a tool for social engineering. In this regard Houston's ideas undoubtedly reflected the more general ethos of New Deal social planning and anticipated Gunnar Myrdal's later application of this approach to the solution of the race problem.[18] Although Houston resigned the post of special counsel in mid-1936, he was succeeded by his most brilliant law student, Thurgood Marshall.

During the 1930s the NAACP's litigation maintained a remarkable continuity with that of the 1920s. Much effort was still devoted to legal redress on behalf of individuals, with the NAACP selecting cases from the many received on the basis of two criteria: 1) an issue of citizenship rights had to be involved, and 2) the racial discrimination had to be clear. By 1940 the volume of this kind of litigation, most of it originating in the local branches, had grown to the point that the legal staff now decided to limit itself to cases that had the potential of establishing a new precedent of constitutional significance. NAACP lawyers also continued the earlier campaigns against restrictive covenants and white primaries. They won three Supreme Court victories against the Texas white primary system, although the Texas Democrats continued to find ways to circumvent the decisions.[19] But legal victories in the restrictive covenant cases proved elusive.

The major new legal initiative, underwritten in part by the American Fund for Public Service, a philanthropy more commonly known as the Garland Fund, was the inauguration of the fight against educational discrimination in the South. A two-pronged strategy was involved: directly attacking the exclusion of blacks from the professional and graduate schools at state universities and indirectly attacking segregation in the primary and secondary grades with litigation calling for full equalization of salaries, length of school term, and physical facilities in the public schools. The rationale for this indirect approach was to make segregated public schooling so expensive that the choice would be desegregation or economic ruin. The plan adopted was to begin with the border states, then move into the upper South, and finally challenge the Deep South. A latent function of this strategy was to use these local cases as opportunities to raise funds for the NAACP and increase its membership.

While the legal program and the campaign for an antilynching law were characterized by significant continuity and were shaped independently of the Great Depression, it would be difficult to overestimate the impact of the economic collapse and the New Deal on other aspects of the NAACP's programs and activities. The NAACP was operating in a radically new environment, and a series of mutually reinforcing developments caused a number of changes. At the initiative of a strengthened executive branch led by Franklin D. Roosevelt, there was a proliferation of federal programs addressing the nation's economic problems. By the end of the 1930s the majority of black voters had shifted from the Republican to the Democratic party. The importance of this shift was heightened by the continued migration of blacks into urban centers generally controlled by Democratic political machines. There was also a general shift to the left on the part of substantial numbers of Americans. One manifestation of this leftward shift was a relatively large and extremely active Communist party that continually criticized the NAACP for its lack of radicalism. Another response to both the depression and government initiatives was the rise of the Congress of Industrial Organizations (CIO), which, while not free of discrimination, had made serious efforts to implement its official policy of organizing all workers. Finally, from within the black community itself came a range of challenges to the NAACP's traditional assumptions and programs.

In response to these circumstances and the accompanying pressures, the NAACP as early as 1930–1931 began to make economic issues more important to its agenda. Blacks were faced with obvious inequities in the implementation of New Deal programs: for example, wage differentials sanctioned by the National Recovery Administration; virtual exclusion of black sharecroppers from the benefits of the Agricultural Adjustment Act; the exclusion of certain occupations in which blacks were heavily represented, such as sharecropping and domestic work, from coverage by Social Security. Even those agencies that were most helpful to blacks—the Works Progress Administration, the National Youth Administration, and the United States Housing Authority—and did the most to attract blacks to the Democratic party also exhibited discriminatory practices. The NAACP monitored the patterns of such discrimination and lodged protests with the appropriate federal agencies. The Association established personal contacts with leaders in the New Deal administration, most notably with Eleanor Roosevelt, who in contrast to her husband was openly supportive of the NAACP. Her warm relationship with Walter White and sincere interest in the NAACP's goals epitomized the growing sensitivity of some left-wing New Dealers to racial discrimination.

Blacks suffered disproportionately from the economic devastation of the Great Depression, and one result was that NAACP members and other segments of the black community put increased pressure on the Association for assistance. Local branches began to entreat the national office for help as the full effects of the depression began to be felt. The majority of the protests that the NAACP filed with New Deal agencies resulted from such complaints. The NAACP had responded as best it could to economic discrimination since its 1909 origin, when at its founding convention it was presented with a petition from a group of black firemen on the Georgia railroads being forced out of their jobs by racist white workers. In the absence of relevant federal law or a favorable legislative consensus, there was almost nothing the NAACP could do. However, after 1930 not only did the urgency and volume of the complaints escalate but the national government was committed to some sort of response.

The Association's most painful internal conflict, although it had negligible long-range consequences, was between Du Bois and Walter White. The contention was rooted in a long-simmering hostility between the two men. Among other reasons, the economic downturn of the 1930s had exacerbated their disagreement over the allocation of funds for the *Crisis,* an issue that had bedeviled Du Bois and other leaders of the Association for two decades. The particular confrontation that led to Du Bois's resignation in 1934 was his proposal, published in the *Crisis,* to solve the economic problems of the black masses by creating all-black cooperative enterprises while downplaying the struggle for integration. In fact Du Bois's willingness to accept a large degree of voluntary separation seemed to represent a repudiation of the founding principles and goals of the NAACP. To White and his colleagues, such a distinction between forced segregation and voluntary separation (a distinction made with much more success under different circumstances by Malcolm X thirty years later) was unacceptable. In the ensuing debate and struggle Du Bois was forced to resign from the organization that he had helped to found and played a leading role in for a quarter of a century.[20]

At the same time a small group of radical intellectuals centered primarily at Howard University urged the NAACP to reorient its programs and approaches toward an alliance with the white working class. The most prominent of these radicals were economist Abram L. Harris, sociologist E. Franklin Frazier, and political scientist Ralph J. Bunche. Charles H. Houston, who in his own law practice represented southern black railway workers, also thought that the NAACP needed to pay greater attention to economic problems and privately nudged White in that direction. After some resistance, the NAACP leadership responded by commissioning Harris to head a committee for making special recommendations. The so-called Harris Report in 1935 advocated such sweeping changes to the Association's organization that it foreclosed any possibility of being adopted. The report did, however, sensitize the NAACP leadership to the importance of the relationship between black and white workers. As a result, the Harris Report had long-range consequences for the organization.

Relations with the Communist party were predictably quite stormy, even during the period of the Popular Front (1935–1940). In addition to fundamental ideological differences, there was a bitter struggle over which of the two organizations would benefit from the increased militancy of black people. This discord became clear in the conflict between the NAACP and the Communist party over defense of the so-called Scottsboro Boys. Thus, long before the Cold War and McCarthyism, the resolutely liberal NAACP had its own reasons for opposing American Communists. That the NAACP saw fit to interact with American Communists at all was due to the Communist party's success among the black population with such militant tactics as picketing, holding marches, organizing unemployment councils, and fighting with landlords over evictions.

The National Negro Congress (NNC) emerged as a result of the intersecting concerns of the Howard radicals (especially Bunche) and the Communist party. The NNC was the outgrowth of a conference on the economic problems of blacks held at Howard University in 1935, underwritten by the Julius Rosenwald Fund and arranged by John P. Davis, a black Harvard graduate who was very close to the Communists. Projected as a broad coalition of racial advancement organizations, the NNC adopted a program quite similar to that of the NAACP but with the promise of more militant action and closer ties to white workers in the new industrial unions. Roy Wilkins, then assistant secretary to Walter White, attended the 1936 founding convention in Chicago as an observer and reported with obvious distaste on the number of Communists he saw active in the proceedings. But the following year black support for the NNC had grown to such an extent that even Walter White agreed to appear as one of the convention speakers. From the NAACP's point of view it was quite fortunate that the NNC and the Popular Front began to fall apart in 1939 over disagreements on Soviet foreign policy.

In contrast, the NAACP formed a lasting relationship with the CIO. The road to cooperation was complicated by mixed motives on both sides. The CIO policy of organizing black workers contrasted greatly with that of the craft unions in the American Federation of Labor (AFL), most of which had herded blacks into impotent Jim Crow locals, excluded them altogether from jobs under AFL control, and even driven black workers from jobs they had already held. Many of the NAACP leaders were impressed by the positions taken by the CIO but were constrained from readily embracing the new union by two factors: the extent of Communist leadership among some unions and the justifiable skepticism many NAACP branch leaders and rank-and-file members felt about unions in general. This distrust was not confined only to the black elite but was widely shared by working-class blacks who had had a long history of bad experiences with racist white workers and their unions. The CIO unions themselves were anxious to capitalize on the militancy of black workers but had earlier turned to the NNC because it had a stronger and more consistently pro-CIO stance than the NAACP did. The collapse of the NNC and the successful collaboration of the United Automobile Workers with the NAACP in the Ford strike of 1941 prompted the NAACP to form an alliance with the CIO, a coalition with labor that continued even after the merger of the AFL and the CIO in 1955.

At the end of the 1930s like the end of the 1920s the NAACP had weathered the storms of both internal and external challenges and emerged as the strongest of all the race advancement organizations. In fact, the membership of the NAACP, although not equal to its earlier peak in 1918, doubled between 1929 and 1939. Surprisingly, membership figures during the Great Depression in the early 1930s held up remarkably well, and numerous branches were revitalized and others founded. The Association was now firmly under black control and direction, and effective power had passed from the board to the executive secretary. Thus the organization was prepared to shape actively the future of the black struggle for equal rights. In the crisis of the depression, blacks, especially those in urban areas outside the South, could be mobilized as never before, and the organization that they chose to join was the NAACP.

Much of the credit for building membership in the local branches should go to countless black women, whose activities have yet to be carefully examined. Women also served in a variety of leadership capacities in the branches, particularly as secretaries and treasurers, some as vice presidents, and, on occasion, as branch presidents or chairs of the executive board. More visible than local women officers were the unusual succession of talented black women on the national staff whose achievements have thus far been overlooked by most historians. In the aftermath of the elevation of James Weldon Johnson to executive secretary, Mary B. Talbert of Buffalo, a past president of the National Association of Colored Women's Clubs, was appointed field secretary. She was followed by Addie W. Hunton of Brooklyn and by Daisy Lampkin of Pittsburgh, who worked with extraordinary success even during the depths of the depression. In the mid-1930s the Association appointed Juanita E. Jackson of the powerful Baltimore branch to increase the involvement of black youth. Ella J. Baker, better known for her later work with the Southern Christian Leadership Conference (SCLC) and Student Nonviolent Coordinating Committee (SNCC), served both as a field secretary and during the 1940s a brief but vigorous term as director of branches. After the war came the appointment of individuals like Lucille Black and Ruby Hurley who served long terms as membership secretary and southeast regional secretary, respectively.

The outbreak of World War II in Europe, the subsequent mobilization of the American economy for war, and the creation of millions of new jobs solidified the NAACP's concern with economic matters. At first white workers were the main beneficiaries of the expanding economy, while black workers still found themselves in the depths of the depression. Protestations to Washington were decidedly unproductive. In this context A. Philip Randolph proposed a march of 100,000 blacks on Washington to take place in June 1941.

Randolph was no stranger to the NAACP. Although he had been one of its most outspoken critics early in his career, the Association had supported his efforts to organize the Pullman porters in the 1920s. Following the recognition of the Brotherhood of Sleeping Car Porters by the AFL in 1935 and the collective bargaining agreement with the Pullman Company in 1937, Randolph was widely hailed as the leading spokesman for black workers. He served as president of the National Negro Congress from 1936 until forced out by the Communists in 1939. Influenced by the success of mass action demonstrations to achieve economic goals, even the NAACP mounted a picket line outside the 1934 AFL convention in San Francisco while inside Randolph was giving a speech that addressed the practice of discrimination by the craft unions. It therefore is not surprising that the NAACP welcomed Randolph's call for a March on Washington and played a key role in helping him use this tactic to force President Roosevelt to establish a Fair Employment Practices Committee (FEPC) in 1941.[21] An important factor in the calculations of both Roosevelt and the NAACP was the growing political strength of northern black voters as part of the Democratic coalition.[22]

In short, the depression and the New Deal proved to be a watershed in the NAACP's history. Unlike many other reform organizations of the Progressive Era, the NAACP had been able to adapt successfully, taking on economic concerns without abandoning its traditional agenda.

World War II provided a more favorable environment for NAACP activism. The goal to defeat Nazi Germany, which expressed an openly racist ideology, promoted concern for domestic racial problems among some white Americans. Although there was much racial tension, even rioting, in wartime America, both official and popular attitudes were significantly different from those of the World War I period. Race riots no longer took the exclusive form of pogroms, for blacks were now better able to defend themselves, inflict casualties on whites, and even attack white property in predominantly black areas.

A telling indicator of the differences between the eras was the soaring NAACP membership, which for the first time surpassed the heights it had reached during World War I. As during the preceding decades, economic and demographic factors loomed large. Continuing job discrimination notwithstanding, wartime labor needs had encouraged a massive increase in black migration to cities in the North and West, which continued at the rate of one million per decade through the 1960s. Although there was some economic reversal following the war, basically blacks had been able to establish firm footholds in semiskilled positions outside southern agriculture.[23]

The wartime gains in employment had stemmed in part from the embarrassing testimony at public hearings conducted by the FEPC, and also from the quiet work of regional FEPC and War Manpower Commission staff members negotiating with industry officials in the North and West. However, the FEPC lacked enforcement powers, was constantly attacked by southern congressmen, and ceased operations at the end of the war. In 1943 A. Philip Randolph created a coalition of organizations known as the National Council for a Permanent FEPC with which the NAACP at first cooperated on an ad hoc basis and eventually joined after the end of the war. For the next two decades the enactment of fair employment legislation would prove to be an elusive goal. But largely through the adroit machinations of Roy Wilkins the National Council evolved by 1952 into an influential lobby for civil rights legislation, the Leadership Conference on Civil Rights (LCCR). This coalition, however, was led not by Randolph but by the NAACP.

This particular development, which has escaped the notice of historians, marked a radical transformation of the NAACP's lobbying strategy from one based on personal contacts by a few top officers of the Association to one that mobilized the resources of scores of civic, labor, and religious organizations. This change was made possible by a significant shift in white public opinion toward accepting the necessity to confront the issue of racial inequality. This influx of support and the new climate of public opinion that it indicated in turn raised the expectations of the NAACP and encouraged it to press its agenda even more forcefully.

The nine years between the end of World War II and the *Brown* decision of 1954 coincided with the onset of the Cold War and the climax of McCarthyism. Although generally unrecognized by scholars, the anti-Communist atmosphere actually had a contradictory impact on the NAACP and the struggle for equal rights. On the one hand, for many white southerners and right-wing conservatives, civil rights for blacks was perceived to be part of an international Communist conspiracy, and the NAACP was attacked repeatedly as being Communist-inspired, -led, and -dominated. On the other hand, the NAACP, which like some other liberal organizations maintained its vigorous opposition to Communist influence, employed the threat posed by the Cold War and the influence of the Soviet Union among nonwhite peoples of the world to press its own agenda. The gist of the argument was that American racial practices played into the Soviet argument about the nature of capitalism, imperialism, and racism.[24] In fact, as an organization, the NAACP entered its most prosperous period during the heyday of the Cold War. Through expanded and effective fundraising mechanisms such as the Life Membership campaigns and the "Freedom Fund" banquets, it established a firm financial footing. This permitted an expansion of the NAACP staff, including maintaining a Washington bureau headed by a full-time lobbyist and the employment of a specialist to deal with organized labor on questions of discrimination.

Late in the war (1944–1945) and in the postwar era, labor and lobbying activities revolved around an alliance between the NAACP and the CIO. The NAACP lobbied in behalf of labor-sponsored social welfare legislation such as minimum wages, public housing, and expansion of unemployment compensation and campaigned against right-to-work laws and the Taft-Hartley Act. From the NAACP's perspective, labor's legislative agenda, if enacted, would also benefit blacks. For its part the CIO not only supported antilynching legislation but was also a vigorous proponent of bills for a permanent FEPC. In part this was a marriage of convenience because, as was frequently said, "both blacks and labor are facing identical enemies in Congress: Southern Democrats and conservative northern and western Republicans." With migration from the South continuing at a high level, blacks were more than ever an essential part of the New Deal-Fair Deal coalition. In 1948 civil rights policy became an important national political issue for the first time since Reconstruction, and black votes in the North and West were key to Harry S. Truman's victory in 1948.[25]

During this period the NAACP also forged alliances with certain leading Jewish secular organizations including the Anti-Defamation League, the American Jewish Committee, and the American Jewish Congress. There has been a mythological tone about what has been called the "Black–Jewish Alliance."[26] For more than three decades after the NAACP was founded, Jewish involvement was limited to the contributions of a handful of individuals. Among the few people of Jewish ancestry connected with the NAACP in the early years were Joel Spingarn and his brother Arthur Spingarn, a lawyer, who as chair of the legal committee played a major role in NAACP litigation until Houston and Thurgood Marshall were hired in the 1930s. Louis Marshall, a constitutional lawyer, was a founder and president of the American Jewish Committee, which played no role in the affairs of the NAACP during this period. Marshall's son-in-law Jacob Billikopf was active in Jewish philanthropic circles during the Great Depression. He arranged for substantial contributions from a few wealthy Jews like Lessing Rosenwald (whose father Julius Rosenwald had given some fairly large contributions to the NAACP during its early years), Joseph Fels of the Fels-Naptha Soap Company, and Herbert Lehman, the prominent Democratic politician. After mid-century, individuals of Jewish ancestry held important positions on the NAACP staff, including Herbert Hill as labor secretary and June Shagaloff as education secretary. However, cooperation between Jewish organizations and the NAACP began only with the campaign to establish a permanent FEPC. This particular alliance played a decisive role in the LCCR legislative coalition that lobbied for the passage of the civil rights acts in 1964 and 1965. In fact, Arnold Aronson, the executive secretary of the LCCR who had had a career in Jewish advancement organizations, became executive secretary Roy Wilkins's most trusted ally. Like most political alliances this one was based on a combination of self-interest, shared goals, and idealism.

President Truman's support for equal rights was not entirely consistent, and he had to be prodded. In 1946 he did appoint a Committee on Civil Rights that issued a report the following year entitled *To Secure These Rights.* Among other recommendations was "the elimination of segregation, based on race, color, creed, or national origin, from American life."[27] In the aftermath Truman issued an order integrating the armed forces. This action illustrates something of the complex maneuvering required for even limited changes. A. Philip Randolph had dramatized the issue by calling for a civil disobedience campaign against the draft; the NAACP, like other race advancement organizations, disavowed the strategy but used the threat posed by Randolph to underline its own concern with the issue. Receiving private assurances that the president would act to integrate the armed forces, Randolph then withdrew his call, and after some delay Truman issued the appropriate executive order.

The NAACP abandoned the seemingly hopeless fight for an antilynching bill. The struggle for a permanent FEPC, which, after early 1949, became the NAACP's top legislative priority, also proved frustrating. The NAACP—unhappy with Randolph's direction of the National Council—had created the LCCR. Probably the most important gains made by the NAACP itself during the period from 1944 to 1954 came through its long-standing program of litigation in the federal courts. Not only had the Supreme Court overturned the system of white primary elections in 1944, but four years later it declared restrictive covenants unenforceable. In the early 1950s came a series of decisions banning the exclusion or segregation of blacks in publicly owned recreation facilities. The NAACP's campaign against Jim Crow schools was coming to a climax. In a series of decisions the Supreme Court required southern states to admit blacks to graduate and professional schools in public universities.

In 1948, possibly capitalizing on the recommendations in *To Secure These Rights,* the NAACP officially undertook a series of suits aimed directly at overthrowing the *Plessy* doctrine of separate but equal. Finally in 1954 in the combination of cases subsumed under *Brown v. Board of Education,* the Supreme Court accepted unanimously the NAACP argument that separate schools were inherently unequal.[28] At the local level coalitions led chiefly by the NAACP and Jewish organizations succeeded in obtaining FEPC laws in a number of states and cities and, in a few places, fair housing laws as well.

During the years following the *Brown* decision, though the pace of change seemed to accelerate, federal court decisions were not self-enforcing and the NAACP had plenty of work to do. In fact, there was a notable expansion of NAACP activity on all fronts. In the southern states white resistance intensified, manifest in a resurgence of the Ku Klux Klan, the formation of white Citizens' Councils, and massive resistance to school desegregation (most notably in the violence at Little Rock that was quelled only when President Dwight D. Eisenhower reluctantly sent in federal troops). Three southern states, Texas, Louisiana, and Alabama, passed laws making it illegal for the NAACP to operate within their boundaries, and across the South violence and intimidation against the NAACP increased. For its part the Association continued to win victories before the courts. The LCCR, backed by a growing array of organizations and sympathetic figures in the Eisenhower administration, was able to secure passage of the civil rights acts of 1957 and 1960. Modest though their provisions were, having been diluted by the compromises of Senate majority leader Lyndon B. Johnson, they were nevertheless significant as the first national civil rights laws passed since 1875.

In retrospect, the policies of the Eisenhower administration could be characterized as moderate Republican.[29] For example, the NAACP labor secretary Herbert Hill utilized well the machinery of the President's Committee on Government Contracts, which was charged with resolving incidents of discrimination practiced by both management and labor in cases involving contracts with the federal government. This sort of mechanism had first been put into place by Truman after the continued failure of the Congress to pass fair employment legislation. Headed by Vice President Richard M. Nixon, Eisenhower's committee performed with surprising efficacy. Acting on complaints from the NAACP and other groups, it resolved a number of the most egregious individual cases.

All of this was taking place against the background of the rise of anticolonial movements in Asia and Africa. Ghana's independence in 1957 prompted the view among black Americans that their brothers and sisters in Africa were achieving freedom at a more rapid pace than blacks in America.

Domestically the pace of events also quickened but at a slower rate. State FEPC laws, Supreme Court decisions, and congressional legislation seemed to promise so much but made only relatively small dents in basic patterns of discrimination. An example of the difficulties faced can be seen in the Supreme Court ruling in 1955, which blunted the thrust of the *Brown* decision by sanctioning "all deliberate speed" and thereby afforded the white South the encouragement and time to mobilize against the movement toward equal rights. Another example was the situation with regard to the franchise. By 1954, a decade after the white primary decision, black voter registration in the South had risen from 250,000 to 1,250,000, with increases chiefly in the upper South but also in repressive areas of the Deep South such as some of the Louisiana parishes. But an important aspect of the development of southern resistance to black advances was the increased use of intimidation and of technicalities such as literacy tests that actually reduced the number of blacks registered.[30]

In this context there was what we may call a "revolution in expectations" among American blacks, a new sense of urgency to speed the dismantling of barriers to racial equality. The result was an outpouring of nonviolent direct action that by the early 1960s came to characterize this most recent phase of the civil rights movement. Tens of thousands of people—black and white—were mobilized for the first time, and the rise of new organizations such as SCLC, SNCC, and many local organizations ended the NAACP's hegemony over the civil rights movement. Ironically the NAACP's successful work in the courts and legislatures had created the impatience and dissatisfaction with its tactics and strategies.

The first organizational challenge to the NAACP came from the Montgomery bus boycott, which led to the rise of Martin Luther King, Jr., and the founding of SCLC in 1957. Unlike the situation with Randolph, the NAACP had had no knowledge of or working relationship with King before his appearance as a leader; King, for his part, did not need the NAACP. Therefore the NAACP leadership was unable to exert substantial influence over his activities. In this changing climate, and given King's personal magnetism, the founding of SCLC posed the most serious threat to the NAACP's leadership that it had faced since the founding of the National Negro Congress in 1936. Even though the Supreme Court case resulting from the Montgomery bus boycott was won by NAACP lawyers, King's charisma was such that this achievement—which effectively clinched the victory—went virtually unnoticed.

During the early 1960s, though vastly overshadowed in the mass media by King, by the southern student revolt and the rise of SNCC, by the resurgence of the Congress of Racial Equality (CORE) under James Farmer's leadership, and by the appearance of Malcolm X, the NAACP was more active and successful than ever before. The sixties was a period of especially intense conflict and competition among civil rights organizations partly over questions of strategy, tactics, and the pace of change but largely over organizational credit. The NAACP was criticized from both within and without the Association's ranks as being a conservative, bureaucratic organization that was out of touch with the new militancy. In the context of the early 1960s this lack of unity was actually quite helpful as civil rights organizations at both the national and local levels competed with one another in their quest for victories in the struggle for equality. Oddly enough its long-established structure enabled the NAACP to reap the benefits from the new racial consciousness, and by 1963 its membership crested at over 400,000, making it by far the largest civil rights organization. Moreover, it was the only civil rights organization that was funded primarily by the black community.

As could be expected in an organization of its age and size, there was an enormous range of attitudes and responses in the branches to the new wave of demonstrations. Some branches figuratively sat on their hands, while others embraced the new activism with enthusiasm. In fact, the NAACP branches were probably the major source of legal aid to the youthful activists of 1960 and 1961, and the Association's own youth councils and college chapters did much to make this phase of the movement effective. In South Carolina, for example, in 1963 and 1964 the NAACP State Conference of Branches led the direct action struggle. As Roy Wilkins said with some justice, "the NAACP branches put up the money and others get the credit." The NAACP was also deeply involved in litigation against de facto school segregation in northern cities and provided support for school boycotts in Boston, New York, and other cities in 1963 and 1964. Numerous NAACP members were also among the demonstrators at construction sites in northeastern cities protesting discrimination in the building trades and among the masses of protesters against job discrimination in such places as the cities in the San Francisco Bay area.

With regard to the issue of racial bias by many labor unions, beginning in the late 1950s the NAACP labor secretary Herbert Hill had adopted an innovative approach to job discrimination. Using a combination of litigation and publicity, Hill kept constant pressure on government, corporations, and labor unions to do their part in opening up more job opportunities for blacks. At the same time Hill was carrying out this aspect of the NAACP program, Clarence Mitchell, head of the Washington bureau, and the whole LCCR strategy were heavily dependent on the AFL–CIO legislative lobby for stronger civil rights legislation. In effect NAACP executive secretary Roy Wilkins was pursuing a skillful two-pronged strategy of confronting labor with specific examples of discrimination while continuing to maintain an alliance with labor on matters of joint legislative interest. This whole strategy depended upon the need for the AFL–CIO's leadership to maintain the liberal image of the labor movement and labor's role and influence in the New Deal coalition. Moreover, the AFL–CIO leadership admitted that on the question of union discrimination it could not clean its own house without the assistance of federal fair employment legislation.

The culmination of direct action North and South came during the year following the Birmingham demonstrations of spring 1963. The August 1963 March on Washington symbolized unprecedented national support for some form of civil rights legislation. In this context of dramatic confrontations displaying both racist repression and individual courage, the NAACP mobilized the

LCCR for the successful lobbying for the passage of the Civil Rights Act of 1964 and the Voting Rights Act of 1965. The support of both the large AFL-CIO lobby in Washington and the representatives of the major religious faiths was vital as was the political pressure applied by President Johnson, but it was the NAACP's executive secretary who made the important decisions, including the one to incorporate a strong employment anti-discrimination clause that became Section 7 of the 1964 Act. One should not discount the role of the direct action organizations in awakening public opinion and exerting tremendous moral and political pressures. But it is important to emphasize the development of a symbiotic relationship between the campaigns led by new waves of demonstrators and the NAACP's skillful translation of their joint concerns into lasting legislative victories.

The civil rights legislation came during the apex of New Deal-style reformism that characterized the war on poverty. This legislation finally removed the legal barriers that had prevented blacks from exercising their basic rights under the Fourteenth and Fifteenth Amendments, which the NAACP had sought since its founding. This legislation also brought into being the legal sanctions against employment discrimination that the NAACP had first included in its national agenda during the Roosevelt era.

The enactment of the civil rights laws of 1964 and 1965 produced what A. Philip Randolph called a crisis of victory. It soon became apparent that the mere passage of legislation and the recognition of constitutional rights were not sufficient to redress three hundred years of racial oppression. The issues associated with economic inequality— widespread poverty, poor and inadequate housing, inferior schools, police brutality, and other inequities in the criminal justice system— proved to be virtually intractable. Much of the black power response consisted of attempts to deal with the difficulties and frustrations of this situation. Ideologically the NAACP resisted this tendency toward separatism, and the national leadership's success in this matter was probably due to the commitment, especially in the South, of its largely middle-aged membership to the struggle for integration. Yet at this point the national board for the first time became all black, and it has remained that way ever since.

Just as the New Deal-style economic and social programs of the Great Society were on the verge of decline, so also the NAACP, from an organizational point of view, was looking at a bleaker future. Finding that its traditional strategies of legal redress and legislative reform were not adequate to deal with problems of this magnitude and that there was no national consensus on how to deal with these matters, the Association began to drift and decline. The NAACP began to lose its membership and its leadership role.

The Voting Rights Act opened up the possibility of significant gains in the political system; consequently much of black leadership has gravitated toward electoral politics. Leadership began to develop from the local level through the Congressional Black Caucus. The irony is that it was the NAACP's success in lobbying for black voting rights that helped lay the groundwork for the drift away from the organization and toward political activism. However, the increase in black voting power caused many white southerners and northern white ethnics to shift to the Republican party, reinforcing the decline in liberalism associated with the Republican ascendancy since the end of the 1960s.

In short, the NAACP, which outlived many of the Progressive and New Deal organizations and had a successful post-World War II career, now appears to have suffered the general fate of liberal reform in the 1970s and 1980s.

Notes

1. This essay is a synthesis based principally upon years of research in the National Association for the Advancement of Colored People (NAACP) Papers in the Manuscript Division of the Library of Congress, selective research in other manuscript and archival collections, extensive reading in all the major black newspapers, interviews with NAACP officials, and insights gained from participation in NAACP branches and in the larger black protest movement. Earlier publications based on this research are August Meier and Elliott Rudwick, "Attorneys Black and White: A Case Study of Race Relations within the NAACP," *Journal of American History,* LXII (March 1976), 913–46; Rudwick and Meier, "The Rise of the Black Secretariat in the NAACP, 1909–35" in Meier and Rudwick, *Along the Color Line: Explorations in the Black Experience* (Urbana, Chicago, and London, 1976), 94–127; Meier and Rudwick, *Black Detroit and the Rise of the UAW* (New York and Oxford, 1979); and John H. Bracey, Jr., and Meier, "Allies or Adversaries: The NAACP, A. Philip Randolph and the 1941 March on Washington," *Georgia Historical Quarterly,* LXXV (Spring 1991), 1–17. We wish to thank David Katzman for suggesting to Professor Meier this topic as an appropriate one for a presidential address.

2. The "Inc." Fund was established in 1940 as a tax-exempt mechanism that carried out the organizations legal strategies. In 1957 changes in Internal Revenue regulations forced its complete separation from the parent body.

3. John Chamberlain, *Farewell to Reform: Being a History of the Rise, Life and Decay of the Progressive Mind in America* (New York, 1932); Richard Hofstadter, *The Age of Reform: From Bryan to F.D.R* (New York, 1956); Eric F. Goldman, *Rendezvous with Destiny* (New York, 1952); Allen F. Davis, *Spearheads for Reform: The Social Settlements and the Progressive Movement, 1890–1914* (New York, 1967); Otis L. Graham, Jr., *An Encore for Reform: The Old Progressives and the New Deal* (New York, 1967), and Graham, *Toward a Planned Society: From Roosevelt to Nixon* (New York, 1976); Wilbur J. Cohen, ed., *The Roosevelt New Deal: A Program Assessment Fifty Years After* ([Austin, Texas], 1986). Other relevant volumes that omit or pay scant attention to blacks and the NAACP include Clarke A. Chambers, *Seedtime of Reform: American Social Service and Social Action, 1918–1933* (Minneapolis, 1963); Robert Higgs, *Crisis and Leviathan: Critical Episodes in the Growth of American Government* (New York and Oxford, 1987); Steve Fraser and Gary Gerstle, eds., *The Rise and Fall of the New Deal Order, 1930–1980* (Princeton, 1989); Alan Dawley, *Struggles for Justice: Social Responsibility and the Liberal State* (Cambridge, Mass., 1991); and James T. Kloppenberg, *Uncertain Victory: Social Democracy and Progressivism in European and American Thought, 1870–1920* (New York and Oxford, 1986).

4. Arthur S. Link and Richard L. McCormick, *Progressivism* (Arlington Heights, Ill., 1983); Link, "What Happened to the Progressive Movement in the 1920's?" *American Historical Review,* LXIV (July 1959), 833–51; Alonzo L. Hamby, *Liberalism and Its Challenges: FDR to Reagan* (New York and Oxford, 1985). The ADA studies are Clifton Brock, *Americans for Democratic Action: Its Role in National Politics* (Washington, D.C., 1962) and Steven M. Gillon, *Politics and Vision: The ADA and American Liberalism, 1947–1985* (New York and Oxford, 1987). The ADA and the NAACP are discussed in Denton L. Watson, *Lion in the Lobby: Clarence Mitchell, Jr.'s Struggle for the Passage of Civil Rights Laws* (New York, 1990).

5. See James M. McPherson, *The Abolitionist Legacy: From Reconstruction to the NAACP* (Princeton, 1975) and Emma Lou Thornbrough, "The National Afro-American League, 1887–1908," *Journal of Southern History,* XXVII (November 1961), 494–512.

6. For a somewhat different version of these matters see Nancy J. Weiss, "From Black Separatism to Interracial Cooperation: The Origins of Organized Efforts for Racial Advancement, 1890–1920," in Barton J. Bernstein and Allen J. Matusow, eds., *Twentieth-Century America: Recent Interpretations* (2d. ed.; New York and other cities, 1972), 58–67.

7. On the early years see for example B. Joyce Ross, *J.E. Spingarn and the Rise of the NAACP, 1911–1939* (New York, 1972). On *The Birth of a Nation* see Thomas R. Cripps, "The Reaction of the Negro to the Motion Picture Birth of a Nation," *Historian,* XXV (May 1963), 344–62.

8. Robert L. Zangrando, *The NAACP Crusade Against Lynching, 1909–1950* (Philadelphia, 1980). All of the cases mentioned are discussed in the NAACP annual reports, and most have been the subject of scholarly monographs. See Dennis B . Downey and Raymond M. Hyser, *No Crooked Death: Coatesville, Pennsylvania, and the Lynching of Zachariah Walker* (Urbana and Chicago, 1991); Elliott M. Rudwick, *Race Riot at East St. Louis, July 2, 1917* (Carbondale, Ill., 1964); Robert V. Haynes, *A Night of Violence: The Houston Riot of 1917* (Baton Rouge, 1976); William M. Tuttle, Jr., *Race Riot: Chicago in the Red Summer of 1919* (New York, 1970); Richard C. Cortner, *A Mob Intent on Death: The NAACP and the Arkansas Riot Cases* (Middletown, Conn., 1988); Scott Ellsworth, *Death in a Promised Land: The Tulsa Race Riot of 1921* (Baton Rouge and London, 1982); Dan T. Carter, *Scottsboro: A Tragedy of the American South* (Baton Rouge, 1969); Stephen J. Whitfield, *A Death in the Delta: The Story of Emmett Till* (New York and London, 1988); and Howard Smead, *Blood Justice: The Lynching of Mack Charles Parker* (New York and Oxford, 1986).

9. See files on Aiken, South Carolina, lynchings, Containers 365 and 366, Group 1, Series C, in NAACP Papers, Library of Congress.

10. Ralph J. Bunche, "The Programs, Ideologies, Tactics and Achievements of Negro Betterment and Interracial Organizations," p. 48 (Unpublished Memorandum for the Carnegie-Myrdal Study, 1940); copy at the Schomburg Center for Research in Black Culture, New York Public Library).

11. For the documentary record of these debates see Theodore G. Vincent, ed., *Voices of a Black Nation: Political Journalism in the Harlem Renaissance* (San Francisco, 1973), Chapters 3 and 4.

12. David Levering Lewis, "The Politics of Art: The New Negro, 1920–1935," *Prospects: An Annual of American Cultural Studies,* III (1977), 237–61.

13. In addition to chapter I in the biography by B. Joyce Ross cited above, Joel E. Spingarn's literary activities are given more extensive treatment in Marshall Van Deusen, *J.E. Spingarn* (New York, 1971). Mary White Ovington wrote in a variety of genres. The most relevant works for our purposes include *The Shadow* (New York, 1920), a novel; *Hazel* (New York, 1913) and *Zeke* (New York, 1931), novels written for black youth; *The Awakening* (New York, 1923) and *Phyllis Wheatley* (New York, 1932), plays about black life; *The Upward Path; A Reader for Colored Children . . .* (New York, 1920); and *Portraits in Color* (New York, 1927), a collection of biographical sketches of twenty prominent black men and women living at that time.

14. James Weldon Johnson was a prolific writer in a variety of genres both fictional and nonfictional. His most significant works during this period include *The Autobiography of an Ex-Colored Man* (Boston, 1912; 2d ed., 1927), a novel; *The Book of American Negro Poetry . . .* (New York, 1922; rev. ed., 1931); *God's Trombones: Seven Negro Sermons in Verse* (New York, 1927); *Black Manhattan* (New York, 1930), a social and cultural history of blacks in New York City; and *Along This Way: The Autobiography of James Weldon Johnson* (New York, 1933). The standard biography of Johnson is Eugene Levy's *James Weldon Johnson: Black Leader, Black Voice* (Chicago and London, 1973). White wrote two novels during this period: *The Fire in the Flint* (New York, 1924) and *Flight* (New York, 1926). His relationship to the Renaissance has been discussed in Edward E. Waldron, *Walter White and the Harlem Renaissance* (Port Washington, N.Y., 1978). Jessie Redmon Fauset's novels include *There is Confusion* (New York, 1924); *Plum Bun* (New York, 1929); *The Chinaberry Tree* (New York, 1931); and *Comedy, American Style* (New York, 1933). William Pickens was the author of *The New Negro: His Political, Civil, and Mental Status; and Related Essays* (New York, 1916); an autobiography, *Bursting Bonds: Enlarged Edition, The Heir of Slaves* (Boston, 1923); a collection of short stories, *The Vengeance of the Gods* (Philadelphia, 1922); and an anthology entitled *American AESOP: Negro and Other Humor* (Boston, 1926). The best overall study of the relation of art to politics in the Harlem Renaissance is David Levering Lewis, *When Harlem Was in Vogue* (New York, 1981).

15. Clement E. Vose, *Caucasians Only: The Supreme Court, the NAACP, and the Restrictive Covenant Cases* (Berkeley and Los Angeles, 1959).

16. Richard L. Watson, Jr., "The Defeat of Judge Parker: A Study in Pressure Groups and Politics," *Mississippi Valley Historical Review,* L (September 1963), 213–34. See also Kenneth W. Goings, "*The NAACP Comes of Age": The Defeat of Judge John J. Parker* (Bloomington and Indianapolis, 1990).

17. See Richard Kluger, *Simple Justice: The History of* Brown v. Board of Education *and Black America's Struggle for Equality* (New York, 1975) and especially Mark V. Tushnet, *The NAACP's Legal Strategy Against Segregated Education, 1925–1950* (Chapel Hill and London, 1987).

18. Gunnar Myrdal, *An American Dilemma: The Negro Problem and Modern Democracy* (New York and London, 1944). See also Walter A. Jackson, *Gunnar Myrdal and America's Conscience: Social Engineering and Racial Liberalism, 1938–1987* (Chapel Hill and London, 1990). For a biography of Houston see Genna Rae McNeil, *Groundwork: Charles Hamilton Houston and the Struggle for Civil Rights* (Philadelphia, 1983); for Hastie see Gilbert Ware, *William Hastie: Grace Under Pressure* (New York and Oxford, 1984).

19. Darlene Clark Hine, *Black Victory: The Rise and Fall of the White Primary in Texas* (Millwood, N.Y., 1979).

20. For a more complete presentation of Du Bois's argument than is found in the *Crisis* or in the NAACP Papers, see his 1936 essay, "The Negro and Social Reconstruction," in W.E.B. Du Bois, *Against Racism: Unpublished Essays, Papers, Addresses, 1887–1961*, edited by Herbert Aptheker (Amherst, Mass., 1985), 103–58.

21. On Randolph's career see Jervis Anderson, *A. Philip Randolph: A Biographical Portrait* (New York, 1973); Paula F. Pfeffer, *A. Philip Randolph, Pioneer of the Civil Rights Movement* (Baton Rouge and London, 1990); William H. Harris, *Keeping the Faith: A. Philip Randolph, Milton P. Webster, and the Brotherhood of Sleeping Car Porters, 1925–37* (Urbana, Chicago, and London, 1977); and Herbert Garfinkel, *When Negroes March: The March on Washington Movement in the Organizational Politics for FEPC* (Glencoe, Ill., 1959). For our understanding of the NAACP's role in the 1941 March on Washington see Bracey and Meier, "Allies or Adversaries?". For general studies of the relationship between blacks and organized labor see especially Sterling D. Spero and Abram L. Harris, *The Black Worker: The Negro and the Labor Movement* (New York, 1931) and Horace R. Cayton and George S. Mitchell, *Black Workers and the New Unions* (Chapel Hill, 1939).

22. For the shift to the Democratic party see especially Harvard Sitkoff's *A New Deal for Blacks: The Emergence of Civil Rights as a National Issue* (New York, 1978) and Nancy J. Weiss, *Farewell to the Party of Lincoln: Black Politics in the Age of FDR* (Princeton, 1983).

23. For general conditions of blacks in industry during the 1940s see Herbert R. Northrup, *Organized Labor and the Negro* (New York and London, 1944) and Robert C. Weaver, *Negro Labor: A National Problem* (New York, 1946).

24. The juxtaposition of these issues was graphically demonstrated on the front page of the *New York Times* of May 18, 1954, the day after the *Brown* decision. A two-line banner headline across the top of the page announced: "HIGH COURT BANS SCHOOL SEGREGATION; 9-TO-0 DECISION GRANTS TIME TO COMPLY." There followed an across-the-page headline in smaller letters, "McCarthy Hearing Off a Week as Eisenhower Bars Report." And in the lower right-hand corner was an article about the Voice of America flashing the court ruling to the world in thirty-four different languages.

25. On the new importance of the black vote in national elections see Henry Lee Moon, *Balance of Power: The Negro Vote* (Garden City, N.Y., 1948).

26. On black-Jewish relations see for example Robert G . Weisbord and Arthur Stein, *Bittersweet Encounter: The Afro-American and the American Jew* (Westport, Conn., 1970); Hasia R. Diner, *In the Almost Promised Land: American Jews and Blacks, 1915–1935* (Westport, Conn., and London, 1977); and David Levering Lewis, "Parallels and Divergences: Assimilationist Strategies of Afro-American and Jewish Elites from 1910 to the Early 1930s," *Journal of American History*, LXXI (December 1984), 543–64.

27. *To Secure These Rights: The Report of the President's Committee on Civil Rights* (Washington, 1947), 166. On Truman's civil rights policies see especially William C. Berman, *The Politics of Civil Rights in the Truman Administration* (Columbus, Ohio, 1970).

28. For a complete list of these cases see Jack Greenberg, *Race Relations and American Law* (New York and London, 1959), 401–2, entitled "Appendix B: NAACP Legal Defense Cases Before the Supreme Court."

29. For differing views on Eisenhower, see Robert Fredrick Burk, *The Eisenhower Administration and Black Civil Rights* (Knoxville, 1984) and Stephen E. Ambrose, *Eisenhower* (2 vols.; New York, 1983–1984), Volume II: *The President.*

30. For a comprehensive treatment of the struggle against disfranchisement see Steven F. Lawson, *Black Ballots: Voting Rights in the South, 1944–1969* (New York, 1976).

Reading 14

Soldiers of Democracy: Black Texans and the Fight for Citizenship, 1917–1921

Steven A. Reich

This is the country to which we Soldiers of Democracy return. . . . But by the God of Heaven, we are cowards and jackasses if now that that war is over, we do not marshal every ounce of our brain and brawn to fight a sterner, longer, more unbending battle against the forces of hell in our own land.

> We *return*.
> We *return from fighting*.
> We *return fighting*.

Make way for Democracy! We saved it in France, and by the Great Jehovah, we will save it in the United States of America, or know the reasons why.

W. E. B. Du Bois, Crisis, May 1919

The world can never be made safe for democracy as long as America is unsafe for its own citizens.

C. F. Richardson Jr., Houston Informer, *June 7, 1919*

On the night of December 8, 1918, Black residents of Kildare, an unincorporated hamlet nestled in the northeast corner of Texas, gathered at the local African Methodist Episcopal Church to hear a lecture "on the War and after the War." The audience, composed mostly of farmers and sharecroppers who struggled to make a living out of the stubborn piney woods soil, listened to the preacher describe how, despite their bravery abroad and sacrifice at home, Blacks were "still being treated badly by the White man." The United States, he grieved, "forced the Negro to go 3000 miles away to fight for Democracy when they should have been fighting for Democracy at home." Now that the war was over, Blacks must no longer "close ranks" with whites but demand their rights as citizens, even if it meant opening "another war for Democracy, right here at home." Black veterans, he envisioned, would lead this fight for citizenship. Although whites drafted "our boys against their will," they also armed them and taught them lessons of combat. "When our boys return," he warned a disciplined army of "trained officers, of men not afraid to die" and experienced "in killing white men," would invade the South. He urged his listeners to "arm themselves with Winchester rifles" and join the returning soldiers of democracy in a united stand against white supremacy.[1]

This call to arms stands out as neither an isolated incident nor the wishful fantasy of a deluded preacher. On the contrary, African Americans echoed these themes in churches, fraternal societies, union halls, and social settings across Texas and throughout the South from 1917 to 1919, the years during and immediately following American involvement in World War I. They took such ideas seriously, seizing upon the idealistic rhetoric of President Woodrow Wilson's Fourteen Points to claim new rights at home. In a multitude of ways—withholding their labor, fleeing the state, evading the draft, stockpiling arms, forming local chapters of political organizations such as the National Association for the Advancement of Colored People (NAACP)—African Americans resisted their oppressions, posing a formidable threat to the status quo. Indeed, during these years southern Blacks mobilized in opposition to white supremacy to an extent that historians have not yet appreciated. Privileging the views of Black elites, most narratives assume that African Americans submerged demands for citizenship, closed ranks, and hoped that whites would reward them for their service and patriotism, a faith that turned out to be misguided.[2] If historians have assumed that African Americans remained patient during the war years, the men and women who applauded the preacher at Kildare were not quiescent. Nor did the Department of Justice's newly created Federal Bureau of Investigation (FBI) remain complacent. It found the preachers comments serious enough to demand "any action . . . necessary."[3]

The story of African American resistance during the war and immediate postwar years challenges prevailing interpretations of Black politics in the age of Jim Crow. Much race relations scholarship posits that the system of Jim Crow was powerful enough to preclude any substantive challenges to it. In an era of declining electoral rights, growing segregation, and rising negrophobia, African Americans, according to this view, remained politically apathetic. For most Blacks, as the historian Lester C. Lamon concluded, "the obvious answer" was simply to ignore elections, "follow the line of least resistance and stay at home." Accordingly, African American history tends to concentrate on arenas where Blacks presumably exercised more agency: community development, family life, emigration, and migration. When this scholarship turns to the politics of the disfranchised, it focuses narrowly on the activities of a few Black Republican party functionaries in their struggle to claim delegate seats to national conventions, combat the influence of lily-whites within the party, and retain control over patronage distribution. This model of an active Black elite and a passive working class contributes to the impression that African Americans consciously separated issues of economic advancement and social justice from politics and that they abandoned serious political struggle between 1877 and 1954. In his pathbreaking study on the origins of segregation, C. Vann Woodward remarked that after southern legislatures passed disfranchisement laws. "Many of the Negroes became apathetic and ceased political activity altogether. Despite over a generation of interest in African Americans as subjects of historical study, such assumptions continue. For example, in his otherwise impressive synthesis of Reconstruction, Eric Foner writes that in the post-Reconstruction South "black activity turned inward," assumed "a defensive cast," and "concentrated on strengthening the black community rather than on directly challenging the new status quo."[4]

Other historians, however, insist that African Americans did not remain politically passive under Jim Crow. Black workers in the South, for example, recognized that demands for higher wages and shorter hours rang hollow without the attainment of full citizenship rights. Recent scholarship on coal miners in West Virginia, waterfront workers in New Orleans, and Communists in Alabama reexamines the several ways Black workers struggled to improve their lives in the Jim Crow South. Historians have also begun to analyze African American women as political actors. Paula Giddings argued for a genuine radical tradition among African American women, many of whom understood the dynamic relationship between sexism and racism. These women recognized that women's rights were empty if Blacks remained crushed under the heel of a racist power structure and, conversely, that women's rights had to be secured in order to assure Black liberation. In a recent pathbreaking article, Robin D. G. Kelley argued for an expansive definition of Black political action. Southern Blacks did not separate politics "from lived experience or the imagined world of what is possible." In fact, political action and resistance among African Americans was going on all the time. Through countless "unorganized, evasive, seemingly spontaneous actions," Kelley writes, Black workers battled "to roll back constraints, to exercise power over, or create space within, the institutions and social relationships that dominated their lives." Such everyday struggles informed African American participation in moments of broader political insurgency.[5]

American participation in World War I proved such a moment. Subterranean resistance briefly erupted into above-ground, organized political action. Local activists understood the implications of a worldwide struggle for democracy and self-determination. The metaphor of a war for democracy, the heroics of Black troops in France, and the anticolonial struggles of Africans served as a powerful basis for organized political action, empowering Blacks to expand their vision of what was possible. They linked their everyday challenges to white supremacy to those of Blacks not only in other parts of the South but in Chicago, New York City, the Caribbean, and Africa. The possibility that daily, unorganized challenges to white supremacy might cohere into something national, even global, in scope threatened the nation's white establishment, who mustered legal and extralegal authority to smash the emergence of such a movement.

A case study of Texas during the war and immediate postwar years brings these themes into focus. A rich and varied collection of sources informs the study including Texas Black newspapers, extensive NAACP branch files, and investigative reports conducted by the FBI and the Military Intelligence Division of the War Department. A careful reading of these sources uncovers a wide spectrum of African Americans—male and female, urban and rural, working-class and professional, comfortable and destitute—involved in political action. These men and women risked their lives to demand social change in a state notorious for lynching and political violence. An examination of the fortunes and failures of these activists can thus serve as a window on power relations in the New South and reveal the "reasons why" Africans Americans were unable to fulfill W. E. B. Du Bois's call to "make way for democracy."

Mobilization for the Great War in 1917 and 1918 presented southern Blacks an unprecedented opportunity to escape white control. African Americans fled Texas in droves, seizing new opportunities in wartime industries and military service. Elijah C. Branch, a Black minister from Galveston, established the International Relief Company in 1917 to secure loans for Blacks who wished to leave. Northern Black newspapers such as the *Chicago Defender* enjoyed a wide circulation in Texas and informed readers of the opportunities available in the North. The letters of the migrants reveal the energy and determination of southern Blacks to improve their lives, not only economically but socially and politically as well. Most migrants likely agreed with the Houston freight handler who wrote to the *Houston Observer* that he would move anywhere north "so long as I Go where a man is a man." Others willingly joined the army, as military service promised relief from repressive conditions at home. By the summer of 1918 the Dallas Exemption Board announced that more negroes ...responded to the calls than could be sent to camp." Black enlistees expected to receive good clothes, three meals a day, shelter, some money, and the chance for travel and adventure.[6]

Migration to the North and the draft precipitated an intense labor shortage, giving those who remained greater leverage in negotiating wages. On some plantation, farm laborers, by withholding their labor, compelled planters to increase daily wages form $1.50 to as high as $4.50. Unregulated by government price controls, cotton prices soared to 35 cents a pound in 1919, as compared to 8 cents and less in 1914. For rural Blacks, the prospects of moving up the tenure ladder and of escaping debt and dependence on oppressive landlords never seemed brighter. Nate Shaw, an Alabama tenant farmer, recalled that "the war was good to me because it meant scarce cotton; and scarce cotton, high price." In 1918 Shaw raised enough money from selling cotton to pay off a five-year debit to his landlord. Other Black workers organized collectively to exploit the labor shortage. At Jefferson, in Marion County, Texas, washerwomen refused to take in laundry for less than two dollars, prompting white women to complain "that it is practically impossible to secure domestic help" because Black women are "so organized and demand so much." Employers in the state's railroads, sawmills, logging camps, and shipyards complained often of labor shortages during these years.[7]

African Americans wedded their aspirations for higher wages and better working conditions to broader demands for civil and political rights. In a letter to the *Fort Worth Record*, an anonymous Black man announced, if "you think that we are going to war, bleed and die and come back here and still be a step stone for you unthankful people, not so." The Black press in Texas and elsewhere across the South celebrated Black soldiers as symbols of a new, more militant race pride. "'Black Devils' Are Sounding Death Knell to Trench Warfare—Germans in Deadly Fear of Our Black 'Boys'" ran one typical headline. Such stories carried an implicit message: Blacks at home should exhibit the same assertiveness, as did the troops abroad. The *Galveston New Idea*, a Black paper, echoed this theme, declaring that "patience will cease to be a virtue" if lynch law and prejudicial juries continue to tyrannize Blacks. Now that America needed to stand united, Blacks should press "to rectify the wrongs done us" by "the bloody, savage vampires of the white race."[8]

Such declarations fed white fears that Black soldiers would return from France to start a social revolution across the South. Indeed, few images haunted the white supremacist's imagination more than a Black man in uniform. African American soldiers exposed potent contradictions within the Jim Crow social order and raise critical questions about the very foundations of citizenship. Could United States soldiers stationed in southern cities be denied seats on a bus, at a lunch counter or in a theater? What authority did civilian police have over servicemen who violated Jim Crow laws? Could a liberal democratic government compel citizens to sacrifice their lives in battle yet continue to deny them the franchise? Would Black soldiers who faced the horrors of death on the battlefield, asked the *New Republic*, "accept the facts of white supremacy with the same spirit as formerly?" And did not white opposition to Black conscription confirm that the southern social order rested on nothing more than fear? The *Houston Chronicle* thought so. In defending the military's decision to station Black battalions at Houston's Camp Logan, the editor wondered, "Can we conscientiously ask our allies to quarter soldiers whom we ourselves profess to be afraid of?" To ban Black troops from the city, he concluded, would be an open admission that Texas governed through an indefensible form of discrimination.[9]

Black soldiers played a crucial role in defining the implications of military service. As Eric Foner noted in reference to the Black troops of the Civil War, "military service has always been a politicizing and radicalizing experience.": Rather than patiently waiting for a grateful nation to grant them the rights and privilege of loyal citizens, Black servicemen proudly assumed the authority of their uniform. Black soldiers stationed in Houston defied the symbols of white supremacy by tearing down "colored only" signs in segregated restaurants and taking seats in "whites only" sections aboard city streetcars. According to United States military intelligence reports, discharged Black soldiers organized secret societies to "protect the interests of the colored race," to combat "any white effort, especially in the South, to re-establish white ascendancy," and to "maintain and strengthen the social equality between the races as established in France." As one Black Texan serving in France wrote, "I have but one desire, and that is to be able to go all over our land and tell of my experiences in the democratic France, and the manly qualities displayed by our soldiers under conditions so very foreign to those at home." Much as their Civil War predecessors had, Black veterans of the Great War used military service to justify bold, forthright demands for equal citizenship.[10]

From the beginning of the war, white Texans acted swiftly with a campaign of terror and violence to restrict the social implications of military service. In August 1917 Black soldiers stationed at Houston's Camp Logan, responding to reports of police brutality against a Black soldier, clashed with armed civilians and police in a riot that left seventeen whites and two Black soldiers dead. The military moved quickly to punish Black suspects. In a court-martial in December 1917; thirteen Black soldiers were found guilty, sentenced to death, and hanged without public notice or opportunity to appeal.[11]

Southern whites also tried to deny returning Blacks the right to continue wearing their uniforms for three months after discharge. When appeals to the War Department went unanswered, whites took matters into their own hands. Nate Shaw recalled hearing stories of how whites would meet discharged Blacks "at these stations where they was gettin off, comin back into the United States, and cut the buttons and armaments off of their clothes, make em get out of them clothes make em pull them uniforms off and if they didn't have another suite of clothes . . . make em walk in their underwear." Shaw insisted that these were not isolated incidents as "I heard too much of it from the ones that come back to this country." Through these acts of public degradation, vigilantes tried to devalue the meaning of Black loyalty and service to the nation. As Shaw explained, "nigger come back, he ain't recognized more than a dog. . . . didn't give you no credit for what you done."[12]

White responses to Black soldiers were inconsistent, however, and underscored the logical contradiction of white supremacy. Whites feared Blacks in uniform, yet vigilantes pursued Black draft dodgers with vengeance. Some Blacks resisted the draft. T. P. Terry confidently asserted that "he knew how to get around the white people, that when all the white boys went to war he would have a good time here." Doubtless, more than a few Black Texans shared the sentiments of Monroe Bean of Buna, who openly declared that "If I have to go to war, I will not fight for the United States but for Germany, for they will equalize themselves with me and the people of the United States will not." Near Huntsville in 1918 whites murdered George Cabiness, who resisted arrest for evading the draft. When his brothers vowed revenge, the white men of the community organized a citizens' posse, surrounded the Cabiness home, and commenced firing when the family refused to surrender. The occupants fought back, but the cabin caught fire in the midst of battle, forcing Cabiness's mother, Sarah, to carry the bodies of her four dead sons and wounded daughter out of the flames and into the yard, where she was shot and killed.[13]

Local draft boards used the selective service system as a vehicle for confiscating Black property. As one Texan explained, whites targeted Blacks "who had just purchased little farms, so that the property would soon return to the original owners." Draft agents would then scour the countryside and gather Blacks "up everywhere" so they could avoid drafting "their white boys." As the man admitted, "the Negroes didn't know any better and just thought they had to come." Not surprisingly, then, a disproportionate number of the state's draftees were African Americans, ironically assuring white Texas a large number of returning Black veterans.[14]

As draft agents and vigilantes tried to restrict the meaning of military service, employers imposed tighter controls over Black workers who sought to exploit the wartime labor shortage. Sheriffs assisted in enforcing laws against vagrancy and idleness. At McKinley, the sheriff arrested Blacks who refused to harvest fields for three dollars a day as part of a campaign to see that no Black "idlers are permitted to go unmolested." When the Black exodus from the piney woods compelled the Kirby Lumber Company temporarily to shut down its planing mills at Browndel and Call, east Texas newspaper editors cooperated with company officials by giving prominent coverage to the 1917 East St. Louis race riot and other negative news about the North. Lumber operators also hired a conservative Black lecturer to tour sawmills and logging camps and deliver addresses designed to discourage Black employees from migrating north.[15]

Local postmasters aided in controlling the flow of information by intercepting publications of Black protest such as the *Chicago Defender* and the *Crisis*. "Please don't allow the word *Crisis* to appear" on my mail, wrote a farmer from Mumford. If it does, "I may not get them at all." *The New York Age* reported that one Texas sheriff objected "so strongly to the circulation in Texas of *The New York Age* that he . . . constituted himself a Board of Censors and in that capacity . . . issued orders to the *Age* representative to stop handling the paper in his community." The sheriff apprehended the

Age's traveling representative, who tried to circulate the paper. Despite these threats, the agent vowed not to back down, declaring that the *Age* had reached "every hole and corner in this country," that "it has put some pep where it was badly needed," and that it "cannot afford to die here."[16]

The wartime labor shortage intensified racial conflict in the Texas countryside. During the first two decades of the twentieth century, thousands of white farmers throughout the Southwest slid into permanent tenancy. Many experienced their impoverishment in racial terms. Consider Red River County in northeast Texas. In 1900 the number of whites who owned and rented farms was equal. Twenty years later, the number of owners remained unchanged, but the number of tenants had increased by 58 percent, driving the overall white tenancy rate countywide to 65 percent. During the same period, tenancy among Black farmers remained constant—78 percent—but the number of Black farm owners climbed 12 percent. Landless whites increasingly competed with Blacks for access to tillable plots. Hoping that the wartime cotton boom might offer a chance to escape dependence on absentee landlords, white tenants struck back at Black farmers, who, they believed, benefited from these conditions at their expense. In February 1918 white tenants of Red River County "organized for the purpose of terrorizing Negro farmers." In "operations that extended clear across the county," these vigilantes attacked Black settlements and burned their dwellings, churches, and schoolhouses forcing many to abandon their farms.[17]

Similar violence erupted just south of Red River County. There, one prominent landowner had over 350 acres under cultivation. "Owing to scarcity of white labor, he constructed several "little houses" and hired a number of Black families to work the plantation. In a series of attacks, a posse of backcountry farmers descended on the plantation and fired upon the Black workers. These assaults forced the planter to send his Black workers "back to town for their own safety" and left him without hired hands, turning "this large crop" into "a total loss." In both cases, federal authorities investigated the bloodshed. In Red River County they jailed seventeen white tenants, charging them "with violating the national defense act." As one sheriff explained, "the labor situation is too critical to permit such action on the part of dissatisfied men." These and numerous other incidents reveal how, under wartime labor conditions, class conflict among whites could explode into open racial warfare.[18]

Although African Americans might find federal authorities willing to protect them from roving bands of discontented white tenants, they could not rely on local lawmen or landlords for protection. Planters, just as quickly as white tenants resorted to violence against Blacks who sought to cash in on the wartime cotton boom. In November 1918, Charlie Shipman, a sharecropper under contract to Ollie Senior of Fort Bend County, gathered and weighed his cotton, paid off his debt to Senior, loaded his wagon, and set out with his wife in search of more favorable living conditions. About two miles from the plantation, Senior accosted the two migrants and attempted to force them to return. When Shipman resisted Senior declared, "You Black son-of-a-bitch, I've got a notion to kill you right now." Senior rode off about twenty yards, turned, and fired three shots at Charlie striking him once. Shipman returned fire, but Senior was out of range. Shipman then fled to his mother's house. Shortly thereafter, Senior and five accomplices stormed the house, dragged Shipman into their car, and drove him to a wooded lot where they shot him. Senior told Shipman's mother to retrieve her son's body and bury him as "the law was not coming" to "hold an inquest."[19]

The pervasiveness of violence throughout the war years parallels what Eric Foner described in his study of Reconstruction as the "'politicization' of everyday life." Following emancipation, Foner explains, "a seemingly insignificant incident" could rapidly escalate "into violence and acquire political meaning." At a moment when "established power relations and commonly understood rules of conduct" had been swept away but not yet replaced with a new social order, everyday encounters between Blacks and whites "became infused with tension" as each group attempted to define in its own way the meaning of freedom.[20] In much the same way, mobilization for World War I created a situation in which Blacks and whites battled to redefine social relations.

An incident at Kerens, Texas, in 1917 illustrates this development. According to federal investigators, Mary Monroe, an African American resident, provided room and board to Edward Chambers, a Black itinerant minister. One afternoon while Monroe and Chambers chatted on the porch, Shelton, a white man and "one of the oldest residents of the county," passed by. Since Shelton knew Monroe "since slavery times," he often paused to speak with her. This day, he stopped in his usual manner, commented on the war, and wondered if many local boys would have to serve. Chambers immediately launched into a verbal attack. He accused newspaper editors of covering up the truth, insisting that "white people did not want the negroes to know [the United States was] being whipped by the Germans." He declared that "President Wilson needn't call on the negroes that they did not intend to fight, that they had no country and no flag." Cursing and shaking his finger at the old man, he predicted "that when the Germans won the negroes would own the country." Since "white people . . . had subjected the race to cruelty . . . the negroes would now have their turn." Chambers's remarks caused an immediate stir throughout town. Suspecting that area whites might accuse her of complicity, Monroe asked Chambers to leave. The local constable contacted the FBI for assistance in apprehending Chambers. Federal agents hunted down Chambers in a deserted cabin on the edge of town and threw him in jail.[21]

The Reverend Chambers's bold defiance of racial etiquette is a powerful example of how international events shaped everyday encounters and reverberated into the deepest corners of the New South. In the context of mobilization for war, Shelton's commonplace visit to Mary Monroe erupted into a tense confrontation. The war gave Chambers the vehicle through which to express openly a lifetime of injustices, to reject the patronizing demeanor of a paternalistic white elder, to explode the myth that Blacks trusted their government, and to imagine a world in which power relations were reversed. Whether she agreed with him or not, Monroe distanced herself from the preacher, fearing that vigilantes would retaliate against Blacks indiscriminately. Finally, the case reveals how local lawmen, upon only the slightest hint of trouble, knew they could rely on federal authority to preserve power relations.

In response to this spreading racial violence, African Americans across the state, beginning in San Antonio in 1918, started organizing branches of the NAACP. As a branch organizer from Mart explained, "we are in need very much of strong organization" so "that we might be protected." Activists quickly enlisted a broad base of support for this organization dedicated to civil rights. The *Dallas Express*, a Black weekly, urged readers, "JOIN NOW AND FIGHT FOR JUSTICE—Lynching, Jim Crowism and Denial of Civil Rights Must Cease." The Fort Worth Branch circulated leaflets and handbills and advertised its meetings in Black-owned grocery stores and drugstores. The Dallas Branch sent representatives to the city's Black churches, where they spoke on the benefits of membership and enrolled new members. Activists distributed the *Crisis* and the *Branch Bulletin*, the NAACP's monthly journal of chapter news, placing them in Black-owned businesses and churches and selling them at association meetings where they reportedly "went like 'hot cakes'".[22]

Through these and other tactics, branches aroused mass support, enlisting recruits outside of the Black business and professional classes. At Galveston, Blacks of the International Longshoremen's Association No. 807 organized a branch, recruiting not only waterfront workers but other laborers as well. Elsewhere, janitors, laborers, letter carriers, housekeepers, laundresses, seamstresses—even the butler at the governor's mansion—joined the ranks of the NAACP. "The people are worked to a 'fever heat,'" exulted the San Antonio Branch secretary. That branch grew from an initial membership of 52 in March 1918 to over 1,700 by the summer of 1919, making it the second largest branch in the South, behind only that in Atlanta. Given the size of some of these branches and the occupational profile of the African American population, the Black working class likely constituted the core of the membership.[23]

The national NAACP office assisted in boosting the Texas movement. In the fall of 1918, Mary B. Talbert, president of the National Association of Colored Women's Clubs (NACW), toured Texas and Louisiana to organize NAACP branches. Talbert dedicated her life to the eradication of mob violence, Jim Crow, and colonial domination of Africa, and she agitated for penal reform, education, and protective legislation. An acclaimed orator who "held the undivided attention" of audiences, Talbert delivered her trenchant message to some forty thousand people during her three-month trip, sparking enthusiasm for the NAACP. She raised several thousand dollars, formed eight new branches, and led membership drives at existing ones. Texas "is thoroughly aroused," she wrote; "everywhere they are anxious to join the Association." Thanks to Talbert's "two sterling addresses," she "will long be remembered in Beaumont," reported Aaron Jefferson; "her convincing argument gained many whom we could not interest." In addition to organizing branches, Talbert recruited volunteers to continue building the Texas NAACP after she returned to New York. "Texas will have 50 branches," she predicted; "of the people I talked with, [many] do not go to sleep."[24]

The work of Mary Talbert demonstrates the centrality of women in building branches. Women took the lead in organizing several branches and constituted the core of the membership in many of them, and at least ten served on branch executive committees (see table 1). Talbert expanded branch membership by appealing to women through the Texas Federation of Colored Women's Clubs (TFCWC). As president of the NACW, Talbert strengthened the relationship between the national organization and its state branches through frequent visits, creating a nationwide network of women who supported and implemented NACW initiatives. Talbert called upon such contacts to build the Texas NAACP. Since the founding of the TFCWC in 1905, women of that organization strove to alleviate social ills in an era of diminishing civil and political rights and struggled to provide for the Black masses what white society systematically denied them. At its fourteenth annual convention in 1919, the TFCWC debated the role Black women should play in reconstructing race relations in the postwar period and gave vigorous support to the NAACP's antilynching campaign. Thus many of the women who joined the Texas branches of the NAACP had experience in social activism. These women sponsored programs of special interest to the branches' female members such as lectures on "The Value of the NAACP to the Colored Women of America." And the San Antonio Branch succeeded in securing the employment of a hundred of the city's Black women in the Quartermaster's Department at Fort Sam Houston.[25]

Activists also sought recruits in rural areas. Farmers and laborers composed the bulk of the rural branch membership. Most of the members of the Silsbee Branch were railroad men, including its president, a switchman, and its vice-president, a brakeman. Farmers swelled the ranks of several rural branches. Some, such as many members of the Leggett Branch in Polk County, owned their farms. Most, however, rented, such as the men and women who organized the branch in Mumford. Professional men and women formed the executive committees of some of the branches in smaller communities. In Wharton, three teachers directed the branch, yet farmers from the surrounding area formed the core of the branch's membership. Some of these branches drew impressive numbers. The branch in the small community of Wharton began with 84 charter members but recruiting quickly brought the total to 345. The hamlets of Jones Prairie and Baileyville combined to form one branch of 158 members. And Mumford, a rural village in Robertson County, enrolled 315.[26]

Letters from rural branches reveal an eagerness for political activity and a faith in democracy among poor people. Not since Reconstruction had an organization emerged that connected Blacks in these isolated regions to the larger struggle for citizenship. Through the NAACP, rural Blacks learned of civil rights battles occurring beyond the confines of their community. "What is the peace council doing, what is the world doing for the neggro," asked the Mumford secretary, J. E. Turner; "send me . . . information to advise my people." Enthused at the prospects of real change, Black Texans were, as Grant Burleson of Waelder proclaimed, eager "to be willing workers." Grant Derry promised to "do my very best to get as many joiners as I can"; Turner declared, "I am uneducated, but I want to do some good for my people"; and T. C. Smith reported, "I am working to make 800 members" and pledged to travel "where ever . . . to astablash this association." Such zeal sparked a

Table 1: Women in the Texas NAACP, 1918–1919

Branch	Number of Charter Members	Number of Women	Percentage
Austin	75	34	45%
Baileyville★	89	36	40%
Beaumont	50	1	2%
Benchley	50	12	24%
Bryan	58	12	21%
Caldwell	59	13	22%
Corsicana	61	34	45%
Cuero	115	0	0%
Dallas	169	63	37%
Fort Worth	117	7	6%
Galveston	50	17	34%
Gonzales	50	23	46%
Greenville	111	31	28%
Hearne	59	14	24%
Highbank	92	14	15%
Jones Prairie★	50	10	20%
Leggett	64	12	19%
Marlin	51	3	6%
Marshall	50	22	44%
Mart	50	5	10%
Mumford	61	5	8%
Orange	186	56	30%
Palestine	129	36	28%
San Antonio	112	36	32%
Seguin	50	7	14%
Silsbee	58	24	41%
Temple	58	0	0%
Texarkana	104	46	61%
Waco	56	3	6%
Waelder	50	11	22%
Wharton	84	29	35%
Yoakum	50	4	8%

Source: Applications for Charter, Branch Files, boxes G-200 to G-205, NAACP Papers.

★Organizers in Baileyville and Jones Prairie submitted separate applications for charter; they later combined to form one branch.

flurry of activity across the Black belt, inspiring rural Black Texans to seek political change. These letters convey the kind of utopian spirit that Eric Hobsbawm described as the millenarian strands "necessary . . . for generating the superhuman efforts without which no major revolution is achieved." Indeed, many African Americans expected that the war now made it possible to complete the unfinished revolution of Reconstruction. "Send me a copy of the 13th, 14th, 15th amendment," requested the Mumford secretary, for "the time has come that the white man and the black man to stand upon terms of social equality."[27]

Returning soldiers stimulated the idealism feeding the Texas NAACP. Many NAACP branches sponsored lectures by ex-soldiers, especially during membership drives. Lt. C. C. Taylor aroused interest in organizing a branch in Wharton with a talk on "The Negro and the War." Taylor discussed his war experiences, but he also "dwelled extremely" on topics such as "Race Pride, Suffrage, Leadership, Segregation, Housing Conditions, and the Color Line." The people of Corsicana "turned out enmasse" to hear Lt. B. A. Jackson and Pvt. W. F. Porter address the local NAACP. In a spirited session that lasted "well into the night," the two veterans related their experiences on the "blood-soaked fields of the war ground of the world . . . exhibited gas masks . . . and in other ways greatly enlightened" the standing-room-only crowd. The Reverend Jeems Lewis concluded the meeting with a "roof raising speech right behind the fighting men, demanding the rights of the race which had been bought by blood." Such declarations gave the movement broad appeal. Laborers, laundresses, and farmers, as well as professionals, attended the gathering and applauded the demand for action.[28]

A new, aggressive Black leadership emerged during these years to articulate the grievances and aspirations of the Black working poor. Clifton F. Richardson Jr., newspaper editor and secretary of the Houston Branch, was such a political activist. Richardson co-founded the *Houston Observer* in 1916 and then established his own paper, the *Informer*, in 1919. In his editorials, he inveighed tirelessly against segregation, disfranchisement, racist reporting, and mob violence. Considering himself an "agitator" and a "radical," he demanded "justice, equality before the law, education, decent wages, living conditions, suffrage rights and privileges" and insisted that Blacks wanted "a man's chance— nothing more, nothing less." The vituperative editor continuously criticized Houston's Black elite as self-interested "Huns of ebony Hue" who neglected the needs of the city's Blacks. As an activist, he used his paper as a recruiting tool for the NAACP and encouraged Black labor unions to report their activities in his weekly. His paper had broad appeal and circulated well beyond Houston.[29]

With an energetic membership and aggressive leadership, these newly organized NAACP branches launched a campaign against racial injustice. The mayors of several Texas cities banned the racist film *Birth of a Nation* after NAACP branches presented petitions protesting the film that had been signed by hundreds of Black residents. The San Antonio Branch secured similar petitions protesting the inflammatory *San Antonio Harpoon*, whose editor slandered Black soldiers. Branch activists succeeded in convincing Secretary of War Newton Baker to pull the racist sheet out of circulation at Camp Fort Sam Houston and Camp Travis. The Dallas and Corsicana branches conducted voter registration drives. When Texas granted limited suffrage to women in 1918, the Houston Branch prepared petitions and secured the services of a local Black attorney in overturning a Harris County decision to exclude Black women from registering to vote in the July 1918 primary election. The Austin Branch orchestrated an effective boycott of a store whose owner bludgeoned a Black patron. When a clerk in a San Antonio shoe store struck a Black woman with a shoe, the local branch succeeded in getting the offending clerk fired, tried, and fined and also won $250 in damages for the victim.[30]

Branch activists conducted their most vigorous campaigns against mob violence. They investigated lynchings. They also assisted Blacks unjustly accused of crime. In rural Gonzales County, for example, a Black sharecropper fired upon a gang of white terrorists who invaded his home. The cropper escaped to the home of W. J. Porter, secretary of the Gonzales Branch, who harbored the fugitive from vigilante justice. Other branches raised funds for Black defendants, and activists flooded the governor's office with petitions demanding the apprehension of lynchers and pleading for the pardon of Black convicts. In 1918 several Texas branches united to push an anti-lynching bill. J. F. Hawkins, a Black attorney and member of the Austin Branch, drafted a tough anti-lynching bill. Hawkins urged Gov. William P. Hobby to endorse the bill "as a fitting tribute" to the "black boys who died to maintain the honor of their state and dignity of their nation." Hobby even appealed to the legislature to pass an anti-lynching measure in the current session. Despite the governor's endorsement and the support of several leading white daily newspapers, the bill failed to pass.[31]

The advent of the NAACP in Texas generated vigorous debate among the state's African Americans. Some questioned the value of organizing. Skeptics charged that the NAACP would heighten, not ease racial tensions and that it would isolate, not redress, Black grievances. Within branches, members quarreled over strategies and tactics. Some preferred to steer a cautious course. Others advocated a more militant approach.

The most heated interracial conflict emerged in Houston. In the wake of the Houston riot, the city's established Black elite formed the Civic Betterment League (CBL), an organization that aimed to work with city and county officials in promoting racial harmony. The controversy began when the CBL applied for a NAACP branch charter in June 1918 and found that a group led by

C. F. Richardson, the militant newspaper editor, had already initiated the formation of a branch. Richardson's group had begun legal proceedings against two white policemen who shot a Black man allegedly escaping arrest. E. O. Smith, a school principal and secretary of the CBL, criticized this approach as counterproductive. As he explained to the national office, "conditions are not so serious that we need to be unduly hasty." He urged Walter F. White of the NAACP national office not to grant a charter to a group of men "whose temperament and reputation would likely defeat our purposes and render the work of the national association unpopular if not impossible." Although Smith promised to fight "hard and relentlessly," he pledged to "exhaust every honorable means" to "avoid legal combats." In contrast, Richardson defended his group's aggressiveness. Since the NAACP "is a fighting as well as enlightening force," argued Henry Lucius Mims, president of Richardson's group, the national office must ally itself with Blacks willing to use the courts, press, and pulpit to fight for their rights. White avoided entangling himself in this bitter rivalry and gave recognition to Richardson's group since it had applied first. The CBL, realizing that it was unable to outmaneuver the fiery editor, withdrew its application and, in a spirit of "team play," urged its members to join the local branch.[32]

The conflict between Richardson and the CBL reveals the many tensions within the movement. More than a debate over strategies and tactics, the dispute reflected a generational conflict that was occurring not only in Houston but in other cities across the country.[33] Like other old-guard elites, CBL leaders depended on their ability to compromise with whites to maintain their jobs and status. Hence, they favored working for municipal improvements and proceeded toward political ends only with "proper tact and diplomacy." Richardson, an outsider, younger, self-employed, and less established, had less to lose. As Mims explained, the officers of his group were "employed in an independent way" and, unlike the CBL leadership, did "not depend for a living upon the city administration." According to Mims, Smith would not "take any steps to remedy crying evils" since he could not "antagonize his source of income." Conflicts continued to erupt, and within a year Richardson resigned. The temporizing forces of the old CBL soon gained control of the branch, and, under Smith's tenure as president, the branch pursued a more cautious course. Consequently, Richardson gave the branch no exposure in the *Informer*, and the branch lost much potential popular support.[34]

Several historians fault the NAACP in this period for failing to capitalize on the popular ground swell for mass organization. Too often, these scholars complain, the association's agenda ignored the immediate problems of the poor and focused narrowly on the interests of Black business. According to this view, the NAACP and other racial organizations of the period failed to sustain a mass movement because of their commitment to what historian Judith Stein calls the "elite model of progress."[35]

Such a perspective overlooks the subversive aspirations of these activists and, by stressing elitism, ignores how working-class African Americans interpreted such a movement on their own terms or otherwise found meaning through membership. True, many branch activists maintained a faith in liberalism, capitalism, progress, and Christianity. But as historian Evelyn Brooks Higginbotham forcefully reminds us, "it is not uncommon for oppressed peoples to adopt the values of their oppressors for reasons of their own."[36] Whether protesting *Birth of a Nation*, challenging police brutality, or agitating for anti-lynching legislation, Texas activists distinguished themselves by demanding the active intervention of the state to protect the citizenship rights of all Americans. Moreover, Black workers energized this movement, exploiting the wartime emergency by migrating, withholding their labor, or seeking political self-activity through participation in the NAACP. In fact, it was not these activists' elitism that proved fatal. On the contrary, their very assertiveness prompted threatened whites to launch a concerted campaign of violence and intimidation aimed at destroying this nascent civil rights movement.

By the summer of 1919, Black activism became increasingly risky. In July a white mob at Longview assaulted a Black man who allegedly accused local officials of covering up a recent lynching. The mob retaliated against Blacks who came to the victim's defense by burning several stores and homes in Longview's Black neighborhood, killing one man. Racial tensions worsened when a score of white and Black longshoremen clashed in Port Arthur just three days after the violence at Longview. At Waco, Blacks aroused public sentiment by soliciting signatures to a petition that proclaimed that the "last war made [Blacks] the equals of the white race, and that this stand must be enforced." From Austin, the branch secretary, P. A. Williams, wrote that "the boys that are returning from over seas are telling of their mistreatment, discrimination, etc. by the Americans thereby arousing a racial feeling that is likely to give vent to rioting upon any provocation." The men "have returned to old homes but are not going to submit to old conditions." And the *Galveston New Idea* called upon Blacks "everywhere to get good guns plenty of ammunition and meet the damnable mob with the same thing the mob meets you."[37]

This resistance among Blacks fed white fears that outside agitators and Black Texans had allied to overthrow the state's racial order. Felix McCord, the state representative from Longview, blamed the "ill feeling" between the races in Gregg County on newspapers "advocating social equality for Negroes." Federal agents in Galveston targeted the *New Idea* as a source of racial enmity. According to FBI investigators, articles "scathing against the white race" convinced "well-thinking people" in Galveston "that these agitators have the negroes in this community in such a state of mind that but the slightest friction is necessary to participate a race war." The FBI investigated reports that the city's Black waterfront workers maintained a stockpile of "high-power rifles and ammunition" at the "Negro Screwman's Union Hall." Throughout July city officials prepared for an emergency. "Owing to an inadequate police force," they requested federal assistance "should the race war break, as they expect it to."[38]

The return of Black veterans throughout the summer further convinced establishment whites of the plausibility of an impending revolution. In August 1919, a terrified white resident of Paris, Texas, reported to federal investigators that he had learned from his African American washerwoman that Black soldiers were conducting meetings with Black residents. She warned him to stay away as "there could be trouble." Alarmists in the War Department's Division of Military Intelligence feared that similar incidents would erupt not just in Texas but across the South. One intelligence officer advised that Black soldiers assumed "new ideas and social aspirations" while serving in France and would no longer "be the same sort of negro" as before "donning the uniform." He insisted that there was a "strong probability" of "numerous racial clashes in the South," the blame for which he placed on "strutting" Black soldiers "inclined to impudence and arrogance." Should Black veterans "attempt to carry those ideas back into the South," he warned, "an era of bloodshed will follow as compared with which the history of reconstruction will be mild reading, indeed."[39]

Fearing imminent racial bloodshed, Governor Hobby enlisted the federal government's help in defending white supremacy. In late July, he requested the assistance of the FBI "in the matter of investigating Race Riot propaganda in Texas." Hobby believed that Bolsheviks, or "some sinister source," sought "to array the negroes against constituted authorities, both State and Federal." After meeting with federal investigators and national guardsmen, Hobby ordered the Texas Rangers to journey through the "Black Belt and sound out the situation," paying special attention to the circulation of Black newspapers and the activities of the NAACP, both of which he believed were now stirring Black Texans into "a frenzy against the government."[40]

Whites across the state now prepared for race war. On his tour of the state, Texas Ranger Frank Matthews urged local sheriffs to prepare for trouble. In some places, as at Fort Worth, law enforcement officials seemed unaware of the activities of local Blacks. After Matthews showed the Fort Worth sheriff the *Crisis* and told him "how extensive they were organized," the sheriff pledged to "keep up with the negroes from now on" and "ordered a dozen sawed off pump shot guns." At neighboring Dallas, lawmen assured Matthews that assistance from the Rangers was unnecessary since a number of white volunteers were "armed" and instructed "to form together on demand" of the police. Whites at Marshall organized a vigilance committee and advised Matthews that they had the "negroes under pretty good control."[41]

Vigilance committees elsewhere took even more forceful measures to bring Blacks "under control." Whites in Leggett, a sawmill town in deep east Texas, compelled Black residents to attend a citizens' council and listen to its resolutions. The council issued a manifesto that set a curfew, prohibited Blacks from holding evening fraternal meetings and worship services, and banned them from the railroad depot and post office. Leggett whites then announced that "if you 'niggers' do these things you can stay here: but five families must leave." The council banished, among other T. S. Davis, organizer of the local NAACP. Leggett whites regarded the NAACP as revolutionary, fearing it would force "white folks do what [Blacks] wanted them to do." To destroy the organization, a mob waylaid Davis's son in broad daylight. That night, the mob besieged Davis's brother's home, sending a fusillade of bullets into it. Davis managed to escape to Houston and then to Ohio. Those who failed to evacuate were subject to further intimidation and ambushing. The Leggett NAACP Branch had barely been organized a month when whites crushed it.[42]

In August 1919, only fifteen months after the first Texas branch of the NAACP was chartered, the governor's office moved to terminate the association's activities in the state. The state attorney general subpoenaed the records of the Austin Branch, contending that it was operating in violation of state law as it was unchartered to "do business" in Texas. Informed of these developments, the white executive secretary of the NAACP, John R. Shillady, traveled to Austin to defend the local branch, explaining to officials that since the NAACP was a nonprofit organization, it did not require a state charter to operate. The next morning a band of men, including a county judge and a local constable, assaulted Shillady outside his hotel, beating him nearly unconscious. The attackers shoved him on the next train north, warning him, on pain of death, not to set foot again in Texas.[43]

Shillady's ill-fated visit to Austin had a disastrous effect on the thirty-three branches of the NAACP in Texas. Within days of the assault, the Austin Branch notified state authorities that it would no longer operate. Fearing reprisals, many branches hesitated to call meetings. In early 1920 the Fort Worth Branch reported that it had experienced "chaotic conditions since Austin affair." Efforts to reorganize the branch failed. The incident left several branches doubting the NAACP's legality in Texas. Despite contrary instructions from Shillady, several branches applied for state charters. Doing so exposed them to state authorities, who then used legal intimidation to terminate their operations. A farmer from Highbank recalled some years later that the attack on Shillady "stop our Progress," and the "law" confiscated "our books and for that Reason we went Down." Shillady solicited the San Antonio Branch's help in assisting those branches that "may be timid and . . . find it difficult to operate." He urged the branch president to write them and "stiffen their backbones and give them confidence to go on."[44]

Such efforts were of no avail. By the end of 1921 all but 7 of the 33 branches had disbanded. Fear of violence frustrated attempts to reorganize branches. Although the Dallas Branch continued to survive after the tragedy at Austin, the Ku Klux Klan's ascent in the early 1920s discouraged branch officers from calling meetings. Despite the efforts of some members, the branch failed to sustain operations. In 1921 the national office sought Mary Talbert's help in reviving the Texas branches as part of a southern tour to renew interest in the NAACP. Talbert agreed to go but only under the auspices of the NACW. "*None* of us can afford to go to Texas as NAACP," she warned; "such Jim Crow travel is not only hard but *hazardous* in that part of *Hell* where we should work." New York heeded her advice, leaving Texas off the itinerary of its southern tour.[45] From a membership of nearly 7,700 in 1919, the Texas NAACP maintained fewer than 1,100 to 1921 (see table 2 on following page).

African American political activism encountered violent suppression elsewhere in the South. Blacks in Georgia and Mississippi also organized NAACP branches during 1918 and 1919. Death threats, lynching, and other acts of terror, however, forced these branches into inactivity. By the end of 1919, nine of Georgia's fifteen branches had ceased operations. To prevent further organizing

Table 2: The Rise and Fall of the NAACP in Texas, 1918–1921

Branch	Date Organized	Charter Members	Total Membership			
			1918	1919	1920	1921
San Antonio	March 1918	112	970	1746	607	177
Fort Worth	April 1918	117	166	267	267	0
Beaumont	June 1918	50	94	475	47	95
Houston	July 1918	301	372	606	123	280
Dallas	September 1918	169	169	1152	317	278
Orange	November 1918	186	186	182	0	0
Gonzales	November 1918	50	50	50	0	0
Silsbee	November 1918	58	58	85	0	0
Galveston	November 1918	50	50	173	259	15
Corsicana	December 1918	61	61	117	70	33
Austin	December 1918	75	75	279	0	0
Texarkana	December 1918	104	104	183	74	196
Marshall	January 1919	50	–	97	0	0
Wharton	February 1919	84	–	345	0	0
Seguin	March 1919	50	–	50	0	0
Temple	March 1919	58	–	58	0	0
Palestine	April 1919	129	–	129	0	0
Marlin	April 1919	51	–	51	0	0
Mumford	April 1919	61	–	315	0	0
Bryan	April 1919	58	–	172	6	0
Benchley	May 1919	50	–	78	0	0
Highbank	May 1919	92	–	121	0	0
Mart	May 1919	50	–	84	0	0
Waelder	May 1919	50	–	50	0	0
Cuero	June 1919	115	–	123	14	0
Waco	June 1919	56	–	99	0	0
Yoakum	June 1919	50	–	103	49	0
Leggett	June 1919	64	–	64	0	0
Greenville	June 1919	111	–	111	0	0
Caldwell	July 1919	59	–	83	0	0
Hearne	July 1919	59	–	86	0	0
Jones Prairie	August 1919	50	–	67	0	0
Baileyville	September 1919	89	–	91	0	0
Total		2,774	2,355	7,692	1,827	1,074

Source: Applications for Charter, Branch Files, boxes G-200 to G-205, NAACP Papers; membership file cards, box L-45, L-47, NAACP Papers, Series II.

efforts among Blacks, the Mississippi legislature passed a law prohibiting the distribution of literature intended "to disturb relations between the races." In Phillips County, Arkansas, Black sharecroppers, many of them ex-servicemen, organized a union to force equitable crop settlements from landlords. Fearing an insurrection, Delta leaders requested and secured over 2,500 federal troops. White vigilantes joined the troops in a massacre of an estimated 250 sharecroppers. Delta officials arrested over 1,000 Black men and women, indicted 122, convicted 79, and sentenced 12 Black men to death.[46]

The fate of African American activism in Texas and throughout the South illustrates that no southern Black protest movement, no matter how vigorous, could survive in such a hostile political environment. The continuing dominance of plantation agriculture and low-wage industry ensured that state and local officials would assist in combating labor shortages. National elites remained uninterested in the aspirations of local African Americans. By investigating the NAACP and other civil rights groups as subversive organizations, the federal government assured white southerners that it would not intervene to overthrow Jim Crow. The press also defended the status quo. In justifying the attack on Shillady, the *New Orleans States* insisted that any organization that championed "a demand for absolute quality" and that tried "to stir up the colored people of the South to demand and fight" for it "is only inviting ill-feeling and disorder."[47]

Such were the conditions that proved conducive to the terrorism that delivered the fatal blow to the nascent civil rights struggle of the postwar years. At Longview, Leggett, Austin, and elsewhere, vigilantes, sheriffs, and federal agents pursued and terrorized Black activists without fear of reprisal. Yet most scholars, as Robin Kelley observed, continue to underrate "the role violence played in quashing radical movements" in the South.[48] The events in Texas, however, reveal that force was an integral means of suppressing Black activism under Jim Crow. The political violence of the postwar years also contradicts characterizations of African Americans as politically indifferent. White Texans may have blamed the unrest of 1919 on outsiders in an effort to restore the fiction that "the great mass of Southern negroes harbor no ideas and no aspirations which challenge the supremacy of the whites or their sense of superiority."[49] But their actions indicated that they thought otherwise. The extent of anti-Black violence attests to how southern whites had become paranoid about Black assertiveness. In fact, the campaign of terror is difficult to explain if we accept images of African Americans as timid, apolitical, or following the path of least resistance.

The campaign of terror, however, did not defeat Black activism entirely. Black resistance and struggle continued, just as it had before the war, in countless ways at the subterranean level. The struggles of 1917 to 1919 left an imprint on participants, and although the NAACP died, memories persisted. Twelve years later, in 1931, the former Highbank Branch secretary remembered the NAACP as "one of the Best origination Ever were organise in Texas" and that his branch had been "sound" and over "100 strong." Activists lost their vehicle of organization, of connecting to boarder national and global struggles, but anti-Black violence, as two historians recently pointed out, never succeeded in its "attempt to crush the African American community which continued to grow and assert itself." Race relations remained unsettled.[50]

African Americans struggled to convert the war to make the world safe for democracy into a fight for citizenship at home. By migrating in search of more favorable economic and political climes, by withholding their labor, by defying the draft, by serving in the military, and by organizing NAACP branches, Blacks waged a political struggle that contested not only exploitative working conditions, but segregation and disfranchisement as well. To the state's planters, industrialists, and elected officials, African Americans, politicized and organized, posed a formidable threat of open rebellion. By deploying the coercive resources of both state and federal governments, the powerful defeated these soldiers of democracy and, for the moment, made Texas safe for white supremacy.

Notes

1. L. H. Henry, Local Officer, Department of Justice, Bureau of Investigation, Texarkana, Texas, to C. E. Breniman, Division Superintendent, San Antonio, Texas, Jan. 7, 1919, in *Federal Surveillance of Afro-Americans (1917–1925): The First World War, the Red Scare, and the Garvey Movement,* ed. Theodore Kornweibel Jr. (microfilm, 25 reels, University Publications of America, 1986), reel 10, frame 11.

2. Among the few accounts acknowledging widespread Black resistance are Neil R. McMillen, *Dark Journey: Black Mississippians in the Age of Jim Crow* (Urbana, 1989), 302–17; Nan Elizabeth Woodruff, "African-American Struggles for Citizenship in the Arkansas and Mississippi Deltas in the Age of Jim Crow," *Radical History Review,* 55 (Winter 1993), 33–51; and Nancy MacLean, *Behind the Mask of Chivalry: The Making of the Second Ku Klux Klan* (New York, 1994), 26–30.

3. Henry to Breniman, Jan. 7, 1919, in *Federal Surveillance of Afro-Americans* (1917–1925), ed. Kornweibel, reel 10, frame 11. The Office of Chief Examiner was established in 1908; four name changes and 27 years later it became the Federal Bureau of Investigation (FBI). It will be referred to as the FBI throughout this article.

4. Lester C. Lamon, *Black Tennesseans,* 1900–1930 (Knoxville, 1977), 37. On the Black community, see Darrel E. Bigham, *We Ask Only a Fair Trial: A History of the Black Community of Evansville, Indiana* (Bloomington, 1987); Douglas Henry Daniels, *Pioneer Urbanites: A Social and Cultural History of Black San Francisco* (Philadelphia, 1980); John Dittmer, *Black Georgia in the Progressive Era,* 1900–1920 (Urbana, 1977); Lamon, *Black Tennesseans*; and George C. Wright, *Life behind a Veil: Blacks in Louisville, Kentucky,* 1865–1930 (Baton Rouge, 1985). On family life, see Herbert Gutman, *The Black Family in Slavery and Freedom,* 1750–1925 (New York, 1976); and Jacqueline Jones, *Labor of Love, Labor of Sorrow: Black Women, Work, and the Family from Slavery to the Present* (New York, 1985). The classic works on emigration include William E. Bittle and Gilbert Geis, *The Longest Way Home: Chief Alfred C. Sam's Back-to-Africa Movement,* (Detroit, 1964); and Edwin S. Redkey, *Black Exodus: Black nationalist and Back-to-Africa Movements,* 1890–1910 (New Haven, 1969). On migration, see Peter Gottlieb, *Making Their Own Way: Southern Blacks' Migration to Pittsburgh,* 1916–1930 (Urbana, 1987); James R. Grossman, *Land of Hope: Chicago, Black Southerners, and the Great Migration* (Chicago, 1989); Florette Henri, *Black Migration: Movement North,* 1900–1920 (Garden City, N.Y., 1975), and Nell Irvin Painter, *Exodusters: Black Migration to Kansas after Reconstruction* (New York, 1976). For examples of discussions on Black politics, see Dittmer, *Black Georgia in the Progressive Era,* 90–109; Lamon, *Black Tennesseans,* 37–58; McMillen, *Dark Journey,* 57–71; I. A. Newby, *Black Carolinians: A History of Blacks in South Carolina from 1895 to 1968* (Columbia, 1973), 160–61; and Wright, *Life behind a Veil,* 176–93. C. Vann Woodward, *The Strange Career of Jim Crow* (New York, 1966), 80. Eric Foner, *Reconstruction: America's Unfinished Revolution,* 1863–1877 (New York, 1988), 598.

5. On Black workers, see Joe William Trotter Jr., *Coal, Class, and Color: Blacks in Southern West Virginia,* 1915–32 (Urbana, 1990); Eric Arnesen, *Waterfront Workers of New Orleans: Race, Class,* and *Politics,* 1863–1923 (New York, 1991); and Robin D. G. Kelley, *Hammer and Hoe: Alabama Communists during the Great Depression* (Chapel Hill, 1990). Works that examine the politicization of Black women include Paula Giddings, *When and Where I Enter . . . The Impact of Black Women on Race and Sex in America* (New York, 1984); Evelyn Brooks Higginbotham, *Righteous Discontent: The Women's Movement in the Black Baptist Church,* 1880–1920 (Cambridge, Mass., 1993); Cynthia Neverdon-Morton, *Afro-American Women of the South and the Advancement of the Race,* 1895–1925 (Knoxville, 1989); Jacqueline Anne Rouse, *Lugenia Burns Hope, Black Southern Reformer* (Athens, Ga., 1989); and Darlene Clark Hine, ed., *Black Women in United States History,* vol. XIV: Dorothy Salem, *To Better Our World: Black Women in Organized Reform,* 1890–1920 (Brooklyn, 1990). In fact, throughout the Jim Crow era, Black women fought on the front line in resistance to segregation. See Willi Coleman, "Black Women and Segregated Public Transportation: Ninety Years of Resistance," in Hine, *ibid.,* vol. V: *Black Women in American History: The Twentieth Century,* 295–301. Robin D. G. Kelley, "'We Are Not What We Seem': Rethinking Black Working-Class Opposition in the Jim Crow South," *Journal of American History,* 80 (June 1993), 76–78. For an important study that adopts some of Kelley's insights and interprets the 1917 lynching of Ell

Persons in Memphis, Tennessee, in the context of ongoing struggle and resistance, see Kenneth W. Goings and Gerald L. Smith, "'Unhidden' Transcripts: Memphis and African American Agency, 1862–1920," *Journal of Urban History*, 21 (March 1995), 372–94.

6. *Houston Observer*, May 11, 1918, in *The Tuskegee Institute News Clippings File*, ed. John W. Kitchens (microfilm, 252 reels, Tuskegee Institute, 1978), reel 244, frame 648; Dallas Exemption Board quoted in Bruce A. Glasrud, "Black Texans, 1900–1930: A History" (Ph.D. diss., Texas Technological College, 1969), 70. Several historians have demonstrated that Blacks moved north not only to seek better jobs but also to gain social and political freedoms: see Gottlieb, *Making Their Own Way*; Grossman, *Land of Hope*; McMillen, *Dark Journey*; Joe William Trotter Jr., *Black Milwaukee: The Making of an Industrial Proletariat, 1915–1945* (Urbana, 1985); and Joe William Trotter Jr., ed., *The Great Migration in Historical Perspective: New Dimensions of Race, Class, and Gender* (Bloomington, 1991). See also Emmett J. Scott, "Letters of Negro Migrants of 1916–1918," *Journal of Negro History*, 4 (July 1919), 290–340; and Emmett J. Scott, "Additional Letters of Negro Migrants of 1916–1918," *ibid.* (Oct. 1919), 412–65.

7. Woodruff, "African-American Struggles for Citizenship," 36; Theodore Rosengarten, *All God's Dangers: The Life of Nate Shaw* (New York, 1974), 161; *Marion County News* reprinted in *Dallas Express*, July 5, 1919. Cotton prices are from George Brown Tindall, *The Emergence of the New South*, 1913–1945 (Baton Rouge, 1967), 33, 60. On the economic effect of the war on agricultural laborers, see Gavin Wright, *Old South, New South: Revolutions in the Southern Economy since the Civil War* (New York, 1986), 203–6.

8. Anonymous of Menard, Texas, to Editor, *Fort Worth Record*, July 23, 1918, in *Federal Surveillance of Afro-Americans (1917–1925)*, ed. Kornweibel, reel 10, frame 16; *Houston Observer*, Sept. 14, 1918, in *Tuskegee Institute News Clippings File*, ed. Kitchens, reel 244, frame 477; *Galveston New Idea*, Oct. 6, 1917, in *Federal Surveillance of Afro-Americans* (1917–1925), ed. Kornweibel, reel 10, frame 69. Efforts to locate issues of the *New Idea* from this period failed. The federal government, however, extensively investigated the *New Idea* as a seditious publication. Transcriptions of several articles are in federal case files.

9. "Negro Conscription," *New Republic*, Oct. 20, 1917, p. 317; *Houston Chronicle*, July 18, 1917, quoted in Robert V. Haynes, *A Night of Violence: The Houston Riot of 1917* (Baton Rouge, 1976), 53.

10. Foner, *Reconstruction*, 9: Haynes, *Night of Violence*, 63–68; D. E. Nolan to Acting Director of Military Intelligence, memo, Jan. 20, 1919, in *Federal Surveillance of Afro-Americans (1917–1925)*, ed. Kornweibel, reel 21, frame 231; Horace G. Burke, France, to Editor, *Houston Observer*, Oct. 19, 1918, in *Tuskegee Institute News Clippings File*, ed. Kitchens, reel 244, frame 659. African American participation in the Spanish-American War raised similar questions among Blacks over domestic concerns about race, citizenship, and political rights. See George P. Marks III, *The Black Press Views American Imperialism* (New York, 1971); and Willard B. Gatewood Jr., "Black Americans and the Quest for Empire, 1898–1903," *Journal of Southern History*, 38 (Nov. 1972), 545–66.

11. For a comprehensive study of the riot, see Haynes, *Night of Violence*.

12. F. Sullens to Major Brown, Nov. 30, 1918, in *Federal Surveillance of Afro-Americans (1917–1925)*, ed. Kornweibel, reel 21, frame 175; Rosengarten, *All God's Dangers*, 161.

13. T. P. Terry quoted in B. C. Baldwin, memo, Aug. 3, 1917, in *Federal Surveillance of Afro-Americans (1917–1925)*, ed. Kornweibel, reel 9, frame 630; Monroe Bean quoted in J. J. Lawrence, memo, Aug. 22, 1917, *ibid.*, frame 688; *Houston Chronicle*, June 2, 1918, in *Tuskegee Institute News Clippings File*, ed. Kitchens, reel 244, frame 744.

14. Addie W. Hunton and Kathryn M. Johnson, *Two Colored Women with the American Expeditionary Forces* (1920; New York, 1971), 199. Despite constituting only 16% of the state population, Blacks made up 25% of the conscripts from Texas—about 31,000 men. See Alwyn Barr, *Black Texans: A History of Negroes in Texas, 1528–1971* (Austin, 1973), 115. On Black resistance to the draft, see Theodore Kornweibel Jr., "Apathy and Dissent: Black America's Negative Response to World War I," *South Atlantic Quarterly*, 80 (Summer 1981), 334–36.

15. Dallas Journal, June 7, 1918, in *Tuskegee Institute News Clippings File*, ed. Kitchens, reel 8, frame 35; C. P. Myer, Assistant General Manager, to B. F. Bonner, Vice President and General Manager, June 25, 1917, box 338, Kirby Lumber Company Records, Forest History Collection (Ralph W. Steen Library, Stephen F. Austin State University, Nacogdoches, Tex.); Bonner to Myer, June 1, 1917, *ibid.*; and Bonner to I. W. Crawford, June 6, 1917, *ibid.*

16. T. C. Smith to National Association for the Advancement of Colored People (NAACP), Dec. 1919, Mumford Branch File, box G-205, Branch Files, National Association for the Advancement of Colored People Papers (Manuscript Division, Library of Congress, Washington, D.C.); *New York Age*, Nov. 1, 1919, in *Tuskegee Institute News Clippings File*, ed. Kitchens, reel 10, frame 254.

17. U. S. Department of Commerce, Bureau of the Census, *Compendium of the Twelfth Census: 1900*, vol. V: *Agriculture*, pt. 1 (Washington, 1902), 128–29; Bureau of the Census, *Compendium of the Fourteenth Census: 1920*, vol. VI: *Agriculture*, pt. 2 (Washington, 1922), 681. For lucid testimony of the struggles of one white tenant in neighboring Lamar County during these years, see U. S. Congress, Senate, Commission on Industrial Relations, *Final Report and Testimony*, 64 Cong., 1 sess., vol. 9 (Washington, 1916), 9006–43; *Dallas Express*, Feb. 23, 1918, in *Tuskegee Institute News Clippings File*, ed. Kitchens, reel 7, frame 617. For an analysis of class conflict in this section of the rural Southwest during the early twentieth century, see James R. Green, *Grass-Roots Socialism: Radical Movements in the Southwest, 1895–1943* (Baton Rouge, 1978).

18. William Houshoffer, investigative report, May 22, 1918, in *Federal Surveillance of Afro-Americans (1917–1925)*, ed. Kornweibel, reel 10, frame 15; *Dallas Express*, Feb. 23, 1918, in *Tuskegee Institute News Clippings File*, ed. Kitchens, reel 7, frame 617; *Dallas Journal*, Aug. 10, 1918, *ibid.*, reel 8, frame 47. For a brilliant account from South African history of how class conflict between marginalized white farmers and capitalizing landowners erupted into violent racial oppression of Black tenant farmers, see Helen Bradford, *A Taste of Freedom: The ICU in Rural South Africa, 1924–1930* (Johannesburg, 1987), 186–212.

19. Dicie Shipman, affidavit, Nov. 14, 1918, San Antonio Branch File, box G-204, NAACP Papers; Aunt Leah Shipman, affidavit, Nov. 14, 1918, *ibid.*

20. Foner, *Reconstruction*, 122–23.

21. J. H. Harper, report, Aug. 29, 1917, in *Federal Surveillance of Afro-Americans* (1917–1925), ed. Kornweibel, reel 19, frames 769–70.

22. Bradford Hammonds to James Weldon Johnson, June 1, 1919, Mart Branch File, box G-204, NAACP Papers; *Dallas Express*, May 24, March 1, Feb. 8, 1919; B. K. Maynard to Walter F. White, March 25, 1918, San Antonio Branch File, box G-204, NAACP Papers.

23. C. B. Johnson to James Weldon Johnson, April 8, 1918, San Antonio Branch File, box G-204, NAACP Papers; San Antonio Branch, publicity release, Oct. 18, 1918, *ibid.* The NAACP's national office sent charter applications to potential branches at this time, requesting that branches list the names and occupations of charter members. Although the applications are somewhat uneven in their listing of occupations, enough information survives to indicate a significant working-class membership. Branches did not submit the names and occupations of subsequent enlistees. Total membership numbers are drawn from membership file cards, Auxiliary Files, box L-45, NAACP Papers, Series II.

24. Hallie Q. Brown, *Homespun Heroines and Other Women of Distinction* (1926; Freeport, N.Y., 1971), 217; Mary B. Talbert to James Weldon Johnson, Dec. 29, 1918, Special Correspondence Files, box C-76, NAACP Papers; *Branch Bulletin* (Dec. 1918), 62; Talbert to Johnson, March 15, 1919, Special Correspondence Files, box C-76, NAACP Papers. In Texas Talbert organized branches of the NAACP at Galveston, Silsbee, Orange, Austin, Corsicana, Marshall, Texarkana, and Gonzales and conducted membership drives at San Antonio, Dallas, Fort Worth, and Beaumont. For details on her trip, see Talbert to John R. Shillady, Dec. 23, 1918, *ibid.* For a more extended summary of Talbert's work for the NAACP, see Salem, *To Better Our World*, 176–79. For a good biographical sketch of Talbert, see Lillian S. Williams, "Mary Morris Talbert," in *Notable Black American Women*, ed. Jessie Carney Smith (Detroit, 1992), 1095–1100.

25. Mrs. C. E. Adams, president of the Texas Federation of Colored Women's Clubs (TFCWC), belonged to the Beaumont Branch and assisted Talbert in doubling branch membership. Mrs. H. E. Williams, vice president of the TFCWC, and Talbert chartered the Corsicana Branch. See Application for Charter, June 6, 1918, Beaumont Branch File, box G-201, NAACP Papers; Application for Charter, Dec. 10, 1918, Corsicana Branch File, *ibid.*; *Galveston News*, July 4, 1919, in *Tuskegee Institute News Clippings File*, ed. Kitchens, reel 11, frame 140; Minutes of the Organization Meeting of the Fort Worth Branch, April 20, 1918, Fort Worth Branch File, box G-202, NAACP Papers; *Branch Bulletin* (June–July 1918), 30. On Talbert and NACW (National Association of Colored Women's Clubs) initiatives, see Williams, "Mary Morris Talbert," 1097, 1099. On the founding and early years of the TFCWC, see A. W. Jackson, *A Sure Foundation* (Houston, 1940), 292–93. On the involvement of women in the early years of the NAACP at both the national and local levels, see Salem, *To Better Our World*, 145–80.

26. Application for Charter, Sept. 8, 1918, Silsbee Branch File, box G-205, NAACP Papers; Application for Charter, Feb. 1, 1919, Wharton Branch File, *ibid.* Membership numbers are drawn from membership file cards, Auxiliary Files, box L-45, NAACP Papers, Series II.

27. J. E. Turner to Shillady, March 25, 1919, Mumford Branch File, box G-204, NAACP Papers; Grant Burleson to Oswald Garrison Villard, May 31, 1919, Waelder Branch File, box G-205, *ibid.*; Grant Derry to Shillady, June 26, 1919, *ibid.*; Turner to Shillady, March 25, 1919, Mumford Branch File, box G-204, *ibid.*; T. C. Smith to Villard, April 2, 1919, *ibid.*; Eric Hobsbawm, *Primitive Rebels: Studies in Archaic Forms of Social Movement in the 19th and 20th Centuries* (New York, 1965), 60–61; Turner to Shillady, March 25, 1919, Mumford Branch File, box G-204, NAACP Papers.

28. *Dallas Express*, Feb. 8, April 19, 1919.

29. For examples of Clifton F. Richardson's energetic rhetoric, see *Houston Informer*, June 28, 1919. For an example of Richardson's efforts to criticize Houston Blacks he considered "antebellum Sambos," see James M. SoRelle, "The Darker Side of 'Heaven': The Black Community in Houston, Texas, 1917–1945" (Ph.D. diss., Kent State University, 1980), 79–81. On Richardson's career as an editor, political activist, and civic booster, see Howard Beeth, "Houston & History, Past and Present: A Look at Black Houston in the 1920s," *Southern Studies*, 25 (Summer 1986), 177–81; and Howard Beeth, "A Black Elite Agenda in the Urban South: The Call for Political Change and Racial Economic Solidarity in Houston during the 1920s," *Essays in Economic and Business History*, 10 (June 1992), 41–55.

30. Clipping from *Fort Worth Star Telegram*, March 3, 1919, Fort Worth Branch File, box G-202, NAACP Papers; *Dallas Express*, March 15, April 5, 1919; San Antonio Branch to Secretary of War Newton D. Baker, petition, April 18, 1918, San Antonio Branch File, box G-204, NAACP papers; J. A. Grubles to W. E. B. Du Bois, April 22, 1918, *ibid.*; *Dallas Express*, Dec. 20, 1919; C. F. Richardson to Walter F. White, July 2, 1918, Houston Branch File, box G-203, NAACP Papers; P. A. Williams to Shillady, July 1, 15, 1919, Austin Branch File, box G-200, *ibid. Branch Bulletin* (June–July 1918), 30.

31. Walter F. White of the NAACP national office recruited G. N. T. Gray, president of the Fort Worth Branch, to investigate the lynching of Bragg Williams at Hillsboro in January 1919. Gray enlisted informants who helped him uncover the names of the perpetrators. G. N. T. Gray to Walter F. White, Feb. 14, 1919, Administrative Files, box C-368, NAACP Papers. The Austin, Houston, and San Antonio branches also investigated mob violence, secured affidavits from victims and witnesses, and pressured the governor to take action. C. F. Richardson also employed the resources of the *Houston Informer* to investigate mob action against African Americans: for two examples, see *Houston Informer*, June 7, 1919. W. J. Porter to Shillady, June 12, 1919, Legal Files, box D-1, NAACP Papers; J. F. Hawkins to W. P. Hobby, Jan. 8, 1919, reprinted in *Dallas Express*, Jan. 25, 1919; *Dallas Morning News*, Jan. 21, 1919. J. F. Hawkins's bill required, among other things, that all lynching cases by tried in Austin and be prosecuted by the attorney general, that the county in which the lynching occurred pay a $10,000 indemnity to the heirs of the victim, and that lynching be defined as taking the life of a citizen without due process. For a full text of the bill, see *Dallas Express*, Jan. 25, 1919.

32. E. O. Smith to White, June 10, 1918, box G203, NAACP Papers; Henry Lucius Mims to Shillady, July 5, 1918, *ibid.*; CBL open letter in Houston Observer, Aug. 10, 1918, clipping, *ibid.* For a more detailed summary of the controversy between the CBL and Richardson, see SoRelle, "Darker Side of 'Heaven,'" 361–66.

33. Kenneth Kusmer, *A Ghetto Takes Shape: Black Cleveland, 1870–1930* (Urbana, 1976), 230–43; Allan Spear, *Black Chicago: The Making of a Negro Ghetto, 1890–1920* (Chicago, 1967), 51–90; Trotter, *Black Milwaukee*, 80–114, 123–28. On factional disputes as generational conflict in Houston, see SoRelle, "Darker Side of 'Heaven,'" 357–58.

34. Smith to White, June 10, 1918, Houston Branch File, box G-203, NAACP Papers; Mims to Shillady, July 5, 1918, *ibid.*; *Houston Informer*, Aug. 2, 1919, May 1, 1920.

35. Judith Stein, *The World of Marcus Garvey: Race and Class in Modern Society* (Baton Rouge, 1986), 5. See also Judith Stein, "Defining the Race, 1890–1930," in *The Invention of Ethnicity*, ed. Werner Sollors (New York, 1989), esp. 95–97. Robing Kelley attributes the failure of the Birmingham NAACP in the 1920s to its focus on the city's Black business interests rather than on "racial violence, denial of civil liberties, and the immediate problems confronting the poor": Kelley, *Hammer and Hoe*, xx.

36. Evelyn Brooks Higginbotham, "Beyond the Sound of Silence: Afro-American Women's History," *Gender & History*, 1 (Spring 1989), 59.

37. For accounts of the Longview riot, see William M. Tuttle Jr., "Violence in a 'Heathen' Land: The Longview Race Riot of 1919," *Phylon*, 33 (Winter 1972), 324–33; Arthur I. Waskow, *From Race Riot to Sit-in, 1919 and the 1960s: A Study in the Connections between Conflict and Violence* (Garden City, N.Y., 1966), 12–16; and *Crisis*, 18 (Oct. 1919), 297–98. *Dallas Morning News*, July 15, 1919; Assistant Director and Chief, Bureau of Investigation, to R. W. Timothy, Waco, Texas, Aug. 9, 1919, in *Federal Surveillance of Afro-Americans (1917–1925)*, ed. Kornweibel, reel 10, frames 22–23; Williams to Shillady, July 15, 1919, Austin Branch File, box G-200, NAACP Papers; *Galveston New Idea*, July 28, 1919, in *Federal Surveillance of Afro-Americans (1917–1925)*, ed. Kornweibel, reel 6, frame 219.

38. George Ohler, "Background Causes of the Longview Race Riot of July 10, 1919," *Journal of the American Studies Association of Texas*, 12 (1981), 50; Report of J. L. Webb, July 28, 1919, *Federal Surveillance of Afro-Americans (1917–1925)*, ed. Kornweibel, reel 6, frames 228–29. The FBI summarized its six-month investigation of the Negro Screwman's Union in W. A. Wiseman, report, Nov. 30, 1919, *ibid.*, reel 3, frames 350–51.

39. Bureau of Intelligence, report, Aug. 3, 1919, in *Federal Surveillance of Afro-Americans (1917–1925)*, ed. Kornweibel, reel 12, frame 391: Sullens to Brown, Nov. 30, 1918, *ibid.*, reel 21, frames 175–77.

40. Report of Special Agent McCaleb, July 31, 1919, *ibid.*, reel 12, frame 389; Hobby to A. Mitchell Palmer, July 29, 1919, Papers of the Governor, box 391, Record Group 301 (Texas State Library, Austin).

41. Ranger Frank W. Matthews, report, Aug. 18, 1919, in *Federal Surveillance of Afro-Americans (1917–1925)*, ed. Kornweibel, reel 10, frame 28; Matthews, report, Aug. 16, 1919, ibid., frame 27; Matthews, report, Aug. 15, 1919, *ibid.*, frame 26.

42. *Houston Informer*, Aug. 16, 1919, in *Tuskegee Institute News Clippings File*, ed. Kitchens, reel 10, frame 404; T. S. Davis to Shillady, Aug. 11, 1919, Leggett Branch File, box G-203, NAACP Papers. See also T. S. Davis to James Weldon Johnson, Oct. 24, 1919, *ibid.*

43. The assault on Shillady in Austin is recounted in several places; see especially Mary White Ovington, *The Walls Came Tumbling Down* (New York, 1947), 172–75.

44. J. Gentry Horace to NAACP, May 22, 1920, Fort Worth Branch File, box G-202, NAACP Paper; S. R. Carter to William Pickens, Feb. 18, 1931, Highbank Branch File, box G-203, *ibid.*; Shillady to Grumbles, Jan. 15, 1920, San Antonio Branch File, box G-204, *ibid.*

45. George F. Porter to James Weldon Johnson, Jan. 30, 1923, Dallas Branch file, box G-201, *ibid.*; Robert Bagnall to Porter, Feb. 6, 1923, *ibid.*; Porter to Bagnall, March 13, 1923, *ibid.*; Bagnall to Porter, March 10, 1923, *ibid.*; Porter to Bagnall, June 6, 1923, *ibid.*; Bagnall to Talbert, Sept. 17, 1921, Special Correspondence Files, box C-76, *ibid.*; Bagnall to Talbert, Sept. 19, 1921, *ibid.*; Talbert to Bagnall, Sept. 22, 1921, *ibid.*; *Branch Bulletin* (Dec. 1921).

46. Dittmer, *Black Georgia in the Progressive Era*, 206–7; McMillen, *Dark Journey* 314–16; *Crisis*, 21 (Dec. 1920), 67–68. For an account of the massacre in Elaine, Phillips County, see Richard C. Cortner, *A Mob Intent on Death*: *The NAACP and the Arkansas Riot Cases* (Middletown, 1988), 1–56; and Woodruff, "African-American Struggles for Citizenship."

47. *New Orleans States*, Aug. 30, 1919, in *Tuskegee Institute News Clippings File*, ed. Kitchens, reel 9, frame 980.

48. Kelley, *Hammer and Hoe*, xiii. Kelley emphasizes antiradical violence *ibid.*, 57–77, 159–75. Other historians who attribute significance to antiradical violence include McMillen, *Dark Journey*, 224–56; Woodruff, "African-American Struggles for Citizenship"; and MacLean, *Behind the Mask of Chivalry*, 149–73. For a recent study of racial unrest in the South during World War I that overemphasizes the cultural and ritual functions of anti-Black violence, as opposed to the political motives that are stressed here, see J. William Harris, "Etiquette, Lynching, and Racial Boundaries in Southern History: A Mississippi Example," *American Historical Review*, 100 (April 1995), 387–410.

49. *Galveston Daily News*, Sept. 7, 1919, in *Tuskegee Institute News Clippings File*, ed. Kitchens, reel 9, frames 987–88.

50. S.R. Carter to William Pickens, Feb. 18, 1931, Hishbank Branch File, Box G-203, NAACP Papers; Goings and Smith " 'Unhidden' Transcripts," 376.

Reading 15

The "Magic" Leak of 1941 and Japanese-American Relations

Ruth R. Harris

Eight months before the attack on Pearl Harbor, Japan learned that its coded diplomatic messages were being read by the United States. For years politicians and historians have believed that Japan's knowledge of this cryptoanalytic breakthrough proved inconsequential, but recently declassified documents suggest otherwise. Japan's knowledge of "Magic," the American codebreaking operation, seems to have contributed to a worsening of relations with Japan and to Washington's unpreparedness for war in Asia in 1941.[1]

One year after World War II had begun in Europe, President Franklin D. Roosevelt was already conducting what historians have termed an "undeclared war" against the Axis. That undeclared war included both open and secret efforts against Japanese territorial expansion. The Japanese attack on China in 1937 eventually led Roosevelt to invoke economic sanctions against Japan. In January 1939 the President imposed a moral embargo on Japan, and in July the United States notified Japan that it would not renew their annual commercial agreement, due to expire in January 1940.

Following the Nazi defeat of France in June 1940, Roosevelt approved talks by Secretary of State Cordell Hull with the Japanese ambassador to resolve disagreements. At the same time, the army and navy intelligence services were penetrating the Japanese diplomatic and military codes. The exposure of the American cryptoanalytic breakthrough to Japan in May 1941 seemed to forecast the loss of that important intelligence source. But the Japanese did not change their cipher system, thus allowing the U.S. to continue reading Japan's diplomatic messages. On the surface at least, the Magic disclosure seemed to elicit no countermeasures by the Japanese government.

Several previous investigations of the intelligence lapse which allowed Japan to learn of the American breakthrough turned up little information about either the origin or consequences of the leak. In 1945 the joint congressional committee investigating the Pearl Harbor attack looked into the matter, and on November 16 Senator Homer Ferguson asked the committee's general counsel, William D. Mitchell, to obtain all available American intelligence information about Japan's awareness of the U.S. penetration of the codes. The subsequent probe revealed that both the Army Military Intelligence Division and the Office of Naval Intelligence (ONI) had discovered by May 1941 that a German official had notified the Japanese about the American breakthrough. The congressional researchers failed, however, to determine the origin of the intelligence leak, and they produced no evidence that the Japanese Foreign Office had taken serious countermeasures.[2]

Historians of the incident have been hampered because the documents that might have clarified matters remained classified. Roberta Wohlstetter, in her classic analysis of Pearl Harbor intelligence, thought the compromise was responsible for Washington's ban on sending Magic disclosures to armed forces field stations from August through November of 1941. Like other scholars, she noted that the Japanese Foreign Office did not change its diplomatic codes after the German warning.[3] She did not, however, deal with the question of whether the Japanese believed the German warning. In his discussion of the leak, David Kahn also acknowledged that the Japanese took only superficial and ineffective security measures. Tokyo, for instance, merely urged officials using codes and ciphers, to exercise utmost caution, but not to change the code itself. Although Kahn noted that the U.S. launched an investigation of the Magic disclosure, he was uncertain about how the leak occurred.[4]

In a less scholarly work, Ladislas Farago placed responsibility for the intelligence revelation on Under Secretary of State Sumner Welles. Farago claimed that Welles had shown American translations of the Japanese messages to the Soviet ambassador who, in turn, passed that information on to the German charge d'affaires in Washington.[5] Barton Whaley, in his *Codeword Barbarossa*, accepted Farago's explanation.[6] Historians writing on other aspects of the Pearl Harbor attack have considered the influence of the Magic messages but have ignored the leak. "The Japanese were quite unaware that the United States was in possession of their diplomatic code . . . ," declared Homer N. Wallin in 1968 in a typical observation.[7]

This article, based on recently released documents unavailable to earlier investigators, attempts to explain more fully the intelligence leak, with emphasis primarily on the effects of the disclosure on the American government. The evidence suggests that the breach of security facilitated Japan's efforts to conceal the surprise attack on the United States at Pearl Harbor.

In 1941 U.S. cryptographers were analyzing several Japanese diplomatic codes of various levels of importance as part of a communications intelligence operation known as Magic. (*Communications intelligence* refers to the process of code breaking as well as intercepting, analyzing, and translating communications.) Reports based on cryptoanalytical intelligence were closely guarded and shown ordinarily only to the highest-ranking government officials with an obvious need to see such material. Even the analysis of unreadable codes sometimes provided helpful information to President Roosevelt. Such was the case on July 13, 1940, when Brigadier General Sherman Miles, acting chief of G–2, advised Roosevelt "that considerable radio traffic is now in progress between Berlin and Tokyo in a code of such extreme secrecy as to permit the deduction that highly important negotiations are in progress."[8] These negotiations resulted in the Tripartite Pact, signed in September 1940 by Japan, Germany, and Italy and aimed at keeping the United States out of the European war. The code utilized in the talks was broken several weeks later by Colonel William Friedman and became known as "Purple," the highest level and most important Japanese diplomatic code read by American intelligence. Rear Admiral Arthur H. McCollum of the Office of Naval Intelligence later described the American reading of Purple in glowing terms: "It looked like real gravy."[9]

The sparse information available on early security arrangements to protect the Magic operation reveals that the army and navy intelligence services sent transcriptions by courier to the White House and State Department. In January 1941, the two services agreed to avoid duplication of effort by taking turns on a monthly basis delivering and picking up the communications intelligence of both offices. Neither the Secretary of State nor President Roosevelt was permitted to retain copies of Magic intelligence.

As Wohlstetter has already pointed out, the usefulness of the Magic operation was limited by the lack of analysis and interpretation within the intelligence services. Only rarely did they combine the Magic information with other sources to assess a particular situation. Generally the memoranda to the President and appropriate senior officials merely summarized the contents of particular messages without relating the significance of the information to the course of Japanese policy. In reporting to Roosevelt, the intelligence services gave equal treatment to the expressions of the Japanese foreign minister and various Japanese ambassadors. Any interpretations and subsequent applications to American policy seemed to rest with the policy makers who read the raw intelligence. Nonetheless, the Magic messages undoubtedly proved helpful to the Roosevelt administration.[11] From Magic came a summary in November 1940 of the conversations of Hitler and Soviet Foreign Affairs Commissar Vyacheslav Molotov.[12] Magic also gave Roosevelt advance notice of the Japanese foreign minister's plans to visit Moscow and Berlin in the spring of 1941 and afforded him insight into Foreign Minister Yosuke Matusoka's personal beliefs about the course of Soviet-American relations.[13] In general, the messages supplemented and helped cross-check information from various sources on Japanese policy. Ambassador Joseph C. Grew in Tokyo and a number of individuals with quasi-governmental ties in Japan also provided information on Japanese policy to Hull and Roosevelt,

The Security lapse that resulted in the revelation about American penetration of the Japanese diplomatic codes occurred in the spring of 1941. Although Ladislas Farago has suggested an explanation of how the Axis learned about this American cryptoanalytic success, his interpretation fails under close examination. Sumner Welles was to blame, insists Farago, because the Under Secretary showed the Soviet ambassador Japanese messages which indicated Hitler's plan to attack the Soviet Union in 1941. But the particular documents cited by Farago do not, as it became clear when they were declassified, say anything about German intentions.[14] Moreover, the Under Secretary would have been among the least likely administration officials to show Japanese diplomatic messages to the Soviet ambassador, for Welles did not trust the Soviet representative. As early as the summer of 1940, the FBI had notified Roosevelt, Hull, and Welles that Soviet Ambassador Constantine Umansky was informing German charge d'affaires Hans Thomsen about his conversations with State Department officials. Welles believed that the German embassy would notify the Japanese embassy of anything reported by Umansky concerning Japan.[15]

By piecing together a number of recently declassified documents, a new explanation of the Magic leak emerges. Under Secretary Welles did play a role, although it was an innocent one. Welles customarily passed on to the British ambassador bits of intelligence, for there was already Anglo-American cooperation on such material. On April 1, 1941, Welles disclosed to Viscount Halifax, newly appointed British ambassador to Washington, the contents of a recent conversation between Foreign Minister Matsuoka and Herman Goering in Berlin. According to Welles, Goering indicated that Germany intended to attack the Soviet Union immediately after the Nazi strike against Britain, whether or not that attempt succeeded. The Under Secretary's information came from a "Purple" coded message that had been translated by the Army Signal Intelligence Service on March 29. On April 2 the British embassy sent Halifax's report of his talk with Welles to London, but not in the regular British diplomatic cipher for classified material. Instead, the British embassy, in order to lessen the burden on the diplomatic ciphering staff and machinery, used a ciphering machine that the Foreign Office had designated "for telegrams of a less confidential nature." When they received this particular message, Foreign Office personnel expressed alarm over the use of the Ministry of Aircraft Production cipher for such a telegram. Sir Orme Sargent, chief of the North American section, believed that a serious error had been committed, and he brought the matter to the attention of Sir Alexander Cadogan, permanent under secretary of state for the Foreign Office.[16]

Orme probably suspected that the information from Welles had emanated from communications intelligence. Matsuoka, after all, was still in Berlin and engaged in talks of the greatest secrecy with German leaders. It was well known, as the American embassy in Berlin reported on April 1, that no neutral diplomat or journalist had been able to learn anything about the carefully protected meetings of Matsuoka with Hitler, Goering, and Joachim von Ribbentrop.[17] To an experienced British diplomat, the most logical source for Welles's report would have been a successful reading of a Japanese diplomatic message. Where else would the United States acquire so rapidly the substance of secret talks in Berlin between two such high-ranking Axis officials? The great concern of the

Foreign Office was thus justified because the Ministry of Aircraft Production cipher obviously gave inadequate communications protection.

Strong circumstantial evidence exists that the German embassy in Washington intercepted and decoded the Halifax message to London on April 2. The German embassy then informed Japan that the U.S. had broken the Japanese diplomatic cipher. American officials already knew that the German embassy was engaging in communications intelligence in 1941,[18] but because the U.S. had been unable to break the German embassy's high-level diplomatic code, Americans did not learn of the embassy's role in the warning to Japan until after World War II had ended. A captured German document later revealed the German embassy's part in that episode. On April 28, 1941, German Chargé Thomsen sent a "Top Secret" message from Washington to the Foreign Ministry in Berlin:

> As communicated to me by an absolutely reliable source, the State Department is in possession of the key to the Japanese coding system and is therefore also able to decipher information telegrams from Tokyo to Ambassador Nomura here regarding Ambassador Oshima's reports from Berlin.[19]

The text of the German message bore clues indicating that the embassy had intercepted the British message reporting Welles's description of Goering's remarks. First, there is evidence that the words "absolutely reliable source" meant a *foreign communication intercepted by German intelligence*. In messages of April 7 and 22 to another embassy, the Foreign Ministry in Berlin used almost identical wording—"reliable, strictly secret source"—to describe a source that later proved to be German interceptions of foreign diplomatic messages.[20] Secondly, Chargé Thomsen credited the State Department with possession of the key to the Japanese diplomatic code at a time when only the army and navy intelligence units were serving as cryptoanalytic agents in the United States. A reader of the British message of April 2 would have believed that the State Department was among the U.S. agencies possessing a cryptoanalytical office because Halifax cited the Under Secretary of State as the source for the Goering statement.[21] Third, the German embassy specifically cited a relay from Tokyo to Washington as the source of reports about Japanese activities in Berlin. Actually, the information had come from the interception of a Japanese message sent from Berlin to Tokyo. A reader of the Halifax communication—although recognizing the source as a Japanese diplomatic message but unable to identify the specific link—could be expected to assume that the source was a message from Tokyo to Washington.

The Germans apparently did not suspect that the Americans had intercepted the Japanese message from Berlin to Tokyo. This seems a reasonable conclusion because the German Foreign Ministry conveyed its warning to Tokyo through the Japanese ambassador in Berlin rather than through the German ambassador in Tokyo. A search of captured German documents reveals no evidence that the Germans had requested their ambassador in Tokyo to advise Matsuoka of the American penetration of the Japanese diplomatic code. In sum, the evidence is very strong that the British communications lapse was the primary cause of the Magic leak in April 1941.

Inasmuch as Hitler had ordered absolute secrecy about his plans to attack the Soviet Union, news of the American accomplishment must have been extremely unwelcome to the German leadership. On May 3, a German foreign ministry official repeated the substance of the Washington message of April 28 to Japanese Ambassador Oshima in Berlin.[22] Three days later, U.S. naval intelligence officers translated Oshima's message of May 3 apprising Matsuoka of the German warning. At that point the Magic operation appeared doomed. For the United States the timing could not have been worse since relations with Japan had recently taken a turn that made information on Japanese intentions increasingly important.

News of the intelligence compromise came shortly after the United States had suffered a setback in its attempt to stop through diplomacy Japanese territorial expansion. For years, and particularly after the fall of France in June 1940, Japanese, American and Soviet officials had discussed the expansionism issue. Since July 1940, Welles had granted several concessions to the Soviet government in hopes of preventing a Soviet rapprochement with Japan. At the time, both the United States and the Soviet Union were siding with China in the Sino-Japanese conflict. The Soviets were not only supplying China with arms, but had also presented Japan with a formidable military establishment on its northern border. In March and April 1941, these developments had prompted Japanese Foreign Minister Matsuoka to visit Berlin and then Moscow in search of a treaty with the Soviet Union.

The U.S. and Japan were also conducting official and unofficial talks. Hull had been meeting with Japanese Ambassador Kichisaburo Nomura since his arrival in the United States in February 1941. At the same time Father James M. Drought, an American Catholic priest, had been sponsoring private exchanges between Japanese and American civilians in an attempt to improve relations between the two nations. On April 9 the State Department had received Father Drought's draft proposal for the settlement of United States-Japanese differences.

On April 13 Welles saw his diplomatic efforts go for naught with the announcement in Moscow of a Soviet-Japanese Neutrality Pact. That agreement undoubtedly influenced the Secretary of State to take seriously the proposal offered by Father Drought and his associates. Gone was one deterrent to Japanese expansion. As early as April 16, Secretary Hull had offered a revised version of the Drought paper as a basis for negotiations with the Japanese ambassador. Hull's efforts were encouraged, but also weakened, by the Soviet-Japanese agreement.[23]

The sudden change in relations between Japan and the Soviet Union increased the importance of the Magic operation to the United States. Hull used the Japanese messages to ascertain Tokyo's instructions to Ambassador Nomura prior to his meet with the ambassador, Roosevelt, on the other hand, lost direct access to the messages because of the leak. Delivery of Magic material to the White House had been stopped as early as March when an intelligence officer discovered a Magic memorandum in the wastebasket of the President's secretary. The navy had continued to supply Roosevelt with intercepted Japanese messages until discovery of the leak when it too discontinued its service to the White House.[24]

Beginning in May 1941, President Roosevelt received only indirect and piecemeal information about intercepted Japanese messages. Naval intelligence arranged for the President's aide, Captain John R. Beardall, to see selected documents, but he was not allowed to show them to Roosevelt and could only orally brief the President. Hull and Welles also could discuss the messages with Roosevelt, but they were not allowed to keep the documents or to take copies to the White House.[25]

The leak and the subsequent curtailment of Magic service to Roosevelt adversely affected American relations with Japan during the initial phase of the German invasion of the USSR in June 1941. The surprise attack on the Soviet Union took place almost seven weeks after the navy had discovered the Magic leak. The Japanese government entered a period of indecision about whether it should strike at Russia's far eastern boundary. Unknown to the U.S., a secret clause in the Tripartite Pact gave Japan an excuse to stay out of the German-Soviet war. Shortly after the German invasion began, Von Ribbentrop urged the Japanese to join in the war against the USSR. On July 2 Japan decided to put aside, for the time being, a strike against the Soviets and to concentrate on its southward expansion. Even though the Japanese Foreign Office quickly notified its ambassadors of the decision, neither the U.S. Army nor Navy intelligence units were able immediately to break the particularly complicated coded message. Ambassador Grew reported only that Japan had decided that southward expansion would be gradual in order to avoid a clash with the United States.[26]

On July 3 President Roosevelt received a warning from Chiang Kai-shek that Japan was about to attack Siberia. Reacting promptly, Roosevelt approved a message that was sent on July 4 urging the Japanese government not to war against the Soviet Union. Ambassador Grew was instructed to deliver the message personally to Prince Konoye.[27] It was traditional, however, for Japanese prime ministers to deal directly only with individuals of comparable rank, and Grew thus had to leave the communication with the prime minister's private secretary. This episode contributed greatly toward the deterioration of relations with Japan.

At a crucial time when the United States could ill afford exacerbating its relations with Japan, the message of July 4 exposed to the Japanese leaders American ignorance of Japanese protocol. Although Ambassador Grew initially denied that the July 4 message had hurt American-Japanese relations, Prime Minister Konoye's own words indicated that it had a devastating effect on the position of Matsuoka. Prince Konoye wrote:

This procedure was unprecedented and showed how seriously the American Government held Foreign Minister Matsuoka in disfavor. . . , [T]he Foreign Minister evinced considerable displeasure at the direct and secret transmission of the message to me. Whereupon Ambassador Grew could hardly hide his disappointment in having had a direct interview with me blocked. After this relationships between the Foreign Minister and Ambassador Grew, which had always been cool, grew increasingly worse.[28]

Prime Minister Konoye's private secretary believed that American pressure had played a significant role in bringing down the Japanese cabinet, which came a few days after the message of July 4 was sent to the prime minister.[29]

The American message undoubtedly strengthened the anti-Matsuoka faction in the Japanese cabinet. The foreign minister had split with his colleagues over where Japan should expand territorially and over how it should deal with the United States. Despite his role in the neutrality agreement with the Soviets, Matsuoka advocated immediate invasion of the Soviet Union and postponement until the end of 1941 of a military move southward. On the other hand, Prime Minister Konoye, along with army and navy leaders, had prevailed at the imperial Conference on July 2 when they had advocated concentration on southward expansion. Whereas Matsuoka considered negotiations with the United States to be hopeless, Konoye wished to pursue bargaining. Arriving shortly after Matsuoka's imperial Conference defeat, the Roosevelt message insulted the foreign minister, disturbed the protocol-conscious Konoye, made Matsuoka appear unacceptable as the person to continue negotiations with the United States, and contributed to the foreign minister's disgrace and downfall. As a diplomatic faux pas, it added to the bad feeling that was mounting between the United States and Japan.[30]

A recently declassified document indicates that a Magic message had been processed in time to make the direct communication with Konoye unnecessary. On July 3, army intelligence had translated a Japanese diplomatic message revealing Tokyo's decision to defer for the time being hostile action against the Soviet Union. The particular communication was the official Japanese rejection of Von Ribbentrop's request that Japan join Germany in the war against the Soviet Union.[31] Roosevelt did not see this communication; the security arrangements that denied him immediate and direct access to Magic documents prevented him from learning of the Japanese decision in time to quash the unwarranted American note sent to Konoye.

As this incident involving the American message suggests, by July 1941 Magic was rapidly becoming the sole source of secret information on Japanese policy available to Washington. Ambassador Grew's sources had dwindled to only a few contacts because of police threats against Japanese citizens who approached the U.S. embassy. The ambassador found himself reduced to seeking material on Japanese policy from the British ambassador, who in turn was getting his information from the British Foreign Office in London.[32] Possibly the most serious consequence of the Magic leak occurred after the fall of the Japanese cabinet on July 16. Reportedly using a ruse to oust Matsuoka, the entire cabinet resigned; but most members later returned. Matsuoka, however, was replaced by Teijiro Toyoda, a naval officer presumably acceptable to right-wing extremists but considered willing to carry out moderate policies.[33] The new cabinet embarked on the more aggressive advance southward which had been endorsed by the Imperial Conference on July 2. Japan took over all of French Indochina on July 24—drawing American ire and the freezing of Japanese assets in the

United States. Although inexperienced in diplomacy, Toyoda—perhaps because of his naval experience—showed a disposition for communications security that appeared to be lacking in the Foreign Office under Matsuoka.

The new foreign minister tightened security in the use of Japanese diplomatic codes. Evidence is absent on the exact causes of the change in the use of codes. Nonetheless, the Japanese appeared to accept at last the German warning of May 3 that the Americans had broken their diplomatic cipher system. The Foreign Office clearly treated the coded communications as vulnerable and no longer trustworthy for transmitting overseas policy secrets. The change in communications policy was revealed to the Americans in August 1941 through a Japanese diplomatic message. In response to a complaint about inadequate intelligence information from Tokyo, Toyoda on August 7 indicated to Ambassador Oshima in Berlin that because of the fear of interception "we cannot touch upon any confidential matters. Please bear in mind also that for the above reasons we are unable to keep those advised at times of our policies."[34] American naval intelligence intercepted the message from Toyoda, but neglected to bring it to the attention of Hull, Captain Beardall, or Roosevelt.[35] It seems clear that Tokyo had decided to continue using what it regarded as insecure codes; the Foreign Office, however, had decided to refrain from sending highly secret policy decisions abroad in those codes.

A survey of intercepted Japanese diplomatic messages appears to support the conclusion that the Foreign Office ceased to send to the field highly secret policy decisions after Matsuoka left office. On August 8, 1941, American cryptanalysts finally processed the Japanese Foreign Office relay to the field of the results of the Imperial Conference on July 2. That message was in a "system . . . considered to be of the highest type of secret classification," according to the cryptanalysts who broke the cipher.[36] The Japanese diplomatic message of July 2 was the last peacetime communication that the Americans read which contained a highly secret policy decision made in Tokyo.

Through most of the fall of 1941 American officials thus were unaware of any subsequent shifting in Japanese policy. Neither the American embassy nor the Magic cryptanalysts knew about the Imperial Conference decision of September 6 to plan for a possible war against the United States. At that meeting Japanese officials decided that, if by early October, there appeared no prospect of winning American consent to their demands, they would prepare for hostilities against the United States as well as Britain and the Netherlands.

On October 16 disagreements over negotiations with the U.S. led to the fall of the Konoye cabinet. In the new cabinet headed by General Hideki Tojo, a career diplomat, Shigenori Togo, became foreign minister and continued negotiations with the United States. Togo served in that capacity until July 16, 1944, and then again from April 7 to 15, 1945.

Writing from a prison cell after World War II, Togo left for historians contradictory accounts about the effects of the intercepted diplomatic messages on Japanese-American relations. Embittered and blaming the U.S. for the war, Togo was tried and convicted of conspiracy by the International Military Tribunal for the Far East. Claiming that he was poorly informed about American-Japanese negotiations when he took office, Togo insisted that he had been assured by a communications official that Japanese diplomatic dispatches were secure. In one place in his memoirs, he acknowledged that the American interception of Japanese messages had little effect on negotiations. Elsewhere in his writings he stated that his telegraphed instructions to Ambassador Nomura in Washington "could not have embarrassed me so far as my actual language would have become known to the adversary."[37] But, complained Togo, the Americans produced incorrect translations of his messages which led the United States to reject his proposals to Hull. Citing an example, he argued that the American translation "might well have been a malicious distortion of the message aimed at creating an impression of perfidy,"[38] Togo used the alleged American errors in translation as part of his defense before the International Military Tribunal.

But did Togo really believe that the Japanese codes were secure? The evidence suggests that he did not. His recollection, of course, differed greatly from the substance of Toyoda's earlier excuse for not sending important policy information abroad. Togo later claimed he transmitted only instructions that he considered harmless to the Japanese cause. And those instructions were the ones that Hull and Roosevelt read in the fall of 1941.

By November 1941, President Roosevelt was once again seeing Magic transcriptions. Although they had changed in value, Roosevelt's interest in them had increased by September. One could speculate endlessly about why the President had not earlier protested the withdrawal of Magic documents from him. In the spring and summer of 1941, he was overwhelmed with other problems, including heated Cabinet debates over whether to transfer the Pacific Fleet to the Atlantic Ocean in order to help the British as well as differences over the wisdom of entering the European war. He was also confronted with the question of whether to aid the Soviet Union in the war against Germany, and he was preparing to meet Prime Minister Winston Churchill for a secret conference off Newfoundland in August. Near the end of September, after some of those matters had been resolved, Roosevelt began pressing his naval aide to bring the Magic documents to the White House.[39] At first, naval intelligence allowed Captain Beardall to show the President only memoranda based on the Magic documents. By November 12 the delivery of Magic transcriptions had been restored to the President through his naval aide. But neither Roosevelt nor Beardall was informed of the limitation placed on these documents as revealed in Toyoda's message to Oshima in August.

Secretary of State Hull was relying heavily on the Magic transcriptions to guide him in the vigorous negotiations he had been pursuing with Japan following the signing of the Soviet-Japanese Neutrality Pact in April 1941. As he later admitted, he frequently read Tokyo's instructions to Ambassador Nomura just prior to their meetings.[40] By late November, the Magic transcriptions and the nature of Hull's negotiations suggested to American officials that Japan intended to take drastic action if its needs were not appreciated or recognized by the U.S. Tokyo set a deadline of November 25 to reach agreement with Washington, but the Magic documents gave no indication as to the specific action contemplated by the Japanese government.[41]

On November 27 Roosevelt's advisors who had access to the Magic transcriptions predicted that if the Hull-Nomura-Kurusu negotiations ended without an agreement, Japan would immediately attack either the Burma Road, Thailand, Malaya, the Netherlands East Indies, the Philippines, the Russian Maritime Provinces, or China. With minor reservations, Stanley Hornbeck, the State Department political advisor on Far Eastern matters, agreed with these forecasts of General George C. Marshall and Admiral Harold Stark.[42]

All—Roosevelt, his senior advisors, and Hull—had, however, allowed themselves to be lulled into a false sense of security by their perceptions of the Magic documents. When Hull and the noted historians William Langer and S. Everett Gleason evaluated the Magic project several years after the war ended, they concluded that it provided the Roosevelt administration with an inside view of Japanese foreign policy.[43] But, as the records show, the Magic transcriptions gave the U.S. no precise understanding of Japan's plans.

Unknown to the U.S.—for there was barely any mention of the later Imperial conferences of 1941 in Magic documents—Japanese leaders had met on September 6, November 5, and December 1. The conference on November 5 set the deadline of November 25 for American accession to Japanese demands; if the negotiations failed, the Emperor would be asked to approve war against the United States. On December 1 the Emperor consented to the Japanese attack on Pearl Harbor. Roosevelt, meanwhile, "really thought that the tactics of the Japanese would be to avoid a conflict with us," according to his advisor, Harry Hopkins.[44] And indeed the tone of the Magic documents that the President saw in the fall of 1941 supported such a view.

The bombing of Pearl Harbor on December 7 thus took the President and his advisors by surprise. The Japanese had planned the strike in such secrecy that very few individuals knew in advance the exact war plans; the silence in the Magic transcriptions about the American target contributed toward the success of Japan's initial victory, which depended on the element of surprise. Although the Japanese probably did not deliberately use the Magic project to deceive the U.S. about their plans, the American officials were nonetheless misled about Japanese intentions because of the false illusion fostered by the Magic documents.

The leak in the Magic operation in the spring of 1941 intensified American misunderstanding on the eve of the Pearl Harbor tragedy. The most notable difficulty, of course, was the lack of a professional intelligence agency to advise the President, Secretary of State, and leaders of the armed forces on secret intelligence concerning foreign policies of other countries. The existing intelligence services exhibited poor judgment in dealing with President Roosevelt by neglecting to acquire other sources of information to supplement the Magic disclosures and by failing to assess continuously the reliability and the limitations of the fragmentary Magic transcripts. With or without the leak, the United States should have considered whether the Japanese Foreign Office would tell its ambassadors much about vital decisions made in Tokyo. American delight over breaking the high-level Japanese diplomatic code apparently caused such a consideration to be overlooked.

The steps taken by the American intelligence services in the wake of the leak were ineffectual at best and damaging at worst. There is no evidence that the Roosevelt administration sought arrangements to protect U.S. intelligence passed on to another government. Disturbed with the White House security, which indeed appeared lax, the intelligence services denied the President immediate and direct access to Magic documents from May to November 1941. The withholding of such intelligence prevented the President from making sound foreign policy decisions and from understanding the nature of Japanese intentions toward the United States. It helped lead to the unnecessary and upsetting message of July 4 sent to Konoye. That incident added to the deterioration of American-Japanese relations in the summer and fall of 1941.

Another blunder by the American intelligence services was their failure to apprise Roosevelt of the Japanese Foreign Office's apparent loss of confidence in the security of its diplomatic codes, as revealed by the message of August 7. Thus, when Magic documents were again sent to the President in November, he mistakenly believed that he was getting an inside picture of secret Japanese foreign-policy decisions rather than merely the view that the Japanese government wanted the rest of the world to believe in the fall of 1941.

Despite the limitations of the Japanese messages interception after August 7, those documents still constituted a valuable intelligence source. They provided useful information on conversations between German leaders and Japanese officials, gave the Roosevelt administration access to the day-to-day instructions sent from Tokyo, and contained a vague warning in late November 1941 that the Japanese were contemplating hostile action. But American officials expected more of Magic than it could produce. Magic did not give the U.S. advance warning that its territory would be the target of a Japanese attack; it did not alert the Roosevelt administration to the time and place of the planned aggression. As the events following the leak of 1941 showed, Magic proved to be less than magical after all.

The author, a consultant for History Associates, Inc., is currently doing research on the U.S. Economic Stabilization Program, 1971–1974.

The author wishes to thank Peter P. Hill of George Washington University, Harry Young and David Patterson of the U.S. Department of State, and William Cunliffe of the National Archives for reading this paper in its initial stages.

Notes

1. Collection of Japanese Diplomatic Messages, July 12, 1938, to Jan. 21, 1942, U.S. Dept. of the Army Intelligence Files, SRH-018, National Archives. Information about Japanese diplomatic messages and additional U.S.-intercepted Japanese telegrams are also in the U.S. Dept. of the Army Intelligence Files. Record Group 165, National Archives (hereafter cited as DAIF, RG 165, NA); U.S. Naval Court of Inquiry, Navy Reports, Record Group 107 (hereafter cited as NCI, RG 107, NA); Records of the Pearl Harbor Liaison Office, Japanese Diplomatic Files, General Records of the U.S. Dept. of the Navy, 1798–1947, Record Group 80. National Archives (hereafter cited as RPHLO, RG 80, NA). A microfilm collection of American-intercepted Japanese diplomatic messages from the Judge Advocate General's files is available in the operational Archives of the Naval History Division, Washington. D.C. (hereafter cited as JAG, NHD). Published American-intercepted Japanese messages appear in U.S. Dept. of Defense, *The "Magic" Background of Pearl Harbor* (8 vols., Washington, D.C., 1977–1978).

2. U.S. Congress, Joint Committee on the Investigation of the Pearl Harbor Attack, *Hearings*, 79 Cong., 1 sess. (1946), IV, 1859–1863 (hereafter cited as *Pearl Harbor Attack*).

3. Roberta Wohlstetter, *Pearl Harbor: Warning and Decision* (Stanford, 1962), 176–186. The same author later wrote *Cuba and Pearl Harbor; Hindsight and Foresight* (Santa Monica, Calif., 1965).

4. David Kahn, *The Codebreakers: The Story of Secret Writing* (New York, 1967), 26–27, 31.

5. Ladislas Farago, *The Broken Seal: The Story of "Operation Magic" and the Pearl Harbor Disaster* (New York, 1967), 191–202.

6. Barton Whaley, *Codeword Barborossa* (Cambridge, Mass., 1973), 42–46.

7. Homer N. Wallin, *Pearl Harbor: Why, How, Fleet Salvage and the Final Appraisal* (Washington, D.C., 1968), 72. Most authors writing about Pearl Harbor are not as explicit as Wallin. Some simply acknowledge the influence on the U.S. of the intercepted messages; others use the texts of the intercepted Japanese communications to analyze Japan's reactions during negotiations with the U.S. The list of works on Pearl Harbor is too lengthy to list here, but the following guides are available: Wayne S. Cole, "American Entry into World War II: A Historiographical Appraisal." *Mississippi Valley Historical Review*, XLIII (1957), 593–617; Louis Morton, "Pearl Harbor in Perspective: A Bibliographical Survey." *U.S. Naval Institute Proceedings*, LXXXI (1955), 461–468; R. H. Ferrell, "Pearl Harbor and the Revisionists," *The Historian*, XVII (1955), 215–233. The most recent works include Martin V. Melosi, *The Shadow of Pearl Harbor: Political Controversy over the Surprise Attack, 1941–1946* (College Station, Texas, 1977); and Lester H. Brune, "Considerations of Force in Cordell Hull's Diplomacy, July 26 to November 26, 1941." *Diplomatic History*, 11 (1978), 389–405. The theme of Brune's article, which might be read in conjunction with this article, is that Hull neglected to coordinate his diplomacy with military leaders.

8. Brig. Gen. Sherman Miles to Gen. E. M. Watson, the president's secretary, in "Pearl Harbor Events," G-2 Files, 1943–1946, box 960, DAIF, RG 165, NA.

9. John T. Mason, Jr., ed., "Oral History of Rear Admiral Arthur H. McCollum," 1,277, NHD. Although Magic was a term applicable to the U.S. communications intelligence efforts directed against foreign countries, the term is used in this paper to refer only to intercepted Japanese diplomatic messages.

10. Memo by Capt. A. D. Kramer, Nov. 12, 1941, on "Dissemination to White House," in *Pearl Harbor Attack*, XI. 5455–5456; survey of Japanese diplomatic messages in Japanese Diplomatic Files, ANB, RG 80, NA.

11. Wohlstetter, *Warning and Decision*, 186; "Magic" memoranda in Japanese Diplomatic Files. RPHLO, RG 80, NA. According to a number of contemporary witnesses, the intelligence services then were extremely rudimentary. John T. Mason, Jr., ed., "The Reminiscences of Alan Goodrich Kirk" (Oral History Research Office, Columbia University, 1962). I, 183; testimony of Major Gen. Sherman Miles, *Pearl Harbor Attack*, II, 899; testimony of Capt. Ellis M. Zacharias before the Roberts Commission, *ibid* XXIII, 1013–1025. Admiral Kirk served as director of ONI in 1941, and Capt. Zacharias served under him. Gen. Miles was acting chief of G-2 in 1941.

12. Gen. Watson to Roosevelt, memo of Jan. 2, 1941, in War Department, Henry L. Stimson, 1941, Departmental correspondence, President's Secretary's Files, Franklin D. Roosevelt Library, Hyde Park. N.Y. (hereafter cited PSF, FDRL).

13. Memo of Feb. 22, 1941, for Roosevelt, in *ibid.*, State Department, PSF, FDRL; Message #68 of Feb. 14, 1941, from Matsuoka, Tokyo, relayed by the Japanese ambassador in Washington to the Japanese ambassador in London, reel #1, JAG NHD.

14. Farago cited documents processed on March 19 and 22, and April 3 and 4, 1941. The March 19 document concerned Matsuoka's trip to the Soviet Union; the March 22 document is missing; and the April 3 and 4 documents dealt with Yugoslavia. Farago, *Broken Seal*, 191–202, 411–412; Japanese Diplomatic Files. RPHLO, RG 80. NA.

15. Memo by the FBI of Oct. 4, 1940, released to the author; transcript of telephone conversation between Welles and Henry Morganthau, Jr.. Sept. 19, 1940, in Henry Morganthau, diaries, 307: 76, FDRL. The Soviet ambassador's meetings with Thomnen reflected Stalin's policy of treating Germany in a friendly fashion. As the captured German documents indicate, Umansky gave the German chargé only routine information about the Soviet-American meetings. U.S. Dept. of State, *Documents on German Foreign Policy, 1918–1945* (Washington, D.C., 1957–1964), series D, X–XII.

16. Halifax to Foreign Office, London, telegram #1436. April 2, 1941, and minutes, F.O. 371/29479/1599, Public Record Office, London (hereafter cited as PRO); Japanese Diplomatic Files. RPHLO. RG 80, NA.

17. Leland Morris to U.S. Dept. of State, April 1, 1941, file 762.94/503. Records of the U.S. Dept. of State, Record Group 59, National Archives.

18. Welles to Roosevelt, April 21, 1941, Sumner Welles, Departmental Correspondence, State Department, Jan.–May 1941, PSF, FDRL.

19. U.S. Dept. of State, *German Foreign Policy*, XII, 661.

20. *Ibid.*, 604–605; U.S. Dept. of State, *Foreign Relations of the United States, 1941* (Washington, D.C., 1956), IV, 939–940.

21. The Department of State had previously participated in a cryptoanalytic project with the army, but it had abandoned that effort during the Herbert Hoover administration at the insistence of Secretary of State Henry L. Stimson, who considered it ungentlemanly for the United States to read the mail of other governments.

22. *Pearl Harbor Attack*, IV, 1861.

23. Memo by Hull of a conversation with Japanese ambassador, April 16, 1941, in Japan File, January 1940–June 1941, subject file, box 60, folder 230. Hull Papers, Library of Congress. The April 9 draft resulted from the collaboration of Father Drought, Col. Hideo Iwakuro, and Japanese embassy officials, according to Robert Butow in his excellent, detailed account of the private negotiations, The *John Doe Associates: Backdoor Diplomacy for Peace* (Stanford, 1974), 147–167. In the view of a specialist in Japanese political history, the Japanese prime minister, Prince Fumimaro Konoye, was apparently unaware then of that particular draft but reportedly approved of the concept of unofficial negotiations because of prevailing public opinion in Japan. See Seiichi Imai, "Cabinet, Emperor, and Senior Statesmen," in Dorothy Borg and Shumpei Olamoto, eds., *Pearl Harbor as History: Japanese-American Relations, 1931–1941* (New York, 1973), 77.

24. Memo by Capt. Kramer. *Pearl Harbor Attack*, XI. 3455–3456; dissemination stamps on "Magic" documents in Japanese Diplomatic Files. RHPLO, RG 80, NA.

25. Kramer memo, in *Pearl Harbor Attack*, XI, 5455–5456; "Pearl Harbor Events," G-2 files, box 960, DAIF, RG 165, NA; testimony of Kramer, July 24, 1944, NCI, RG 107, NA.

26. "An Outline of the Policy of the Imperial Government in View of the Present Developments," in *Pearl Harbor Attack*, XX, 4018–4019; translated message, *ibid.*, XII, 1–2; Grew to Hull, July 6, 1941, in U.S. Dept. of State, *Foreign Relations, 1941*, IV, 999–1001.

27. Chiang Kai-shek to Roosevelt by way of SEGAG to Lauchlin Currie, administrative assistant to Roosevelt, telegram probably received on July 3, 1941, *ibid.*, 289; Welles to Grew, approved by Roosevelt, July 3, 1941; telegram sent on July 4, 1941, *ibid.*, 994–993.

28. *Pearl Harbor Attack*, XX, 3993

29. Joseph C. Grew, *Ten Years in Japan* (New York, 1944), 428, 431.

30. Scholars have suggested other factors that contributed to the ouster of Matsuoka. According to Takashi Ito, an extreme right-wing faction favored an immediate Japanese attack on the Soviet Union after the initiation of the German-Soviet war; other groups, however, sided with the cabinet majority. Ito, "The Role of Right Wing Organization in Japan," in Borg and Okamoto, eds., *Pearl Harbor History*, 508. Some historians have also suggested that Matsuoka was emotionally disturbed, if not insane. Butow, *John Doe Associates*, 399–400; Barbara Teters, "Matsuola Yosuke: The Diplomacy of Bluff and Gesture," in Richard Dean Burns and Edward M. Bennett, eds., *Diplomats in Crisis: U.S. Japanese Relations, 1919–1941* (Santa Barbara, Calif., 1974), 293. Surprisingly, the July 4 message is not discussed in most secondary accounts. William L. Langer and S. Everett Gleason considered it an expression of the Anglo-American desire that Japan not hasten collapse of the Soviet Union. Langer and Gleason, *The Undeclared War, 1940–1941* (New York, 1953), 635. Teters believes that Matsuoka's ouster had been decided in early July 1941, but see Herbert Feis, *The Road to Pearl Harbor: The Coming of the War Between the United States and Japan* (Princeton, NJ., 1950), 223.

31. Matsuolka to Oshima, Berlin, telegram no. 585, translated by the army on July 3, 1941, reel 1, vol. 3, JAG, NHD.

32. Grew to Welles, telegram no. 970, July 10, 1941. in U.S. Dept. of State, *Foreign Relations, 1941*, IV, 299–300.

33. Butow, *John Doe Associates*, 238.

34. Toyoda's message is in GZ-5, memo of Aug. 10, 1941, from Capt. Kirk, director of ONI, to Chief of Naval Operations, Japanese Diplomatic Messages. RHPLO, RG 80, NA.

35. Roosevelt was at sea for the Atlantic Conference with Churchill; Capt. Beardall was not listed as a recipient of this memorandum, probably because he was accompanying Roosevelt.

36. This notation was appended to the circular of July 2, 1941, which was translated on Aug. 8, 1941, reel 1, vol. 3, JAG, NHD.

37. Togo Shigenori, *The Cause of Japan* (New York, 1956), 55–57, 61, quotation on p. 167.

38. *Ibid.*, 169.

39. Memo by Capt. Kramer, in *Pearl Harbor Attack*, XI, 5453–5456.

40. Cordell Hull, *The Memoirs of Cordell Hull* (New York, 1948), 11, 998.

41. The Americans actually may have been confused about Japanese intentions in mid-November 1941, because of at least two sets of peculiar warning codes that Tokyo sent to the field for possible future use. The codes, if used, presumably would have notified Japanese diplomats what action Japan would take. The United States, however, did not intercept any coded warnings prior to December 7. The appendix to volume V of U.S. Dept. of Defense, *The "Magic" Background of Pearl Harbor*, includes special studies of those "winds" and "stop" codes. See also Trumbull Higgins. "East Wind Rain," *Naval Institute Proceedings*, LXXXI (1955), 1198–1203.

42. Military estimate of Nov. 27, 1941, signed by Gen. George C. Marshall and Admiral Harold R. Stark, for the President, in *Pearl Harbor Attack*, XIV, of Nov. 27, 1941, by Hornbeck on "Problems of Far Eastern Relations—Estimate of Situation and Certain Probabilities," in U.S. Dept. of State, *Foreign Relations, 1941*, IV, 672–675.

43. Hull, *Memoirs*, II. 999; Langer and Gleason, *The Undeclared War*, 637.

44. Robert E. Sherwood, *Roosevelt and Hopkins: An Intimate History* (New York, 1948), 428.

Reading 16

Women, Work, and War

Alice Kessler-Harris

Depression and war have opposite effects on the economy. One prompts efficiency, constraint, cautious investment; the other encourages industrial expansion—even a spirit of reckless gambling. If the 1930s depression sloughed off workers, making every fourth one redundant, the war gobbled them up, then searched for more. Where workers had to plead for jobs in the thirties, in the early forties industry begged for workers. And when the army had soaked up the residue of unemployed men, employers turned to women. Unprecedented opportunity now confronted women who months earlier had pleaded for work. Was this to be a breakthrough?—a turning point that would signal the end of discrimination against women in the labor market?

It certainly looked like it. In many ways, this war duplicated the experience of World War I. Women found jobs in areas previously closed to them and, once there, proved to be effective workers. The statistical data reveal a dramatic influx of women—five million between 1940 and 1944—into the labor force and new openings in the heavy industries that had been tightly defended against them. Historians like William Chafe, Chester Gregory, and Sheila Tobias and Lisa Anderson have concluded, as a result, that World War II was, in Chafe's words, "a milestone for women in America." From that perspective, the war serves to explain and justify the new expectations of the fifties. Tobias and Anderson see demobilization as the central issue raised by the war years. The war, they argue, opened doors, changed attitudes, made women aware of possibilities they had not previously considered.

To some extent this is undoubtedly true. As in World War I, women who had always worked fought hard to retain their gains when the war ended. But viewing the war this way places too much weight on the role of a single unpredictable event in altering women's behavior. And, whereas women came to the first war out of a lengthy period of struggle for minimal wages and working conditions, they entered the second from a depression-fostered certainty of their economic importance. In fact, women had already begun to change their working patterns in the two preceding decades. They responded to war not as shiny new instruments honed to do their bit in a larger design, but out of the continuity of their own historical experience. In the twenties and thirties different women had struggled to participate in the labor market in their own way—some seeking the challenge of a career, others organizing for higher standards of living. The war provided opportunities for both kinds of women to continue these struggles. It did not relieve the tensions surrounding their dual roles, but did cast a different light on them.

The second World War provides a place to see these tensions from a different perspective than the depression. Asked their reasons for wage-earning in both periods, women offered the same explanations. Wage work contributed to family life; financial need justified potential neglect of the home. Wartime appeals to patriotism turned the defensive posture these arguments had in the depression into an aggressive stance. Where the depression had prompted women to apologize for paid work—to present it as a last resort to preserve family life—the war focused attention on women's positive contributions to labor force needs. Satisfying family requirements, once a seemingly insurmountable barrier to wage work, became a practical problem to be solved quickly so that the nation could meet the war machine's insatiable hunger for personnel.

The changed perspective made all the difference in the reception women met in the labor force, and there is no doubt that the war raised the level of their material well-being. But whether it permanently altered their relation to wage work is another question. Women would not willingly have given up their family roles even if social sanctions were lifted and support services helped them to do so. And employers and male workers could not readily overcome a tradition of segmentation so closely related to masculinity. Economist Theresa Wolfson put it this way: "It is not easy to forget the propaganda of two decades even in the face of a national emergency such as a great war. Women themselves doubted their ability to do a man's job. Married women with families were loath to leave their homes; society had made so little provision for the thousands of jobs that a homemaker must tackle. And when they finally come into the plants, the men resent them as potential scabs." The resulting ambivalence led women to weigh the tremendous pressure to take jobs against the sacrifices required of their time and by their families. It penetrated every facet of women's work force experience.

As the European was stimulated production in 1940 and 1941, the residue of unemployment began to lessen, though men, not women, benefited from the early build-up. Women were told to "Do the home job better" or channeled into volunteer jobs. As one jocular civil defense official put it, "Give the women something to do to keep their hands busy as we did in the last war—then maybe they won't bother us." As government programs began early in 1941 to "warm up" the unemployed to heavy industry, twenty men were offered places to every woman. Some 700,000 workers received training in industrial skills in the last half of 1941. Only 1 percent of these were female. Employers believed women were not suited to most jobs and declared themselves unwilling to hire women for 81 percent of available production jobs.

Attitudes began to change after Pearl Harbor. Early in 1942, it became clear that the draft would decimate the ranks of production workers. The government issued a nondiscrimination directive. For the first time, employers sought out women, for nontraditional jobs, and occasionally offered the kinds of services that made wage work more viable for those who had households and children to care for. They sometimes provided day care centers on site. Shopping and banking facilities appeared in plants. Convenient transportation and hot lunches attracted women to factory work. As men left jobs for the armed services, women entered them. Still, from September 1942 to September 1943, the number of people in the work force remained at the 1940 level.

By mid-1942 it was clear that this was not enough. Calculating that only 29 percent of America's fifty-two million adult women had jobs, the War Manpower Commission started a campaign to recruit women in areas of labor shortage. Journalist Eleanor Herrick accused half the women in New York City of shirking their war obligations. The federal government lowered the age limit for the employment of women from eighteen to sixteen years. Patriotic appeals to women accompanied tales of their special stake in winning this war in order to stop Hitler from reducing women to "sex slaves" or driving them back to their kitchens. The Women's Bureau described desperate entrepreneurs who harangued women at street corners to come to work, or bribed high school principals to send workers to their plants. The radio did its bit, popularizing tunes like "Rosie the Riveter," which told listeners about "red, white and blue" Rosie who was "making history working for victory." Rosie kept

... a sharp lookout for sabotage
Sitting up there on the fuselage
That little frail can do,
More than a male can do,
Rosie—(Brrrr) the riveter.
Rosie's got a boyfriend, Charlie;
Charlie, he's a marine
Rosie is protecting Charlie
Working overtime on the riveting machine.

By February 1943, *Fortune* magazine declared the margin for victory to be "woman power" and suggested drafting them if they did not come forward voluntarily to work in industry. And in July 1943 the War Production Board declared itself in need of a million and a half more women within a year.

Women responded to these appeals in large numbers but not with the kind of unthinking enthusiasm that the statistics seem to demonstrate. Fully three-quarters of the women who worked for pay during the war had worked before, and one and a half million more would have entered the labor force anyway in the normal course of events. Less than five million of the nineteen million women who worked for wages at some time during the war emergency had not been in the labor force before the war began.

What looks like massive mobilization of women in the war years breaks down on examination to something less startling. Nearly 11.0 million women held jobs in 1940. At the peak of wartime production in 1945, 19.5 million women were actually earning wages: an apparent increase in absolute numbers of nearly 8.7 million people or 80.5 percent. But a closer look at the figures forces us to modify our assessment of the real change this number implies. In addition to the women actually working in 1940, the Census Bureau counted some 3.0 million unemployed and looking for work. An additional number, unknown except by estimate, were discouraged but would have worked if they thought jobs were available. A million such workers seems a safe estimate. The difference between the resulting figure of 14.8 million and 19.5 million reduces the increase in women workers to 43 percent or 4.7 million new workers in the war years.

But we need to make still further modifications. What percentage of the 4.7 million would have entered the labor force anyway as a result of population growth and maturity? And what percentage would have entered as a product of the continuing twentieth-century trend of women moving into the work force? The first figure can be calculated on the basis of population growth. In 1940, 27.6 percent of the female population over fourteen was in the labor force. They constituted 25.3 percent of all workers. If the same percentage had been in the labor force in 1945, when the population of women numbered 52,860,000, an additional 750,000 workers in round numbers would have joined the labor force, war or no war. But the proportion of women wage earners had been increasing steadily since 1900 and in all likelihood would have climbed in this decade as well. From 1900 to 1940, the female labor force participation rate had increased 23.5 percent, or an average of nearly 6 percent each decade—though there were in fact wide fluctuations from decade to decade. For the half-decade from 1940 to 1945 we can safely add another 3 percent, or 400,000 women, to the 1940 figure as normal growth. In fact, the figures would in all likelihood have been higher, given the possibility that the depression, having discouraged women from wage work, had created a backlog of women eager to try their wings. Subtracting these two groups, then, one might argue that only 3.5 million workers who might not otherwise have entered the labor force did so in the war years—in addition of 25.28 percent to the female work force above the natural and expected increases. Seventy-five percent of these new female workers were married.

Wartime figures reflect the latent tendency of women to seek wage work when normative pressures to stay at home are removed. Considering the unusual (if still inadequate) child care and food services available; the absence of men to whom women ordinarily catered; attractive wages and job opportunities; and a temporary suspension of overt animosity, these data may represent a peak of the number of women willing to work for wages in that period. In the two years after the war ended, women's participation in the work force dropped by a factor of 19 percent—a figure only a trifle lower than the estimated "additional" women who entered wage work as a result of the war. In other words, after the wartime emergency receded, most of the women who remained in the labor force would have been working for wages anyway. There is no way of knowing if the three and a half million new women workers were the same women who dropped out, or were forced out, of the labor force when the war ended. But it seems clear that wartime surveys reporting that 75 to 85 percent of wage-earning women wanted to keep their jobs at the war's end probably reflected the normal proportion of wage-earning women. Of the two million additional women (above the 1940 level) still in the labor force in 1947, the Women's Bureau estimated that all but 250,000 would have been working in any event. By 1950, the rate of women's participation in the work force had increased to 32 percent—for a net gain of 16 percent over the entire decade. The Census Bureau estimated that without war, natural factors would have yielded seventeen million wage-earning women in 1950. There were in fact eighteen million in that year—only a slight increase above expected growth.

Much has been made of the number of women who entered the work force as an indication of changes in attitude and breakdown of traditional socialization patterns. But from another perspective the figures reflect continuity with previous attempts by some women to break out of traditional roles. Married women had entered the work force during the depression. In the war years, older married women contributed most of the increase that occurred among female workers. Despite publicity given to children left in locked cars while their mothers worked, a government report noted in 1943 that "practically no net expansion occurred among women between 20 and 30 years of age, and only a 6 percent increase of actual over normal employment is estimated for women in the next five year bracket." In contrast, women over forty-five appeared in the labor force in numbers about 20 percent above what would normally be expected. And of the nearly five million women at work in the spring of 1945 who had not been in the labor force five years earlier, three million were over thirty-five.

These rapid rises in participation rates exceeded those of any other age group in the labor force. They were more rapid for the married than for the unmarried, indicating both the degree to which single women had already been engaged in paid labor and the latent trend for the married with no children at home to want to work. This tendency continued after the war. By November 1946, half of all wage-earning women were over 34.8 years old. And the inclination of younger married women to leave the work force when husbands returned home meant that the proportion of older workers in the labor force would continue to rise. By 1950 there had been a net drop in the rate at which married women aged 25–34 went out to work. Correspondingly, half again as many women aged 45–54 were working for wages as had worked in 1940.

Given the high level of previous work experience among most women in the labor force during the war, it is not surprising that the emergency presented itself as an opportunity to get ahead. Memories of the depression urged women wage earners to get what they could while they could. So for those who had been accustomed to working, war-born opportunities encouraged an aggressive stance and resulted in real gains, at least for the duration of hostilities. Black women, older women, and professional women all took advantage of a reduction in discrimination to enter well-paying jobs.

For black women, the change was especially dramatic. For generations, they had been denied access to good, skilled jobs that now opened to them. The proportions who entered the labor force did not expand as rapidly as those of white women reflecting high prewar participation rates. But black women took advantage of their previous work experience and the labor shortage to move into more desirable jobs. About 20 percent of those who had been domestic servants found work in areas that had previously snubbed them. Where white women moved from laundries into factories, especially in the South, black women readily took the jobs they vacated. But it took effort to move up into factory jobs. The threat of a mass demonstration in Washington in 1941, while the United States was building up its armaments in preparation for war, drew public attention to discrimination against all blacks. To head off demonstrations, the federal government created the Fair Employment Practices Commission in July 1941.

Sustained by the FEPC as well as by rulings of the War Manpower Commission against discrimination, and actively aided by the National Council of Negro Women, black women pressed for lucrative factory jobs. In cities like Detroit, where defense work was widespread, large factories imported huge numbers of rural whites to fill jobs for which they initially refused to hire blacks. Black women there led a series of demonstrations, beginning early in 1942 and lasting for nearly two years, to force local authorities to hire them. These demonstrations—for housing as well as jobs—culminated in the storming of a Ford plant by two busloads of women protesting discriminatory hiring policies. Progress was slow. Yet for once, protesters had the active support of union locals, some civic agencies, and government policy. Members of UAW locals threatened to walk out of one plant in 1943 unless black women got jobs. At another plant, union representatives took nine months to win an agreement to hire black women, and then only after a threat of citywide action. The War Production Board and the U.S. Employment Service repeatedly urged employment of blacks in Detroit and elsewhere.

By war's end the position of black women workers had improved substantially. They never got some of the best-paying jobs—in steel mills, as welders, ship fitters, and riveters. But the numbers involved in low-paid and low-status domestic work dropped by 15 percent while the number of factory operatives more than doubled, and clerical, sales, and professional workers substantially increased. Ninety percent of the black women at work after the war had been in the labor force in 1940. Their movement into better jobs reflects not changed attitudes but their ability to take timely advantage of enlarged opportunities.

Professional women were equally aggressive. Historian Susan Hartmann has documented the extent to which they worked through their clubs and organizations to press for economic equality. Groups like the American Association of University Women and the National Federation of Business and Professional Women's Clubs met with the Women's Bureau to design "programs to promote the training, equal treatment and full utilization of women in war production," as well as "to plan for the retention of women's gains after reconversion." These organizations had little understanding of, or sympathy for, the economic problems of poor women or the racial discrimination faced by black women. Rather, they pushed to get women into policy-making positions in war agencies, even denying the need for special black representation on the Women's Advisory Committee—the only direct pipeline for women into the wartime agencies concerned with utilizing labor effectively. Despite the opposition of organizations representing poorer women, business and professional women continued to support the ERA and paid little attention to such mundane issues as day care. For them, the important thing, as always, was not resolving the home and family issues that might equalize work force opportunities for all women, but improving their own relative economic positions. They became entrenched in civil service jobs at the federal and state levels, made inroads into banking and insurance, and moved into administrative jobs in education and health. Though gains remaining after the war ended were relatively small, professional women had nevertheless succeeded in moving out of the holding pattern in which the Depression had placed them.

Two other pieces of evidence suggest that what happened in the war and immediate postwar years represented a response to emergency rather than a shift in attitude. The first emerges from a look at what women did when hostilities ceased; the second, from examining what happened to them in the demobilization period.

When war production ended, large numbers of women simply quit their jobs. The rate at which women chose to leave jobs was at least double, and sometimes triple the rate at which they were discharged. And it was consistently higher than quit rates for men. In the food, clothing, and textile industries, where they had traditionally been employed, women quit jobs at an incredible pace. Women in well-paid jobs—chemical, rubber, and petroleum—quit more slowly than from any other manufacturing jobs. Apparently, more experienced workers who had moved into better-paid jobs wanted to keep their jobs. More newer workers who had spent the war in traditionally female sectors willingly gave their places up.

Employers countered low quit rates by laying off women in the heavy industrial sectors where returning soldiers wanted jobs back. In the two months immediately following V-J Day, women were laid off at a rate of 175 per 1,000, double that of men. As the rate of layoffs slackened, women still lost their jobs at a slightly higher rate than men—especially in some durable goods industries. The biggest involuntary reduction came in the jobs where they had made the biggest gains in wartime and which presumably represented the biggest shift in social attitude—the durable heavy goods industries. Iron and steel manufactories, automobile and machinery makers fired women faster than they fired men. On the other hand, employers clearly sought to retain female employees in the nondurable goods sectors, where they were laid off more slowly than men.

Women's net gains in the war years were, therefore, negligible. They managed to retain a slightly greater share of manufacturing jobs, especially in the durable goods industries, but the general pattern of their employment remained the same as before the war. Even within manufacturing, the big gains occurred in electrical goods, where the task of assembling tiny parts was said to be suited to nimble fingers. The shift to clerical and office jobs continued. Few women retained skilled crafts jobs. The Women's Bureau concluded a study of Bridgeport, Connecticut, after the war sadly: "Only a few women have been allowed to continue in the newer fields of employment, and thus to continue to use skills learned during the war." Older women, married women, women without at least a high school education, and black women again had a hard time finding jobs.

Wartime necessity may have required women's wage work, but it did not release women who worked from the pressure to adhere to old social roles. Women's own urges for better jobs and wages met their match in the pleas for patriotism and service to the community that came from employers, the Labor Department, and the War Manpower Commission. These rationales for wage work produced policies that effectively skirted women's desires for work for its own sake. The never-ending fear that women might be unwilling to leave when the war ended led government policy makers and employers to make it clear that women ought to work only temporarily. And this too required continuing patterns of behavior that perpetuated the divided labor market with all of its psychic underpinnings.

Because of the ambivalence surrounding women's work, policies designed to make it easier for them to enter the labor force emerged erratically. Women found themselves without representation on the influential War Manpower Commission. Instead, the Commission created a Women's Advisory Committee in September 1942. That committee was authorized to recommend policy regarding women. But its recommendations were channeled through a Management-Labor Committee and thence to the WMC. The commission turned down Mary Anderson's request for one or two representatives on the Management-Labor Committee, offering instead a seat without a vote to Margaret Hickey, who chaired the Women's Advisory Committee. Three steps removed from the seat of power, the WAC operated in a vacuum. According to the Women's Bureau, it took seven months "before the WMC and its staff advisers sat down to consider the problem of how to improve communications."

While confusion persisted in administrative ranks, women in good jobs found themselves facing male pressure to be feminine, and sometimes hostility for violating traditional roles. To keep women's images of themselves as intact as possible, administrators focused attention on the ways women managed to remain feminine despite hardships. The director of War Public Services for the Federal Works Authority—in charge of expanding facilities for the war effort—told an interviewer in 1943 that women war workers deserved special commendation for the attention they paid to grooming. "They bring glamour to the job," she said. The personnel manager of a plant confirmed the importance of grooming: "We like the girls to be neat and trim and well put together. It helps their morale. It helps our prestige too." Women workers sustained and supported this stance. They struggled to be able to wear their own clothing, even where it might be dangerously floppy. One plant posted drawings of scalped women to get them to tuck hair into bonnets or nets. Overt hostility kept women in their places too. Nell Giles, a reporter for the Boston *Herald* who worked in a defense factory for a period of months, described being hooted down for carrying a black tin lunch box. Only men, it seemed, carried lunch boxes. Women used paper bags, even though they couldn't put soup or milk in them. Giles didn't have the courage, she admitted, "to buck that line." Catcalls, whistles, and hisses faced women who walked onto the production floor for the first time. Young girls who became pages on the floor of the New York Stock Exchange met wolfish whistles.

Employers adopted promotion and training policies that played into these role divisions. At the suggestion of the War Department, female training included frequent analogies to household work. Supervisors attempted to convince new recruits that any woman who could use a needle could handle a welding rod, or that cutting out sheet metal resembled cutting a pattern for a dress. Employers' willingness to use women was governed by immediate needs. They refused to integrate women into training programs that might provide access to skills beyond those essential for their initial tasks. For temporary help, management reasoned, that would have been a wasted investment. One group of women complained in late 1944 that "management is engaging in a vicious and deliberate campaign to induce women to quit by transferring them from one department to another, by assigning women the least desirable jobs, and by an unceasing psychological drive to harass women out of the plants."

The struggle for equal pay illustrates another level of ambivalence. For years, trade unions had argued for equal pay for women only when the jobs of unionists were threatened by women's lower wages. Women's quest for equal pay on the grounds of equity had met little response. Now women were literally taking men's jobs, as earlier it had been feared they would do. To pay them at a man's scale undermined the barriers that divided women's work from men's. To pay them below it undermined the value of the job and threatened men's scales when they returned to reclaim their jobs. Manufacturers under contract to the government, and paid on a cost-plus basis, could readily agree to raise wages. Those in the private sector preferred to retain barriers. Trade unions concerned with job protection tended to fight for equal pay (although only the left-wing unions espoused genuinely egalitarian values). Wishing to avoid chaos in the labor market as well as to promote "mobility of the labor force and maximum utilization of women workers," government agencies agreed to support labor and attempted to persuade management to go along with equal pay. A Bureau of Labor statistician acknowledged the realities involved when she wrote in 1947 that there were three reasons for granting equal pay to women: justice, sustaining men's wage rates, and increasing purchasing power. The second, she argued, was by far the most powerful.

Recognizing the pressures to sustain wages in a period when wage rises were strictly limited, the National War Labor Board issued General Order No. 16 in November 1942, permitting employers to "equalize the wage or salary rates paid to females with rates paid to males for comparable quantity of work." But the Congress failed to pass a companion bill that would have prohibited wage differentials based on sex. And only five states with about a quarter of the nation's female wage earners enacted their own laws. Furthermore, since these laws were concerned primarily with the issue of sustaining men's wages, they addressed themselves only to preventing women from wage-cutting that could depress men's earnings, not to the major source of discriminatory wages for women— the historic differentiation of male and female jobs, where jobs defined as female carried a lower wage rate. As a result, the gap between men's and women's wages increased during the war. Women were earning far more in dollar terms than before the war, and more than they would earn thereafter. Still, the average full-time woman worker earned only 55 percent of what her male co-worker earned: a drop from the 1939 figure of about 62 percent.

Women protested the vagueness of federal guidelines and agitated for additional protection. In Dayton, Ohio, angry women told Elizabeth Christman of the Women's Bureau that despite federal guidelines on equal pay embodied in General Order No. 16, the Frigidaire plant in which they worked continued to hire women at lower rates than men would be paid for the same jobs, and to violate their seniority. Book binders in the Government Printing Office complained of getting thirty to fifty-two cents an hour less than men for the same work. Christman reported that hundreds of grievances had been filed by female employees of General Motors in Ohio against rate discrimination. The same women objected to the War labor Board's use of "comparable" to define work that should be paid equally. They wanted to substitute "same pay for same work" in order to avoid misunderstanding and confusion.

Like the struggle for equal pay, the struggle for access to trade unions suffered from the ambiguity of women's presence under sufferance owing to wartime emergency. Unions that had never had women members, like the International Boilermakers, Iron Shipbuilders, Welders and Helpers, continued to deny them membership until it was clear that the war emergency necessitated it. Unionized men complained that women would "spoil the job" or "break the morale of the plant." Women who did not understand informal work rules tended to exhaust themselves in rapid bursts of work and to work without stint. Some unionists struck to prevent women from being hired. Others, like those in steel, auto, rubber, and machine tools, accepted or actively recruited women into their ranks but denied them upgrading and frequently continued discriminatory job classifications. Most trade unions maintained separate seniority lists of men and women and tolerated job classifications and job rates on the basis of sex. They bypassed issues of particular interest to women workers. Women complained that men were not fighting hard enough for such things as equal pay. And they wanted maternity leaves without loss of seniority, good day care centers, and time off to care for sick children.

Yet the women who joined unions benefited nonetheless. In the aftermath of the great organizing drives of the 1930s, unionization had spread over the industrial Northeast. Union shops and maintenance of membership agreements—under which incoming workers automatically joined the collective bargaining unit—provided unions with a steady influx of members as war industry expanded. Recruiting three and a half million women into heavy industry where they had not previously been employed increased fourfold the number of female union members within two years. Economist Gladys Dickason estimated that at the beginning of the war only 800,000 wage-earning women were unionized. They made up 9.4 percent of unionized workers. By 1944 more than three million women constituted 22 percent of trade union membership. . . .

The war turned out to be less a milestone than a natural response to the call for patriotism, to lucrative jobs, to husbands' absences, and to more readily available household and childcare services. The milestone came after. It was marked by the dawning recognition within families that women's functions of cushioning depression and fighting inflation, traditionally performed by economies within the household, might be more effectively handled by wage-earning. A woman's income, still supplementary, and her job, still less than a career, could make the difference between sheer survival and minimal comfort. If the entry of women into war work was a response to opportunity, the continuing rise in their work force participation after demobilization reflects a response to increasing economic demands on the family. Briefly, a reordered set of ideas—what Betty Friedan called the "feminine mystique"—managed in the 1950s to reconcile the competing interests of home and work. Though middle-class and working-class communities responded to postwar ideology differently, the home remained central to the aspirations of most women. It took a new set of pressures on the family and a dramatic shift in the labor market to challenge that ideology.

Reading 17

Loyal and Heroic Service: The Navajos and World War II

Jeré Franco

During World War II a Navajo trudged several miles on foot to his reservation's trading post and gave thirty cents for the war effort. This represented ten cents each for himself, his wife, and his son. Considering that the man had no visible means of support, the money constituted a veritable fortune. Furthermore, his contribution, in comparison to other tribal members, ranked as a commonplace occurrence. Navajos, enduring a century of poverty, illiteracy, and ill-health, overwhelmingly supported their nation's war effort through military enlistment, defense work, and tribal resources. A deep, abiding love for a country which had mistreated them in the past and would discriminate against them in the future prompted this patriotic response.[1]

In 1868 ten thousand Navajos lost their long, hard-fought battle against the United States, signed the Treaty of Bosque Redondo and agreed to live peaceably on a reservation one-fifth the size of their previous country, 3.5 million acres. Trusting the government's treaty promises, they returned to their former lifestyle of grazing sheep, weaving blankets, and planting crops. "The advantages and benefits conferred by this treaty" included annuities, goods, and educational opportunities for every Navajo child.[2]

Less than a century later, the Navajos faced tremendous problems with poverty, illiteracy, and ill-health, all originating in the failure of the federal government to live up to its obligations. Land scarcity and a rising population contributed to the poor conditions. By 1934 a fivefold increase in population resulted in an overcrowded, overgrazed reservation. The government, therefore, ordered the destruction of 400,000 head of livestock, an economic mainstay, with little remuneration for owners. Per capita income placed Indians at the poverty level. Whereas the average American family of five in 1942 earned $900 yearly, at least half of all Indian families made less than $500 per year.

Unable to depend entirely on rural resources, Navajos also failed to compete successfully on the job market. The tribal illiteracy rate stood at eighty percent; fifty-seven percent spoke only their native language. By 1942 U.S. abrogation of treaty promises resulted in such a dearth of educational facilities that 14,000 school-age reservation children had never attended school. Death and disease further handicapped the Navajos. Unsanitary housing, lack of medical facilities with qualified personnel, and food shortages so severe that some people fasted for days resulted in trachoma, tuberculosis, and a high mortality rate. In 1940 the Indian death rate stood at thirteen per thousand, exceeding the white rate of ten per thousand. The infant mortality rate ranked forty percent above the white rate and accounted for twenty-five percent of all Indian deaths.[3]

At the outbreak of World War II, Navajos struggled with problems caused primarily by governmental inefficiency. Given this background, their response to the war should have been apathy. Instead, immediately after the United States declared war on December 8, 1941, American Indians rushed to enlist in the armed forces. On some reservations in other parts of the country, half the male inhabitants volunteered for army duty. Southwestern Indians, however, displayed the most enthusiasm. When on December 9, 1941, Congress passed the Conscription Bill, so many men from New Mexico and Arizona enlisted that the first draft, according to one observer, "was almost a dead letter." Navajos at Fort Defiance, Arizona, stood in the snow for hours to sign their draft cards while others took along their own rifles, prepared for battle, when they joined. With more Indians in uniform than any other part of the country, New Mexico claimed 5.9% Indian volunteers and Arizona counted 7.7% of their total enlistees as Native American. Navajos responded to their nation's call by sending 3,000 people, or six percent of their population, into service. Out of 3,600 Ramah Navajos, 800 men signed up immediately.[4]

Nationwide Indian enlistment jumped from a low of 7,500 in the summer of 1942 to a high of 44,500 at the end of the war. At all times during the war years, Indian enlistees composed a larger proportion of their population than any other segment of the American public. In 1942, according to the Selective Service, at least ninety-nine percent of all eligible Native Americans had registered for the draft. Army officials maintained that if the entire country had enrolled in the same proportion, selective service would have been unnecessary.[5]

Motivations for enlistment ranged from the pragmatic to the patriotic. Many enlistees claimed that they signed up early to avoid the draft. Keats Begay, a veteran of the Bataan Death March, recalled that he learned about conscription while teaching silversmithing at the Albuquerque Indian School. "Some said if we wanted to join the Army, we could, but otherwise, we would be drafted even though we didn't want to join." In March, 1941, Begay and twenty other Navajos joined the army. Shipped to Manila, they fought at the outbreak of the war. Like Begay, Dan Benally decided to enlist early. In 1940 he unsuccessfully tried to enter the navy "because I didn't want them to draft me and place me in a position that I would not like or be satisfied with." Because he lacked college credentials, the navy refused to accept him until the war began. Another prisoner-of-war veteran, Begay served his time in Germany.[6]

Navajo women enlisted to further their education, acquire skills, and aid their fighting men. In 1942 Myrtle Waybenais, who had worked as a cook, an interpreter, and a teacher's aide on the reservation, joined the Women's Army Corps. During her army service, she trained as a nurse and traveled in several countries. Upon completing high school, Peggy Jones also desired more education and a career other than sheepherding, the traditional role for Navajo women. Enlisting the same year as Myrtle, she became an army cook and butcher. Both women expressed loyal support for Indian soldiers. "The soldiers would be on the front lines," explained Peggy, "and we would be in the back of the lines to help."[7]

All practicalities aside, most veterans voiced deep, idealistic motivations for volunteering. These motivations combined American patriotism and Navajo religious beliefs. Cozy Stanley Brown, a former marine code talker, stated, "my main reason for going to war was to protect my land and my people because the elderly people said the Earth was our mother." Brown compared his Navajo sacred beliefs with American patriotism, asserting, "the Anglos say 'Democracy,' which means they have pride in the American flag. We Navajos respect things the same way they do." Raymond Nakai, an ex-navy code talker, concurred with Brown. "Many people ask why we fight the white man's wars. Our answer is that we are proud to be Americans. We're proud to be American Indians."[8]

Rejections by the military for health or illiteracy hurt men with such deeply ingrained emotions. Nationally, military physicians rejected at least thirty-seven and one-half percent of all eligible Indian males as opposed to thirty-two percent of the white population. Doctors disqualified Native Americans primarily for trachoma and tuberculosis, two diseases rampant on large reservations. Trachoma, a highly contagious eye disease usually transmitted from one individual to another through the use of a common wash basin, affected the largest number of Indians. Of those rejected for trachoma, Navajos constituted thirty-seven percent. Navajos accounted for forty-one percent of all Indians turned down because of tuberculosis, which had been virtually eliminated in the United States. Possibly 1,000 tribal members had unacceptable health problems.[9]

Illiteracy and inability to speak English ranked as the most humiliating reasons for rejection by the draft board. Because of the high rate of illiterate and non-English-speaking Navajos, possibly another 1,000 men failed to serve their country. More than any other situation, the lack of Native American education prompted criticism against the government from both Indians and whites. In January, 1942, realizing the enormous task confronting them in aiding the military effort, the Navajo Tribal Council requested that young men be trained and taught English on the reservation utilizing Navajo interpreters. Despite promises from a government representative that a military post would be established on the reservation, none materialized.[10]

One year into the war, stories of discrimination and mistreatment of illiterate Navajos began to surface. The Tribal Council charged that many of their young men spoke English so poorly they could not communicate with their officers. Treated as undesirables and passed around from camp to camp, they often endured hunger, thirst, and other deprivations because of their handicap. Concerned Indian leaders reminded the government that "2,000 Navajo soldiers who can speak the white man's language are making an outstanding record everywhere in loyal and heroic service to their country." They urgently requested that the Selective Service Board allow non-English speakers to work in civil defense industries or agricultural work under the supervision of tribal translators. As an alternative the Council asked that all uneducated recruits be trained together under English-speaking Navajo officers.[11]

Again the government refused to incorporate tribal recommendations. In February, 1943, however, the Army Air Corps inaugurated a program to teach a group of Arizona Navajos the English language. Private Frank Becker, a former schoolteacher, originated a class for illiterate, non-English speakers in Atlantic City, New Jersey. Roger Davis, Tribal Council member and Presbyterian minister, assisted Becker as interpreter during the soldiers' training. After teaching the recruits and becoming knowledgeable about their background, the instructor criticized their treatment by government and military officials. He termed the lack of educational facilities a "terrible indictment" against the government and considered their previous treatment by army officers as "passing the proverbial buck." Later Becker reminisced, "I learned that in spite of everything, my Navajo friends still fought a good war."[12]

The Navajos not only fought a good war; they also exhibited skill and enthusiasm in military training and duty. Army Major Lee Gilstrap fought with Indians in World War I, coached Native Americans in football at the Oklahoma Military Academy, and commanded 2,000 Indians, representing fifty tribes, at an Oklahoma basic-training camp during World War II. After long experience with Native Americans, Gilstrap cited their outstanding abilities in marksmanship, patrol work, bayonet fighting, and leadership. He unhesitatingly stated, "the Indian is the best damn soldier in the army . . . [they] make such fine soldiers that they soon become noncommissioned or regular officers." The major described Indians who easily completed twenty-five-mile hikes, including one man who returned from combat maneuvers with eighty-seven "scalps" or identifying armbands.[13]

Arizona Navajos, who still scouted the uplands and frontier reservations, became particularly adept at physical-endurance tasks and marksmanship. In the summer of 1942 an all-Indian marine platoon, stationed in San Diego, outshot all other platoons. This Navajo group, who enlisted en masse at Fort Defiance, Arizona, included one expert, fourteen sharpshooters, and twelve marksmen. Evidently they had acquired much of their skill at home. Cozy Stanley Brown, one of the group, recalled that in the army "we were trained for only eight weeks because the war was going on and they were lacking soldiers."[14]

Utilizing their talents, Navajos distinguished themselves in battle. When the Japanese imprisoned Keats Begay and twenty other men on Bataan, fellow tribal members from New Mexico and Arizona, known as the Bushmasters, avenged the defeat when they recaptured the island. As part of the 158th Infantry Regiment twenty Indian tribes, including Pimas and Navajos, trained in Panama to become expert jungle fighters. Gifted in the use of rifles and knives, the soldiers conducted assaults upon Japanese-held Pacific islands. In January, 1944, they fought in one of the most successful battles of the war. In a rare instance whereby the Indians rescued the cavalry, Bushmasters reinforced the Texas Cavalry at Arawe, New Britain, drove back the Japanese 1,000 yards, captured field artillery, smashed twenty-eight machine guns, and killed 139 of the enemy.[15]

New Mexico and Arizona Indians also participated in the European theatre. Originally belonging to a National Guard unit, one group joined the Forty-fifth Division, which took as its insignia the Thunderbird, an Indian symbol. At least 1,500 Indians, including Navajos, fought at Salerno, Sicily; in southern France; and at Munich from 1943 to war's end. Officers lauded these Native Americans for their bravery, sacrifice of life, and contribution to the morale of the entire division. On the night before the soldiers sailed to Europe, Native Americans staged a full-dress battle dance around a campfire and prayed for their fellow warriors' success in battle.[16]

Indians in every branch of the service, at every level, won every available medal and honor, including the nation's highest award, the Congressional Medal of Honor. Out of 414 Medals of Honor awarded, Native Americans received two. Neither of these soldiers, however, was a Navajo, and a few veterans felt that the government practiced discrimination in awarding medals. Dan Benally described killing a German who had crawled close to American headquarters and pulled a grenade. Before the soldier could throw the weapon, Benally grabbed him and cut his throat. In the process, he saved his company commander. "If a White soldier had done it," stated Benally, "he would have received the Congressional Medal of Honor right then."[17]

As eagerly as Indians offered their people to fight, they also funded the war program. Native Americans existed well below the average national income level but they bought more war bonds and stamps, pro ratio, than any other racial group. By 1944 national war bond sales to Indians, both privately and tribally, amounted to fifty million dollars. The Navajos included bond sales in their comprehensive war relief program. Salaried Indians, government employees, and wealthy sheepmen and cattlemen allotted twenty percent of their monthly pay for war bonds. Poorer Navajos also contributed, often in ingenious ways. In 1942, after Canoncito Indians gathered tons of scrap iron, they discovered that they were unable to sell it because the tribe had no scales with which to weigh the metal. They solved the problem by calling upon a woman who knew her body weight, seating her on one end of a teeter-totter, and placing hunks of metal on the other end. In this manner they weighed and sold five tons, using the seventy-five dollar proceeds for war bonds.

Navajos pledged a Red Cross quota of 3,000 dollars, 1,000 dollars above the request, and even the poorest contributed. One man gave his entire fortune of seven cents. Indians who had no money volunteered goods. "We have no record of all the contributions the Indians have made to war relief societies," said Commissioner of Indian Affairs John Collier, "but such reports as we do get indicate that the Indians are giving all they can." In lieu of cash, many Pueblos and Navajos gave mutton, silver jewelry, rugs, and corn (their staff of life) to the Red Cross. With this spirit the Navajos dedicated their entire reservation resources to the war effort. These included the use of their sawmill, converted for war-preparation projects, a packing plant, a flour mill, victory gardens, and an increase in the wool clip. Urged on by the Tribal Council, Navajos cut down on social gatherings to preserve food, gasoline, and tires.[18]

Many tribal members, anxious enough to aid the war effort, felt that past injustices rendered full assistance difficult and asked for a change in policy. Small, as well as large, livestock owners contributed meat to the armed forces, often at a sacrifice to themselves. In 1942 the Tribal Council requested that livestock reduction be slowed down in order to aid both the small owner and the war effort. "We hear from out East a cry from our government to use that extra penny or nickel or quarter in buying war savings stamps," urged council member Yellowman, "and how can we help our government if we have to dispose of our stock?"[19]

Stock reduction, nevertheless, continued and so did Navajo contributions. The most significant utilization of Arizona Indian resources concerned the removal of thousands of Japanese evacuees onto three reservations in southwestern Arizona. In April, 1942, 20,000 Japanese were relocated to the Colorado River Indian Reservation which held the Mojave, Chemehuevi, Hopi, and Navajo tribes. Four months later another 15,000 Japanese traveled to the Gila River Reservation, belonging to the Pima-Maricopa tribes, for the remainder of the war. On June 24, 1942, the Navajo Tribal Council granted permission to the director of the War Relocation Authority to use the Leupp Indian School and Hospital, located near Winslow, Arizona, on the condition that all improvements left by the wartime inmates accrue to the benefit of the tribe. The following August the government placed 1,500 Japanese in these facilities. Strangely enough John Collier, who had denounced the Germans for their racial attitudes and had warned Indians of possible slavery under a Nazi regime, saw nothing contradictory in cooperating with the War Relocation Authority to imprison thousands of Japanese.[20]

As the Japanese moved onto Navajo reservations, the Indians moved out to work in the nation's defense plants, making a successful, if often temporary, adjustment to mainstream society. Because of the national manpower shortage, employers turned to Indian reservation superintendents, requesting any available labor. Native Americans, who had previously lacked employment opportunities, left their homes in unprecedented numbers. From 1942 to 1945, 40,000 Indians, ten percent of the national population, entered defense work. Navajos contributed the greatest number as a total of twenty percent entered industrial occupations.[21]

In 1942 Sam Akheah, vice-chairman of the Navajo Tribal Council, encouraged young people to undertake industrial training. He related that Colonel Smith, Navajo Ordnance Depot officer, expressed a willingness to aid people to learn any trade. Enthused by the promises, 2,500 Navajos worked on the construction of a large ordnance depot at Fort Wingate, New Mexico, and another 500 gained employment at the Navajo Ordnance Depot near Flagstaff, Arizona. Others traveled to Clearfield, Utah, to work at the Naval Supply Depot, while many labored on railroad construction in Gallup, New Mexico. Employers praised tribal members for their industry, intelligence, hardiness, and constancy. But those same employers continued to discriminate. Although many Navajos qualified as skilled technicians, a result of Indian Service training, managers hired them as common laborers. Paid less and dismissed first, Navajos operated bulldozers, loaded ships, or handled construction machinery. And as the war ended, so did most of the jobs, often abruptly. At Bellemont Corporation, part of the Navajo Ordnance Depot, Agnes Begay reported that Colonel Huling thanked the workers on the final day of the war. "We were the ones who helped win the war," she recalled him saying. "He said we could all pack and go home to the Reservation."[22]

Because of the labor shortage, Navajo women contributed their own skills both on and off the reservation. At home they worked as chemists and truck drivers, and learned the traditionally male-dominated art of silversmithing. Some reservation women joined the American Women's Voluntary Service, took American Red Cross courses and sewed armed forces insignia, while almost everyone planted victory gardens. Others left the reservation to serve as nurses and cooks in the Women's Army Corps, to work in industrial plants, and to labor on farms. Large produce farmers praised Navajo women, comprising half of all Navajo off-reservation agricultural laborers, as good workers. These employers, however, lamented their inability to entice more women away from their "hogans, sheep, and children" to more distant points.

Women did not enjoy every aspect of their new roles. At Bellemont, Agnes Begay remained with her family while enjoying two-bedroom housing and child care. In her non-traditional role of guard, however, she carried a pistol and searched incoming people on buses. Although she admitted she hated the job, Agnes added that she never had trouble because people "were good and cooperative."[23]

Navajos fought the war as bravely on the homefront as they did in the armed forces. Unfortunately the American victory, which brought lasting economic and social success for many Indians, both on and off reservations, brought disillusionment and frustration to the Navajos. Their wartime optimism turned to anger as a postwar generation clamored for their rights. Indian veterans returned to reservations, their self-esteem buoyed by skills newly acquired from the armed forces. To take full advantage of their opportunities, most Indians planned to use the 1944 G.I. Bill of Rights. Under this act, the government paid a fifty-dollar monthly stipend, an additional twenty-five dollars for spouses, and 500 dollars yearly for tuition and fees to state-approved institutions, including many authorized Indian schools. Closest to the Navajos was the Indian school at Wingate, New Mexico, which offered vocational courses. In addition to educational opportunities, the G.I. Bill guaranteed half of a loan up to 2,000 dollars to build a home, purchase a farm, or acquire business property.[24]

Many returning Navajos could neither take advantage of the educational opportunities offered by the G.I. Bill nor the bank benefits guaranteed by the Veterans Administration. Because of their inadequate education, they found themselves as handicapped after the war as they had been during the conflict. Many veterans, with only a few years of elementary instruction, desired to further their education, but overcrowded reservation schools had room only for children. An unwillingness to leave their reservations and families, coupled with the inability to function adequately in a non-reservation society, kept many former soldiers from attending any school.[25]

Although the G.I. Bill also provided for on-the-job training in some areas, none of these programs originated in the Southwest. Therefore, Navajo veterans could either return to their old jobs or be employed in another job of equal pay and status. Since most Navajos held no jobs prior to the war, they instead turned to the readjustment allowance, which paid twenty dollars weekly for fifty-two weeks. Their quest for employment became complicated as the defense industries laid off thousands of workers in the reconversion to a civilian economy. Hundreds of Navajos, ex-servicemen and ex-defense workers alike, applied for every available job.[26]

In addition to educational and employment problems, Navajos felt cheated by the loan provisions of the G.I. Bill. Lending agencies refused credit to the majority of Indians who owned restricted land. Bankers believed that the reservation agencies, which had severely limited funds, should handle all Indian loans. On December 19, 1945, tribal leaders recommended that credit be extended to Navajos, with preference to veterans, by direct government loans. Instead the Indian Bureau, in a reversal of policy, allowed superintendents to use land income and livestock as collateral against a local bank loan. Despite this adjustment, which aided some Native Americans, many Navajos simply became frustrated at the unintelligible red tape and ceased their loan requests.[27]

Civil rights concerned Native Americans to the same extent as economic problems. Indians who had tasted freedom in World War II demanded the same freedom in their postwar lives. Veterans, impressed that they had purchased liquor without difficulty while in the service, returned home to face restrictions or even prohibitions on buying alcoholic beverages. Understandably resentful that local bars refused to sell to them, Navajos often bought bootleg liquor. Overwhelmed by poor finances and lack of opportunities, many veterans went on binges and, while inebriated, faced discrimination. One Navajo bitterly recalled being incarcerated for public drunkenness, along with another Navajo veteran, two Anglos, and several Spanish Americans. Although authorities released the others immediately, they kept the Indians for ten days.[28]

Many congressmen and the American legion voiced disapproval of the liquor laws and called for an end to the ban. Various tribes joined the campaign by passing resolutions urging the sale of alcoholic beverages to off-reservation Indians. In 1946 the Office of Indian affairs, cooperating with the Secretary of the Interior, introduced a bill in Congress which would have permitted such sales.

Lawmakers refused to repeal the Liquor Law, however, until 1953; and even then the law remained in force on reservations. New Mexico and Arizona continued the ban on off-reservation sales of liquor to Indians.[29]

Voting ranked as a higher priority with most Indian groups. Democratic voting procedures had always constituted an integral part of tribal life and, as American citizens, Indians resented the injustice of disfranchisement. The Snyder Act of 1924 granted full citizenship to all American Indians. Congress reiterated the bequest in the Nationalities Act of 1940, which specifically named Indians as citizens. Although most states granted Native Americans the franchise, New Mexico and Washington disqualified them from voting because of their tax-exempt status. Arizona and Idaho barred Indians because the federal government exercised guardianship and controlled their lands held in trust. Because Arizona and New Mexico had the largest Indian tribes, these regulations disfranchised a considerable portion of the Indian population. "These states should do the American thing and grant the Indians the franchise," criticized John Collier, irate at America's ungratefulness for the Indian war effort. "All over the world we are preaching democracy and should grant a little more of it at home."[30]

In 1946 a Navajo delegation traveled to Washington to protest the legal ban against Indian suffrage in New Mexico and Arizona. Backed up by tribal veterans and the Indian Bureau, they cited their wartime achievements and contributions. Asking for congressional support, they won half the battle almost immediately. Two years later, in response to federal requests, the Arizona Supreme Court declared Indian disfranchisement unconstitutional. In 1962 New Mexico finally allowed Native Americans to vote in state elections. The Literacy in English Act of 1970, allowing non-English speakers to vote, reinforced these state decisions.[31]

The Navajos accomplished much more than earning the right to buy liquor and vote. They had proved their patriotism and loyalty to America, demonstrated an ability to function in off reservation environments, and earned national respect and recognition for their contributions. Native Americans also learned a valuable lesson as they saw postwar America overlook their loyalty, patriotism, and sacrifices. Wartime veterans, soldiers and civilians alike, began to protest their third-class status and demanded first-class honors. This protest would grow in later decades and be intensified by Native American involvement in two more wars. Finally culminating in the radicalism of the sixties and seventies, the American Indian Movement would contain elements of unresolved expectations by the Navajo Nation which stemmed from World War II.

The author is a graduate student in the History Department at the University of Arizona.

Notes

1. Commissioner of Indian Affairs, *Annual Report*, 1942 (Washington, D.C: Government Printing Office, 1942), p. 239.

2. "1868 Treaty with the Navajo," in Charles J. Kappler, ed, *Indian Affairs, Laws and Treaties*, 5 vols, (Reprint, Washington, D.C.: Government Printing Office, 1971), vol. 2, pp. 1015–1019. Two comprehensive studies of Navajo social, economic, and political history are John Upton Terrell, *The Navajos: The Past and Present of a Great People* (New York: Weybright and Talley, 1970), and Peter Iverson, *The Navajo Nation* (Westport, Connecticut: Greenwood Press, 1981).

3. "Establishment of Joint Committee to Investigate Claims Against the United States," Senate Joint Resolution 79, *Congressional Committee Hearings*, 79 Congress, 2 Session, pp. 2–4. *Time*, August 12. 1946, p. 42. Iverson, *Navajo Nation*, pp. 42–45.

4. Stanley Vestal, "Plains Indians and the War," *Saturday Review of Literature*, May 16, 1942, p. 10; John Adair and Evon Vogt, "Navajo and Zuni Veterans: A Study of Contrasting Modes of Cultural Change," *American Anthropologist*, vol. 51 (October–December, 1949), p. 551; *Second Report of the Director of Selective Service, 1941–1942* (Washington, D. C.: Government Printing Office, 1942), p. 617. "Establishment of Joint Committee to Investigate Claims," Senate Joint Resolution 79, p. 15.

5. New York *Times*, January 23, 1945; Richard Neuberger, "The American Indian Enlists," *Asia and the Americas*, vol. 42 (November, 1942), p. 628; J. R. McGibony, "Indians and Selective Service," *Public Health Reports No. 1*, January 2, 1942, p. 57. McGibony claims that 100% of eligible Indians had registered. By the end of the war, according to the Assistant Secretary of Defense in 1982, 27,221 American Indians had served. However, in the 1980 census, 44,500 Native Americans listed themselves as veterans of World War II. From "Veterans Administration Statistical Brief on Native American Veterans" (1986), author's files.

6. "Interview with Keats Begay," in *Navajos and World War II* (Chinle, Arizona: Navajo Community College Press, 1977), p. 13; and "Interview with Dan Benally," *ibid.*, p. 66.

7. "Interview with Myrtle Waybenais," and "Interview with Peggy Jones," both in *ibid.*, pp. 32 and 120, respectively.

8. "Interview with Cozy Stanley Brown," *ibid.*, p. 61; Dan B. McCarthy, "Samuel Smith and Son Michale . . . Plus 32 Other Navajo U.S. Marines," *VFW Magazine* (January, 1982), p. 26.

9. McGibony, "Indians and Selective Service," pp. 3–4; *Time*, August 12, 1946, p. 42; S. R. Winters, "Health for the Indians," *Hygeia*, vol. 22 (September, 1944), pp. 680–83.

10. Frank E. Becker, *Navajo Way* (New York: The Indian Association of America, Inc., 1956), p. 22; Estelle Webb Thomas, "America's First Families on the Warpath," *Common Ground*, vol. 2 (Summer, 1942), p. 99. Photographs of Navajo code talkers are in the Still Picture Branch, National Archives (NA).

11. Becker, *Navajo Way*, p. 22; *Navajo Tribal Council Resolutions, 1922–1951* (Washington, D.C.: Government Printing Office, 1952), pp. 7–8.

12. Becker, *Navajo Way*, pp. 25, 53.

13. Elmer Thomas, "Indians as Soldiers," *Congressional Record*. 77 Cong., 2 Sess., p. A4125.

14. Thomas, "America's First Families on the Warpath," p. 97; New York *Times*, July 5, 1942; "Interview with Cozy Stanley Brown," *Navajos and World War II*, p. 54.

15. New York *Times*, January 19, 1944.

16. *Ibid.*, August 4, 1945.

17. "Interview with Dan Benally," *Navajos and World War II*, p. 82; Claiborne D. Haughton, Jr., Director of Equal Opportunity Programs, "Memorandum from the Office of the Assistant Secretary of Defense," copy in author's files.

18. New York *Times*, May 10, May 20, 1942, and January 23, 1945; Commissioner of Indian Affairs, *Annual Report, 1944*, pp. 238–39; "Proceedings of the Meetings of the Navajo Tribal Council, Window Rock, Arizona, June 25, 1942." p. 126, Special Collections, University of Arizona Library, Tucson.

19. "Proceedings of the Meetings of the Navajo Tribal Council, June 25, 1942," pp. 39–40.

20. "Memoranda of April 15, 1942, August 31, 1942, and June 15, 1943, Concerning Executive Order 9102." Record Group 78, NA. Secretary of War, *Final Report of the Japanese Evacuation from the West Coast* (Washington, D.C.: Government Printing Office, 1942), p. 250; "Proposed Revision to Transfer Surplus Property from War Relocation Authority to Indian Affairs Office," *House Document 487*, 79 Cong., 2 Sess. (Serial 11055), p. 1.

21. "Establishment of Joint Committee to Investigate Claims," Senate Joint Resolution 79, p. 15.

22. "Proceedings of the Meetings of the Navajo Tribal Council, June 25, 1942," p, 42; J. A. Tadlock, "Navajos Respond to Nation's Need," *Manpower Report* (April, 1938), p. 8; Bureau of Indian Affairs, *Indians in the War* (Washington, D.C; Government Printing Office, 1945), p. 42; John Collier, "The Indian in a Wartime Nation," *Annals of the American Academy of Political and Social Science*, vol. 223 (September, 1942), p. 31; "Interview with Agnes Begay," *Navajos and World War II*, p. 49.

23. New York *Times*, February 6, 1943. Commissioner of Indian Affairs, *Annual Report, 1944*, pp. 237; Bureau of Indian Affairs, *Indians in the War*, p. 49; *Indians at Work*, March 25, 1943, p. 26; Tadlock, "Navajos Respond to Nation's Need," p.8; "Interview with Agnes Begay," *Navajos and World War II*, pp. 48–49.

24. "Servicemen's Readjustment Act of 1944," *U.S. Statutes at Large*, vol, 58, pt. 1, pp. 287–89; Walter Crosby Eels, "Educational Opportunities for the Indian Veteran," *The American Indian*, vol. 2 (Fall, 1945), pp. 19–20; Bureau of Indian Affairs, *Indians in the War*, p. 44; Commissioner of Indian Affairs, *Annual Report, 1946* (Washington D.C.: Government Printing Office, 1946), pp. 356–57.

25. Evon Z. Vogt, "Between Two Worlds: Case Study of a Navajo Veteran," *Indian Affairs*, vol, 5 (May, 1949), pp. 19–20; Oliver LaFarge, "They Were Good Enough for the Army," *Harper's Magazine*, vol. 195 (November, 1947), p. 444; Commissioner of Indian Affairs, *Annual Report, 1945* (Washington D.C.: Government Printing Office, 1945), pp. 233, 246.

26. LaFarge, "They Were Good Enough for the Army," p. 444; "Servicemen's Readjustment Act of 1944," pp. 287–89.

27. "Loans to Indian Veterans Under Servicemen's Readjustment Act of 1944," *Congressional Record*, 79 Cong., 1 Sess., p. A3342; "Emancipation," House Report 3681, *Congressional Committee Hearings*, 79 Cong., 2 Sess., p. 9; "Investigation to Determine if Revision of Laws Regarding Indians is Required," *House Report 2091*, 78 Cong., 2 Sess., (Serial 10848), p. 14; *Navajo Tribal Council Resolutions*, p. 375.

28. Vogt, "Between Two Worlds," p. 16; "To Permit Sale of Liquor to Indians," *Congressional Record*, 79 Cong., 2 Sess., p. 4534; Burt W. Aginsky, "The Interaction of Ethnic Groups: A Case Study of Indians and Whites," *American Sociological Review*, vol. 14 (April, 1949), p. 290; LaFarge, "They Were Good Enough for the Army," p. 444.

29. "An Act Making Appropriations for the Department of the Interior for the Fiscal Year ending June 30, 1946 . . . ," *U.S. Statutes at Large*, vol. 69, pt. 1, pp. 324–38; "An Act to Eliminate Certain Discriminatory Legislation Against Indians in the United States," and "An Act to Terminate Certain Federal Restrictions Upon Indians," *ibid.*, vol. 67, pp. pp. 586–87 and 590, respectively; Theodore W. Taylor, *The States and Their Indian Citizens* (Washington, D.C.: Government Printing Office, 1972), p. 62; "Revision of Laws and Legal Status," House Resolution 166, *Congressional Committee Hearings*, 78 Cong., 2 Sess., p. 69; "Investigation to Determine if Revision of Laws Regarding Indians is Required," *House Report 2091*, p. 11.

30. "Nationality Act," *U.S. Statutes at Large*, vol. 54, pt. 1, p. 1138. *Constitutions of the United States: National and State*, vol. 2, p. 25; vol. 3, pp. 23–24; vol. 4, p. 26, January 1, 1961 to December 31, 1962. Theodore W. Taylor, *The States and Their Indian Citizens* (Washington, D.C.: Bureau of Indian Affairs, 1972), p. 90; New York *Times*, September 21, 1943; "Revision of Laws and Legal Status," *House Resolution 166*, p. 50.

31. Taylor, *The States and Their Indian Citizens*, p. 91; Commissioner of Indian Affairs, *Annual Report, 1946*, p. 381; Collier, "The Indian in a Wartime Nation," p. 30.

Reading 18

Spanish-Speaking Americans in Wartime

Gerald D. Nash

World War II had a significant effect on the Spanish-speaking people of the United States. Few other events in the twentieth century did so much to sharpen their ethnic consciousness and to focus the attention of the federal government on their particular problems. These included economic deprivation and poverty, since the annual income of Hispanics fell below the general average for Americans. Most Spanish-speaking Americans were rural or had recently emerged from rural backgrounds and lacked requisite educational training or skills to compete effectively in an industrialized society. Moreover, in many parts of the West, members of this minority faced economic and social discrimination which further impeded their mobility in American society. These conditions were not new; they had characterized their lives for generations. But World War II dramatized the plight of groups such as Hispanics and opened up new opportunities. As Americans fought for democracy throughout the world they became more conscious of the inequalities within their own borders. And the massive war effort created hitherto undreamed of possibilities for jobs, education, and training. Invariably, these drew Spanish-speaking Americans to towns and cities, thus accelerating their urbanization. As it did for other minorities, World War II had a liberating effect on Spanish-speaking Americans, and resulted in the development of federal programs to improve their welfare.

At the outbreak of World War II, Spanish-speaking Americans constituted the largest minority in the West. In the area west of the Mississippi River (excluding Texas) lived about 1.5 million Spanish-speaking Americans who were concentrated in the Southwest, in the Rocky Mountain area, and along the Pacific Coast. Of the 354,432 Mexican-Americans in California in 1940, 219,000 lived in Los Angeles. That city's barrio was the largest concentration of Mexican-Americans outside of Mexico City. During the War the numbers increased significantly, although precise figures are not available due to problems with census enumeration and the flow of illegal aliens. Until 1941 the great majority were unskilled workers, excluded by labor unions and largely outside the mainstream of American life.

The precise number of these people was in dispute. It was believed by the Coordinator of Inter-American Affairs (CIAA) that the U.S. Census had undercounted Spanish-speaking Americans in the Southwest. Some, because of their illegal status in the United States, had avoided census takers, while others had language problems or shrank from all government officials. Moreover, the census takers did not distinguish between rural and urban Spanish-speaking individuals, and missed some in outlying areas. Therefore, Dora Hettower of the CIAA staff in 1943 made independent estimates that were considered to be a closer approximation, which the agency used to develop its programs. Hettower noted:

The following breakdown of the Spanish-speaking population in the Southwest into urban and rural dwellers is an estimate based on our knowledge of the social and economic situations in the Southwest. Census figures give a rural-urban breakdown only for the entire population; there are no such figures for the Spanish-speaking people. Our estimates consider the distribution of the total population and also the general social and economic conditions of the Spanish-speaking people and its special effect on their distribution.

	Urban	Rural
Texas	300,000	700,000
Colorado	30,000	120,000
New Mexico	75,000	225,000
Arizona	25,000	175,000
California	300,000	20,000

All authorities agree that the census figures on the Spanish speaking are too low.

The problems of Hispanics were eminently visible on the Pacific Coast. Many of those in the barrio of East Los Angeles existed on a poverty level. The median income of a Mexican-American family in 1940 was $790 a year—compared to the federal minimum standard of $1,310 for a family of five. And in the barrio Mexican-Americans lived in a world apart: with their own values and institutions. To escape from this enclave was difficult. Financial stringencies alone were a major impediment. In addition, restrictive real estate covenants prevailed throughout Los Angeles. Thus, when Alex Bernal, a California-born Mexican-American, moved into a "restricted" part of Fullerton in March of 1943, three of his neighbors objected, claiming that Mexicans were dirty, noisy, and lawless, and went to court to enforce a 1923 deed restriction. Although the Superior Court declared such deed restrictions to be unconstitutional, the case demonstrated one common American image of Mexicans as lazy, dirty peons.

In Southern California, job discrimination was not uncommon in the early stages of the war. "Any United States Employment Service office in California could testify that the placement of even well qualified Mexican youths necessitated a struggle with prejudiced employers," reported a contemporary observer. Most defense plants and citrus packing operations refused to hire Mexican-Americans, claiming that whites would not work beside them. A survey of the Los Angeles City and County Civil Service Commission in 1944 revealed that although Mexican-Americans constituted 10 percent of the population, they held only 2.5 percent of the jobs in local government.

If discrimination against Spanish-speaking Americans was not as vehement as against blacks in the West, nevertheless enough injustices occurred to arouse concern. The Rocky Mountain minority representative of the War Manpower Commission reported in 1944 about Denver employers who refused to hire "Mexicans" (in the particular case the young man was descended from an old New Mexico family), of the segregation of Spanish-speaking laborers in a Colorado war construction project, of differential wage scales. But the extraordinary shortage of labor during the war and the concerted efforts of the Fair Employment Practices Committee and the War Manpower Commission to break down discriminatory practices were yielding more results, he believed, than individual efforts of the previous eighty years.

The problems of Spanish-speaking Americans in Denver were not unique. By 1945 at least 30,000 resided there, most of them unskilled workers. Some were migratory Mexican field workers who had come to labor in sugar beet and vegetable fields of the Rocky Mountain area and who sensed greater opportunities in an urban environment. As the newest large minority in Denver they lived under undesirable conditions. A contemporary estimated that 88 percent lived in substandard housing. Their infant mortality rate was twice the city's average. Employment opportunities were limited. In a sample survey of employment opportunities in Denver, of 189 business establishments Charles Graham and Robert Perkin reported that 107 employed no blacks and 80 no Hispanics. Clearly, employment opportunities for minorities were restricted, but World War II began to open up new fields that drew increasing numbers of Spanish-speaking Americans to Denver in succeeding years.

In the more urban areas of the Southwest such as Tucson, conditions for Spanish-speaking Americans approximated those in Los Angeles. In 1940 the U.S. census had recorded 34,000 Anglos, 12,000 Mexicans and Mexican-Americans, 1,678 blacks, and 417 Indians in Tucson. By 1946 the tallies showed 69,000 Anglos, 18,000 Mexicans and Mexican-Americans, 3,000 blacks, 1,500 Indians, and 500 Chinese. Minorities in Tucson were usually subject to various forms of discrimination. Most Americans in the area did not consider them as "white" and until 1941 excluded them from white collar occupations. A few business establishments were owned by Mexican-Americans, but the majority were unskilled workers. Most Spanish-speaking residents lived in dilapidated adobe apartments in the downtown neighborhoods, and knew they were not welcome in the city's better restaurants or hotels. Local business schools reported problems in placing Mexican-Americans in white collar or secretarial jobs. And the Southern Pacific Railroad, a major employer in the city, refused to hire Spanish-speaking individuals or Indians as firemen or brakemen.

The responses of the Spanish-speaking communities to such problems varied. A majority, especially the older generation, endured their lot in silence. They had been culturally attuned to deprivation in and outside the United States for centuries, had limited aspirations, and reflected a conservatism often associated with people from peasant backgrounds. Many were strongly patriotic. The enlistment rate of Hispanics in the armed forces was well above the average for Americans. Their ethnic pride was strengthened during the war by the distinguished military records of Spanish-speaking Americans, seventeen of whom earned the Congressional Medal of Honor. In fact, the first draftee to win this distinction was José Martinez from Colorado. Others won a wide range of decorations for meritorious service and bravery under fire. But not all Spanish-speaking Americans shared the same values, as is the case in any ethnic group. Some of those in their teens and twenties reacted against the conservative values of their parents. They seemed suspended between two worlds, half Mexican or Hispanic, and half American. On the one hand, they rejected the Mexican peasant culture of their parents, with its clear sense of rural values derived from a rural Mexican environment. On the other hand, they were aware that they were not fully accepted in the mainstream of American society. Half Mexican and half American, the young generation growing up in World War II sought its own identity.

Some of them found it by joining special gangs. These were not unique to Mexican-American youths, of course, but they were especially drawn into this type of social organization because of their particular cultural background. Gangs that had a purely social function became known as *palomillas*, while those who displayed some antisocial tendencies became known as *pachucos*. The latter developed their own language (patois), standards of behavior, and modes of dress. For some youths the gangs provided a sense of status. Also, as one observer remarked, they relieved boredom with "smut sessions, dancing, gambling, and narcotic drug parties; gang fighting, raiding, robbing, and committing acts of vandalism." Octavio Paz, a noted Mexican writer and social critic, aptly noted about the *pachuco*: "Their attitude reveals an obstinate, almost fanatical will-to-be, but this will affirms nothing specific except their determination . . . not to be like those around [them]. . . . [Their] whole being is sheer negative impulse, a tangle of contradictions." Often, the result was to engage in exaggerated forms of behavior, whether in dress, language, or personal interaction. Those *pachucos* who rejected their parents, a contemporary sociologist observed, and aspired to become full-fledged Americans frequently exaggerated what they considered to be "American" characteristics. They rebelled against their fathers and their families and often drifted into juvenile delinquency. Although wartime jobs boosted family income, they loosened ties in the traditionally close-knit Mexican-American family.

The origins of the *pachuco* movement are unclear. According to one account, it began in El Paso, Texas, during the 1930s (*Pachuco* is a slang name for El Paso). There a group of members of the 7X gang congregated in the area of Florence and 8th Streets in that city's barrio. Involved in the local drug culture, they popularized a distinctive style of speech adapted from the Calo of the Mexican underworld. It remained a local El Paso dialect until 1942 when a large group of El Paso youths of Mexican-American descent migrated to Los Angeles. Most of them hopped Southern Pacific freight trains on this migration, and numbers of them scattered in towns along the way, such as Tucson. This wholesale migration of 1942 was prompted by the police chief of El Paso who threatened to arrest the youths on various charges unless they left the city. Once in Los Angeles the *pachucos* adopted the zoot suit as a distinctive style of dress. This was marked by a long coat, pancake hat, pants with narrow cuffs, and thick soled shoes. Heavy gold chains adorned the suits. *Pachuco* men wore their hair long, slicked to a ducktail effect in the back of the head. By late 1942 these self-styled *pachucos* had formed distinctive gangs in Los Angeles and other Southwestern cities like Tucson and became an increasing problem for law enforcement authorities in the region.

Most Mexican-American youths were law abiding. As Karl Holton of the Los Angeles County Probation Department said in wartime: "The great majority of Mexican children are not involved in these delinquent activities . . . [but] there is a specific problem of gang violence that must be, and is being dealt with." But the minority who were in *pachuco* gangs increasingly attracted attention in the newspapers since they contributed to increasing crime in the Los Angeles area during 1942 and 1943. Arrests for juvenile delinquency, burglary, and theft rose significantly during these years.

Throughout 1942 ethnic tensions mounted in the Los Angeles area. The Hearst newspapers in particular sensationalized what their editors perceived as a Mexican crime wave. The Chandler-owned *Los Angeles Times* was equally strident, as indicated by the tone of the following account on August 10, 1942:

City and County authorities last night continued their relentless drive against youthful "pachuco" gangs, arresting 30 additional suspects to boost the two-day total of arrests to more than 300 in what was termed the biggest roundup since prohibition days. . . . Captain Joe Reed . . . who directed the roundup of the youthful terrorists, announced the following "breakdown" of charges against the suspects: suspicion of robbery, 48, suspicion of assault with deadly weapon, 39, violation of selective service registration, 20. . . . The law enforcement officials stationed themselves at scores of intersections throughout the eastern edge of the city and nearby points in the county, checking all automobiles that passed and arresting suspicious youths. Police seized more than 100 knives with blades ranging from 3 to 6 inches in length, half a dozen butcher knives, three revolvers, several daggers and stilettos, several lengths of steel chain, which the police said the youths wrap around their hands to slug opponents in their gang fights.

During the first half of 1942 the Los Angeles Police Department became more nervous about the *pachucos* and tended to view perfectly innocent Mexican-Americans on the streets as potential criminals. That was reflected in their arrests of groups of Mexican-American youths for alleged crimes, for loitering, gambling, or merely on suspicion of possible illegal activities. Increasing tensions, exacerbated by the hectic wartime pace, created conditions for overt violence.

The violence came in August 1942 in the well known case of the Sleepy Lagoon. On Saturday evening, August 1, 1942, a brawl took place between two rival Mexican-American gangs near an East Los Angeles watering hole known as the Sleepy Lagoon, in the vicinity of Slauson and Atlantic Boulevards. A member of the 38th Street gang, Henry Leyvas, had taken his girl friend to the Lagoon, where he was set upon by a rival gang, the Downey Boys. Intent on revenge, Leyvas returned a few hours later with his buddies. Eventually they found their rivals, and a free-for-all ensued. No one could testify just what precisely happened on that night. But on the next morning the

Los Angeles police found the unconscious body of José Diaz, a Downey Boy. He appeared to have been drinking and had repeatedly fallen. Although rushed to a hospital, he died a few hours after he had been discovered. Despite the fact that the police could find no murder weapon they speedily rounded up 22 gang members. Soon thereafter the youths were charged with the murder of Diaz. At the same time the police arrested 300 other Mexican-Americans on a variety of lesser charges.

During the fall of 1942 the much publicized trial of the accused took place. One of the defendants' lawyers, Anne Zacsek, charged that the police beat one of her clients, and that deputy district attorney Shoemaker denied them a change of clothes and a haircut before their appearance in front of a jury. Moreover, the California Appellate Court later found that the trial judge, C. W. Frick of the Los Angeles Superior Court had conducted the proceedings in a prejudicial manner. On January 12, 1943, the jury in the Superior Court rendered its verdict. It convicted three of the defendants of first degree murder, nine of second-degree murder and assault, held five guilty on lesser charges, and acquitted the five remaining gang members. Judge Frick sentenced the three accused of first-degree murder to San Quentin Prison while the others were remanded to the Los Angeles County Jail.

The conviction of the Sleepy Lagoon defendants aroused high emotions in the Mexican-American community. While the initial verdict was on appeal a group of interested citizens formed a Sleepy Lagoon Defense Committee. Its organizer was La Rue McCormick, accused at the time by the California Legislature's Un-American Activities Committee (headed by Jack Tenney) of being a member of the Communist Party. Its indefatigable executive secretary was Alice Greenfield, a young activist reformer. Its chairman was Carey McWilliams, a socialist who was a well-known writer on California, a strong advocate of civil rights, and chief of the Division of Immigration and Housing of the California Department of Industrial Relations in Governor Culbert Olson's administration. Los Angeles Police Chief C. B. Horrall accused the group of being a Communist Front although its members were of various political persuasions.

Some members of the movie colony and Hollywood celebrities rallied to the cause of the defendants and raised money to help pay legal costs for an appeal. A prime source of income was a pamphlet by a noted screen writer, Guy Endore, *The Sleepy Lagoon Mystery* (Los Angeles, 1944), which did much also to publicize the case. Benefit dinners and concerts headlined by such stars as Henry Fonda and Anthony Quinn brought in additional funds. Orson Welles succinctly summarized their prevailing mood when he told the Parole Board at San Quentin Prison that "After a very careful examination of the records and facts of the trial, I am convinced that the boys in the Sleepy Lagoon case were not given a fair trial, and that their conviction could only have been influenced by anti-Mexican prejudice. I am convinced, also, that the causes leading up to this case, as well as its outcome, are of great import to the Mexican minority in this community." The committee collected about $100,000, enough to hire lawyers who filed the case with the District Court of Appeals. In October 1944 that tribunal reversed the guilty verdict and ordered all the accused freed. The court cited a lack of evidence and condemned the prejudicial conduct of Judge Frick in rendering the decision.

In 1964, Guy Endore, who during the McCarthy era had been blacklisted by Hollywood studios because of his alleged Communist affiliations, reflected on the case. Endore thought that Judge Frick had been particularly hard on the Sleepy Lagoon Boys because he was known to be harsh with first offenders, and hoped to dissuade them from a life of crime. As he reminisced, Endore said that he did not think the Sleepy Lagoon Boys were "nice," although he did not condone the rather strident anti-Mexican prejudice fomented by the Los Angeles newspapers in 1942 and 1943. Perhaps Carey McWilliams, one of the most ardent champions of the Sleepy Lagoon Boys and of zoot suiters in World War II, summarized the situation most aptly when he said in 1978 that "I wouldn't say the zoot suiters were mother's angels but they weren't devils, either. The papers were dreadful. The officials were no better."

The significance of the Sleepy Lagoon case was to heighten tensions between the Mexican-American community and others whom they regarded as Anglos. In a sincere effort to improve intergroup relations the Los Angeles Grand Jury appointed a Special Committee on the Problems of Mexican Youth. This group contained a variety of viewpoints, and numbered among its members not only Carey McWilliams but Mexican Associate Consul Manuel Aguilar, UCLA Anthropology Professor Harry Hojer, Guy Nunn of the War Manpower Commission, and others. On December 22, 1942, this committee made a report to the Grand Jury in which it noted that "young people of Mexican ancestry have been more sinned against than sinning, in the discriminations and limitations that have been placed on them and their families." It recommended the abandonment of discrimination against Mexicans in public places such as playgrounds and swimming pools (open to Mexicans only one day a week), and in defense industries. It also urged more vocational training as well as an increase in the number of Spanish-speaking police.

Although the report aroused some attention, it had little immediate impact. The Los Angeles newspapers continued their extensive coverage of *pachuco* gangs; city officials remained passive; and a local coordinating council organized by Manuel Ruiz to increase Mexican enrollment in trade schools made little progress.

As 1943 began, therefore, ethnic tensions were even more strained than they had been in the previous year. By this time the zoot suit had gained considerable popularity among Mexican-American youths. Zoot suits appealed to lower class youths of different ethnic or racial backgrounds, but enjoyed special favor among blacks in New York and the *pachucos* of the Southwest and Los Angeles. A contemporary sociologist, Beatrice Griffith, estimated that two-thirds of the Mexican-American boys in Los Angeles wore zoot suits although perhaps only 5 percent were members of the *pachuco* gangs that engaged in criminal behavior. In the popular mind, however, most zoot suiters were stereotyped as *pachucos* and as common criminals. And just as the zoot suit was a symbol of Mexican-American identity to Anglos, the uniforms of servicemen became symbolic as a badge of the dominant Anglo society.

Such a sharpening of ethnic consciousness triggered numerous incidents that created a tense atmosphere. During the spring of 1943 zoot suiters often attacked servicemen, whom they saw also as rivals for the affections of their girl friends. Servicemen in the barrio were subjected to beatings, robberies, and harassment at the hands of *pachucos*. The uniforms of each group provided instant visibility—and instant conflict. And the situation in Los Angeles was duplicated in other western cities, if not as pronounced. In April 1943 a group of sailors and Marines attacked Mexican and black zoot suiters in Oakland. A month later servicemen in Venice (just south of Los Angeles) became involved in a disturbance with zoot suiters at a dance hall. By the middle of May 1943 the attacks by zoot suiters on servicemen had increased both in volume and in intensity. A special report made by Lt. Glenn A. Littin to the commander of the Eleventh Naval District detailed 83 separate incidents involving Navy men only in the Los Angeles area during the last week of May.

In many cases zoot suiters did not go beyond name calling and verbal abuse, harassment, and some shoving. Thus, "on Saturday, June 5 about 2200 [Radio Man 3d Class Chauncey A.] Bengiveno was on a Pacific Electric car with several sailors, going to Long Beach. When the car stopped at Compton, several zoot suiters appeared by the car and dared the sailors to come out. At the same time a group of other zoot suiters came from behind the station and attempted to break into the car; but the door was closed and they were not able to enter." Another reputed incident involved Seaman 2d Class Cecil Maggard. "On Sunday morning, May 29 at 0600 Maggard and G. C. Lee were walking passed [*sic*] New Depot Street on Figueroa, coming to the Armory," wrote Littin. "A group, of Mexican zoot suiters, about ten or fifteen in number, ran after the sailors, throwing rocks at them and cursing them. No provocation of any kind for the assault was given by the sailors. No injuries resulted."

In some cases the zoot suiters reportedly harassed the families of servicemen. Littin noted the case of George R. King, whose wife worked at Lockheed Corporation. For several nights after May 27, he charged, groups of zoot suiters accosted her on the way to work, seeking to pick her up on the corner of Euclid and Whittier Streets where she usually boarded a streetcar. In the following week King had to arrange an escort for his wife. Then, "on Sunday, June 6 while sitting on his front porch with his family, zoot suiters began to appear in increasing numbers, cruising back and forth in front of King's house. They began cursing him and threatened to 'get him.' It became necessary for King to telephone the police. . . . The zoot suiters have on several occasions pushed King's children from the sidewalk into the street and fear for their safety made it necessary for him to send them to Sacramento."

Various incidents resulted in more serious injuries to Navy men, however, according to the Navy version. Thus, "on the 31st of May Seaman 2d Class Homer C. Draper, along with several other servicemen, were on their way downtown about 2030. Very suddenly, without any warning of any kind, zoot suiters attacked the service men from all directions, throwing rocks and bottles, and a general fight ensued. . . . Someone hit Coleman on the head from the rear. Coleman was knocked unconscious and remembers nothing further. . . . His jaw was broken in two places. Coleman is receiving medical treatment from the Navy doctor." And, the report continued, "About the middle of April, Seaman 2d Class Robert J. Short and W. H. Bushman were returning to the Armory from downtown Los Angeles, about 2145. Just south of the viaduct on Figueroa three men dressed in zoot suits approached from the opposite direction and blocked the sidewalk. Short and Bushman stepped off the sidewalk in order to pass, and as they did so one of the zoot suiters hit Short in the jaw, and then all three ran, calling the sailors 'suckers.' Short's jaw was considerably swollen. He was given treatment at Sick Bay." In another of the scores of incidents Seaman 2d Class Dale C. Henderson, "coming off liberty on Saturday night, May 22, about 2230, was crossing Pershing Square when two zoot suiters walked up and one hit Henderson in the eye. Two service men came to the rescue of Henderson and the zoot suiters left. The one that hit Henderson said, 'Oh, the Navy!' as he struck him. Henderson reports that on several occasions before, he had been cursed by Mexicans in passing cars and in restaurants."

Hostile feelings between zoot suiters and servicemen mounted steadily during the second half of May. By that time taxis filled with men from military bases were cruising the city streets in the barrio of East Los Angeles to harass zoot suiters. Meanwhile, attacks by *pachucos* on servicemen increased. As Captain Martin Dixon, Commander at the Chavez Ravine Naval Base in the heart of Palo Verde, a Mexican district, later said: "We had about ten of our boys insulted or attacked in April, and double that amount in May." Then, on Sunday, May 30, eleven soldiers and sailors walked along the 1700 block of North Main Street—in the worst slum area in Los Angeles. They were attacked by 35 zoot suiters but fought off their assailants. The Los Angeles police did little, aware that their civilian authority over military personnel was limited. But the sailors who had been attacked were furious and sought to take the law into their own hands. "We're out to do what the police have failed to do," said one petty officer among them. "We're going to clean up this situation. . . ." And another added angrily: "We don't intend to be beaten and seriously injured while on leave here. If the police can't handle the little gangsters then we will."

During the first week of June the pent-up emotions erupted in a full-fledged riot. On Thursday evening, June 3, 1943, several hundred servicemen left the Chavez Ravine Armory armed with rocks and sticks and rampaged through the barrio. Ironically, some of their first victims were members of a Mexican-American crime prevention group known as the Alpine Club. Through the streets they went, on foot and in taxis, sometimes invading buildings such as movie houses and dragging out such hapless zoot suiters as they could find. Most of the violence was directed against Mexican-Americans, but blacks were also attacked. The Los Angeles police found itself unable to contain the rioters. On successive nights, on Friday and Saturday in particular, the rioting worsened as thousands of servicemen poured into East Los Angeles to strike at zoot suiters. The *Los Angeles Times* of June 8, 1943, described the battle zone:

> Thousands of servicemen joined by thousands of civilians last night surged along Main Street and Broadway hunting zoot-suiters. Chief of Police Horrall declared riot alarm at 10:30 P.M. and ordered every policeman on duty. More than fifty zoot-suiters had clothing torn off as servicemen and civilians converged on bars, restaurants, penny arcades and stores in downtown areas searching for zoot-suiters. Streetcars were halted and theaters along Main Street were scrutinized for hiding zoot-suiters. . . . Police were handicapped by the tremendous crowds of civilians who apparently had listened to the police riot calls on the radio and had rushed into downtown. . . . Traffic blocked as groups raced into streets after victims.

According to the records of the 11th Naval District (San Diego), the military authorities in the area made deliberate efforts to restrain their men. Rear Admiral David W. Bagley, commander of the 11th Naval District, sent a memo to those under his command on June 9, 1943, noting that "irrespective of what may have been the original cause of these disorders the enforcement of laws rests in the hands of the civilian police and is not a matter which should be undertaken by any unauthorized groups of Navy personnel." He urged "the enlisted men concerned . . . [to] refrain from such disorders." At the same time Bagley wrote to Senor Alfredo Elias Calles, the Mexican consul in Los Angeles: "I deeply regret that individual incidents of hoodlumism in Los Angeles have been interpreted as acts specifically involving nationals of either Mexico or the United States." Admiral Bagley stated, "You and I are sympathetic to each other's position in a situation which should have been classified as simple rowdyism." By June 10, 1943, the Los Angeles police had reestablished a semblance of order, aided by military police and a military curfew, and the worst race riot in Los Angeles history came to an end.

Army commanders were concerned that such incidents be prevented in the future. On June 11, 1943, Major General Maxwell Murray of the Southern California sector of the Western Defense Command sent a release to his subordinates urging them to inform the troops "of the serious nature of riot charges," which could result "in sentences to death or long confinement. Military personnel of all ranks must understand that no form of mob violence or rioting will be tolerated."

Within a month after the zoot suit riots the Eleventh Naval District was also developing plans for more effective control of possible large scale mob actions in the future. By August 2 Commandant S. F. Heim of the Naval Operating Base on Terminal Island had formulated standardized instructions for Riot Duty Personnel. He also worked out cooperative arrangements for securing additional Army troops for the Southern California sector. At the same time detailed instructions for riot control were also formulated by J. D. Colodny, the Commanding Officer of the Marine Detachments stationed at Terminal Island.

Immediately after the June zoot suit riots not only the military but also civilian officials were anticipating further racial disturbances during the summer of 1943. "A tense situation is existant [*sic*]," noted the Senior Patrol Officer of the Navy Shore Patrol on July 29, 1943, "and serious racial disorders may break out in this area at any time." Mayor Bowron held an "off the record" conference on the race problem on July 20 with police officials and representatives of minority groups in the Los Angeles area. The mayor noted that he expected more racial violence and was particularly worried since the Los Angeles Police Department was short 500 men. Thus he requested the use of Army troops, if needed. Meanwhile, representatives from the black community argued that while tensions might be high, they could be relieved by relaxation of discrimination in housing and recreation. Mayor Bowron promised to look into the suggestions and to establish community action and educational programs to ease racial strains.

Bowron and business leaders in the Chamber of Commerce were greatly concerned about the national and international image of the city of Los Angeles as a result of the riots. Bowron's correspondence reveals numerous efforts on his part to dispel the image of Los Angeles as a city beset with racial strife. One of his efforts was directed at Elmer Davis, Director of the Office of War Information:

> I do not question either the right or advisability of representatives of your office getting the facts and we would greatly appreciate anything that could be done in the ascertainment and declaration of the truth in order that the garbled, highly colored, wholly misleading and detrimental news accounts that went out to the entire country and relayed to the people of our neighboring American Republics could be corrected.

And then he leveled his shafts at "Mr. Allen Cranston of your office who rushed here from Washington, ostensibly to get information, but who has busied himself with many things that are not appreciated either by myself or others who feel that the responsibility for local conditions is our own." Cranston had publicly blamed city authorities for the disturbances and had organized a local committee allegedly to investigate the situation. The mayor's sensitivity to negative publicity was also noted by Captain Heim of the 11th Naval District. After attending a meeting in Bowron's office with other military and community leaders, Heim reported to his superior, Rear Admiral Bagley, by telephone: "Admiral, what they are hurt about the situation—and oh, how they are hurt—is the City of Los Angeles being placed out of bounds and the publicity they are getting."

In Washington, Nelson Rockefeller's Office of the Coordinator of Inter-American Affairs was similarly concerned about the impact of the riot on America's Good Neighbor policy and sought to take direct action to ease racial tensions in Los Angeles. (Ironically, the regional office of the CIAA in Los Angeles opened its doors on the same day that the zoot suit riots began.) As John Clark of the CIAA noted, "Mr. Rockefeller is personally greatly concerned with the problem."

One of the major results of the zoot suit riots was to focus greater attention of many Angelenos on the Mexican-American community in its midst. For many, the disturbances had a shock effect, and much soul searching commenced to ascertain the reasons for the troubles. The Los Angeles County Grand Jury undertook a thorough investigation, and concluded rather curiously that racial and ethnic tensions were not a primary cause. California Governor Earl Warren also established a special committee headed by Attorney General Robert Kenny to investigate the riots. In their report they dealt with a variety of influences without stressing ethnic tensions as a major factor. Public resentment of zoot suiters continued. In fact, the City Council passed an ordinance outlawing zoot suits.

But various city and voluntary groups went to work to ameliorate bad feelings. Thus, the city of Los Angeles increased its budgets for education and recreation in the East Los Angeles area and embarked on a five-year community development program for Mexican-Americans. Mayor Bowron appointed a new Committee for Home Front Unity to facilitate communication between city officials and the Mexican-American community. Rockefeller's Office of the Coordinator of Inter-American Affairs activated its new Los Angeles office to develop improved cultural relations between Mexicans and Americans. During the summer of 1943 the city and county of Los Angeles sponsored teacher workshops dealing with Mexican culture and developed adult job training programs. The Los Angeles County Probation Department meanwhile developed a Group Guidance Program in 1943 designed to diminish violence among juveniles. And in the following year the Los Angeles County Board of Supervisors created a Committee on Human Relations. Composed of county government department heads and community leaders, the group was designed to develop intercultural programs for better mutual understanding. Meanwhile, voluntary groups like the Catholic Youth Organization provided special counseling for Mexican-American juvenile delinquents and established a scholarship program for Spanish-speaking graduate students who promised to return to work in the home communities.

Whether all of these activities did much to defuse tensions in wartime Los Angeles is difficult to judge. What can be said with greater certainty is that they represented efforts to prevent the outbreak of violence such as had disrupted the city during early June 1943.

The Los Angeles zoot suit riots had reverberations throughout the West in communities where Spanish-speaking Americans resided. In Tucson, for example, throughout 1943, 1944, and 1945, street fights and public brawls revealed the increasing militancy of the Mexican-American community. In one incident—a reflection of the zoot suit riots in Los Angeles—a group of Anglo high school boys paraded through the Mexican areas of downtown Tucson to harass *pachucos*, and minor scuffles ensued. The end of the war lessened, but did not end such tensions. But the emergence of *pachucoism* during the war heightened ethnic consciousness and a sense of identity of Mexican-Americans in Tucson as elsewhere.

The long, hot summer of 1943 convinced not only city but also state and federal officials of the need to redouble their efforts to cope with some of the special problems of Hispanics. States like California and Texas began educational programs to train teachers to be more aware of cultural and language problems of Spanish-speaking students. At the federal level the Fair Employment Practices Committee (FEPC) and particularly the Coordinator of Inter-American Affairs (CIAA) developed policies designed exclusively to help this minority. The activities of these agencies in wartime were to be a prototype of public policies developed in the ensuing four decades.

The FEPC had been seeking to thwart discrimination in employment since it was created by presidential order in 1941. Although nationwide many of its energies were devoted to investigation of complaints by blacks, regional offices in the West paid increasing attention to cases brought by Hispanics outside California. One of the major supporters of the FEPC in Congress during the war years was Senator Dennis Chavez (N.M.), who sponsored a succession of bills to give it legislative sanction. Although President Roosevelt liked Chavez and viewed him as a spokesman for Hispanics in the United States, full White House support for such legislation was not forthcoming during wartime. As the only Spanish-speaking American in the United States Senate Chavez frequently urged his supporters to speak out against discrimination.

But by 1942 the increasing breakdown of discrimination due to a growing shortage of labor was making job opportunities available for Mexican-Americans. Surprisingly, however, the Spanish-speaking population of the Pacific Coast made little effort to utilize the help of the FEPC, in direct contrast to blacks. A reading of the complete files of the more than 500 cases that came before Region 12 of the Fair Employment Practices Committee reveals that only one discrimination complaint was made by a Spanish-speaking person, despite the fact that Director Harry Kingman appointed a special agent in Los Angeles for Hispanic-Americans in the hope of publicizing the work of the commission and facilitating the use of its good offices. Many of the Spanish-speaking population in California were Mexican-Americans with little education who as yet were not well acquainted with the workings of the American governmental system. Sociologists have noted that they depended more on community or family leaders than on unfamiliar American institutions. It was hardly surprising, therefore, that the special examiner, Ignacio L. Lopez, was quite disappointed with the results his efforts brought. "The need for information about FEPC and its functions to the Spanish-speaking Americans is great," he wrote to Kingman. "Very few of these people know that such an agency as FEPC exists, and still fewer understand how it works. This is true of those living in California as well as those from Texas, Colorado, Arizona, and New Mexico." He contacted Maurice Hazen in the Office of the Coordinator of Inter-American Affairs to suggest that a publicity program regarding FEPC be developed in cooperation with the Mexican Affairs Committee of the

Southern California Inter-American Council, but he found this group positively hostile. He also suggested a series of radio programs aimed at the Spanish-speaking community in the West because "radio is by far the best medium available in reaching the Spanish-speaking public."

Although some discrimination against Spanish-speaking Americans undoubtedly occurred in Colorado and the Northern Rockies, the regional office of the FEPC (Region 10) received more complaints from Texas, Arizona, and New Mexico. The regional director for the Rocky Mountain and Southwest Region was Carlos Castaneda, who heard a wide range of cases, such as that of W. H. Ural, who charged that he had been a laborer with the Santa Fe Railroad in Albuquerque for twenty-five years and had not received a promotion because he was a Spanish-speaking American. If the number of cases handled was fewer than those on the Pacific Coast, yet the complaints revealed some discriminatory patterns.

The FEPC made extensive investigations of discrimination in the Southwest and in the Rocky Mountain area. The Washington office sent one of its examiners, E. G. Trimble, into the Southwest in 1943 to gather evidence concerning discrimination against Spanish-speaking Americans. In El Paso, Texas, Trimble received complaints about discrimination by workers in the copper industry, particularly by employees of the Phelps-Dodge Corporation and Nevada Consolidated Company (a subsidiary of Kennecott Copper Company). About one-third of the 15,000 workers in the region's copper mines (New Mexico, Arizona, Nevada) were New Mexican, Mexican-American, Indian, or black. But the complainants to the FEPC were almost all Hispanic-Americans. They charged that their wage rates were lower than those of whites for similar work and that they were not advanced as rapidly as whites. Most also complained about being frozen in the lowest category of ordinary laborer. Trimble concluded that a general pattern of discrimination against Mexicans existed throughout the copper industry of the Southwest and that better paying jobs were simply out of reach for them on purely ethnic grounds. Moreover, within the industry Trimble felt that it was characterized by segregation, on the basis of patterns that had grown over the previous half century. Change would come only slowly, and so he recommended that the FEPC hold public hearings to expose these practices since the fear of publicity would induce most employers to abandon their discriminatory policies.

More extensive in its programs for Spanish-speaking Americans than the FEPC was the CIAA, which embarked on a wide range of activities throughout the West. The primary aim of this agency, headed by Nelson Rockefeller during the war years, was to improve the Good Neighbor policy of the Roosevelt administration. One means of strengthening the ties between the United States and its neighbors in the Western hemisphere was to extend more direct aid to the Spanish-speaking people within the United States and to use them as a bridge to more cordial relations with Central and South America. In a very real sense, wartime pressures led Rockefeller and his staff to point to Spanish-speaking Americans as a model of American attitudes toward Hispanics. It was toward that end that the CIAA sponsored programs that anticipated most federal policies toward Hispanics during Lyndon B. Johnson's Great Society era and in the two decades thereafter. These included establishing institutes at colleges and universities to develop greater sensitivity to Hispanic culture and to train community leaders. The CIAA also sponsored conferences to deal with the issue of bilingualism and the educational problems of Spanish-speaking school children, and awarded scholarships to Hispanic college students. In many cities the agency provided direct aid for local governments engaged in community action programs in the barrios. It also made grants to states and localities to stimulate vocational training programs designed to aid Spanish-speaking Americans in acquiring skills which would qualify them for newly emerging wartime jobs. In their entirety, the CIAA wartime policies constituted the most comprehensive federal effort to deal with Hispanic problems yet made during the first half of the twentieth century.

CIAA official Joseph E. Weckler clearly summed up the major goals of these programs:

> The Division of Inter-American activities in the United States is in part concerned with the problem of securing a higher degree of integration between the Spanish speaking residents and citizens of this country and the Anglo population. Our program is directly related to the war effort. . . . If the Spanish-speaking people in this country are given the proper training and opportunities, they will be able to aid considerably the war production. To achieve this end considerable social rehabilitation needs to be done in many sections of the country. It will also be necessary to break down, so far as possible, Anglo prejudices against resident Latin Americans which have done so much to prevent them from securing training or jobs. This discrimination is also directly injurious to our relations with the other Americas, particularly Mexico.

The CIAA made a conscious effort to stimulate cultural awareness through a variety of programs, including a Cultural Relations Division and a Radio and Motion Pictures Division. By 1943 Rockefeller had created a full-fledged Division of Inter-American Activities. That group prepared materials for teachers concerning the Hispanic heritage of the Americas and encouraged the teaching of Spanish in the United States. In Texas it inaugurated a statewide program to train teachers for Spanish-speaking communities while at Claremont College in California it conducted a workshop to train community leaders. It also sponsored Inter-American Centers in Denver, Salt Lake City, and Los Angeles which involved community, business, and educational leaders in activities relating to Hispanic-American culture in the United States and in Latin America.

One of the CIAA's key programs was involvement with Spanish-speaking minorities in the United States, particularly in Texas, New Mexico, Arizona, and California. "Among these groups it was found that problems arising from discrimination and lack of understanding offered fertile ground for the development of movements which would hinder the war effort and weaken hemispheric solidarity" wrote the agency's historian. The CIAA made grants to universities and chambers of commerce in the Southwest to ameliorate discrimination and improve teaching among Spanish-speaking minorities.

Of the CIAAs numerous conferences on the condition of Hispanic-Americans in the Southwest one of the most important was held in Washington in July 1943. Attending were various government officials, the agency's field representatives, and numerous educators. In focusing on the importance of bilingual education the Conference agreed on the primacy of the Spanish language in any broadly gauged effort to improve the conditions of Spanish-speaking Americans in the Southwest. "The Conference agreed emphatically upon the importance of a knowledge of the Spanish language," the reporter noted, "so as to aid in the elimination of attitudes unfavorable to an understanding of the problems of the Spanish speaking minority."

One example of the manifold activities of the CIAA was the sponsorship of a Conference on the Educational and Community Problems of Spanish-speaking People in the Southwest in cooperation with the University of New Mexico and New Mexico Highlands University in Santa Fe, New Mexico, August 19 - 24, 1943. Participants were educators and public officials from the region, including representatives of Spanish-speaking peoples, such as Professors George T. Sanchez of the University of Texas and Joaquin Ortega from the University of New Mexico. "The presence in the area of some two and one-half million Spanish-speaking people," noted Rockefeller's representative, historian Harold E. Davies, "a large proportion of them falling into the ranks of the low income groups, gives rise to many problems which are peculiar and common to the region." That region included California, Arizona, New Mexico, and Texas. The conference discussants approached five major issues, issues that had a familiar ring even four decades later. These included problems involved in teaching the Hispanic cultural heritage in the schools and the special conditions surrounding bilingual instruction. The conferees also devoted time to bettering school-community relations. Another major concern was occupational training for Spanish-speaking Americans, especially in mechanical, agricultural, and manual industries. As a committee of the conference noted, however, it was "especially careful to guard against using manual industries as a means of perpetuating the low income status of the Spanish-speaking people." The group estimated that 800,000 Spanish-speaking people were available for the labor market, but urged special training "to give the Spanish-speaking individuals full opportunity to acquire the skill and knowledge necessary to raise their standard of living to those prevalent in the nation."

The CIAA used federal funds to train Spanish-speaking Americans for wartime jobs. One example of its multifaceted programs was that of the New Mexico State Department of Trade and Industrial Education. Henry A. Gonzales, acting supervisor of the agency, reported in 1943 that while his department made some effort to train Spanish-speaking people in traditional crafts, "we have now shifted from crafts work to the metal working trade, to train people for defense jobs. . . . The boys and girls who two years ago were doing artistic tin work are today still working on metals, as riveters and airplane engine mechanics in war industries. . . . Similarly, our master wood carvers and joiners are constructing airplanes. . . . Girls from isolated communities who have had training in weaving and spinning . . . will make good workers in the fabrication and covering of airplanes. . . . This department [hopes] to bring these girls to our defense centers for training and subsequent placement." The New Mexico agency taught classes in aircraft engine manufacture, riveting, oil field technology, and other subjects directly related to the war effort. Gonzales' brief report hinted at the far-reaching economic and social changes which the war had brought to the rural Spanish speaking villagers of the Southwest.

For many Spanish-speaking people of New Mexico, Joaquin Ortega of the University of New Mexico explained, the major problems related not so much to discrimination as to poor economic and health conditions. The key to solving their problems, he believed, was further educational and vocational training. Improvements in nutrition were bound to lead to increased productivity. Ortega also hoped the CIAA could involve Hispanic Americans more closely in community groups like the Boy Scouts, the Red Cross, and similar organizations to achieve greater social integration.

Although the primary functions of the Inter-American institutes were educational, they often entered upon the administration of local action programs. The CIAA's Spanish and Portuguese Section approached Ben Cherington of the University of Denver and asked him to develop projects to increase participation of Hispanic Americans in community activities, particularly those that promised to improve their economic, educational and health milieu. Joseph Weckler of the CIAA was especially concerned with reaching the migratory beet sugar field workers of northeastern Colorado, city slum dwellers in Denver, and poor rural Hispanic-Americans in the San Luis Valley. In Albuquerque, New Mexico, the CIAA was involved in a similar program with Joaquin Ortega of the University of New Mexico and the local chapter of the League of United Latin American Citizens to improve conditions in Barelas, a depressed barrio in that city. Similar programs were sponsored by the CIAA in Texas, where the University of Texas served as a major focus for its programs and where the CIAA also maintained a full-time field representative.

The Second World War wrought great changes in the lives of Spanish-speaking Americans in the West, changes no less profound than the Mexican War of 1848 which had brought the transfer of the Southwest from Mexico to the United States. The war tended to uproot them from their placid rural environment and thrust them more directly into the mobilization effort. Fiercely patriotic, the high percentage who served in the American armed forces came back with an enhanced self-image and sometimes with new skills. Eager for economic betterment, young people especially migrated to towns and cities to take advantage of new job opportunities. Military service and urbanization tended to break down traditional values and life styles, and accelerated social and cultural integration into

American society. At the same time Spanish-speaking Americans became more conscious of their own identity and of such discrimination to which they were subjected.

Discriminatory practices against Hispanics weakened during the wartime years. In a city like Tucson, for example, Spanish-speaking Americans now began to have access to white collar jobs, while the Southern Pacific Railroad abrogated its discriminatory hiring policies in the midst of war. An inventory of occupations in which Spanish-speaking Americans were engaged in 1946 revealed a broad range, reflecting the impact of the war. Meanwhile, Tucson's school superintendent between 1941 and 1945 made conscious efforts to integrate schools where there was evidence of *de facto* segregation. Thus, the war changed the aspirations of Hispanics, heightened their ethnic awareness, and accelerated their assimilation. As few other events, it changed the direction of their lives. And at the same time it prompted federal and state governments to inaugurate programs for Spanish-speaking Americans that created important precedents for succeeding decades.

Reading 19

Jackie Robinson Breaks Baseball's Color Line

Jules Tygiel

Opening Day of the baseball season was always a festive occasion in Jersey City on the banks of the Passaic River. Each year Mayor Frank Hague closed the schools and required all city employees to purchase tickets, guaranteeing a sellout for the hometown Giants of the International League. The Giants sold 52,000 tickets to Roosevelt Stadium, double the ball park capacity. For those who could not be squeezed into the arena, Mayor Hague staged an annual pre-game jamboree. Jersey City students regaled the crowd outside the stadium with exhibitions of running, jumping, and acrobatics, while two bands provided musical entertainment.

On April 18, 1946, the air crackled with a special electricity. Hague's extravaganza marked the start of the first major league baseball season since the end of the war. But this did not fully account for the added tension and excitement. Nor could it explain why people from nearby New York City had burrowed through the Hudson Tubes for the event. Others had arrived from Philadelphia, Baltimore, and even greater distances to witness this contest. Most striking was the large number of blacks in the crowd; many undoubtedly attending a minor league baseball game for the first time. In the small area reserved for reporters chaotic conditions prevailed. "The press box was as crowded as the subway during rush hours," wrote one of its denizens in the Montreal *Gazette*. On the field photographers "seemed to be under everybody's feet." The focus of their attention was a handsome, broad-shouldered athlete in the uniform of the visiting Montreal Royals. When he batted in the first inning, he would be the first black man in the twentieth century to play in organized baseball. Jackie Robinson was about to shatter the color barrier.

"This in a way is another Emancipation Day for the Negro race," wrote sportswriter Baz O'Meara of Montreal's *Daily Star*, "a day that Abraham Lincoln would like." Wendell Smith, the black sportswriter of the Pittsburgh *Courier* who had recommended Robinson to Brooklyn Dodger President Branch Rickey, reported, "Everyone sensed the significance of the occasion as Robinson . . . marched with the Montreal team to deep centerfield for the raising of the Stars and Stripes and the 'Star-Spangled Banner.' We sang lustily and freely for this was a great day." And in the playing area, the black ballplayer partook in the ceremonies "with a lump in my throat and my heart beating rapidly, my stomach feeling as if it were full of feverish fireflies with claws on their feet."

Six months had passed since Rickey had surprised the nation by signing Robinson to play for the Dodgers' top farm club. It has been a period of intense speculation about the wisdom of

Rickey's action. Many predicted that the effort to integrate baseball would prove abortive, undermined by opposition from players and fans, or by Robinson's own inadequacies as a ballplayer. Renowned as a collegiate football and track star, Robinson had played only one season in professional baseball with the Kansas City Monarchs of the Negro National League. Upon Robinson's husky, inexperienced shoulders rested the fate of desegregation in baseball.

Robinson's experiences in spring training had dampened optimism. Compelled to endure the indignities of the Jim Crow South, barred by racism from many ball parks, and plagued by a sore arm, Robinson had performed poorly in exhibition games. One reporter suggested that had be been white, the Royals would have dropped him immediately. Other experts also expressed grave doubts. Jim Semler, owner of the New York Black Yankees, commented before the opener, "The pace in the IL is very fast . . . I doubt that Robinson will hit the kind of pitching they'll be dishing up to him." And Negro League veteran Willie Wells predicted, "It's going to take him a couple of months to get used to International League pitching."

Robinson, the second Montreal batter, waited anxiously as "Boss" Hague threw out the first ball and lead-off hitter Marvin Rackley advanced to the plate. Rackley, a speedy center fielder from South Carolina, grounded out to the shortstop. Robinson then strode to the batter's box, his pigeon-toed gait enhancing the image of nervousness. His thick neck and tightly muscled frame seemed more appropriate to his earlier gridiron exploits than to the baseball diamond.

Many had speculated about the crowd reaction. Smith watched anxiously from the press box to see "whether the fears which had been so often expressed were real or imagined." In the stands Jackie's wife, Rachel, wandered through the aisles, too nervous to remain in her seat. "You worry more when you are not participating than when you are participating," she later explained, "so I carried the anxiety for Jack." Standing at home plate, Jackie Robinson avoided looking at the spectators, "for fear I would see only Negroes applauding—that the white fans would be sitting stony-faced or yelling epithets." The capacity crowd responded with a polite, if unenthusiastic welcome.

Robinson's knees felt rubbery; his palms, he recalled, seemed "too moist to grip the bat." Warren Sandell, a promising young left-hander opposed him on the mound. For five pitches Robinson did not swing and the count ran to three and two. On the next pitch, Robinson hit a bouncing ball to the shortstop who easily retired him at first base. Robinson returned to the dugout accompanied by another round of applause. He had broken the ice.

Neither side scored in the first inning. In the second the Royals tallied twice on a prodigious home run by right fielder Red Durrett. Robinson returned to the plate in the third inning. Sandell had walked the first batter and surrendered a single to the second. With two men on base and nobody out, the Giants expected Robinson, already acknowledged as a master bunter, to sacrifice. Sandell threw a letter-high fastball, a difficult pitch to lay down. But Robinson did not bunt. The crowd heard "an explosive crack as bat and ball met and the ball glistened brilliantly in the afternoon sun as it went hurtling high and far over the left field fence," 330 feet away. In his second at-bat in the International League, Robinson had hit a three-run home run.

Robinson trotted around the bases with a broad smile on his face. As he rounded third, Manager Clay Hopper, the Mississippian who reportedly had begged Rickey not to put Robinson on his team, gave him a pat on the back. "That's the way to hit 'em, Jackie," exclaimed Rackley in his southern drawl. All of the players in the dugout rose to greet him, and John Wright, a black pitcher recruited to room with Robinson, laughed in delight. In the crowded press box Wendell Smith turned to Joe Bostic of the *People's Voice* and the two black reporters "laughed and smiled. . . . Our hearts beat just a little faster and the thrill ran through us like champagne bubbles." Most of their white colleagues seemed equally pleased, though one swore softly, according to one account, and "there were some very long faces in the gathering" as well.

The black second baseman's day had just begun. In the fifth inning, with the score 6–0 Robinson faced Giant relief pitcher Phil Oates. The "dark dasher," as Canadian sportswriters came to call Robinson, bunted expertly and outraced the throw "with something to spare." During spring training Rickey had urged the fleet-footed Robinson "to run those bases like lightning. . . . Worry the daylights out of the pitchers." Robinson faked a start for second base on the first pitch. On the next he took off, easily stealing the base. Robinson danced off second in the unnerving style that would become his trademark. Tom Tatuin, the Montreal batter, hit a ground ball to third. Robinson stepped backwards, but as the Jersey City fielder released the ball, he broke for third, narrowly beating the return throw.

Robinson had stolen second base and bluffed his way to third. He now determined to steal home to complete the cycle. He took a long lead, prompting Oates to throw to third to hold him on base. On the pitch he started toward home plate, only to stop halfway and dash back. The crowd, viewing the Robinson magic for the first time, roared. On the second pitch Robinson accelerated again, causing Oates to halt his pitching motion in mid-delivery. Oates had balked and the umpire waved Robinson in to score. Earlier Robinson had struck with power; now he had engineered a run with speed. The spectators, delighted with the daring display of baserunning, went wild, screaming, laughing, and stamping their feet. Blacks and whites, Royal fans and Giant fans, baseball buffs and those there to witness history, all joined in the ensuing pandemonium.

One flaw marred Robinson's performance. "By manner of proving that he was only human after all," according to one reporter, Robinson scarred his debut with a fielding error in the bottom of the inning. Acting as middleman in a double play, he unleashed an errant throw that allowed the Giants to score their only run. Otherwise, Robinson affirmed his reputation as an exceptional fielder.

In the seventh-inning Robinson triggered yet another Royal rally. He singled sharply to right field, promptly stole another base, and scored on a triple by Johnny Jorgenson. Before the inning had ended two more runs crossed the plate to increase the Royal lead to 10–1. In the eighth frame Robinson again bunted safely, his fourth hit in the contest. Although he did not steal any bases, he scrambled from first to third on an infield hit. Once again he unveiled his act, dashing back and forth along the baseline as the pitcher wound up. Hub Andrews, the third Jersey City pitcher, coped with this tactic no better than his predecessor. Andrews balked and for the second time in the game umpires awarded Robinson home plate. According to a true baseball aficionado, this established "some kind of a record for an opening day game."

The Royals won the game 14–1. Montreal pitcher Barney DeForge threw an effortless eight-hitter and Durrett clubbed two home runs. But, as the Pittsburgh *Courier's* front page headline gleefully announced, JACKIE "STOLE THE SHOW". "He did everything but help the ushers seat the crowd," crowed Bostic. In five trips to the plate Robinson made four hits, including a three-run home run, scored four times, and drove in three runs. He also stole two bases and scored twice by provoking the pitcher to balk. "Eloquent as they were, the cold figures of the box score do not tell the whole story," indicated the New York *Times* reporter in an assessment that proved prophetic of Robinson's baseball career. "He looked as well as acted the part of a real baseball player."

"This would have been a big day for any man," reported the *Times*, "but under the special circumstances, it was a tremendous feat." Joe Bostic, who accompanied his story in the *People's Voice* with a minute-by-minute account of Robinson's feats in the game, waxed lyrical. "Baseball took up the cudgel for Democracy," wrote Bostic, "and an unassuming, but superlative Negro boy ascended the heights of excellence to prove the rightness of the experiment. And prove it in the only correct crucible for such an experiment—the crucible of white hot competition."

II

Two years before Robinson's triumphant Jersey City debut, Swedish sociologist Gunna Myrdal had published *An American Dilemma*, a landmark study of the race problem in the United States. In it he concluded that "Not since Reconstruction has there been more reason to anticipate fundamental changes in race relations, changes which will involve a development towards the American ideal." Few people shared Myrdal's optimistic viewpoint. His work described a society characterized by northern indifference and ignorance of the plight of blacks and a firmly entrenched system of racial segregation in the South, where Jim Crow laws forbade whites and blacks from attending the same schools, riding in the same sections of trains and buses, receiving treatment in the same hospitals, or competing in the same athletic contests. In Birmingham, Alabama, it was "unlawful for a Negro and white to play together or in the company with each other" at dominoes and checkers. These legal restrictions did not adequately reflect the extent of southern discrimination and segregation. As historian C. Vann Woodward noted, "There is more Jim Crow practiced in the South than there are Jim Crow laws on the books." Common custom required separate toilets and water fountains, entrances and exits, and waiting rooms and ticket windows. "Segregation is becoming so complete," Myrdal discovered, "that the white Southerner practically never sees a Negro except as his servant and in other standardized and formalized caste situations."

Southern whites reinforced this Jim Crow regime with a combination of economic and physical coercion. Blacks who challenged racial conventions jeopardized not only their meager sources of income but their lives as well. Although violence had abated since the early decades of the century when mobs lynched scores of blacks each year, the threat of physical reprisals remained a vivid reality. In 1946 at least nine blacks were lynched; and authorities rescued twenty-one others from angry mobs. Any attempt to dismantle the southern caste system, warned Richmond *Times-Dispatch* editor Virginius Dabney, would result in an "interracial explosion" which would leave "hundreds, if not thousands, killed."

The prevalence of these conditions renders all the more remarkable Myrdal's prescient conclusion. Myrdal argued that during the 1930s, the "popular theory behind race prejudice" in the United States had gradually "decayed." The inclusion of blacks in New Deal relief programs, several Supreme Court decisions limiting discriminatory practices, and a growing exasperation with the South among northern liberals reflected this shift in attitudes. In addition, the growing militancy among blacks, whom, said Myrdal, "America can never more regard . . . as a patient, submissive minority" would contribute to the forthcoming transition. This process would be accelerated by "the world conflict and America's exposed position as the defender of the American faith." Ultimately, Myrdal argued, the opponents of segregation would discover "a powerful tool in the caste struggle" in the "American Creed"—"the glorious American ideals of democracy, liberty, and equality to which America is pledged not only by its political constitution, but also by the severe devotion of its citizens."

In the immediate aftermath of World War II, the forces that Myrdal predicted would transform the nation's racial practices merged most dramatically and visibly on the playing fields of America. For a half century, baseball had provided a mirror image of American society; blacks and whites played in two realms, separate and unequal. Within weeks of the end of the war, Brooklyn Dodger president Branch Rickey announced his intention to end Jim Crow in baseball by signing Jackie Robinson. In the eyes of some contemporary observers, Rickey had initiated a "great" or "noble experiment." Could an American institution, steeped in the traditions of racial prejudice and populated by large numbers of southerners, accept the introduction of blacks peacefully? During the following decade and a half the desegregation experiment unfolded in baseball's major and minor leagues. In a formal sense, it was completed in 1959 when the Boston Red Sox, the last all-white major league team, inserted young Elijah "Pumpsie" Green into a game as a pinch runner. In reality, the experiment continues into the present.

The integration of baseball represented both a symbol of imminent racial challenge and a direct agent of social change. Jackie Robinson's campaign against the color line in 1946–47 captured the imagination of millions of Americans who had previously ignored the nation's racial dilemma. For civil rights advocates the baseball experience offered a model of peaceful transition through militant confrontation, economic pressure, and moral suasion. In 1954 when the Supreme Court declared school segregation illegal in the famous *Brown v. Board of Education* decision, a majority of major league teams already fielded black athletes. Minor league integration had penetrated not only the North and West, but most of the South as well. For more than a decade before the explosion of sit-ins and freedom rides of the 1960s challenged Jim Crow accommodations in the Deep South, black athletes had desegregated playing facilities, restaurants, and hotels in many areas of the country.

Baseball was one of the first institutions in modern society to accept blacks on a relatively equal basis. The "noble experiment" thus reflects more than a saga of sport. It offers an opportunity to analyze the integration process in American life. An examination of the forces that led to Robinson's hiring, the reaction among both blacks and whites, the institutional response of the baseball establishment, and the resulting decline of the Jim Crow leagues reveals much about the United States in the 1940s and 1950s. The halting and incomplete nature of baseball's achievement notwithstanding, few other businesses have equalled its performance. The dynamics of interracial relationships among players, coaches, and managers provide rare insights into what occurs when nonwhites are introduced into a previously segregated industry.

"The American Negro problem is a problem in the heart of America," wrote Myrdal. "It is there that interracial tension has its focus. It is there that the decisive struggle goes on." From 1945 to 1959 Jackie Robinson and the blacks who followed him into baseball appealed to the "heart of America." In the process they contributed to the transformation of the national consciousness and helped to usher in a new, if still troubled, age of race relations in the United States.

> A lone Negro in the game will see caustic comments. He will be made the target of cruel, filthy epithets. Of course, I know the time will come when the ice will have to be broken. Both by the organized game and by the colored player who is willing to volunteer and thus become a sort of martyr to the cause.
>
> *Washington Senators owner, Clark Griffith, 1938*

Reading 20

Neither Victim nor Villain: Nurse Eunice Rivers, the Tuskegee Syphilis Experiment, and Public Health Work

Susan L. Smith

From 1932 to 1972 white physicians of the United States Public Health Service (USPHS) carried out an experiment on approximately 400 rural black men in Macon County, Alabama. The study, which historian James Jones has described as "the longest nontherapeutic experiment on human beings in medical history," was predicated on following the course of untreated syphilis until death.[1] Historians have focused on the study as scientifically unjustifiable and as an unethical experiment that highlights the racism of American medicine and the federal government. While affirming the validity of these assessments, I reexamined the experiment to return to the troubling questions of why black professionals, such as nurse Eunice Rivers (Laurie), supported the project.

Black health workers and educators associated with Tuskegee Institute, a leading black educational institution founded by Booker T. Washington in Alabama, played a critical role in the experiment. Robert Moton, head of Tuskegee Institute in the 1930s, and Dr. Eugene Dibble, the Medical Director of Tuskegee's Hospital, both lent their endorsement and institutional resources to the government study. However, no one was more vital to the experiment than Eunice Rivers, a black public health nurse. Rivers acted as the liaison between the men in the study and the doctors of the USPHS. She worked in the public health field from 1923 until well after her retirement in 1965. She began her career with the Tuskegee Institute Movable School during the 1920s in rural Alabama. This traveling school for African Americans provided adult education programs in agriculture, home economics, and health. After a decade of service with the school, Rivers became involved in the infamous Tuskegee Syphilis Study in 1932. How could a nurse dedicated to preserving life participate in such a project?

Although historians have noted the key role that Rivers played in the experiment, they have presented her as a victim by virtue of her status as a woman, an African American, and a nurse. Groundbreaking work by James Jones, for example, interpreted much of Rivers's participation as driven by obedience to higher authority. A more satisfactory consideration of her role as an historical subject is in order; yet, examination of Rivers's role does not necessarily lead to an interpretation of her as an evil nurse. What does it mean, then, to talk about the historical agency of black women within racist and sexist social structures? Indeed, Rivers was neither a victim nor a villain but a complex figure who can only be understood within her historical context. She acted in ways she determined to be in her best interests and in the interests of promoting black health. Consistent with the responses of at least some black health professionals and educators at the time, Rivers did not question the experiment because she did not find it objectionable.

I became curious about the response of Rivers and other black professional to the syphilis experiment during my work on the National Negro Health Movement, a black public health movement during the first half of the twentieth century. A small but active group of black professionals in medicine, dentistry, nursing, and education, along with community women, organized public health programs across the nation to improve the health of African Americans. By 1930 black nursing schools and medical institutions had produced some 5,000 black nurses and 3,700 black physicians, many of whom were involved in community health projects.[2]

Drawing on federal records from the USPHS, manuscript collections at Tuskegee University (the black college formerly known as Tuskegee Institute), and an oral history of Eunice Rivers, this article analyzes the meanings of the experiment from the perspective of black health professionals, especially Rivers. Her story raises important questions about the gendered nature of public health work, the constraints on black middle-class reform efforts, and the costs and benefits to the poor.

The actions of Eunice Rivers can best be understood when set within the context of twentieth-century public health work. In her capacity as a public health nurse, Rivers acted as the mediator between black clients and the government, implementing health policy at the local level. Indeed, she was the key to maintaining subject interest in the experiment for forty years.[3] Paradoxically, it is a "tribute" to her years of hard work at developing relationships with people in the surrounding countryside through her public health work with the Tuskegee Moveable School that the men in the Tuskegee Syphilis Study continued to cooperate year after year.

In order to better understand the work of Eunice Rivers in the Tuskegee Syphilis Experiment, it is important to analyze her activities with the Tuskegee Moveable School. When Tuskegee Institute established the Movable School in 1906, it marked the beginning of organized black agricultural extension work in the United States. Booker T. Washington referred to this form of rural schooling for adults as "A Farmer's College on Wheels." Washington and his assistants convinced government leaders to fund part of the costs of the Movable School and include it within the extension service work of the U.S. Department of Agriculture and the state of Alabama, although housed at Tuskegee Institute. The Movable School was one of the programs through which Washington attempted to secure government assistance and financial support during an era in which government neglect of the needs of African Americans was the norm.[4]

In the spirit of Washington's racial uplift philosophy, black extension agents from the Movable School tried to turn black tenant farmers into healthy, thrifty landowners. Landownership was a key to black freedom from white control. Extension agents wanted to liberate poor black people from the oppressive nature of the southern agricultural system, an economic arrangement which left many people trapped in a cycle of debt and poverty. Most African Americans in Alabama worked on white-owned cotton plantations where they rented their land and faced a losing financial battle. In 1925 in Macon County, home of Tuskegee Institute, 90 percent of the rural African Americans were tenant farmers.[5]

In the early twentieth century, many rural African Americans lived in unhealthy surroundings and faced a range of health problems including malaria, typhoid fever, hookworm disease, pellagra, and venereal disease, along with malnutrition and high infant and maternal mortality rates. Black extension agents and health workers throughout the South tried to address these problems in several ways. They launched programs to promote diversified farming, including vegetable gardens to improve the diet, to screen homes against insects that carried diseases, to build sanitary privies or toilets to minimize contact with human wastes, and to educate people about personal hygiene.[6]

Extension programs such as the Tuskegee Movable School tried to improve living conditions and reduce the migration of black farmworkers out of rural areas. The Movable School, a mule-drawn wagon later replaced by a truck, carried several Tuskegee graduates in agriculture, home economics, and nursing to work in the countryside among the rural poor. Initially the extension agents held teaching sessions in community institutions, such as churches, but by 1920 they decided that they could reach more people by going directly to their homes, either tenant houses on plantations or the homes of the few black landowners. The educational philosophy of the Movable School like that of all extension work was to teach by example and to win the trust of the farmworkers.[7]

The black educators from Tuskegee Institute who worked with the traveling school urged the rural black poor to participate in their programs. Based on previous experiences with local government and its history of upholding white supremacy, many poor African Americans initially were reluctant to participate in rural development programs for fear of being exploited. They were distrustful of the state and its representatives, given their mistreatment at the hands of landlords, the courts, railroads, and law enforcement agents.[8]

Health concerns were an integral part of the agenda of rural development programs, including the work of the Movable School. Although male farm agents and female home demonstration agents addressed health issues informally as part of their lessons in agriculture and home economics, the inclusion of a public health nurse with the Movable School in 1920 marked the beginning of formal health education work.

Throughout the early twentieth century the black nurse was a key figure in spreading the gospel of health or health education to African Americans. As the field of public health nursing expanded in the twentieth century and public health workers placed more emphasis on individual hygiene, nurses came to symbolize the ideal teachers. Public health nurses were especially important in rural areas where access to doctors was severely limited. They had more independence and autonomy than nurses in other fields. Despite discrimination in training, wages, and promotion, black nurses felt a sense of responsibility for the health needs of black communities. By 1930 there were 470 black public health nurses in the country, 180 of whom worked in the South where they constituted 20 percent of all public health nurses.[9]

The public health nurse was in an excellent position to assess the health needs of rural African Americans. Uva M. Hester, a Tuskegee graduate in nursing, became the first black public health nurse to work for the Movable School. She found the health conditions of rural families simply unbearable because of the unsanitary state of many homes. Hester stated that she was appalled by the flies, the dirt, and the small rooms in the cabins she visited. Her first week's report chronicled the inadequate health services available in rural Alabama:

> Tuesday: I visited a young woman who had been bedridden with tuberculosis for more than a year. There are two openings on her chest and one in the side from which pus constantly streams. In addition, there is a bedsore on the lower part of the back as large as one's hand. There were no sheets on her bed. . . . The sores had only a patch of cloth plastered over them. No effort was made to protect the patient from the flies that swarmed around her.[10]

These same themes of unhealthy conditions and inadequate bedside care recurred frequently in Hester's reports from her travels throughout the county. Public health nurses provided health education, comfort, and care where they could, but they usually operated with limited resources.

Eunice Rivers (1899–1986) joined the Movable School in January 1923, happy to have a job and also steeped in Tuskegee's philosophy of service to the rural poor. Like others who worked with the traveling school, Rivers attended Tuskegee Institute, graduating from the School of Nursing in 1922. Born in rural Georgia, she was the oldest of three daughters of a farming family. Rivers became a nurse because of parental encouragement. She remembered that, before her mother died when Rivers was only fifteen years old, her mother had told her to "get a good education, so that I wouldn't have to work in the fields so hard." Her father also promoted education for his daughters, working long hours in a sawmill to help finance it. Rivers eventually followed her father's advice to study nursing despite her protesting, "but Papa, I don't want to be no nurse, I don't want folks dying on me."[11]

Gender prescriptions influenced the shape of Rivers's public health work as she traveled from county to county. She directed most of her health education messages, including discussion of sanitation, ventilation, and cleanliness, to rural women. Public health programs focused on women because they were expected to be the ones most responsible for the health of their families. Rivers informed women about specific diseases, such as malaria and typhoid fever, and taught them how to make bandages from old clothes, care for bedridden patients, and take a temperature. Women often asked questions at these health meetings and seemed eager for information. In addition, Rivers gave dental hygiene lectures to children on how to brush their teeth, and she handed out tubes of Colgate toothpaste donated by the company. Her public health work with men focused on "social hygiene," which usually meant information about the dangers of venereal disease.[12]

In 1926 Rivers redirected some of the focus of her public health work. The state transferred her from the Alabama Bureau of Child Welfare, in which she performed her Movable School work, to the Bureau of Vital Statistics. Her new mandate was to assist the state in creating a system of registration for births and deaths, as well as aid efforts to regulate lay midwifery and lower infant mortality rates. She continued to travel throughout Alabama with the Movable School, but she focused her attention on pregnant women and midwives.[13]

Rivers was well liked by her clients who appreciated her visits. She reached many people through her Movable School position and worked in over twenty counties in her first year alone. She visited hundreds of people every month; during one particularly busy month she tended to 1,100 people. J. D. Barnes, a white extension agent in Greene County, reported to Tuskegee Institute in 1928 that rural women remembered Rivers's visits and the way she made people feel good in her company. He wrote, "one woman asked me when I was going to have that sweet little woman come back to the county again."[14]

Rivers, who grew up with a class background similar to that of the people she aided, attributed her successful relationships with rural people to her attitude toward them. "As far as I was concerned," she explained, "every individual was an individual of his own. He didn't come in a lump sum." She remembered that sometimes people would ask her how she ever received entry into certain homes where visitors were not welcomed. Rivers would reply:

> Well, darling, I don't know. I was brought in there. They're people as far as I'm concerned. I don't go there dogging them about keeping the house clean. I go there and visit a while until I know when to make some suggestions. When I go to the house I accept the house as I find it. I bide my time.[15]

Her approach, she concluded, was nothing more than mutual respect between herself and those she assisted. The trust and close relationships that she developed with rural African Americans through her work with the Movable School proved to be a tremendous asset in her work for the USPHS.

In 1932 Eunice Rivers, along with leaders of Tuskegee Institute, became involved with a study by the USPHS that appears to contradict her efforts to improve black health. Rivers's need for employment, as well as her interest in black health conditions, influenced her decision to accept employment with the USPHS. During the early 1930s, financial cutbacks caused by the onset of the Depression ended her job with the Movable School. Facing unemployment, she accepted a job as night supervisor at the John A. Andrew Memorial Hospital at Tuskegee Institute and worked there eight months until she learned of the position with the federal government. When asked in later years why she went to work with the Syphilis Study she replied: "I was just interested. I mean I wanted to get into everything that I possibly could."[16] An equally compelling reason, no doubt, was her statement: "I was so glad to go off night duty that I would have done anything."[17] Thereafter, Rivers worked part-time for the USPHS and part-time in maternal and child health for Tuskegee's hospital and then later for the county health department.

In the early twentieth century, private foundations and the federal government focused attention on controlling venereal disease. The USPHS first addressed the topic of venereal disease during World War I when the federal government became concerned about the results of tests of military recruits that showed that many men, black and white, were infected with syphilis. The USPHS formed the Division of Venereal Disease to promote health education in black and white communities.[18] In the late 1920s the Julius Rosenwald Fund, a philanthropic foundation with strong interests in health care for African Americans, assisted the federal government in venereal disease control work. The foundation provided financial support to develop a demonstration control program for African Americans in the South. This project to detect and treat syphilis began in 1928 in Bolivar County, Mississippi, among thousands of black tenant farmers and sharecroppers, and it appeared to show that nearly 20 percent of the men and women had syphilis. The Rosenwald Fund next expanded the program from Mississippi to counties in other southern states, including Macon County in Alabama.[19] In 1932, when the Depression led the Rosenwald Fund to discontinue its financial support, leaders of the USPHS launched the Tuskegee Syphilis Study in Alabama. Initially, the study was to continue for about six to twelve months.

White assumptions about the health and sexuality of African Americans influenced the way medical authorities interpreted statistical data on venereal disease. Some black leaders criticized the high syphilitic rate always cited for African Americans as well as the expectation that syphilis was endemic to black populations because of sexual promiscuity. For example, Dr. Louis T. Wright, a leader of the National Association for the Advancement of Colored People (NAACP) and surgeon at Harlem Hospital in New York, wrote that even if there were high rates "this is not due to lack of morals, but more directly to lack of money, since with adequate funds these diseases can be controlled easily."[20]

Confident that racial differences affected health and disease, white physicians of the USPHS expected the Tuskegee study to provide a useful racial comparison to an Oslo study that traced untreated syphilis in Norway. However, the Oslo study was a retrospective study examining previous case records of white people whose syphilis went untreated, unlike the Tuskegee study, which was designed to deliberately withhold available treatment from black people. The development in 1910 of Salvarsan, a toxic arsenic compound that was the first effective treatment for syphilis, prompted the end of the Oslo study. Dr. Raymond Vonderlehr, an official at the USPHS, even proposed that they expand their investigation, suggesting that "similar studies of untreated syphilis in other racial groups might also be arranged." He suggested that they conduct a study of Native Americans with untreated syphilis.[21]

Black leaders at Tuskegee Institute endorsed the government study, to the relief of the federal officials, in the belief that it would help the school in its work for African Americans. The government doctors selected Macon County because they had identified it as having the highest rate of syphilis of all the Rosenwald study groups, with a rate of about 35 percent, and because they rightly concluded that Tuskegee Institute could provide valuable assistance. Dibble, the medical director of Tuskegee's hospital, supported the experiment on the grounds that it might demonstrate that costly treatment was unnecessary for people who had latent or third-stage syphilis, echoing the justifications provided by the USPHS. More importantly, Dibble urged Moton, head of Tuskegee Institute, to support the study because Tuskegee Institute "would get credit for this piece of research work," and the study would "add greatly to the educational advantages offered our interns and nurses as well as the added standing it will give the hospital." Moton agreed to allow the school's employees to examine the men in the study at Tuskegee's Andrew Hospital. Apparently, he believed that federal attention to the poor health conditions in the county would help the school get more funding for programs.[22]

Black educators and doctors at Tuskegee envisioned future financial benefits from cooperating with the federal government in the study. Such a belief grew out of Tuskegee's long history of lobbying the federal government for funding and assistance. Since the days of Booker T. Washington, black leaders at Tuskegee had witnessed evidence of at least limited government cooperation. For example, Washington and, later, Moton garnered government support for the Movable School and the National Negro Health Movement and succeeded in getting a black veterans' hospital located at Tuskegee, despite the absence of a black medical school.[23]

The experiment, officially known as "the Tuskegee Study of Untreated Syphilis in the Negro Male," was not a government secret, kept hidden from health professionals. It lasted for forty years and was publicized widely in the black and white medical community without evoking any protest. In the mid-1930s Dr. Roscoe C. Brown, the black leader of the Office of Negro Health Work at the USPHS, convinced the National Medical Association (the black medical organization) to display an exhibit on the study provided by the USPHS. Dr. Brown argued that it "would be an excellent opportunity for the use of this timely exhibit on one of our major health problems." Members of the black medical establishment knew the subjects of the experiment were poor black men, but they did not see this as problematic. Not until 1973, after a journalist broke the story to general public, did the black medical establishment denounce the study as morally, ethically, and scientifically unjustified. By then, a modern black civil rights movement and a popular health movement critical of medicine resulted in an atmosphere of changed consciousness about rights and responsibilities.[24]

Why did black health professionals, including Rivers, not challenge the study? Dr. Paul B. Cornely of Howard University, a black public health leader since the 1930s, remembered with regret that he knew about the experiment from the beginning. He understood the nature of the study and had followed it all along, never questioning it. He explained in retrospect: "I was there and I didn't say a word. I saw it as an academician. It shows you how we look at human beings, especially blacks who were expendable." Cornely taught about the study in his classes at the Medical School of Howard University, a black college in Washington, D.C., yet no student ever raised a challenge to what he now sees as its racist premise. Dr. Cornley asked himself why he did not see the full ramifications of the projects. "I have guilt feelings about it, as I view it now," he explained, "because I considered myself to be an activist. I used to get hot and bothered about injustice and inequity, yet here right under my nose something is happening and I'm blind."[25]

No doubt a number of factors contributed to the response of black professionals, including class consciousness, professional status, and racial subordination. Historian Tom W. Shick argued that the black medical profession did not challenge the experiment because "black physicians were clearly subordinates, never co-equals, within the medical profession." Furthermore, he believed that the process of professionalization in medicine led them to defend the status quo. James Jones stated that class consciousness permitted black professionals to deny the racism of the experiment.[26]

Although subordinate status no doubt constrained the response of black professionals, they did not protest the syphilis study because they did not view it as unjust. Indeed, black educators and health professionals supported the study because they saw it directing federal attention toward black health problems—a primary goal of the black public health movement. As far as they were concerned, this was a study that focused the objective gaze of science on the health conditions of African Americans. It was one more way to increase the visibility of black needs to the federal government. Rivers shared the viewpoint of black health professionals and assisted with the experiment in the belief that the study was itself a sign of government interest in black health problems.

Why, despite a history of well-founded suspicion of government, did black tenant farmers take part in the government study? Large numbers of poor African-American men and women came to the government clinics because of the impact of the Tuskegee Movable School and Rivers. The experiment began in October 1932 as Rivers assisted the USPHS in recruiting and testing rural black people in Macon County for syphilis so physicians could identify candidates for the study. Rivers was familiar with this work because she had assisted with the earlier syphilis treatment project sponsored by the Rosenwald Fund. Most likely her presence contributed to local interest in the clinics; Rivers and the government physicians were overwhelmed by the number of people who showed up at the sites to have their blood tested.[27]

Equal numbers of women and men appeared at the clinic sites, which proved to be a problem because the government doctors had decided to study only men. Dr. Joseph Earle Moore of Johns Hopkins University School of Medicine suggested the study focus on men because, he argued, women's symptoms of syphilis at the early stage were usually mild, and it was more difficult for physicians to examine internal organs.[28] Yet, as much as the doctors and Rivers tried to test only men, women showed up at the clinics, too. Attempts to segregate the men led to new problems. According to Dr. Vonderlehr, "In trying to get a larger number of men in the primary surveys during December we were accused in one community of examining prospective recruits for the Army."[29] Rivers reported that some of the women, especially the wives of the men selected for the study, were mad that they were not included because "they were sick too." Some even told her, "Nurse Rivers, you just partial to the men."[30]

Jones cited Charles Johnson's 1934 investigation of African Americans in Macon County, *Shadow of the Plantation*, as evidence that poor African Americans participated in the study because of their tradition of dependence and obedience to authority.[31] Yet, Jones's own work suggests that poor African Americans in fact questioned authority, including that of white physicians. For example, Jones described one man who criticized the way a government doctor drew blood samples and recounted how "he lay our arm down like he guttin' a hog." The man reported: "I told him he hurt me. . . . He told me 'I'm the doctor.' I told him all right but this my arm."[32] Rivers remembered that sometimes the young white doctors would behave rudely toward the men and the men would ask her to intervene. A man told her once: "Mrs. Rivers, go in there and tell that white man to stop talking to us like that." So she went in and said: "Now, we don't talk to our patients like this. . . . They're human. You don't talk to them like that." The doctor even apologized.[33]

Rural African Americans cooperated not out of deference to white doctors but because they wanted medical attention and treatment for their ailments, and they had come to trust Nurse Rivers as someone who helped them. Even though the government doctors in the study changed over the years, Rivers provided the continuity. Without her assistance it is doubtful that the experiment would have been able to continue for so long with such cooperation from the subjects of the experiment. In addition, participating in the study gave these tenant farmers increased status as they gained an official association with both the prestigious Tuskegee Institute and the federal government, relationships typically unavailable to men of their class.

The men stayed with the study for forty years because they believed that they received something worthwhile. Rivers found that the men who joined the study "had all kinds of complaints" about what ailed them, and they continued with the study in order to get free treatments. However, the men joined under false pretenses because the health workers never informed the men that they had syphilis or that they would not receive treatment. Instead, the men were told they would be treated for "bad blood," a vague term that referred to a range of ailments, including general malaise. The men were not told that they could spread the disease to their sexual partners or that they were part of an experiment predicated on nontreatment of syphilis until death. What the USPHS provided was annual physical examinations, aspirin, free hot meals on the day the government physician's visited, and financial support for burial expenses. In a rural community where there was almost no formal health care available, and if poor black people could locate it they could not afford it, the study did provide certain types of limited benefits that convinced the men to stay with the study.[34]

As for Rivers, what motivated her to work for the experiment for so many years? Historians have argued that Rivers participated because, first, she could not have understood the full ramifications of the study, and second, as a black female nurse she was in no position to challenge the authority of white male physicians.[35] Evidence suggests, however, that Rivers had sufficient knowledge of the study to know that the men were systematically denied treatment. Rivers was one of the authors, listed first, of a follow-up paper about the study published in 1953 in *Public Health Reports*. However, even if Rivers herself did not write the report, which read like a tribute to her role in the study, her actions made clear that she was well aware of the terms of the experiment. After all, she was one of the people who helped to implement the policy, designed by the leaders of the USPHS, to prohibit the subjects of the study from receiving treatments for syphilis from anyone else. This meant denying the treatment available during the 1930s, even if it was highly toxic mercury ointment and a long series of painful salvarsan injections, after World War II when penicillin became available. At the same time that Rivers assisted with the treatment of syphilis in other public health programs, she helped carry out the experiment's plan to bar the men in the study from treatment.[36]

Finally, based upon how Rivers operated as a nurse, suggestions that she merely deferred to authority are not convincing. She no doubt knew how to tailor her comments and behavior to a given situation to preserve her position and dignity. However, despite the racial, gender, and medical hierarchies under which she operated, she saw herself as an advocate for her patients and acted accordingly. She did not hesitate to intervene on their behalf, even consulting one doctor when she questioned the procedures of another.

If ignorance and deference do not explain her behavior, what does? Her need for employment and the prestige of working for the federal government certainly contributed to her participation. She was proud of her work, and the federal government honored her for her assistance in the experiment. For example, in 1958 she received an award from the Department of Health, Education, and Welfare "for an outstanding contribution to health, through her participation in the long-term study of venereal disease control in Macon County, Alabama."[37]

Most importantly, Rivers considered her participation in the study merely a continuation of her previous public health work. Public health work as gendered to the extent that women, especially in their capacity as nurses, implemented health policy at the local level and had the most contact with people in the community. In Rivers's case, since the early 1920s her job had been to provide health education directly to people in the communities surrounding Tuskegee. Her duty as a nurse was to care for her clients, and she did. In her work with the experiment, she genuinely cared about the men with whom she worked. One of the government physicians even told her that she was too sympathetic with the men. As Rivers explained: "I was concerned about the patients 'cause I had to live here after he was gone." Indeed, she knew each man individually and, after he died, she attended the funeral service with the man's family."[38] In nominating Rivers for an award in 1972, Thelma P. Walker revealed that Rivers "has been my inspiration for entering public health. She made her own work so attractive because of her enthusiasm. . . . She inspired such confidence in her patients and they all seem so endeared to her." Walker discovered "how deeply loved she was by the men in her follow-up program. They felt that there just was no one like Mrs. Rivers."[39]

When the press exposed the study in 1972, it was confusing and heartbreaking for Rivers to hear the criticism after receiving so much praise. Rivers responded by defending her actions. "A lot of things that have been written have been unfair," she insisted. "A lot of things." First, Rivers argued that the effects of the experiment were benign. In her mind it was important that the study did not include people who had early syphilis because those with latent syphilis were potentially less infectious and would be less likely to transmit it to their sexual partners. As she explained, "syphilis had done its damage with most of the people."[40] Yet, as historian Allan Brandt noted, "every major textbook of syphilis at the time of the Tuskegee Study's inception strongly advocated treating syphilis even in its latent stages."[41] Furthermore, evidence suggests that not all of the men had latent syphilis, given that when men in the control group (about 200 black men without syphilis) developed syphilis, the physicians merely switched them over to the untreated syphilitic group.

Second, Rivers accounted for her participation by stating that the study had scientific merit. Even as she admitted, "I got with this syphilitic program that was sort of a hoodwink thing, I suppose," she offered justification. With great exaggeration, she depicted Macon County as "overrun with syphilis and gonorrhea. In fact, the rate of syphilis in the Negro was very, very high, something like eighty percent or something like this."[42] She recalled that the USPHS doctors planned to compare the results of the study with one in Norway on white people and that "the doctors themselves have said that the study has proven that syphilis did not affect the Negro as it did the white man."[43]

Finally, based on the available health care resources, Rivers believed that the benefits of the study to the men outweighed the risks. She knew the men received no treatment for syphilis, but she explained:

> Honestly, those people got all kinds of examinations and medical care that they never would have gotten. I've taken them over to the hospital and they'd have a GI series on them, the heart, the lung, just everything. It was just impossible for just an ordinary person to get that kind of examination.[44]

She continually asserted that the men received good medical care despite the fact that the men received mostly diagnostic, not curative, services. Yet she maintained:

> They'd get all kinds of extra things, cardiograms and . . . some of the things that I had never heard of. This is the thing that really hurt me about the unfair publicity. Those people had been given better care than some of us who could afford it.[45]

What bothered Rivers was not the plight of the men in the study but that of the women and men, who came to her begging to be included, even leading her occasionally to sneak in some additional men. As for the men in the experiment, Rivers concluded that they received more, not less, than those around them: "They didn't get treatment for syphilis, but they got so much else."[46]

Racism, extreme poverty, and health care deprivation in rural Alabama, where so little medical attention could mean so much, contributed to a situation in which white doctors from the federal government could carry out such an experiment. One of the legacies of the syphilis experiment is the reluctance of many African Americans to cooperate with government public health authorities in HIV/AIDS health education and prevention programs out of the fear of a genocidal plot.[47]

The Tuskegee Syphilis Study also relied on the assistance of black professionals. Nurse Eunice Rivers, as well as health workers and educators from Tuskegee Institute, Howard University, and the National Medical Association, never challenged the study because they believed that it was an acceptable way to gather knowledge. Rivers and other black professionals shared the dominant vision of scientific research and medical practice and did not consider issues of informed consent or the deadly consequences of such an experiment. Perhaps professionalization and class consciousness blinded them to the high price paid by the poor, rural black men in the study.[48]

Yet, ironically, black professionals saw this experiment as consistent with their efforts to improve black health. After public censure forced the halt of the experiment, Rivers declared her innocence in the face of criticism, not on the grounds that she was a victim who was uniformed about the true nature of the experiment but rather because she insisted that she had acted on her convictions. She emphasized:

> I don't have any regrets. You can't regret doing what you did when you knew you were doing right. I know from my personal feelings how I felt. I feel I did good in working with the people. I know I didn't mislead anyone.[49]

Rivers remained convinced that she had acted in the best interests of poor black people.

Black professionals faced a dilemma imposed by American racism in how best to provide adequate health services to the poor within a segregated system. Furthermore, the gendered nature of public health work meant that the nurse, invariably a woman, was at the center of public provisions, both good and bad. Thus, the role of Eunice Rivers has drawn particular attention. As her actions show most starkly, black professionals demonstrated both resistance to and complicity with the government and the white medical establishment as they attempted to advance black rights and improve black health. Rivers and other black professionals counted on the benefits of public health work to outweigh the costs to the poor. In the case of the Tuskegee Moveable School they were undoubtedly right, but as the Tuskegee Syphilis Experiment shows, there were dire consequences when they were wrong.

Notes

1. James H. Jones, *Bad Blood: The Tuskegee Syphilis Experiment* (New York: Free Press; 1981; expanded edition 1993), 91 (page numbers refer to the 1981 edition). See also Allan Brandt, "Racism and Research: The Case of the Tuskegee Syphilis Study," in *Sickness and Health in America: Readings in the History of Medicine and Public Health*, ed. Judith Walzer Leavitt and Ronald L. Numbers (Madison: University of Wisconsin Press, 1985), 331–343; Tom W. Shick, "Race, Class, and Medicine: 'Bad Blood' in Twentieth-Century America," *Journal of Ethnic Studies* 10 (Summer 1982): 97–105; and Todd L. Savitt, "The Use of Blacks for Medical Experimentation and Demonstration in the Old South," *Journal of Southern History* 48 (August 1982): 331–348.

2. Herbert M. Morais, *The History of the Negro in Medicine* (New York: Publishers Company for the Association for the Study of Negro Life and History, 1967), 100–101.

3. Eunice Rivers Laurie, interview by A. Lillian Thompson, 10 October 1977, in *The Black Women Oral History Project*, vol. 7. ed. Ruth Edmonds Hill (New Providence, N.J.: K. G. Saur Verlag, A Reed Reference Publishing Company, 1992), 213–242, from the Arthur and Elizabeth Schlesinger Library, Radcliffe College. See also Jones, *Bad Blood*, 6, 158; Brandt, "Racism and Research," 337; Darlene Clark Hine, *Black Women in White: Racial Conflict and Cooperation in the Nursing Profession*, 1890–1950 (Bloomington: (Indiana University Press, 1989), 154–156.

4. M. M. Hubert to Thomas Campbell, May 26, 1922, Box 101, Correspondence 1922, Record Group 33, U.S. Extension Service, National Archives, Washington, D.C.; B. D. Mayberry, "The Role of Tuskegee University in the Origin, Growth and Development of the Negro Extension Service," unpublished manuscript (1988), 111, author's possession; Thomas Monroe Campbell, *The Movable School Goes to the Negro Farmer* (Tuskegee Institute: Tuskegee Institute Press, 1936; reprint, New York: Arno Press and the New York Times, 1969), 145.

5. Monroe Work, "Racial Factors and Economic Forces in Land Tenure in the South," *Social Forces* 15 (December 1936): 214–215; Charles S. Johnson, *Shadow of the Plantation* (Chicago: University of Chicago Press, 1934), 7, 104, 109, 112, 128; Pete Daniel, *Standing at the Crossroads: Southern Life Since 1900* (New York: Hill and Wang, 1986), 7.

6. Dr. Hildrus A. Poindexter, "Special Health Problems of Negroes in Rural Areas," *Journal of Negro Education* 6 (July 1937): 400, 403, 412; U.S. Public Health Service "Report to Congress on the Extent and Circumstances of Cooperation by the Public Health Service with State and Local Authorities in the Drought Stricken Areas Under the Provisions of the Deficiency Act of February 6, 1931," March 1, 1931 to November 30, 1931, General Files, 1924–1935, Box 99, Record Group 90, United States Public Health Service (hereafter USPHS), National Archives, Washington, D.C.

7. Campbell, *The Movable School*, 118, 121, 126; Thomas Campbell, "Extension Work Among Negroes in the South," Correspondence 1935, Box 290, Record Group 33, U.S. Extension Service; *Rural Messenger* 1 (26 May 1920): 9; Thomas Campbell, Report of Movable School Work to Washington, D.C., August 1922, Box 6, Tuskegee Institute Extension Service Collection, Hollis Burke Frissell Library, Tuskegee University, Tuskegee, Ala.

8. Monroe N. Work, "The South's Labor Problem," *South Atlantic Quarterly* 19 (January 1920): 7–8 (located in finding aids folder, Monroe Nathan Work Papers, Hollis Burke Frissell Library, Tuskegee

University, Ala. See also Pete Daniel, *The Shadow of Slavery*: *Peonage in the South*, 1901–1969 (Urbana: University of Illinois Press, 1972, 1990); Daniel, Standing at the Crossroads, 54–58.

9. Stanley Rayfield, Marjory Stimson, and Louise M. Tattershall, "A Study of Negro Public Health Nursing," *Public Health Nurse* 22 (October 1930): 525; Karen Buhler-Wilkerson, "False Dawn: The Rise and Decline of Public Health Nursing in America, 1900–1930," in *Nursing History: New Perspectives, New Possibilities*, ed. Ellen Condliffe Lagemann (New York: Teachers College Press, 1983), 89–106; Barbara Melosh, "*The Physician's Hand*": *Work, Culture and Conflict in American Nursing* (Philadelphia: Temple University Press, 1982), chapter 4; Hine, *Black Women in White,* Introduction.

10. Uva M. Hester's report for her work in Montgomery County for the week of June 19, 1920 is reprinted in Campbell, *The Movable School*, 113–115, especially 113.

11. Eunice Rivers Laurie interview, *The Black Women Oral History Project*, 220, 224; see also 216–219. See also Henry Howard, Report of Movable School, 1923, Extension Agents Reports, Alabama, microfilm reel 11, p. 2, Record Group 33, U.S. Extension Service; Jones, *Bad Blood*, 109–110; Hine, *Black Women in White*, 134, 154; Susan M. Reverby, "Laurie, Eunice Rivers (1899–1986)," in *Black Women in America: An Historical Encyclopedia*, ed. Darlene Clark Hine (New York: Carlson Publishing, 1993), 699–701.

12. Eunice Rivers, "Health Work with a Movable School," *Public Health Nurse* 18 (November 1926): 575–577; Eunice Rivers, reports on her Movable School work, monthly reports for 1924, Box 6, Tuskegee Institute Extension Service Collection; Eunice Rivers Laurie, interview, *The Black Women Oral History Project*, 228; Jones, *Bad Blood*, 110; Hine, *Black Women in White*, 154.

13. *Proceedings of Session on Negro Social Work at the Alabama Conference of Social Work*, Birmingham, April 9, 1929, Box 1, Work Papers, p. 15; T. J. Woofter, "Organization of Rural Negroes for Public Health Work," *National Conference of Social Work Proceedings*, fiftieth session (1923): 72.

14. J. D. Barnes, "Serving the Community," printed in *Southern Letter* 45 (March–April 1929): 2.

15. Eunice Rivers Laurie, interview, *The Black Women Oral History Project*, 234.

16. *Ibid.*, 230

17. Rivers, quoted in Jones, *Bad Blood*, 111.

18. *Annual Report of the Surgeon General of the Public Health Service of the United States for the fiscal year 1918* [hereafter *Annual Report of the USPHS*] (Washington, D.C.: U.S. Government Printing Office, 1918), 97; *Annual Report of the USPHS* (1919), 281, 297; Allan M. Brandt, *No Magic Bullet: A Social History of Venereal Disease in the United States Since 1880* (New York: Oxford University Press, 1987), 56, 77.

19. Paul Carley and O. C. Wenger, "The Prevalence of Syphilis in Apparently Healthy Negroes in Mississippi," *Journal of the American Medical Association*, June 7, 1930, Box 356, Record Group 51, Mississippi Department of health, Mississippi Department of Archives and History, Jackson, Miss.; *Annual Report of the USPHS* (1929), 273; "Recent Progress in the Program of the Julius Rosenwald Fund in Negro Health" [1938?], p. 9, Central File 1937–1940, Box 599, Record Group 102, Children's Bureau, National Archives, Washington, D.C.; Jones, *Bad Blood*, 54, 59–60.

20. Louis T. Wright, "Factors Controlling Negro Health," *Crisis* 42 (September 1935): 264. See also Jones, *Bad Blood*, 23; Brandt, *No Magic Bullet*, 157–158; Brandt, "Racism and Research," 332; Elizabeth Fee, "Sin vs. Science: Venereal Disease in Baltimore in the Twentieth Century," *Journal of the History of Medicine and Allied Sciences* 43 (April 1988): 141–164.

21. Report to the Public Health Service by Dr. Vonderlehr, July 10, 1933, Division of Venereal Diseases, general records 1918–1936, Box 182, Record Group 90, USPHS; Jones, *Bad Blood*, 27, 88, 92–95, 167. See also Brandt, *No Magic Bullet*, 40; Brandt, "Racism and Research," 333–334. My thanks to Vanessa Northington Gamble for clarifying the ways in which the Oslo study differed from the Tuskegee Syphilis study.

22. Robert Moton to Hugh Cumming, October 10, 1932, general correspondence, Box 180, Robert Russa Moton Papers; Eugene Dibble to Robert Moton, September 17, 1932, general correspondence, box 180, Moton Papers; Jones, *Bad Blood*, 74, 76.

23. Pete Daniel, "Black Power in the 1920s: The Case of Tuskegee Veterans Hospital," *Journal of Southern History* 36 (August 1970): 368–388; Vanessa Northington Gamble, "The Negro Hospital Renaissance: The Black Hospital Movement, 1920–1945," in *The American General Hospital: Communities and Social Contexts*, ed. Diana E. Long and Janet Golden (Ithaca: Cornell University Press, 1989), 101–2.

24. Roscoe C. Brown to W. Harry Barnes, president of the National Medical Association, May 27, 1936, and Roscoe C. Brown to Assistant Surgeon General Robert Olesen, September 2, 1936, Group IX, general records 1936–1944, Box 195, Record Group 90, USPHS; "Final Report of the National Medical Association Tuskegee Syphilis Study Ad Hoc Committee," August 1, 1973, p. 13, Moorland-Spingarn Research Center, Howard University, Washington, D.C.; Jones, *Bad Blood*, 7; Brandt, *No Magic Bullet*, 158.

25. Dr. Paul B. Cornely, interview by the author, tape recording, Howard University, Washington, D.C., July 24, 1989.

26. Shick, "Race, Class and Medicine," 104–105; Jones, *Bad Blood*, 167–168.

27. Eugene Dibble to Monroe Work, September 9, 1933, general correspondence, Box 180, Moton Papers; *Annual Report of tthe USPHS* (1933), 96–97; Jones, *Bad Blood*, 68–69, 111, 114; Brandt, "Racism and Research," 335.

28. Jones, *Bad Blood*, 104.

29. Vonderlehr, quoted in Jones, *Bad Blood*, 120.

30. Eunice Rivers, quoted in Jones, *Bad Blood*, 165.

31. Jones, *Bad Blood*, 68.

32. Quoted in Jones, *Bad Blood*, 80.

33. Eunice Rivers Laurie, interview, *The Black Women Oral History Project*, 232.

34. Eunice Rivers, Stanley H. Schuman, Lloyd Simpson, and Sidney Olansky, "Twenty Years of Follow-up Experience In a Long-Range Medical Study," *Public Health Reports* 68 (April 1953): 393; Jones, *Bad Blood*, 6, 69, 71, 72, 114; Brandt, "Racism and Research," 335, 339; Hine, *Black Women in White*, 155–156.

35. Jones, *Bad Blood*, 163–164, 166, Brandt, "Racism and Research," 337 (note at bottom of page).

36. Eunice Rivers *et al.*, "Twenty Years of Follow-up," 391–395; Catherine Corley, Department of Public Health, Alabama, to Eunice Rivers Laurie, Macon County Health Department, May 26, 1953, Eunice Rivers Laurie folder, Biographical files, Hollis Burke Frissell Library, Tuskegee University, Tuskegee, Ala.; Jones, *Bad Blood*, 7, 46, 161–162, 178.

37. Eunice Rivers Laurie, interview, *The Black Women Oral History Project*, 237; Jones, *Bad Blood*, 169.

38. Jones, *Bad Blood*, 128, 155, 160–161.

39. Thelma P. Walker, nomination letter for Eunice Rivers Laurie, January 11, 1972, Eunice Rivers Laurie folder, Biographical Files.

40. Eunice Rivers Laurie, interview, *The Black Women Oral History Project*, 231. See also Jones, *Bad Blood*, 107.

41. Brandt, "Racism and Research," 333.

42. Eunice Rivers Laurie, interview, *The Black Women Oral History Project*, 229–230.

43. Eunice Rivers Laurie, interview, *The Black Women Oral History Project*, 232; see also 230–232; Jones, *Bad Blood*, 167.

44. Eunice Rivers Laurie, interview, *The Black Women Oral History Project*, 231.

45. Eunice Rivers Laurie, interview, *The Black Women Oral History Project*, 232.

46. Jones, *Bad Blood*, 164–165. Darlene Clark Hine found the explanations of James Jones "compelling" but suggested the possibility that Rivers "viewed the study as a way of ensuring for at least some blacks an unparalleled amount of medical attention." Hine, *Black Women in White*, 156.

47. Stephen B. Thomas and Sandra Crouse Quinn, "The Tuskegee Syphilis Study, 1932 to 1972; Implications for HIV Education and AIDS Risk Education Programs in the Black Community," *American Journal of Public Health* 81 (November 1991): 1498–1505.

48. Jones, *Bad Blood*, 97, 188–189; Jay Katz, *The Silent World of Doctor and Patient* (New York: The Free Press, 1984), xvi, 1–4, David J. Rothman, *Strangers at the Bedside* (New York: Basic Books, 1991), 10, 47–48, 90, 247.

49. *Jet* [1973?], Eunice Rivers Laurie folder, Biographical Files.

Reading 21

Letter from Birmingham Jail

Martin Luther King, Jr.

April 16, 1963
My Dear Fellow Clergymen:

While confined here in the Birmingham city jail, I came across your recent statement calling my present activities "unwise and untimely." Seldom do I pause to answer criticism of my work and ideas. If I sought to answer all the criticisms that cross my desk, my secretaries would have little time for anything other than such correspondence in the course of the day, and I would have no time for constructive work. But since I feel that you are men of genuine good will and that your criticisms are sincerely set forth, I want to try to answer your statement in what I hope will be patient and reasonable terms.

I think I should indicate why I am here in Birmingham, since you have been influenced by the view which argues against "outsiders coming in." I have the honor of serving as president of the Southern Christian Leadership Conference, an organization operating in every southern state, with headquarters in Atlanta, Georgia. We have some eighty-five affiliated organizations across the South, and one of them is the Alabama Christian Movement for Human Rights. Frequently we share staff, educational and financial resources with our affiliates. Several months ago the affiliate here in Birmingham asked us to be on call to engage in a nonviolent direct-action program if such were deemed necessary. We readily consented, and when the hour came we lived up to our promise. So I, along with several members of my staff, am here because I was invited here. I am here because I have organizational ties here.

But more basically, I am in Birmingham because injustice is here. Just as the prophets of the eighth century B.C. left their villages and carried their "thus saith the Lord" far beyond the boundaries of their home towns, and just as the Apostle Paul left his village of Tarsus and carried the gospel of Jesus Christ to the far corners of the Greco-Roman world, so am I compelled to carry the gospel of freedom beyond my own home town. Like Paul, I must constantly respond to the Macedonian call for aid.

Moreover, I am cognizant of the interrelatedness of all communities and states. I cannot sit idly by in Atlanta and not be concerned about what happens in Birmingham. Injustice anywhere is a threat to justice everywhere. We are caught in an inescapable network of mutuality, tied in a single garment of destiny. Whatever affects one directly, affects all indirectly. Never again can we afford to live with the narrow, provincial "outside agitator" idea. Anyone who lives inside the United States can never be considered an outsider anywhere within its bounds.

You deplore the demonstrations taking place in Birmingham. But your statement, I am sorry to say, fails to express a similar concern for the conditions that brought about the demonstrations. I am sure that none of you would want to rest content with the superficial kind of social analysis that deals merely with effects and does not grapple with underlying causes. It is unfortunate that demonstrations are taking place in Birmingham, but it is even more unfortunate that the city's white power structure left the Negro community with no alternative.

In any nonviolent campaign there are four basic steps: collection of the facts to determine whether injustices exist; negotiation; self-purification; and direct action. We have gone through all these steps in Birmingham. There can be no gainsaying the fact that racial injustice engulfs this community. Birmingham is probably the most thoroughly segregated city in the United States. Its ugly record of brutality is widely known. Negroes have experienced grossly unjust treatment in the courts. There have been more unsolved bombings of Negro homes and churches in Birmingham than in any other city in the nation. These are the hard, brutal facts of the case. On the basis of these conditions, Negro leaders sought to negotiate with the city fathers. But the latter consistently refused to engage in good-faith negotiation.

Then, last September, came the opportunity to talk with leaders of Birmingham's economic community. In the course of the negotiations, certain promises were made by the merchants—for example, to remove the stores' humiliating racial signs. On the basis of these promises, the Reverend Fred Shuttlesworth and the leaders of the Alabama Christian Movement for Human Rights agreed to a moratorium on all demonstrations. As the weeks and months went by, we realized that we were the victims of a broken promise. A few signs, briefly removed, returned; the others remained.

As in so many past experiences, our hopes had been blasted, and the shadow of deep disappointment settled upon us. We had no alternative except to prepare for direct action, whereby we would present our very bodies as a means of laying our case before the conscience of the local and the national community. Mindful of the difficulties involved, we decided to undertake a process of self-purification. We began a series of workshops on nonviolence, and we repeatedly asked ourselves: "Are you able to accept blows without retaliating?" "Are you able to endure the ordeal of jail?" We decided to schedule our direct-action program for the Easter season, realizing that except for Christmas, this is the main shopping period of the year. Knowing that a strong economic withdrawal program would be the by-product of direct action, we felt that this would be the best time to bring pressure to bear on the merchants for the needed change.

Then it occurred to us that Birmingham's mayoralty election was coming up in March, and we speedily decided to postpone action until after election day. When we discovered that the Commissioner of Public Safety, Eugene "Bull" Connor, had piled up enough votes to be in the run-off, we decided again to postpone action until the day of the run-off so that the demonstrations could not be used to cloud the issues. Like many others, we waited to see Mr. Connor defeated, and to this end we endured postponement after postponement. Having aided in this community need, we felt that our direct-action program could be delayed no longer.

You may well ask: "Why direct action? Why sit-ins, marches and so forth? Isn't negotiation a better path?" You are quite right in calling for negotiation. Indeed this is the very purpose of direct action. Nonviolent direct action seeks to create such a crisis and foster such a tension that a community which has constantly refused to negotiate is forced to confront the issue. It seeks so to dramatize the issue that it can no longer be ignored. My citing the creation of tension as part of the work of the nonviolent-resister may sound rather shocking. But I must confess that I am not afraid of the word "tension." I have earnestly opposed violent tension, but there is a type of constructive, nonviolent tension which is necessary for growth. Just as Socrates felt that it was necessary to create a tension in the mind so that individuals could rise from the bondage of myths and half-truths to the unfettered realm of creative analysis and objective appraisal, so must we see the need for non-violent gadflies to create the kind of tension in society that will help men rise from the dark depths of prejudice and racism to the majestic heights of understanding and brotherhood.

The purpose of our direct-action program is to create a situation so crisis-packed that it will inevitably open the door to negotiation. I therefore concur with you in your call for negotiation. Too long has our beloved Southland been bogged down in a tragic effort to live in monologue rather than dialogue.

One of the basic points in your statement is that the action that I and my associates have taken in Birmingham is untimely. Some have asked: "Why didn't you give the new city administration time to act?" The only answer that I can give to this query is that the new Birmingham administration must be prodded about as much as the outgoing one, before it will act. We are sadly mistaken if we feel that the election of Albert Boutwell as mayor will bring the millennium to Birmingham. While Mr. Boutwell is a much more gentle person than Mr. Connor, they are both segregationists, dedicated to maintenance of the status quo. I have hope that Mr. Boutwell will be reasonable enough to see the futility of massive resistance to desegregation. But he will not see this without pressure from devotees of civil rights. My friends, I must say to you that we have not made a single gain in civil rights without determined legal and nonviolent pressure. Lamentably, it is an historical fact that privileged groups seldom give up their privileges voluntarily. Individuals may see the moral light and voluntarily give up their unjust posture; but, as Reinhold Niebuhr has reminded us, groups tend to be more immoral than individuals.

We know through painful experience that freedom is never voluntarily given by the oppressor; it must be demanded by the oppressed. Frankly, I have yet to engage in a direct-action campaign that was "well timed" in the view of those who have not suffered unduly from the disease of segregation. For years now I have heard the word "Wait!" It rings in the ear of every Negro with piercing familiarity. This "Wait!" has almost always meant "Never." We must come to see, with one of our distinguished jurists, that "justice too long delayed is justice denied."

We have waited for more than 340 years for our constitutional and God-given rights. The nations of Asia and Africa are moving with jet-like speed toward gaining political independence, but we still creep at horse-and-buggy pace toward gaining a cup of coffee at a lunch counter. Perhaps it is easy for those who have never felt the stinging darts of segregation to say, "Wait." But when you have seen vicious mobs lynch your mothers and fathers at will and drown your sisters and brothers at whim; when you have seen hate-filled policemen curse, kick and even kill your black brothers and sisters; when you see the vast majority of your twenty million Negro brothers smothering in an air-tight cage of poverty in the midst of an affluent society; when you suddenly find your tongue twisted and your speech stammering as you seek to explain to your six-year-old daughter why she can't go to the public amusement park that has just been advertised on television, and see tears welling up in her eyes when she is told that Funtown is closed to colored children, and see ominous clouds of inferiority beginning to form in her little mental sky, and see her beginning to distort her personality by developing an unconscious bitterness toward white people; when you have to concoct an answer for a five-year-old son who is asking: "Daddy, why do white people treat colored people so mean?"; when you take a cross-country drive and find it necessary to sleep night after night in the uncomfortable corners of your automobile because no motel will accept you; when you are humiliated day in and day out by nagging signs reading "white" and "colored"; when your first name becomes "nigger," your middle name becomes "boy" (however old you are) and your last name becomes "John," and your wife and mother are never given the respected title "Mrs."; when you are harried by day and haunted by night by the fact that you are a Negro, living constantly at tiptoe stance, never quite knowing what to expect next, and are plagued with inner fears and outer resentments; when you are forever fighting a degenerating sense of "nobodiness"—then you will understand why we find it difficult to wait. There comes a time when the cup of endurance runs over, and men are no longer willing to be plunged into the abyss of despair. I hope, sirs, you can understand our legitimate and unavoidable impatience.

You express a great deal of anxiety over our willingness to break laws. This is certainly a legitimate concern. Since we do diligently urge people to obey the Supreme Court's decision of 1954 outlawing segregation in the public schools, at first glance it may seem rather paradoxical for us consciously to break laws. One may well ask: "How can you advocate breaking some laws and obeying others?" The answer lies in the fact that there are two types of laws: just and unjust. I would be the first to advocate obeying just laws. One has not only a legal but a moral responsibility to obey just laws. I would agree with St. Augustine that "an unjust law is no law at all."

Now, what is the difference between the two? How does one determine whether a law is just or unjust? A just law is a man-made code that squares with the moral law or the law of God. An unjust law is a code that is out of harmony with the moral law. To put it in the terms of St. Thomas Aquinas: An unjust law is a human law that is not rooted in eternal law and natural law. Any law that uplifts human personality is just. Any law that degrades human personality is unjust. All segregation statutes are unjust because segregation distorts the soul and damages the personality. It gives the segregator a false sense of superiority and the segregated a false sense of inferiority. Segregation, to use the terminology of the Jewish philosopher Martin Buber, substitutes an "I-it" relationship for an "I-thou" relationship and ends up relegating persons to the status of things. Hence segregation is not only politically, economically and sociologically unsound, it is morally wrong and sinful. Paul Tillich has said that sin is separation. Is not segregation an existential expression of man's tragic separation, his awful estrangement, his terrible sinfulness? Thus it is that I can urge men to obey the 1954 decision of the Supreme Court, for it is morally right; and I can urge them to disobey segregation ordinances, for they are morally wrong.

Let us consider a more concrete example of just and unjust laws. An unjust law is a code that a numerical or power majority group compels a minority group to obey but does not make binding on itself. This is *difference* made legal. By the same token, a just law is a code that a majority compels a minority to follow and that it is willing to follow itself. This is *sameness* made legal.

Let me give another explanation. A law is unjust if it is inflicted on a minority that, as a result of being denied the right to vote, had no part in enacting or devising the law. Who can say that the legislature of Alabama which set up that state's segregation laws was democratically elected? Throughout Alabama all sorts of devious methods are used to prevent Negroes from becoming registered voters, and there are some counties in which, even though Negroes constitute a majority of the population, not a single Negro is registered. Can any law enacted under such circumstances be considered democratically structured?

Sometimes a law is just on its face and unjust in its application. For instance, I have been arrested on a charge of parading without a permit. Now, there is nothing wrong in having an ordinance which requires a permit for a parade. But such an ordinance becomes unjust when it is used to maintain segregation and to deny citizens the First Amendment privilege of peaceful assembly and protest.

I hope you are able to see the distinction I am trying to point out. In no sense do I advocate evading or defying the law, as would the rabid segregationist. That would lead to anarchy. One who breaks an unjust law must do so openly, lovingly, and with a willingness to accept the penalty. I submit that an individual who breaks a law that conscience tells him is unjust, and who willingly accepts the penalty of imprisonment in order to arouse the conscience of the community over its injustice, is in reality expressing the highest respect for law.

Of course, there is nothing new about this kind of civil disobedience. It was evidenced sublimely in the refusal of Shadrach, Meshach and Abednego to obey the laws of Nebuchadnezzar, on the ground that a higher moral law was at stake. It was practiced superbly by the early Christians, who were willing to face hungry lions and the excruciating pain of chopping blocks rather than submit to certain unjust laws of the Roman Empire. To a degree, academic freedom is a reality today because Socrates practiced civil disobedience. In our own nation, the Boston Tea Party represented a massive act of civil disobedience.

We should never forget that everything Adolf Hitler did in Germany was "legal" and everything the Hungarian freedom fighters did in Hungary was "illegal." It was "illegal" to aid and comfort a Jew in Hitler's Germany. Even so, I am sure that, had I lived in Germany at the time, I would have aided and comforted my Jewish brothers. If today I lived in a Communist country where certain principles dear to the Christian faith are suppressed, I would openly advocate disobeying that country's antireligious laws.

I must make two honest confessions to you, my Christian and Jewish brothers. First, I must confess that over the past few years I have been gravely disappointed with the white moderate. I have almost reached the regrettable conclusion that the Negro's great stumbling block in his stride toward freedom is not the White Citizen's Councilor or the Ku Klux Klanner, but the white moderate, who is more devoted to "order" than to justice; who prefers a negative peace which is the absence of tension to a positive peace which is the presence of justice; who constantly says: "I agree with you in the goal you seek, but I cannot agree with your methods of direct action"; who paternalistically believes he can set the timetable for another man's freedom; who lives by a mythical concept of time and who constantly advises the Negro to wait for a "more convenient season." Shallow understanding from people of good will is more frustrating than absolute misunderstanding from people of ill will. Lukewarm acceptance is much more bewildering than outright rejection.

I had hoped that the white moderate would understand that law and order exist for the purpose of establishing justice and that when they fail in this purpose they become the dangerously structured dams that block the flow of social progress. I had hoped that the white moderate would understand that the present tension in the south is a necessary phase of the transition from an obnoxious negative peace, in which the Negro passively accepted his unjust plight, to a substantive and positive peace, in which all men will respect the dignity and worth of human personality. Actually, we who engage in nonviolent direct action are not the creators of tension. We merely bring to the surface the hidden tension that is already alive. We bring it out in the open, where it can be seen and dealt with. Like a boil that can never be cured so long as it is covered up but must be opened with all its ugliness to the natural medicines of air and light, injustice must be exposed, with all the tension its exposure creates, to the light of human conscience and the air of national opinion before it can be cured.

In your statement you assert that our actions, even though peaceful, must be condemned because they precipitate violence. But is this a logical assertion? Isn't this like condemning a robbed man because his possession of money precipitated the evil act of robbery? Isn't this like condemning Socrates because his unswerving commitment to truth and his philosophical inquiries precipitated the act by the misguided populace in which they made him drink hemlock? Isn't this like condemning Jesus because his unique God-consciousness and never-ceasing devotion to God's will precipitated the evil act of crucifixion? We must come to see that, as the federal courts have consistently affirmed, it is wrong to urge an individual to cease his efforts to gain his basic constitutional rights because the quest may precipitate violence. Society must protect the robbed and punish the robber.

I had also hoped that the white moderate would reject the myth concerning time in relation to the struggle for freedom. I have just received a letter from a white brother in Texas. He writes: "All Christians know that the colored people will receive equal rights eventually, but it is possible that you are in too great a religious hurry. It has taken Christianity almost two thousand years to accomplish what it has. The teachings of Christ take time to come to earth." Such an attitude stems from a tragic misconception of time, from the strangely irrational notion that there is something in the very flow of time that will inevitably cure all ills. Actually, time itself is neutral; it can be used either destructively or constructively. More and more I feel that the people of ill will have used time much more effectively than have the people of good will. We will have to repent in this generation not merely for the hateful words and actions of the bad people but for the appalling silence of the good people. Human progress never rolls in on wheels of inevitability; it comes through the tireless efforts of men willing to be co-workers with God, and without this hard work, time itself becomes an ally of the forces of social stagnation. We must use time creatively, in the knowledge that the time is always ripe to do right. Now is the time to make real the promise of democracy and transform our pending national elegy into a creative psalm of brotherhood. Now is the time to lift our national policy from the quicksand of racial injustice to the solid rock of human dignity.

You speak of our activity in Birmingham as extreme. At first I was rather disappointed that fellow clergymen would see my nonviolent efforts as those of an extremist. I began thinking about the fact that I stand in the middle of two opposing forces in the Negro community. One is a force of complacency, made up in part of Negroes who, as a result of long years of oppression, are so drained of self-respect and a sense of "somebodiness" that they have adjusted to segregation; and in part of a few middle-class Negroes who because of a degree of academic and economic security and because in some ways they profit by segregation, have become insensitive to the problems of the masses. The other force is one of bitterness and hatred, and it comes perilously close to advocating violence. It is expressed in the various black nationalist groups that are springing up across the nation, the largest and best-known being Elijah Muhammad's Muslim movement. Nourished by the Negro's frustration over the continued existence of racial discrimination, this movement is made up of people who have lost faith in America, who have absolutely repudiated Christianity, and who have concluded that the white is an incorrigible "devil."

I have tried to stand between these two forces, saying that we need emulate neither the "do-nothingism" of the complacent nor the hatred and despair of the black nationalist. For there is the more excellent way of love and nonviolent protest. I am grateful to God that, through the influence of the Negro church, the way of nonviolence became an integral part of our struggle.

If this philosophy had not emerged, by now many streets of the South would, I am convinced, be flowing with blood. And I am further convinced that if our white brothers dismiss as "rabble-rousers" and "outside agitators" those of us who employ nonviolent direct action, and if they refuse to support our nonviolent efforts, millions of Negroes will, out of frustration and despair, seek solace and security in black-nationalist ideologies—a development that would inevitably lead to a frightening racial nightmare.

Oppressed people cannot remain oppressed forever. The yearning for freedom eventually manifests itself, and that is what has happened to the American Negro. Something within has reminded him of his birthright of freedom, and something without has reminded him that it can be gained. Consciously or unconsciously, he has been caught up by the *Zeitgeist*, and with his black brother of Africa and his brown and yellow brothers of Asia, South America and the Caribbean, the United States Negro is moving with a sense of great urgency toward the promised land of racial justice. If one recognized this vital urge that has engulfed the Negro community, one should readily understand why public demonstrations are taking place. The Negro has many pent-up resentments and latent frustrations, and he must release them. So let him march; let him make prayer pilgrimages to the city hall; let him go on freedom rides—and try to understand why he must do so. If his repressed emotions are not released in nonviolent ways, they will seek expression through violence; this not a threat but a fact of history. So I have not said to my people: "Get rid of your discontent." Rather, I have tried to say that this normal and healthy discontent can be channeled into the creative outlet of nonviolent direct action. And now this approach is being termed extremist.

But though I was initially disappointed at being categorized as an extremist, as I continued to think about the matter I gradually gained a measure of satisfaction from the label. Was not Jesus an extremist for love: "Love your enemies, bless them that curse you, do good to them that hate you, and pray for them which despitefully use you, and persecute you." Was not Amos an extremist for justice: "Let justice roll down like waters and righteousness like an ever-flowing stream." Was not Paul an extremist for the Christian gospel: "I bear in my body the marks of the Lord Jesus." Was not Martin Luther an extremist: "Here I stand; I cannot do otherwise, so help me God." And John Bunyan: "I will stay in jail to the end of my days before I make a butchery of my conscience." And Abraham Lincoln: "This nation cannot survive half slave and half free." And Thomas Jefferson: "We hold these truths to be self-evident, that all men are created equal. . . ." So the question is not whether we will be extremists, but what kind of extremists we will be. Will we be extremists for hate or love? Will we be extremists for the preservation of injustice or for the extension of justice? In that dramatic scene on Calvary's hill three men were crucified. We must never forget that all three were crucified for the same crime—the crime of extremism. Two were extremists for immorality, and thus fell below their environment. The other, Jesus Christ, was an extremist for love, truth and goodness, and thereby rose above his environment. Perhaps the South, the nation and the world are in dire need of creative extremists.

I had hoped that the white moderate would see this need. Perhaps I was too optimistic; perhaps I expected too much. I suppose I should have realized that few members of the oppressor race can understand the deep groans and passionate yearnings of the oppressed race, and still fewer have the vision to see that injustice must be rooted out by strong, persistent and determined action. I am thankful, however, that some of our white brothers in the South have grasped the meaning of this Social revolution and committed themselves to it. They are still all too few in quantity, but they are big in quality. Some, such as Ralph McGill, Lillian Smith, Harry Golden, James McBride Dabbs, Ann Braden and Sarah Patton Boyle—have written about our struggle in eloquent and prophetic terms. Others have marched with us down nameless streets of the South. They have languished in filthy, roach-infested jails, suffering the abuse and brutality of policemen who view them as "dirty nigger-lovers." Unlike so many of their moderate brothers and sisters, they have recognized the urgency of the moment and sensed the need for powerful "action" antidotes to combat the disease of segregation.

Let me take note of my other major disappointment. I have been so greatly disappointed with the white church and its leadership. Of course, there are some notable exceptions. I am not unmindful of the fact that each of you has taken some significant stands on this issue. I commend you, Reverend Stallings, for your Christian stand on this past Sunday, in welcoming Negroes to your worship service on a nonsegregated basis. I commend the Catholic leaders of this state for integrating Spring Hill College several years ago.

But despite these notable exceptions, I must honestly reiterate that I have been disappointed with the church. I do not say this as one of those negative critics who can always find something wrong with the church. I say this as a minister of the gospel, who loves the church; who was nurtured in its bosom; who has been sustained by its spiritual blessings and who will remain true to it as long as the cord of life shall lengthen.

When I was suddenly catapulted into the leadership of the bus protest in Montgomery, Alabama, a few years ago, I felt we would be supported by the white church. I felt that the white ministers, priests and rabbis of the South would be among our strongest allies. Instead, some have been outright opponents, refusing to understand the freedom movement and misrepresenting its leaders; all too many others have been more cautious than courageous and have remained silent behind the anesthetizing security of stained-glass windows.

In spite of my shattered dreams, I came to Birmingham with the hope that the white religious leadership of this community would see the justice of our cause and, with deep moral concern, would serve as the channel through which our just grievances could reach the power structure. I had hoped that each of you would understand. But again I have been disappointed.

I have heard numerous southern religious leaders admonish their worshippers to comply with a desegregation decision because it is the law, but I have longed to hear white ministers declare:

"Follow this decree because integration is morally right and because the Negro is your brother." In the midst of blatant injustices inflicted upon the Negro, I have watched white churchmen stand on the sideline and mouth pious irrelevancies and sanctimonious trivialities. In the midst of a mighty struggle to rid our nation of racial and economic injustice, I have heard many ministers say: "Those are social issues, with which the gospel has no real concern." And I have watched many churches commit themselves to a completely other-worldly religion which makes a strange, un-Biblical distinction between body and soul, between the sacred and the secular.

I have traveled the length and breadth of Alabama, Mississippi and all the other southern states. On sweltering summer days and crisp autumn mornings I have looked at the South's beautiful churches with their lofty spires pointing heavenward. I have beheld the impressive outlines of her massive religious-education buildings. Over and over I have found myself asking: "What kind of people worship here? Who is their God? Where were their voices when the lips of Governor Barnett dripped with words of interposition and nullification? Where were they when Governor Wallace gave a clarion call for defiance and hatred? Where were their voices of support when bruised and weary Negro men and women decided to rise from the dark dungeons of complacency to the bright hills of creative protest?"

Yes, these questions are still in my mind. In deep disappointment I have wept over the laxity of the church. But be assured that my tears have been tests of love. There can be no deep disappointment where there is not deep love. Yes, I love the church. How could I do otherwise? I am in the rather unique position of being the son, the grandson and the great-grandson of preachers. Yes, I see the church as the body of Christ. But, oh! How we have blemished and scarred that body through social neglect and through fear of being nonconformists.

There was a time when the church was very powerful—in the time when the early Christians rejoiced at being deemed worthy to suffer for what they believed. In those days the church was not merely a thermometer that recorded the ideas and principles of popular opinion; it was a thermostat that transformed the mores of society. Whenever the early Christians entered a town, the people in power became disturbed and immediately sought to convict the Christians for being "disturbers of the peace" and "outside agitators." But the Christians pressed on, in the conviction that they were "a colony of heaven," called to obey God rather than man. Small in number, they were big in commitment. They were too God-intoxicated to be "astronomically intimidated." By their effort and example they brought an end to such ancient evils as infanticide and gladiatorial contests.

Things are different now. So often the contemporary church is a weak ineffectual voice with an uncertain sound. So often it is an archdefender of the status quo. Far from being disturbed by the presence of the church, the power structure of the average community is consoled by the church's silent—and often even vocal—sanction of things as they are.

But the judgment of God is upon the church as never before. If today's church does not recapture the sacrificial spirit of the early church, it will lose its authenticity, forfeit the loyalty of millions, and be dismissed as an irrelevant social club with no meaning for the twentieth century. Every day I meet young people whose disappointment with the church has turned into outright disgust.

Perhaps I have once again been too optimistic. Is organized religion too inextricably bound to the status quo to save our nation and world? Perhaps I must turn my faith to the inner spiritual church, the church within the church, as the true *ekklesia* and the hope of the world. But again I am thankful to God that some noble souls from the ranks of organized religion have broken loose from the paralyzing chains of conformity and joined us as active partners in the struggle for freedom. They have left their secure congregations and walked the streets of Albany, Georgia, with us. They have gone down the highways of the South on tortuous rides for freedom. Yes, they have gone to jail with us. Some have been dismissed from their churches, have lost the support of their bishops and fellow ministers. But they have acted in the faith that right defeated is stronger than evil triumphant. Their witness has been the spiritual salt that has preserved the true meaning of the gospel in these troubled times. They have carved a tunnel of hope through the dark mountain of disappointment.

I hope the church as a whole will meet the challenge of this decisive hour. But even if the church does not come to the aid of justice, I have no despair about the future. I have no fear about the outcome of our struggle in Birmingham, even if our motives are at present misunderstood. We will reach the goal of freedom in Birmingham and all over the nation, because the goal of America is freedom. Abused and scorned though we may be, our destiny is tied up with America's destiny. Before the pilgrims landed at Plymouth, we were here. Before the pen of Jefferson etched the majestic words of the Declaration of Independence across the pages of history, we were here. For more than two centuries our forebears labored in this country without wages; they made cotton king; they built the homes of their masters while suffering gross injustice and shameful humiliation—and yet out of a bottomless vitality they continued to thrive and develop. If the inexpressible cruelties of slavery could not stop us, the opposition we now face will surely fail. We will win our freedom because the sacred heritage of our nation and the eternal will of God are embodied in our echoing demands.

Before closing I feel impelled to mention one other point in your statement that has troubled me profoundly. You warmly commend the Birmingham police force for keeping "order" and "preventing violence." I doubt that you would have so warmly commended the police force if you had seen its dogs sinking their teeth into unarmed, non-violent Negroes. I doubt that you would so quickly commend the policemen if you were to observe their ugly and inhumane treatment of Negroes here in the city jail; if you were to watch them push and curse old Negro women and young Negro girls; if you were to see them slap and kick old Negro men and young boys; if you were to observe them, as they did on two occasions, refuse to give us food because we wanted to sing our grace together. I cannot join you in your praise of the Birmingham police department.

It is true that the police have exercised a degree of discipline in handling the demonstrators. In this sense they have conducted themselves rather "nonviolently" in public. But for what purpose? To preserve the evil system of segregation. Over the past few years I have consistently preached that nonviolence demands that the means we use must be as pure as the ends we seek. I have tried to make clear that it is wrong to use immoral means to attain moral ends. But now I must affirm that it is just as wrong, or perhaps even more so, to use moral means to preserve immoral ends. Perhaps Mr. Connor and his policemen have been rather nonviolent in public, as was Chief Pritchett in Albany, Georgia, but they have used the moral means of nonviolence to maintain the immoral end of racial injustice. As T. S. Eliot has said: "The last temptation is the greatest treason: To do the right deed for the wrong reason."

I wish you had commended the Negro sit-inners and demonstrators of Birmingham for their sublime courage, their willingness to suffer and their amazing discipline in the midst of great provocation. One day the South will recognize its real heroes. They will be the James Merediths, with the noble sense of purpose that enables them to face jeering and hostile mobs, and with the agonizing loneliness that characterizes the life of the pioneer. They will be old, oppressed, battered Negro women, symbolized in a seventy-two-year-old woman in Montgomery, Alabama, who rose up with a sense of dignity and with her people decided not to ride segregated buses, and who responded with ungrammatical profundity to one who inquired about her weariness: "My feets is tired, but my soul is at rest." They will be the young high school and college students, the young ministers of the gospel and a host of their elders, courageously and nonviolently sitting in at lunch counters and willingly going to jail for conscience's sake. One day the South will know that when these disinherited children of God sat down at lunch counters, they were in reality standing up for what is best in the American dream and for the most sacred values in our Judaeo-Christian heritage, thereby bringing our nation back to those great wells of democracy which were dug deep by the founding fathers in their formulation of the Constitution and the Declaration of Independence.

Never before have I written so long a letter. I'm afraid it is much too long to take your precious time. I can assure you that it would have been much shorter if I had been writing from a comfortable desk, but what else can one do when he is alone in a narrow jail cell, other than write long letters, think long thoughts and pray long prayers?

If I have said anything in this letter that overstates the truth and indicates an unreasonable impatience, I beg you to forgive me. If I have said anything that understates the truth and indicates my having a patience that allows me to settle for anything less than brotherhood, I beg God to forgive me.

I hope this letter finds you strong in the faith. I also hope that circumstances will soon make it possible for me to meet each of you, not as an integrationist or a civil-rights leader but as a fellow clergyman and a Christian brother. Let us all hope that the dark clouds of racial prejudice will soon pass away and the deep fog of misunderstanding will be lifted from our fear-drenched communities, and in some not too distant tomorrow the radiant stars of love and brotherhood will shine over our great nation with all their scintillating beauty.

Yours for the cause of Peace and Brotherhood,
Martin Luther King, Jr.

Reading 22

Message to the Grass Roots

Malcolm X

In late 1963, the Detroit Council for Human Rights announced a Northern Negro Leadership Conference to be held in Detroit on November 9 and 10. When the council's chairman, Rev. C. L. Franklin, sought to exclude black nationalists and Freedom Now Party advocates from the conference, Rev. Albert B. Cleage, Jr., resigned from the council and, in collaboration with the Group On Advanced Leadership (GOAL), arranged for a Northern Negro Grass Roots Leadership Conference. This was held in Detroit at the same time as the more conservative gathering, which was addressed by Congressman Adam Clayton Powell among others. The two-day Grass Roots conference was climaxed by a large public rally at the King Solomon Baptist Church, with Rev. Cleage, journalist William Worthy and Malcolm X as the chief speakers. The audience, almost all black and with non-Muslims in the great majority, interrupted Malcolm with applause and laughter so often that he asked it to desist because of the lateness of the hour.

We want to have just an off-the-cuff chat between you and me, us. We want to talk right down to earth in a language that everybody here can easily understand. We all agree tonight, all of the speakers have agreed, that America has a very serious problem. Not only does America have a very serious problem, but our people have a very serious problem. America's problem is us. We're her problem. The only reason she has a problem is she doesn't want us here. And every time you look at yourself, be you black, brown, red or yellow, a so-called Negro, you represent a person who poses such a serious problem for America because you're not wanted. Once you face this as a fact, then you can start plotting a course that will make you appear intelligent, instead of unintelligent.

What you and I need to do is learn to forget our differences. When we come together, we don't come together as Baptists or Methodists. You don't catch hell because you're a Baptist, and you don't catch hell because you're a Methodist. You don't catch hell because you're a Methodist or Baptist, you don't catch hell because you're a Democrat or a Republican, you don't catch hell because you're a Mason or an Elk, and you sure don't catch hell because you're an American; because if you were an American, you wouldn't catch hell. You catch hell because you're a black man. You catch hell, all of us catch hell, for the same reason.

So we're all black people, so-called Negroes, second-class citizens, ex-slaves. You're nothing but an ex-slave. You don't like to be told that. But what else are you? You are ex-slaves. You didn't come here on the "Mayflower." You came here on a slave ship. In chains, like a horse, or a cow, or a chicken. And you were brought here by the people who came here on the "Mayflower," you were brought here by the so-called Pilgrims, or Founding Fathers. They were the ones who brought you here.

We have a common enemy. We have this in common: We have a common oppressor, a common exploiter, and a common discriminator. But once we all realize that we have a common enemy, then we unite—on the basis of what we have in common. And what we have foremost in common is that enemy—the white man. He's an enemy to all of us. I know some of you all think that some of them aren't enemies. Time will tell.

In Bandung back in, I think, 1954, was the first unity meeting in centuries of black people. And once you study what happened at the Bandung conference, and the results of the Bandung conference, it actually serves as a model for the same procedure you and I can use to get our problems solved. At Bandung all the nations came together, the dark nations from Africa and Asia. Some of them were Buddhists, some of them were Muslims, some of them were Christians, some were Confucianists, some were atheists. Despite their religious differences, they came together. Some were communists, some were socialists, some were capitalists—despite their economic and political differences, they came together. All of them were black, brown, red or yellow.

The number-one thing that was not allowed to attend the Bandung conference was the white man. He couldn't come. Once they excluded the white man, they found that they could get together. Once they kept him out, everybody else fell right in and fell in line. This is the thing that you and I have to understand. And these people who came together didn't have nuclear weapons, they didn't have jet planes, they didn't have all of the heavy armaments that the white man has. But they had unity.

They were able to submerge their little petty differences and agree on one thing: That there one African came from Kenya and was being colonized by the Englishman, and another African came from the Congo and was being colonized by the Belgian, and another African came from Guinea and was being colonized by the French, and another came from Angola and was being colonized by the Portuguese. When they came to the Bandung conference, they looked at the Portuguese, and at the Frenchman, and at the Englishman, and at the Dutchman, and learned or realized the one thing that all of them had in common—they were all from Europe, they were all Europeans, blond, blue-eyed and white skins. They began to recognize who their enemy was. The same man that was colonizing our people in Kenya was colonizing our people in the Congo. The same one in the Congo was colonizing our people in South Africa, and in Southern Rhodesia, and in Burma, and in India, and in Afghanistan, and in Pakistan. They realized all over the world where the dark man was being oppressed, he was being oppressed by the white man; where the dark man was being exploited, he was being exploited by the white man. So they got together on this basis—that they had a common enemy.

And when you and I here in Detroit and in Michigan and in America who have been awakened today look around us, we too realize here in America we all have a common enemy, whether he's in Georgia or Michigan, whether he's in California or New York. He's the same man—blue eyes and blond hair and pale skin—the same man. So what we have to do is what they did. They agreed to stop quarreling among themselves. Any little spat that they had, they'd settle it among themselves, go into a huddle—don't let the enemy know that you've got a disagreement.

Instead of airing our differences in public, we have to realize we're all the same family. And when you have a family squabble, you don't get out on the sidewalk. If you do, everybody calls you uncouth, unrefined, uncivilized, savage. If you don't make it at home, you settle it at home; you get in the closet, argue it out behind closed doors, and then when you come out on the street, you pose a common front, a united front. And this is what we need to do in the community, and in the city, and in the state. We need to stop airing our differences in front of the white man, put the white man out of our meetings, and then sit down and talk shop with each other. That's what we've got to do.

I would like to make a few comments concerning the difference between the black revolution and the Negro revolution. Are they both the same? And if they're not, what is the difference? What is the difference between a black revolution and a Negro revolution? First, what is a revolution? Sometimes I'm inclined to believe that many of our people are using this word "revolution" loosely, without taking careful consideration of what this word actually means, and what its historic characteristics are. When you study the historic nature of revolutions, the motive of a revolution, the objective of a revolution, the result of a revolution, and the methods used in a revolution, you may change words. You may devise another program, you may change your goal and you may change your mind.

Look at the American Revolution in 1776. That revolution was for what? For land. Why did they want land? Independence. How was it carried out? Bloodshed. Number one, it was based on land, the basis of independence. And the only way they could get it was bloodshed. The French Revolution—what was it based on? The landless against the landlord. What was it for? Land. How did they get it? Bloodshed. Was no love lost, was no compromise, was no negotiation. I'm telling you—you don't know what a revolution is. Because when you find out what it is, you'll get back in the alley, you'll get out of the way.

The Russian Revolution—what was it based on? Land; the landless against the landlord. How did they bring it about? Bloodshed. You haven't got a revolution that doesn't involve bloodshed. And you're afraid to bleed. I said, you're afraid to bleed.

As long as the white man sent you to Korea, you bled. He sent you to Germany, you bled. He sent you to the South Pacific to fight the Japanese, you bled. You bleed for white people, but when it comes to seeing your own churches being bombed and little black girls murdered, you haven't got any blood. You bleed when the white man says bleed; you bite when the white man says bite; and you bark when the white man says bark. I hate to say this about us, but it's true. How are you going to be nonviolent in Mississippi, as violent as you were in Korea? How can you justify being nonviolent in Mississippi and Alabama, when your churches are being bombed, and your little girls are being murdered, and at the same time you are going to get violent with Hitler, and Tojo, and somebody else you don't even know?

If violence is wrong in America, violence is wrong abroad. If it is wrong to be violent defending black women and black children and black babies and black men, then it is wrong for America to draft us and make us violent abroad in defense of her. And if it is right for America to draft us, and teach us how to be violent in defense of her, then it is right for you and me to do whatever is necessary to defend our own people right here in this country.

The Chinese Revolution—they wanted land. They threw the British out, along with the Uncle Tom Chinese. Yes, they did. They set a good example. When I was in prison, I read an article—don't be shocked when I say that I was in prison. You're still in prison. That's what America means: prison. When I was in prison, I read an article in *Life* magazine showing a little Chinese girl, nine years old; her father was on his hands and knees and she was pulling the trigger because he was an Uncle Tom Chinaman. When they had the revolution over there, they took a whole generation of Uncle Toms and just wiped them out. And within ten years that little girl became a full-grown woman. No more Toms in China. And today it's one of the toughest, roughest, most feared countries on this earth—by the white man. Because there are no Uncle Toms over there.

Of all our studies, history is best qualified to reward our research. And when you see that you've got problems, all you have to do is examine the historic method used all over the world by others who have problems similar to yours. Once you see how they got theirs straight, then you know how you can get yours straight. There's been a revolution, a black revolution, going on in Africa. In Kenya, the Mau Mau were revolutionary; they were the ones who brought the word "Uhuru" to the fore. The Mau Mau, they were revolutionary, they believed in scorched earth, they knocked everything aside that got in their way, and their revolution also was based on land, a desire for land. In Algeria, the northern part of Africa, a revolution took place. The Algerians were revolutionists, they wanted land. France offered to let them be integrated into France. They told France, to hell with France, they wanted some land, not some France. And they engaged in a bloody battle.

So I cite these various revolutions, brothers and sisters, to show you that you don't have a peaceful revolution. You don't have a turn-the-other-cheek revolution. There's no such thing as a non-violent revolution. The only kind of revolution that is nonviolent is the Negro revolution. The only revolution in which the goal is loving your enemy is the Negro revolution. It's the only revolution in which the goal is a desegregated lunch counter, a desegregated theater, a desegregated park, and a desegregated public toilet; you can sit down next to white folks—on the toilet. That's no revolution. Revolution is based on land. Land is the basis of all independence. Land is the basis of freedom, justice, and equality.

The white man knows what a revolution is. He knows that the black revolution is world-wide in scope and in nature. The black revolution is sweeping Asia, is sweeping Africa, is rearing its head in Latin America. The Cuban Revolution—that's a revolution. They overturned the system. Revolution is in Asia, revolution is in Africa, and the white man is screaming because he sees revolution in Latin America. How do you think he'll react to you when you learn what a real revolution is? You don't know what a revolution is. If you did, you wouldn't use that word.

Revolution is bloody, revolution is hostile, revolution knows no compromise, revolution overturns and destroys everything that gets in its way. And you, sitting around here like a knot on the wall, saying, "I'm going to love these folks no matter how much they hate me." No, you need a revolution. Whoever heard of a revolution where they lock arms, as Rev. Cleage was pointing out beautifully, singing "We Shall Overcome"? You don't do that in a revolution. You don't do any singing, you're too busy swinging. It's based on land. A revolutionary wants land so he can set up his own nation, an independent nation. These Negroes aren't asking for any nation—they're trying to crawl back on the plantation.

When you want a nation, that's called nationalism. When the white man became involved in a revolution in this country against England, what was it for? He wanted this land so he could set up another white nation. That's white nationalism. The American Revolution was white nationalism. The French Revolution was white nationalism. The Russian Revolution too—yes, it was—white nationalism. You don't think so? Why do you think Khrushchev and Mao can't get their heads together? White nationalism. All the revolutions that are going on in Asia and Africa today are based on what ?—black nationalism. A revolutionary is a black nationalist. He wants a nation. I was reading some beautiful words by Rev. Cleage, pointing out why he couldn't get together with someone else in the city because all of them were afraid of being identified with black nationalism. If you're afraid of black nationalism, you're afraid of revolution. And if you love revolution, you love black nationalism.

To understand this, you have to go back to what the young brother here referred to as the house Negro and the field Negro back during slavery. There were two kinds of slaves, the house Negro and the field Negro. The house Negroes—they lived in the house with master, they dressed pretty good, they ate good because they ate his food—what he left. They lived in the attic or the basement, but still they lived near the master; and they loved the master more than the master loved himself. They would give their life to save the master's house—quicker than the master would. If the master said, "We got a good house here," the house Negro would say, "Yeah, we got a good house here." Whenever the master said "we," he said "we." That's how you can tell a house Negro.

If the master's house caught on fire, the house Negro would fight harder to put the blaze out than the master would. If the master got sick, the house Negro would say, "What's the matter, boss, *we* sick?" *We* sick! He identified himself with his master, more than his master identified with himself. And if you came to the house Negro and said, "Let's run away, let's escape, let's separate," the house Negro would look at you and say, "Man, you crazy. What you mean, separate? Where is there a better house than this? Where can I wear better clothes than this? Where can I eat better food than this?" That was that house Negro. In those days he was called a "house nigger." And that's what we call them today, because we've still got some house niggers running around here.

This modern house Negro loves his master. He wants to live near him. He'll pay three times as much as the house is worth just to live near his master, and then brag about "I'm the only Negro out here." "I'm the only one on my job." "I'm the only one in this school." You're nothing but a house Negro. And if someone comes to you right now and says, "Let's separate," you say the same thing that the house Negro said on the plantation. "What you mean, separate? From America, this good white man? Where you going to get a better job than you get here?" I mean, this is what you say. "I ain't left nothing in Africa," that's what you say. Why, you left your mind in Africa.

On that same plantation, there was the field Negro. The field Negroes—those were the masses. There were always more Negroes in the field than there were Negroes in the house. The Negro in the field caught hell. He ate leftovers. In the house they ate high up on the hog. The Negro in the field didn't get anything but what was left of the insides of the hog. They call it "chitt'lings" nowadays. In those days they called them what they were—guts. That's what you were—gut-eaters. And some of you are still gut-eaters.

The field Negro was beaten from morning to night; he lived in a shack, in a hut; he wore old, castoff clothes. He hated his master. I say he hated his master. He was intelligent. That house Negro loved his master, but that field Negro—remember, they were in the majority, and they hated the master. When the house caught on fire, he didn't try to put it out; that field Negro prayed for a wind, for a breeze. When the master got sick, the field Negro prayed that he'd die. If someone came to the field Negro and said, "Let's separate, let's run," he didn't say "Where we going?" He'd say, "Any place is better than here." You've got field Negroes in America today. I'm a field Negro. The masses are the field Negroes. When they see this man's house on fire, you don't hear the little Negroes talking about "*our* government is in trouble." They say, "*The* government is in trouble." Imagine a Negro: "*Our* government"! I even heard one say "*our* astronauts." They won't even let him near the plant—and "*our* astronauts"! "*Our* Navy"—that's a Negro that is out of his mind, a Negro that is out of his mind.

Just as the slavemaster of that day used Tom, the house Negro, to keep the field Negroes in check, the same old slavemaster today has Negroes who are nothing but modern Uncle Toms, twentieth-century Uncle Toms, to keep you and me in check, to keep us under control, keep us passive and peaceful and nonviolent. That's Tom making you nonviolent. It's like when you go to the dentist, and the man's going to take your tooth. You're going to fight him when he starts pulling. So he squirts some stuff in your jaw called Novocaine, to make you think they're not doing anything to you. So you sit there and because you've got all of that Novocaine in your jaw, you suffer—peacefully. Blood running all down your jaw, and you don't know what's happening. Because someone has taught you to suffer—peacefully.

The white man does the same thing to you in the street, when he wants to put knots on your head and take advantage of you and not have to be afraid of your fighting back. To keep you from fighting back, he gets these old religious Uncle Toms to teach you and me, just like Novocaine, to suffer peacefully. Don't stop suffering—just suffer peacefully. As Rev. Cleage pointed out, they say you should let your blood flow in the streets. This is a shame. You know he's a Christian preacher. If it's a shame to him, you know what it is to me.

There is nothing in our book, the Koran, that teaches us to suffer peacefully. Our religion teaches us to be intelligent. Be peaceful, be courteous, obey the law, respect everyone; but if someone puts his hand on you, send him to the cemetery. That's a good religion. In fact, that's that old-time religion. That's the one that Ma and Pa used to talk about: an eye for an eye, and a tooth for a tooth, and a head for a head, and a life for a life. That's a good religion. And nobody resents that kind of religion being taught but a wolf, who intends to make you his meal.

This is the way it is with the white man in America. He's a wolf—and you're sheep. Any time a shepherd, a pastor, teaches you and me not to run from the white man and, at the same time, teaches us not to fight the white man, he's a traitor to you and me. Don't lay down a life all by itself. No, preserve your life, it's the best thing you've got. And if you've got to give it up, let it be even-steven.

The slavemaster took Tom and dressed him well, fed him well and even gave him a little education—a *little* education; gave him a long coat and a top hat and made all the other slaves look up to him. Then he used Tom to control them. The same strategy that was used in those days is used today, by the same white man. He takes a Negro, a so-called Negro, and makes him prominent, builds him up, publicizes him, makes him a celebrity. And then he becomes a spokesman for Negroes—and a Negro leader.

I would like to mention just one other thing quickly, and that is the method that the white man uses, how the white man uses the "big guns," or Negro leaders, against the Negro revolution. They are not a part of the Negro revolution. They are used against the Negro revolution.

When Martin Luther King failed to desegregate Albany, Georgia, the civil-rights struggle in America reached its low point. King became bankrupt almost, as a leader. The Southern Christian Leadership Conference was in financial trouble; and it was in trouble, period, with the people when they failed to desegregate Albany, Georgia. Other Negro civil-rights leaders of so-called national stature became fallen idols. As they became fallen idols, began to lose their prestige and influence, local Negro leaders began to stir up the masses. In Cambridge, Maryland, Gloria Richardson; in Danville, Virginia, and other parts of the country, local leaders began to stir up our people at the grass-roots level. This was never done by these Negroes of national stature. They control you, but they have never incited you or excited you. They control you, they contain you, they have kept you on the plantation.

As soon as King failed in Birmingham, Negroes took to the streets. King went out to California to a big rally and raised I don't know how many thousands of dollars. He came to Detroit and had a march and raised some more thousands of dollars. And recall, right after that Roy Wilkins attacked King. He accused King and CORE [Congress Of Racial Equality] of starting trouble everywhere and then making the NAACP [National Association for the Advancement of Colored People] get them out of jail and spend a lot of money; they accused King and CORE of raising all the money and not paying it back. This happened; I've got it in documented evidence in the newspaper. Roy started attacking King, and King started attacking Roy, and Farmer started attacking both of them. And as these Negroes of national stature began to attack each other, they began to lose their control of the Negro masses.

The Negroes were out there in the streets. They were talking about how they were going to march on Washington. Right at that time Birmingham had exploded, and the Negroes in Birmingham—remember, they also exploded. They began to stab the crackers in the back and bust them up 'side their head—yes, they did. That's when Kennedy sent in the troops, down in Birmingham. After that, Kennedy got on the television and said "this is a moral issue." That's when he said he was going to put out a civil-rights bill. And when he mentioned civil-rights bill and the Southern crackers started talking about how they were going to boycott or filibuster it, then the Negroes started talking—about what? That they were going to march on Washington, march on the Senate, march on the White House, march on the Congress, and tie it up, bring it to a halt, not let the government proceed. They even said they were going out to the airport and lay down on the runway and not let any airplanes land. I'm telling you what they said. That was revolution. That was revolution. That was the black revolution.

It was the grass roots out there in the street. It scared the white man to death, scared the white power structure in Washington, D.C., to death; I was there. When they found out that this black steamroller was going to come down on the capital, they called in Wilkins, they called in Randolph, they called in these national Negro leaders that you respect and told them, "Call it off." Kennedy said, "Look, you all are letting this thing go too far." And Old Tom said, "Boss, I can't stop it, because I didn't start it." I'm telling you what they said. They said, "I'm not even in it, much less at the head of it." They said, "These Negroes are doing things on their own. They're running ahead of us." And that old shrewd fox, he said, "If you all aren't in it, I'll put you in it. I'll put you at the head of it. I'll endorse it. I'll welcome it. I'll help it. I'll join it."

A matter of hours went by. They had a meeting at the Carlyle Hotel in New York City. The Carlyle Hotel is owned by the Kennedy family; that's the hotel Kennedy spent the night at, two nights ago; it belongs to his family. A philanthropic society headed by a white man named Stephen Currier called all the top civil-rights leaders together at the Carlyle Hotel. And he told them, "By you all fighting each other, you are destroying the civil-rights movement. And since you're fighting over money from white liberals, let us set up what is known as the Council for United Civil Rights Leadership. Let's form this council, and all the civil-rights organizations will belong to it, and we'll use it for fund-raising purposes." Let me show you how tricky the white man is. As soon as they got it formed, they elected Whitney Young as its chairman, and who do you think became the co-chairman? Stephen Currier, the white man, a millionaire. Powell was talking about it down at Cobo Hall today. This is what he was talking about. Powell knows it happened. Randolph knows it happened. Wilkins knows it happened. King knows it happened. Every one of that Big Six—they know it happened.

Once they formed it, with the white man over it, he promised them and gave them $800,000 to split up among the Big Six; and told them that after the march was over they'd give them $700,000 more. A million and a half dollars—split up between leaders that you have been following, going to jail for, crying crocodile tears for. And they're nothing but Frank James and Jesse James and the what-do-you-call-'em brothers.

As soon as they got the setup organized, the white man made available to them top public-relations experts; opened the news media across the country at their disposal, which then began to project these Big Six as the leaders of the march. Originally they weren't even in the march. You were talking this march talk on Hastings Street, you were talking march talk on Lenox Avenue, and on Fillmore Street, and on Central Avenue, and 32nd Street and 63rd Street. That's where the march talk was being talked. But the white man put the Big Six at the head of it; made them the march. They became the march. They took it over. And the first move they made after they took it over, they invited Walter Reuther, a white man; they invited a priest, a rabbi, and an old white preacher, yes, an old white preacher. The same white element that put Kennedy into power—labor, the Catholics, the Jews, and liberal Protestants; the same clique that put Kennedy in power, joined the march on Washington.

It's just like when you've got some coffee that's too black, which means it's too strong. What do you do? You integrate it with cream, you make it weak. But if you pour too much cream in it, you won't even know you ever had coffee. It used to be hot, it becomes cool. It used to be strong, it becomes weak. It used to wake you up, now it puts you to sleep. This is what they did with the march on Washington. They joined it. They didn't integrate it, they infiltrated it. They joined it, became a part of it, took it over. And as they took it over, it lost its militancy. It ceased to be angry, it ceased to be hot, it ceased to be uncompromising. Why, it even ceased to be a march. It became a picnic, a circus. Nothing but a circus, with clowns and all. You had one right here in Detroit—I saw it on television—with clowns leading it, white clowns and black clowns. I know you don't like what I'm saying, but I'm going to tell you anyway. Because I can prove what I'm saying. If you think I'm telling you wrong, you bring me Martin Luther King and A. Philip Randolph and James Farmer and those other three, and see if they'll deny it over a microphone.

No, it was a sellout. It was a takeover. When James Baldwin came in from Paris, they wouldn't let him talk, because they couldn't make him go by the script. Burt Lancaster read the speech that Baldwin was supposed to make; they wouldn't let Baldwin get up there, because they know Baldwin is liable to say anything. They controlled it so tight, they told those Negroes what time to hit town, how to come, where to stop, what signs to carry, what song to sing, what speech they could make, and what speech they couldn't make; and then told them to get out of town by sundown. And every one of those Toms was out of town by sundown. Now I know you don't like my saying this. But I can back it up. It was a circus, a performance that beat anything Hollywood could ever do, the performance of the year. Reuther and those other three devils should get an Academy Award for the best actors because they acted like they really loved Negroes and fooled a whole lot of Negroes. And the six Negro leaders should get an award too, for the best supporting cast.

Reading 23

In Quest of African American Political Woman

Jewel L. Prestage

ABSTRACT: African American women, political activists for their entire history on the American continent but long denied the right to vote and hold office, have resorted to nontraditional politics. This article explores the nature and extent of African American women's political participation, beginning with the slave era. As victims of racial and sexual discrimination, these women have been active in the African American liberation movement and the women's movement. Along the way they developed a rich array of innovative alternatives to the traditional political activities from which they were excluded. After the 1965 Voting Rights Act, nontraditional activities began to give way to more traditional ones. Currently, they are the prime users of the ballot, hold a higher percentage of their race's elective offices than do white women, and as officeholders exhibit higher levels of women's organization membership than do white women and are highly supportive of women's issues. African American women receive high praise for their performance as officeholders. Unlike their white counterparts, African American adults have not experienced a gender gap.

The complete history of African American women's participation in American politics must recognize not only their involvement in traditional political acts such as registering, voting, and holding office but also those nontraditional activities in which they engaged long before gaining the ballot. Because African American women are simultaneously members of the two groups that have suffered the nation's most blatant exclusion from the normal channels of access to civic life, African Americans and women, their political behavior has been largely overlooked by political scientists, who have tended to focus primarily on those actions that conform to the more restrictive definitions of politics.[1] Because African American women have only recently been granted access to the political arena as voters and officeholders in significant numbers, there is a paucity of information about them in these roles and even less about their nontraditional actions that predated these roles.[2]

The purpose of this article is to begin a full exploration of the types and extent of political participation and behavior in which African American women have engaged. Utilizing extant social science literature and recent survey research findings by political science scholars, this quest for African

American political women will encompass a historical overview in which traditional and nontraditional political actions will be examined. Three basic contentions will permeate and guide the discussion.

The first contention is that throughout their existence on the American continent, African American women have been engaged in political activity, the nature of which has been determined by the legal and cultural circumstances they faced at the time. The second is that African American women's political activities have been directed toward altering their disadvantaged status both as African Americans and as women. Third is the observation that, historically, African American women have escalated their political activity progressively, moving from a predominance of nontraditional activity to a predominance of traditional activity, and have emerged as prime users of these traditional avenues in contemporary American politics.

In the discussion that follows, four major historical periods will be delineated and the extent and nature of African American women's political activity will be examined in each. The designated periods are preemancipation, Reconstruction, post-Reconstruction through World War II, and the Second Reconstruction. Legal and cultural circumstances of African American women in each period will be summarized, as these are assumed to be the basic impetus for their political actions.

Preemancipation (1619–1865)

While a few held free status, most women of African descent living in the American colonies and in the United States before the Emancipation Proclamation in 1865 were chattel slaves. As enslaved African females, they were the victims of dual oppression, one issuing from race and the other from sex. Subjected to the slave status ascribed to their African male kin, they were further victimized by a body of hostile public policy directed toward them as women. Among the most inhumane and devastating provisions were the lack of legal protection from physical sexual abuse and rape by white males, legally enforced separation from their children, the absence of a legal right to marriage and family life, legally enforced cohabitation with other slaves for breeding purposes, and laws requiring that children born as a result of cohabitation with white males be assigned the slave status of the mother even if the father were white and free, a contradiction of then prevailing common law practices. Abolitionist Frederick Douglass described the African American woman as one "'consigned to a life of revolting prostitution,'" "'a mere chattel,'" pointing out that if she even "'lifted her hand'" in defense of her own innocence she could be lawfully put to death.[3]

The political implications of the physical abuse and rape of African American women have been studied by several social scientists. Angela Davis, for example, argues that rape of slave women was an indirect attack on the slave community as a whole, intended to induce in the African American male doubts about his ability to resist the slave system in any manner whatever since he could not protect the women. For the slave woman, the rape was meant to reinforce her vulnerability as a female.[4]

Most free African Americans of this era, including women, found that their status was not fundamentally different from that of slaves.[5] Restrictive legislation and cultural practices, reflecting the general situation of African Americans and of women, served as a double bind for African American women.

How did African American women respond to their status in the premancipation period? Without the ballot or any other traditional mode of access to the political arena, they resorted to a wide range of other options. Because their nontraditional modes of action were designed to alter public policy provisions and legally condoned cultural practices defining their status and the behaviors mandated for that status, African American women's actions in this period can be appropriately labeled political.[6]

African American enslaved women took leading roles in organizing their community in order to lessen the hostile impact of the slave system on individual and family life. They engaged in physical retaliatory violence on an individual and group basis, systematically refused to carry unwanted children to term and helped others who were so inclined, became runaways whose acumen and skill were cited as unique and superior to those of males, organized and participated in outright slave revolts, and became organizers and operatives—like Harriet Tubman—in the Underground Railroad. They sued for freedom, and in some states they won. During the Civil War, African American slave women escaped to work with the Union Army as laundresses, cooks, and scouts and in other capacities as well.[7]

Free African American women were no less active than their enslaved sisters. Records of antislavery societies, the editorial pages of newspapers and periodicals, available pamphlets, and other records of public discourse reveal the identities of many black women whose attention and talents were devoted to the cause of abolition.[8] In their private capacities, numerous African American free women purchased slaves and granted them freedom, while others went north to find employment to pay for freedom for husbands and other relatives. African American women had their own antislavery societies in addition to being active in the principal abolitionist organizations. It was one of these societies that first defied the prevailing cultural pattern by inviting a black woman feminist and abolitionist, Maria Stewart, to speak to a mixed audience of men and women in Boston in 1832. Women were generally not permitted to speak publicly on an issue as controversial as abolition.[9]

Some other free African American women were active in the women's rights movement in this era.[10] Perhaps the most popular was Sojourner Truth, also a strong force in the abolitionist movement. Author Paula Giddings states that "although the Black woman's contribution to the suffrage campaign is rarely written about, Blacks, including women, had a more consistent attitude toward the vote than Whites, as Blacks had fewer conflicts about women's voting." Furthermore, "one would be hard pressed to find any Black woman who did not advocate getting the vote."[11]

No doubt tensions between women along racial lines within the abolitionist societies and in the women's rights movement, along with the eventual split between the abolitionist movement and the women's movement,[12] had a negative impact on the role of African American women prior to emancipation. While a few African American women whose education and wealth exceeded that of white women were found acceptable as potential members and officers in abolition societies dominated by white women, the question of mass black participation was a matter of bitter conflict.[13] Maria Stewart opined that for black women, race was the priority issue and it was the issue that initially sparked their feminism.[14]

A review of the preemancipation era would seem to suggest that African American women, while deprived of access to traditional channels of political participation, were nonetheless active in a wide range of efforts designed to alter their status as slaves and as women.

Reconstruction

The Emancipation Proclamation, and the constitutional amendments and federal troop occupation of the southern states that followed, provided the legal changes necessary for African Americans to enter the political arena as full participants for the first time and ushered in the period of Reconstruction. During this period, African American males achieved the right to register and vote, and they were elected and appointed to public office in significant numbers. African American women, like women generally, were excluded from these privileges, however.

How did African American women react to this exclusion? Denied the privilege of personal suffrage, these women are reputed to have found means of influencing the political decisions of their male kin and friends. Accounts from Louisiana provide an interesting group profile. According to one state politician and former state senator, they followed their men from morning to night telling them how to vote, formed a large segment of the audiences at political meetings, and evidenced a deep interest "in all that pertained to" politics.[15] Sensitive to the importance of their exclusion from the suffrage, a New Orleans group published a document in 1878 demanding for themselves, former slave women, "every right and privilege" guaranteed under the United States Constitution to men, and vowed to use every power in their hands to get them.[16]

For African American women, Reconstruction brought other problems, which had roots in the political system. Establishment of family life through marriage, searching for relatives, education of themselves and family members, achieving personal and family economic stability, and developing a consensus concerning the role and status of women in the African American community after emancipation were among the challenges they faced. A disproportionate share of the African American women's energies and organizational efforts was devoted not only to finding solutions to these problems but also to getting the ballot for women. Notable among the African American female suffragettes were three South Carolina sisters, Frances, Louisa, and Lottie Rollin. Active also were Charlotte Ray and Mary Ann Shadd Cary, in the District of Columbia. Cary actually registered to vote in 1871.[17]

In Louisiana, African American women are credited with organizing the several exoduses that took thousands of African Americans out of the state to the North.

Although Reconstruction did not bring to the African American woman the privilege of traditional political involvement, it did not dull her penchant for the utilization of nontraditional forms of influence. Because the options available to her actually expanded beyond those of the previous era, so did her involvement.

Post-Reconstruction and World War II (1890–1943)

The withdrawal of federal troops from the South facilitated by the Compromise of 1877 proved to be the death knell for Reconstruction and for the African American's maiden voyage into the turbulent waters of American electoral politics. Inherent in the ending of Reconstruction and the return of white control to the southern states were major problems for African American women. Legal constraints on African American political activity in combination with widely used and condoned illegal forms of violence and intimidation instituted by the white power structure resulted in the creation of a very unstable and threatening situation for the race as a whole.

One form of violence of particular concern for post-Reconstruction African American women was the practice of lynching. Although the most frequent victims were African American males, African American women and whites were sometimes targeted also. Lynchings numbered over 2500 between 1884 and 1900 and over 1100 between 1900 and the start of World War I.[18] Disenfranchisement of African American males through newly enacted state laws, lack of adequate educational opportunities resulting from state segregation laws and underfunding of African American schools, racial segregation of all public accommodations, extensive abuse of African American women by white men, and segregation and discrimination in employment were among the other legal and cultural impediments that African American women faced.

Still denied the ballot, these women continued to resort to nontraditional political action. They took the lead in the antilynching movement by staging national and international campaigns that involved meeting with the president of the United States, protest activity in the nation's capital, and even travel outside the United States to generate external pressure on the national government to make lynching a federal crime. Leadership roles in the antilynching campaign were assumed by Ida Wells Barnett and Mary Church Terrell.[19] Also, when the National Association for the Advancement of Colored People (NAACP) was established in 1909 as a general-purpose civil rights organization, African American women were among the principal players. Convinced that the education and social uplifting of women were essential to overall development of the race, women like Mary McLeod Bethune and Charlotte Hawkins Brown operated schools. College-educated African American women formed sororities and clubs with political education and uplifting as goals. Generally, historical accounts of the continuous struggles waged to overturn the plethora of legal and de facto barriers to equality for African Americans reveal the presence and influence of African American women whether the focus is on education, transportation, or criminal justice.

During this period, relations between the women's movement and African American women ranged from troubled to conflictual. Deckard reports that the women's movement had grown out of the abolitionist movement and that the two had close ties until the Civil War, after which relations deteriorated when the women were not given the vote along with African Americans.[20]

By 1890 the women's movement had dissociated itself from African Americans in an effort to make itself respectable in the eyes of white males. Within a decade its rhetoric and goals had become blatantly racist. Leaders highlighted the potential white outnumbering of total African American voters that would result from the granting of suffrage to white women. White supremacy was touted and appeals to Negrophobia made, out of either expediency or commitment. In a strange turn of events, however, the final congressional arguments against granting the vote to women included expressions of fear that enfranchisement would indeed extend the ballot to African American women. In the bid to achieve ratification of the amendment, Alice Paul, head of the Woman's Party, is quoted as having responded in these words to questions about the possibility of African American women's gaining the vote in South Carolina if the Nineteenth Amendment passed: "Negro men cannot vote in South Carolina and therefore negro women could not vote if women were to vote in the nation. We are organizing white women in the South . . . but have heard of no activity or anxiety among the 'Negresses.'"[21]

Efforts to exclude African American women from the mainstream women's political organizations and from the voting privilege sought for white women did not go unchallenged. The NAACP was mobilized by African American women to bring pressure on Alice Paul and her party. In addition, African American women's groups confronted the white women's major organizations with a petition for membership and requests for policy clarification on the question of race and woman suffrage, and the African American groups proved to be effective debaters and negotiators in the foray that emerged in the final states of the fight for ratification of the Nineteenth Amendment.[22] It was clear even then that African American women were not regarded by their white female counterparts as fully deserving the ballot.

Immediately after the amendment's ratification, African American women were reported to have registered in large numbers in the South. In reaction, Southern states were quick to develop procedures and tactics to slow their registration, including making them wait in line for hours until all white women had registered. Curiously, the enthusiasm for registering to vote displayed by African American women was not reported for white women.[23] In their fight to eliminate this and other forms of discrimination against them as voters, African American women received no real support from the National Woman's Party, but rather hostility and discourteous treatment.

Overall it seems fair to generalize that African American women found that in their post-Reconstruction push to become full members of the body politic, it was necessary not only to fight the antisuffragists but also to wrestle the ballot from the hands of the white suffragettes. In spite of efforts to the contrary, the success of the tactics used to disenfranchise the entire African American population, women included, is reflected in records from 1940 in Louisiana. There the number of African Americans registered to vote was only 886, while the adult African American population was estimated at 473,562. This pattern was replicated throughout the Southern region, where the majority of African Americans resided.[24]

The Second Reconstruction (1944–Present)

One of the mainstays of white political control in the South, the white primary election, was declared unconstitutional in 1944, creating a more positive environment for African Americans to realize their goal of becoming practitioners of traditional politics. Through individual and group initiatives, African Americans mounted an uphill battle against those legal and cultural norms that had militated against their aspirations in previous eras. African American women were made acutely aware of the irrelevance of the Nineteenth Amendment to their enfranchisement desires and earnestly joined in these race-based strategies.

Nontraditional activities were still necessary in the post–World War II broadside against racial discrimination at the polls. In litigation challenging state laws requiring segregation and discrimination in a variety of areas, including voter registration, and in lobbying for legislative remedies at the national level, African American women played prominent roles. Constance Baker Motley, legal counsel for the NAACP, and Thomasina Norford, lobbyist for the American Council on Human Rights in Washing, D.C., are examples. When the "outside of the courtroom" dimension of the movement emerged in the late 1950s and early 1960s, women again played significant roles in grass-roots organizations in local communities, in national coordination structures, and in confrontations with hostile police officers and anti-integration groups and individuals. Studies of demonstrations by African American college students show that 48 percent of those personally involved in sit-ins and freedom rides were female.[25] A study of participation in protests and more traditional antidiscrimination activity by New Orleans African American adults indicated only minimal overall differences between men and women.[26] Among those persons who achieved high visibility as pioneers in integrating previously segregated higher educational settings were African American women like Autherine Lucy, Ada Sipuel, Edith Jones, Vivian Malone, and Charlene Hunter. Other major activists in the civil rights movement were Rosa Parks, Daisy Bates, Fannie Lou Hamer, and Victoria DeLee. In the NAACP leadership ranks were Margaret Bush Wilson, Althea Simmons, and Jean Fairfax.

Writing about the civil rights movement, Professor William Chafe notes the pivotal, initiating role of African American women in defining issues of sex and race liberation for white women.[27] Within the context of the civil rights movement, African American women experienced and chose to consciously confront the issue of sexism. Through church organizations, women's clubs, sororities, and educational organizations, they provided monetary and moral support for civil rights workers, ranging from those registering voters to those engaged in more revolutionary politics.

Voting

With the passage of the 1965 Voting Rights Act, African American women received their first real opportunity to participate in traditional politics, since both the Fifteenth Amendment, which enfranchised men, and the Nineteenth, which benefited women, had in effect excluded them. Underscoring this is a 1966 publication declaring that African American women were, at the time, "frozen out" of the Southern political scene.[28] Clayton, in 1964, found that only a score or so of these women had achieved "success" in politics and that the "less than a dozen" in political offices across the nation had gained them through political parties.[29]

The 1965 Voting Rights Act was significant empowering legislation for African American women. It produced a remarkable escalation in the levels of African American voter registration and voting, especially in Southern states. For example, in Mississippi registration increased from about 8.0 percent to 62.0 percent between 1964 and 1968. In 1964 in Louisiana only 31.7 percent of the African American voting-age population was registered, but by 1970 over 55.0 percent was and by 1975 the figure had reached almost 67.0 percent.[30] These figures represent total registration of African Americans and comparable figures are not available along gender lines. Later voter-registration projections and voter-participation figures that are available along gender lines, however, lend some credibility to a projection that women were significantly represented among these new voters.

Studies of overall African American voter turnout show that it trailed white turnout from 1960 to 1980 and then surpassed it between 1980 and 1984. The total gain in turnout was 5.3 percent.[31] In fact, reported African American voting in 1984 was 5 percentage points higher than reported white voting when state-level political and contextual variables and demographic characteristics are held constant.[32] Clearly there has been a striking increase in overall African Americans voter turnout.

When the focus is narrowed to recent voting patterns of African American women, studies show that young African American women voted at a higher rate than did young African American men and that the gap in voting between African American men and women overall was less than the gap for whites. African American women from white-collar and manual occupations had slightly higher turnout rates than did their male counterparts until 1976, when parity emerged. White professional women voted at higher rates than did African American men of similar status, rates for the men in farm occupations were higher than for African American farm women. Regarded as undergirding this pattern of male-female voting differences were egalitarian sex-role orientations and assertive behavior of African American women at both the low and high ends of the economic scale. Feminist orientations were also associated with higher voter turnout. No single explanation was offered for the unusual pattern, however.[33] African American women who expressed the highest levels of political cynicism and the lowest levels of political efficacy increased their voting strength at greater levels than did any of the other race-sex groups.

As of 1988, African American women were reported to be 4 percentage points more likely to cast ballots than were African American men of comparable socioeconomic status. Especially remarkable, in historical context, is the finding that African American women who were heads of their households were 11 percent more likely to exercise the franchise than were white males, after controlling for demographic factors.[34]

Current available information would seem to suggest that African American women, the last group to acquire the ballot, have emerged as its prime users.

Holding office

The holding of political office by African American women is a rather recent experience. The first African American woman elected to a state legislature took office in 1938, the first to ascend to the bench did so in 1939, the first to become a member of the federal bench was appointed in 1966, and the first elected to Congress was elected in 1968. The first roster of African American women officeholders widely available was prepared by the Joint Center for Political Studies in 1973 and contained 337 names. Table 1 reveals the progressive increase in the number of women on the rosters published annually. As of 1989, some 1814 of the 7226 African Americans elected officials on the roster, or roughly one-fourth, were women.

Probings of the characteristics of African American women officeholders have yielded both selected group profiles and a general profile. African American women state legislators serving in the mid-1970s were found to have mostly Southern origins, to be better educated than their parents and most Americans, to have been elected to office after age 40, to have experienced marriage, and to have children mostly over the age of 18. Most of them had no relative who had held political office. Most had exhibited pre-adult interest in politics, had occupations outside the home, and had little prior political experience and yet felt they took office with special advantage in some policy areas. Overall, women's liberation was not opposed, but it was not given high priority. Support of husbands, children, and other family members was considered important and was reportedly given to them to a great degree. All were Democrats representing urban areas.[35]

African American women judges display many of the same traits as do the legislators. Nearly half were born in the South and identified their background as working-class. Almost all reported affiliation with an organized religious denomination. Most were without a lawyer role model in

Table 1: Black Women as a Percentage of Black Elected Officials (BEOs)

Year	BEOs (Total)	Female BEOs	Female BEOs as a Percentage of Total	Increased Number of Female BEOs as a Percentage of Total
1969	N.A.	131	N.A.	N.A.
1970	1469	N.A.	N.A.	N.A.
1971	1860	N.A.	N.A.	N.A.
1972	2264	N.A.	N.A.	N.A.
1973	2621	337	12.8	N.A.
1974	2991	N.A.	N.A.	N.A.
1975	3503	530	15.1	N.A.
1976	3979	684	17.2	2.0
1977	4311	782	18.1	1.0
1978	4503	843	18.7	0.6
1979	4607	882	19.1	0.4
1980	4912	976	19.9	0.7
1981	5038	1021	20.3	0.4
1982	5160	1081	20.9	0.7
1983	5606	1223	21.8	0.9
1984	5654	1259	22.3	0.4
1985	6056	1359	22.4	0.2
1986	6424	1469	22.9	0.5
1987	6681	1564	23.4	1.0
1988	6829	1625	23.8	0.4
1989	7226	1814	25.1	1.3

Source: *Roster of Black Elected Officials* (Washington, DC: Joint Center for Political Studies, published annually).
Note: N.A. = not available.

their families, as only one female lawyer was reported among family members. About half were products of historically black colleges and universities, and a quarter of them received legal training at one of the five law schools at these institutions. The vast majority had experienced marriage and a smaller majority were mothers. Husbands were mostly labeled "overwhelmingly supportive," but for nearly half of the women, self-motivation was the source of inspiration for running for office. With reference to age, the majority were in their thirties and forties. Only one of the jurists gained initial office as a result of election. Appointment was the principal facilitator for access.[36]

When a 1983 study compared African American and white women elected officials with each other and with men, it was found that African American women, as a group, were "highly qualified, politically experienced and self-confident, outdoing women officeholders overall, who are themselves outdoing men."[37] They were also more likely than males and than women overall to have attended college, and they were more likely than men to have come from professional, technical, and managerial/administrative positions. While they were less likely than women overall to have political experience, they were more likely to have had staff experience and campaign experience.

Some race-specific differences in the experiences of African American and white women en route to office emerged. One was that groups and organizations were more important in gaining political access for African American women. Another was that, more than white women, the African Americans cited representation of minorities or civil rights issues and the ability to combat discrimination as the main reasons why they ran for office.

In terms of family characteristics, African American women were less likely to be married, less likely to evaluate spousal support as important in decisions to seek office, more likely to be college professors or lawyers, and less likely to have children, but more likely to have children under the age of 12. African American women overall were more likely than white women to be Democrats.

Like African American officeholders generally and women officeholders overall, African American women are concentrated most heavily in local positions. In fact, of the 1814 currently serving, 501 serve on local school boards, and 651 are members of municipal governing bodies, while 1 serves in the United States Congress, and 99 serve in state legislatures. Among the jurists, only 1 serves on a state court of last resort, 88 are on other courts, and 22 are magistrates or justices of the peace.

African American women officeholders seem to have found their major successes in the same electoral settings in which their male brethren have achieved.

Even after obtaining access to traditional political channels, African American women continue to be involved in a variety of nontraditional activities. For example, they hold leadership positions in civil rights organizations and in interest groups with special relevance for African Americans.

The 1980s brought into being several organizations to accommodate and promote political activity among African Americans in which women have been quite active. Other organizations have been created exclusively for African American women. In the former category are the Congressional Black Caucus and the National Black Caucus of Local Elected Officials. The organizations especially for women include the National Political Congress of Black Women held its first national assembly in 1985, with Shirley Chisholm, the nation's first black congresswoman, at the helm.

Women's liberation

African American women's relationship to the contemporary women's liberation movement has been a mixed bag. A few African American women have been in the leadership cadre in the major organization, the National Organization for Women, but for most, the women's movement has not been accorded high priority. As early as 1973, the National Black Feminist Organization was formed as an option for African Americans to address feminist issues not dealt with to their satisfaction within the National Organization for Women. Over the last two decades, white women and African American women have worked together when their interests coincided, but, as Deckard points out, "friction does arise."[38] Despite the friction, African American women legislators, as well as African American male lawmakers, have been mostly supportive of women's issues. Curiously, the lack of high-priority status for the women's liberation movement among African American female officeholders has not translated into a lack of membership in women's liberation organizations. Nearly two-thirds of women state legislators who are African American belong to the Women's Political Caucus, compared to one-third of all women legislators. NOW membership is held by one-third of African American women, compared to only one-fifth of all women.[39]

Political parties

African American women's political-party membership and work have increased progressively. While no complete authoritative record is available, the high visibility of Democratic women like Patricia Roberts Harris, Yvonne Burke Braithwaite, C. Dolores Tucker, Barbara Jordan, Cardiss Collins, and Maxine Waters as well as Republicans Jewel LaFontant, Gloria Toote, and LeGree Daniels indicates a change in the role of African American women in the major parties. Shirley Chisholm was the first to seriously contest for presidential nomination, but Charlotta Bass had been the vice presidential candidate on the Progressive Party ticket in 1952.

Political socialization

Some interesting findings have emerged from studies of the political socialization of African American women, especially of those who hold political office. For example, the basic assumption undergirding ambition theory is that wanting political office is a prerequisite for winning office.[40]

Studies show no significant difference in the political ambition of African American male and female officeholders, in spite of the overall lower social status, educational level, and occupational status of women.[41] Also, among African American women state legislators in the mid-1970s, only one stated unequivocally that she would not seek reelection or aspire to a higher office.[42] Comparisons of political ambition between African American women and white women indicate parity in ambition, but white women's ambition is more closely linked to nontraditional sex-role beliefs acquired early while African American women's ambition is associated more with their current activities.[43] This would seem to lessen the possible impact on African American women of the suppressive legal prescriptions and community practices that prevailed in the period before passage and implementation of the 1965 Voting Rights Act.

Do African American women possess coping skills that separate them from other women officeholders? Work by several scholars indicates that this is true for African American women professionals[44] and for political activists.[45] One scholar even contends that it was the independence of direction and action exhibited by African American women domestic workers that raised the consciousness of their white middle-class employers.[46]

Some African American women scholars have recently addressed the question of African American women's liberation as an issue separate from that of women's liberation, on the one hand, and from African American liberation, on the other. Largely because this kind of perspective has been divisive in both the African Americans' and the women's struggles, African American women have generally opted to pursue a two-pronged struggle without taking a radical or self-interested posture in either of the existing movements. Political scientist Shelby Lewis has advised that African American women must construct and implement an independent liberation strategy, as no help can be expected from either of the three other race-sex groups—not even the admission that African American women are oppressed.[47] For either group to do so would acknowledge their culpability in that oppression. Lewis instructs that independence in thought is a prerequisite for independence in action. Given this line of argument, the extent to which there is an African American gender gap equivalent to that reported among white adults takes on special relevance. Research findings to date reveal no comparable division of African American political attitudes along gender lines, however.[48]

Summary and Conclusion

Historical precedence, as examined in this article, suggests that as long as both race and gender remain critical factors in determining life chances, quality of life, and access to what are considered the preferred values in American society, African American women will continue to respond both as African Americans and as women. The nature of that response will involve creative, innovative structures and strategies if the traditional ones are not available or prove to be ineffective. When and where the traditional channels have opened up, African American women have made optimum use of them. One critical issue that must be subjected to continuing and agonizing reappraisal by these women, however, is the efficacy of the traditional political machinery, to which they have only recently gained access, in the achievement of contemporary social and economic goals. In short, have African American women gained access only to find that access has lost its utility for delivering the resources sought? Are there lessons to be learned from the desertion of the ballot box by white males? Does the existence of powerful single-issue groups signal a fundamental change in American politics to which African American women must adapt?

In the search for indications of African American women's political behavior in the future, it would seem that the contingency orientation that has dominated their political behavior historically, the absence of a gender gap among African American adults, and the finding that race issues rather than gender issues are their priorities provide the best clues.

Jewel L. Prestage is Honors Professor of Political Science and interim dean of Benjamin Banneker Honors College at Prairie View A & M University. She is co-author, with Marianne Githens, of A Portrait of Marginality: The Political Behavior of the American Women *and has contributed articles on African American politics and women in politics to scholarly journals and edited volumes. Her current research interests are African American women officeholders and African American women political scientists. She holds a B.A. degree in political science from Southern University and an M.A. and Ph.D. in political science from the University of Iowa.*

Notes

1. In Barbara J. Nelson, *American Women and Politics: A Selected Bibliography and Resource Guide* (New York: Garland, 1964), of 1611 entries, only 39 are under "black women."

2. John J. Stucker, "Women as Voters: Their Maturation as Political Persons in American Society," in *Women in the Professions*, ed. Laurily Keir Epstein (Lexington, MA: D. C. Heath, 1975), pp. 97–121.

3. As quoted in Herbert Aptheker, ed., *A Documentary History of the Negro People in the United States* (New York: Citadel Press, 1969), p. 313.

4. Angela Davis, "Reflections on the Black Woman's Role in the Community of Slaves," *Black Scholar*, 3:2–15 (Dec. 1971).

5. John Hope Franklin, *From Slavery to Freedom* (New York: Knopf, 1974), pp. 214–19.

6. For a less restrictive definition, see Harold Lasswell, *Politics: Who Gets What When How?* (New York: McGraw-Hill, 1936). Jewel L. Prestage and Carolyn S. Williams define politics as encompassing "the totality of the power relationships in society as those relationships impinge upon the ultimate use of coercive powers of the society." See Prestage and Williams, "Blacks in Politics," in *Louisiana Politics: Festival in a Labyrinth*, ed. James Bolner (Baton Rouge: Louisiana State University Press, 1982), p. 285.

7. Accounts of women's participation in slave resistance are given in John Blasingame, *The Slave Community* (New York: Oxford University Press, 1972), pp. 116–53; Paula Giddings, *When and Where I Enter: The Impact of Black Women on Race and Sex in America* (New York: Bantam Books, 1984), pp. 39–40; Jewel L. Prestage, "Political Behavior of American Black Women: An Overview," in *The Black Woman*, ed. La Frances Rodgers-Rose (Beverly Hills, CA: Sage, 1984), p. 238.

8. Aptheker, *Documentary History*, pp. 126, 253, 380–87, 441–42; Susie King Taylor, *A Black Woman's Civil War Memoirs* (New York: Markus Wiener, 1988).

9. For the content of that speech, see Marilyn Richardson, ed., Maria W. Stewart; *America's First Black Woman Political Writer: Essays and Speeches* (Bloomington: Indiana University Press, 1987), pp. 43–49. Also see Giddings, *When and Where I Enter*, p. 49.

10. Barbara Sinclair Deckard, *The Woman's Movement: Political, Socioeconomic and Psychological Issues*, 3d ed. (New York: Harper & Row, 1983), p. 255.

11. Giddings, *When and Where I Enter*, pp. 119–20.

12. Deckard, *Woman's Movement*, p. 260; Giddings, *When and Where I Enter*, p. 68.

13. Giddings, *When and Where I Enter*, p. 55.

14. Ibid.

15. Aptheker, *Documentary History*, pp. 721–22.

16. Ibid.

17. Giddings, *When and Where I Enter*, pp. 70–71.

18. Prestage and Williams, "Blacks in Louisiana Politics," p. 298.

19. See "Black Women Attack the Lynching System," in *Black Women in White America: A Documentary History*, ed. Gerda Lerner (New York: Vintage Books, 1972), pp. 196–98.

20. Deckard, *Woman's Movement*, pp. 264–66.

21. Giddings, *When and Where I Enter*, p. 160.

22. Ibid., pp. 159–65.

23. Stucker, "Women as Voters," p. 98.

24. Prestage and Williams, "Blacks in Louisiana Politics," p. 299.

25. Donald A. Matthews and James W. Prothro, *Negroes and the New Southern Politics* (New York: Harcourt, Brace & Jovanovich, 1966), pp. 416–19.

26. John Pierce, William Avery, and Addison Carey, Jr., "Sex Differences in Black Political Beliefs and Behaviors," *American Journal of Political Science*, May 1973, 422–30.

27. *Women and Equality* (New York: Oxford University Press, 1977), pp. 108–10.

28. Matthews and Prothro, *Negroes and the New Southern Politics*, p. 68.

29. Edward T. Clayton, *The Negro Politician* (Chicago: Johnson, 1964), pp. 122–48.

30. See the discussion in Jewel L. Prestage, "Black Politics and the Kerner Report: Concerns and Directions," *Social Science Quarterly*, 49:453–64 (Dec. 1968).

31. Patricia Gurin, Shirley Hatchett, and James S. Jackson, *Hope and Independence: Blacks' Response to Electoral and Party Politics* (New York: Russell Sage, 1989), p. 53.

32. Gerald Davis Jaynes and Robin M. Williams, Jr., eds., *A Common Destiny: Blacks and American Society* (Washington, DC: National Academy Press, 1989), pp. 234–35.

33. See Majorie Lansing, "The Voting Patterns of American Black Women," in *A Portrait of Marginality: The Political Behavior of the American Woman*, ed. Jewel L. Prestage and Marianne Githens (New York: David McKay, 1977), pp. 379–94; Sandra Baxter and Majorie Lansing, *Women and Politics: The Visible Majority* (Ann Arbor: University of Michigan Press, 1983), pp. 73–112.

34. *Common Destiny*, pp. 234–35.

35. Jewel L. Prestage, "Black Women State Legislators: A Profile," in *Portrait of Marginality*, ed. Prestage and Githens, pp. 401–18.

36. Jewel L. Prestage, "Black Women Judges: An Examination of Their Socio-Economic, Educational and Political Backgrounds, and Judicial Placement," in *Readings in American Political Issues*, ed. Franklin D. Jones and Michael O. Adams (Dubuque, IA: Kendall-Hunt, 1987), pp. 324–44.

37. Susan J. Carroll and Wendy S. Strimling, *Women's Routes to Elective Office: A Comparison with Men's* (Rutgers, NJ: State University Center for the American Woman and Politics, 1983), pt. 1, pp. 141–209.

38. Deckard, *Woman's Movement*, p. 346.

39. Carroll and Strimling, *Women's Routes*, pp. 141–209. See also Susan E. Marshall, "Equity Issues and Black-White Differences in Women's ERA Support," *Social Science Quarterly*, 71:299–314 (June 1990).

40. Joseph A. Schlesinger, *Ambition and Politics: Political Careers in the United States* (Chicago: Rand McNally, 1966), p. 1.

41. Pauline T. Stone, "Ambition Theory and the Black Politician," *Western Political Quarterly*, 33:94–107 (Mar. 1980).

42. Prestage, "Black Women State Legislators."

43. Jerry Perkins, "Political Ambition among United States Black and White Women: An Intergenerational Test of the Socialization Model," *Women and Politics*, 6:27–40 (1986).

44. Cynthia Fuchs Epstein, "Positive Effects of the Multiple Negative: Explaining the Success of Black Professional Women," *American Journal of Sociology*, Jan. 1973, pp. 913–35.

45. Chafe, *Women and Equality*, p. 109.

46. Charles V. Willie, "Marginality and Social Change," *Society*, 12:12 (July–Aug. 1975).

47. Shelby Lewis, "A Liberation Ideology: The Intersection of Race, Sex and Class," in *Women Rights, Feminism and Politics in the United States*, ed. Mary L. Shanley (Washington, DC: American Political Science Association, 1982) pp. 38–42.

48. Susan Welch and Lee Sigelman, "A Black Gender Gap?" *Social Science Quarterly*, 70:120–23 (Mar. 1989).

Appendix

Questions

Name _____

Date _____

Time _____

Reading 1: Abraham Lincoln and the Second American Revolution

1. What are the major arguments of the author to prove that the Civil War was a second American Revolution?

2. What role did the abolitionists play in changing Abraham Lincoln's position on the emancipation of slaves?

Name _____

Date _____

Time _____

Reading 2: The Robber Barons

1. What led the robber barons to create big business? Explain.

2. Detail the socio-economic and political effects the robber barons had on America at the turn of the 20th Century.

Name _____

Date _____

Time _____

Reading 4: Russian Jews in the United States

1. Detail the distinct aspects of Russian Jewish culture on America.

2. How were Russian Jews discriminated against in America?

Name _____

Date _____

Time _____

Reading 5: Booker T. Washington's Atlanta Exposition Address

1. What are the major points of Washington's address? Explain.

2. What advice did Washington give to southern whites? Explain.

Name _____

Date _____

Time _____

Reading 6: Of Mr. Booker T. Washington and Others

1. What are Du Bois's major criticisms of Washington?

Name _____

Date _____

Time _____

Reading 7: The Bitter Cry of the Children

1. Discuss the working conditions of children in the late 19th century. Explain.

Name _____

Date _____

Time _____

Reading 8: The Diplomacy of Discrimination: Chinese Exclusion, 1876–1882

1. Why were Chinese immigrants singled out as the "yellow peril"?

2. After James Burril Angell's visit to San Francisco's Chinatown, what did he conclude about the real reason motivating immigration limitation of the Chinese? Explain.

Name _____

Date _____

Time _____

Reading 10: The Progressive Movement and the Negro

1. What effect did the Progressive Movement, according to the author, have on African Americans? Explain.

2. What role did southern liberals play in the Progressive Movement? Explain.

Name _____

Date _____

Time _____

Reading 11: The Flowering of Black Nationalism: Henry McNeal Turner and Marcus Garvey

1. According to the author, what forces led to the development of black nationalism?

2. Discuss the differences between Turner's and Garvey's views of black nationalism. Explain.

Name _____

Date _____

Time _____

Reading 12: Reckoning with Violence:
W. E. B. Du Bois and the 1906 Atlanta Race Riot

1. How did Du Bois's concept of duality allow him to view himself and race relations?

2. How did Du Bois respond to the Atlanta Riot (militantly, philosophically, passively, etc.)? Explain.

Name _____

Date _____

Time _____

Reading 13: The NAACP as a Reform Movement, 1909–1965

1. How important was the hiring of Charles Hamilton Houston as legal counsel for the NAACP? Explain.

2. How did the legal success of the NAACP affect the "Revolution" in expectations among African Americans and what event was the NAACP's first organizational challenge?

Name _____

Date _____

Time _____

Reading 15: The "Magic" Leak of 1941 and Japanese–American Relations

1. Was the article successful in disputing the claim of Roosevelt's prior knowledge of the attack on Pearl Harbor? Explain.

2. Were the efforts to decode Japanese intelligence messages significant enough to warn of a breakdown in Japanese–American relations? Why? Why not?

Name _____

Date _____

Time _____

Reading 16: Women, Work, and War

1. Discuss the struggles of working women during the war. Explain.

2. What effect did the war have on working women? Explain.

Name _____

Date _____

Time _____

Reading 18: Spanish-Speaking Americans in Wartime

1. Detail the causes and results of the zoot suit riots.

2. What effects did World War II have on Latino Americans? Explain.

Name _____

Date _____

Time _____

Reading 19: Jackie Robinson Breaks Baseball's Color Line

1. What were Anglo-American's attitudes to Jackie Robinson's breaking of baseball's color barrier?

2. How did African Americans view his historic break through? Explain.

Name _____

Date _____

Time _____

Reading 20: Neither Victim nor Villain

1. Does the author present enough information about Nurse Rivers to cast her as "neither victim, nor villain"? Why? Why not?

2. What were some external factors which shaped the scope of the Tuskeegee experiment which did not exist with the same study from Oslo, Norway?

Name _____

Date _____

Time _____

Reading 21: Letter from Birmingham Jail

1. What reasons did Martin L. King, Jr. give to his fellow clergymen for leading the Birmingham demonstration?

2. Detail King's views on white moderates and the Civil Rights Movement. Explain.

Name _____

Date _____

Time _____

Reading 22: Message to the Grass Roots

1. Detail the major points of Malcolm X's "grass roots" speech. Explain.

2. What were Malcolm's views on modern day "Uncle Toms"?

Name _____

Date _____

Time _____

Reading 23: In Quest of African American Political Woman

1. According to the author, what are some of the nontraditional political activities engaged in by African American Women?

2. Identify some of the characteristics of African American women office holders.